MOON

D0746330

EL SALVADOR

JAIME JACQUES

GUATEMALA

Lago
de Güija

Parque
Nacional
Montecristo-
El Trifinio

▲ Cerro
El Pital

EL

CIHUATAN

Lago
Suchitlán

Chalatenango

Santa
Ana

CASA
BLANCA ★

Laguna de
Las Nymphas

TAZUMAL ★

Laguna
Verde

Ahuachapán

Lago de
Coatepeque

SAN
ANDRÉS
★

★ JOYA DE
CERÉN

Suchitoto

▲ Cerro de
Guazapa

Cinquera

Concepción
de Ataco

Apaneca

Los Naranjos

Juayúa

Parque Nacional
El Imposible

Salcoatitán

Parque Nacional
Los Volcanes
(Cerros Verdes)

Nahuizalco

Volcán ▲
San Salvador

SAN
SALVADOR ★

Sonsonate

Barra de
Santiago

Santa
Tecla

Panchimalco

Lago de
Ilopango

Puerto
de Acajutla

CARRETERA   LITORAL

Parque
Nacional
Walter Thilo
▲ Deininger

Playa
Los Cóbanos

Playa
El Sunzal

Puerto
de la Libertad

COMALAPA ✈
INTERNATIONAL
AIRPORT

P A C I F I C

Playa Costa
del Sol

CARRETERA   PANAMERICANA

CARRETERA   TRONCAL   EL   NORTE

0   20 mi

0   20 km

© AVALON TRAVEL

El Salvador

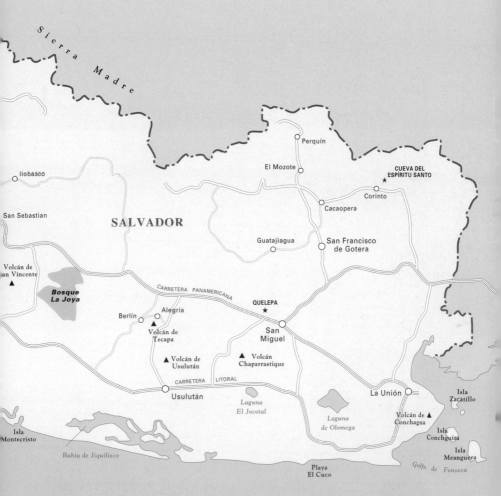

HONDURAS

Sierra Madre

SALVADOR

Ilobasco

San Sebastian

Perquín

El Mozote

CUEVA DEL
ESPÍRITU SANTO

Corinto

Cacaopera

Guatajiagua

San Francisco
de Gotera

Volcán de
an Vincente

Bosque
La Joya

CARRETERA PANAMERICANA

QUELEPA

Berlín   Alegría

Volcán de
Tecapa

San
Miguel

Volcán de
Usulután

Volcán
Chaparrastique

CARRETERA   LITORAL

Usulután

La Unión

Isla
Zacatillo

Laguna
El Jocotal

Laguna
de Olomega

Volcán de
Conchagua

Isla
Montecristo

Isla
Conchaguita

Bahía de Jiquilisco

Isla
Meanguera

Playa
El Cuco

Golfo de Fonseca

O C E A N

Contents

If wealth were measured in kindness, El Salvador would be the richest country in the world. This tiny place with a big heart is famous for softening even the most hardened cynics, and showing them a damn good time while it's at it.

Until recently the only people passing through were intrepid backpackers and devout surfers. But it was only a matter of time before the secretive whispers about crystal green lakes, misty cloud forests, and mysterious ruins got out. Throw some of the best surf breaks in the world into the mix and El Salvador's a hidden gem that's soon to be discovered.

Volcano hikes, national parks teeming with birds and butterflies, and a rugged Pacific coastline dotted with secluded getaways make this country an outdoor enthusiast's dream. But by far, El Salvador's most valuable asset is its people. Hard working and fast-talking, Salvadorans always have time to help someone in need. The country seems to run on the perfect balance of play and productivity. Perhaps it is the many and varied hardships the people of this land have endured that has taught them that life is too short to be taken too seriously. If you ask a Salvadoran where something is, you may be offered a ride, asked to join a meal, then be offered

Clockwise from top left: Iglesia El Rosario in San Salvador; doorway in Suchitoto; wall painting in La Palma; Volcán Chaparrastique; traditional baskets in Nahuizalco; view of islands in the Golfo de Fonseca from Conchagüita.

half the plate. And if somebody invites you over to their home, chances are you will have a forged a friendship for life.

The land of El Salvador is as colorful as the people. The abundance of volcanoes lends it a mythical appeal; flowering trees pepper the landscape with orange, lavender, and fuchsia hues; and the diverse coastline offers huge waves, surreal estuaries, and expansive white-sand beaches. El Salvador is the smallest country in Central America, making it possible to take a morning hike in the cool northern mountains, eat fresh seafood on the beach for lunch, and then shimmy the night away at a salsa bar in San Salvador.

Unfortunately, many people exploring Central America opt out of El Salvador, scared off by reports of violence and crime. Yes, gang activity is high, but it's also localized in terms of where and who is targeted. Incidents involving visitors are extremely rare. The El Salvador you hear about in the news and the El Salvador you are about to discover are two very different places. Leave your preconceptions at the border, expect the unexpected, and prepare to be pleasantly surprised.

Clockwise from top left: along El Salvador's east coast; Los Chorros de la Calera in Juayúa; a wall mural in Concepción de Ataco; handicrafts in Ilobasco, near Suchitoto.

Planning Your Trip

Where to Go

San Salvador

San Salvador sits in a fertile valley and has a history as eruptive as the volcanoes that surround it. The churches and plazas of the **Centro Histórico** all have stories of protest and revolution. The museums, restaurants, and bars of **Zona Rosa** are perfect for an afternoon of art and culture, and day trips to the natural attractions of **Parque Nacional El Boquerón** or **Puerta del Diablo** are just a quick drive to the outskirts of the city.

Western El Salvador

Just west of San Salvador, the scenic rolling **Ruta de Las Flores** takes you through the Sierra Apaneca-Ilamatepec mountain range, punctuated with charming little towns including **Juayúa,** home of El Salvador's most popular weekend food fair and **Concepción de Ataco,** the colorful cobblestone village. **Parque Nacional Los Volcanes (Parque Cerro Verde)** is where you can climb volcanoes, including Izalco and Santa Ana. Nearby **Lago de Coatepeque** is one of the largest crater lakes in the country, and the ruins of **Tazumal** in Chalchuapa are just a short bus ride from El Salvador's second-largest city, **Santa Ana.**

The Pacific Coast

With just over 300 kilometers of Pacific coastline, there's something for everyone on the beaches of El Salvador. The western coast offers several world-class beach breaks for surfers, and the bustling backpacker hub of **Playa El Tunco** is the perfect base from which to explore them all.

Festival de las Flores y Palmas procession in Panchimalco, near San Salvador

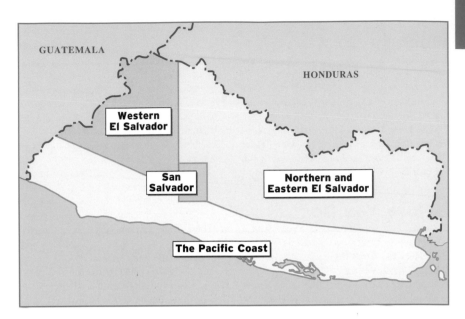

Farther west, the remote **Barra de Santiago** is a peaceful escape with mangroves and bird-watching. The east coast also offers top-notch surfing at **Playa Las Flores** and **Punta Mango,** or sunbathing and swimming at **Playa Maculis** or **Playa Esterón.** The more adventurous can continue east to the Bajo Lempa region, where the Río Lempa meets the Pacific Ocean. Here, **Bahía de Jiquilisco** and **Isla Montecristo** offer community-based ecotourism and opportunities to release baby turtles. Finally, the rugged undeveloped islands in the **Golfo de Fonseca** offer remote beaches and spectacular views.

Northern and Eastern El Salvador

The first Spanish settlement in El Salvador, Suchitoto still shows its colonial roots, with cobblestone streets and crumbling century-old homes. The nearby ruin of **Cihuatán** is the largest pre-Hispanic site found in the country, and farther north the whimsical town of **La Palma** showcases the art of famed artist Fernando Llort. Continue up to the cloud forest of **Cerro El Pital,** the highest and coolest point in the country. The wild east starts in the major city of **San Miguel,** its nightclubs and big hotels in sharp contrast to the nearby rural towns of **Perquín** and **El Mozote,** where the **Museo de la Revolución Salvadoreña** and the El Mozote memorial are stark reminders that not so long ago this country was in the throes of a bloody civil war. The east also offers prehistoric cave art in the **Cueva del Espíritu Santo.**

When to Go

There are two seasons in El Salvador—the **rainy season** and the **dry season.** Rain falls from June to November, and usually during the night. The ideal time to go is right after the rainy season in December-January when things are still lush and green. The best time to go surfing is March to October.

The **high season** is considered Semana Santa (the week leading up to Easter), the month of August (when there are school holidays and San Salvador celebrates its Fiestas Agostinas), and December, when there are extended holidays for Christmas.

Before You Go

Passports, Tourist Cards, and Visas

Travelers to El Salvador must have a **passport** that is valid for at least six months beyond the date of entry. A visa is not required to enter El Salvador, but a **tourist card,** which costs $10, must be purchased upon entry at Aeropuerto Internacional Comalapa or through any of the four land-border entry points. When you buy the tourist card, you will be given a receipt to keep with your passport. You will not be required to pay it again if you exit and reenter El Salvador, as long as you have your receipt and your tourist card remains valid.

Vaccinations

Although no immunizations are required to enter El Salvador (aside from **yellow fever,** if you are arriving directly from a tropical region), visitors should make sure their **routine immunizations** are up to date. In addition, dengue fever (for which there is no vaccine) has become quite prevalent in the last few years, so it is advised to take extra precaution when it comes to avoiding mosquitoes.

Transportation

El Salvador has one **international airport,** Aeropuerto Internacional Comalapa, and a very comprehensive and economical **bus system** within the country, but riding on old American school buses might not suit everyone's tastes. Hiring a private **taxi** to get around is an option but is quite costly. It's cheaper to **rent a car,** and El Salvador has an excellent road system.

The Best of El Salvador

If you have two weeks, you have enough time to get in all the best that El Salvador has to offer. The western beaches of the Pacific Coast are the perfect way to kick off your vacation, enjoying the famous sun, surf, ceviche, and *cerveza*. The ruins, volcanoes, and quaint, colorful towns of Ruta de Las Flores in Western El Salvador are not to be missed. Although San Salvador gets a bad rap, there are plenty of hidden gems in and around this heavily populated city. The northern part of El Salvador is a welcome respite from the heat, with cool cloud forests and a peaceful hike to the highest point in the country. The wild east is the least frequented part of El Salvador, but an absolute must for anyone interested in the history of the civil war. Finally, the eastern beaches offer raucous surf or quiet untouched estuaries—you choose.

The Pacific Coast: Western Beaches

DAY 1

Fly into Comalapa airport and head straight for the beaches near La Libertad. Go to **Playa El Tunco** if you want action, or **Playa El Zonte** if you want a more laid-back vibe. Take a **surf lesson** or hike to **Tamanique Waterfalls.** Enjoy the spectacular sunset over a seafood dinner.

Western El Salvador

DAY 2

Take the bus to **Juayúa** via Sonsonate. This route, known as **Ruta de Las Flores,** is a pretty, winding road with wonderful views of the surrounding coffee fields and volcanoes. When you get to Juayúa, drop your luggage off at your hotel and then hop on the bus and head to **Concepción de Ataco** for the afternoon. Stroll the cobblestone streets, pick up some arts and crafts, and enjoy dinner in one of Ataco's unique restaurants.

Playa El Zonte

Feria Gastronómica in Juayúa

Catedral Metropolitana in San Salvador

Come back to Juayúa to get a good night's sleep before tomorrow's hike.

DAY 3

Get up early and hike the **Siete Cascadas Tour.** If it is the weekend, stay in Juayúa for the **Feria Gastronómica,** the food fair around *parque central*. If not, catch the afternoon bus to **Santa Ana.** When you get to Santa Ana, walk around the center of the city and take in the impressive architecture built during the coffee boom of the late 19th century. Don't miss the beautiful **El Teatro Nacional** and the **Catedral de Santa Ana.**

DAY 4

Take the bus to **Lago Coatepeque** in the morning. Have lunch, enjoy the view of the shimmering emerald green lake, and return to Santa Ana. If you have more time in the afternoon, hop on another bus and head to the Mayan ruins at **Tazumal** in Chalchuapa.

DAY 5

Get up early and go to **Parque Nacional Los Volcanes,** home to three of the country's most noteworthy volcanoes. Climb **Volcán Santa Ana,** an intermediate hike that ends with the iconic view of a striking green sulfur lake. Come back to Santa Ana to sleep.

San Salvador

DAY 6

Take the bus to **San Salvador.** Tour the **Centro Histórico** in the morning and **Parque Nacional El Boquerón,** a volcanic complex that opens up into a massive crater, in the afternoon. Have dinner at one of the restaurants on the road that heads toward the park, enjoying an unrivalled view of the city.

Northern El Salvador

DAY 7

Take the bus to **Suchitoto.** Take a **bird-watching** tour or hike to **Cascada Los Tercios,** then check out the **Casa Museo de los Recuerdos Alejandro Cotto,** an eclectic museum in the home of El Salvador's most iconic patron of the arts. In the afternoon take the bus to **La Palma.** Explore the tiny town and buy souvenirs. Sleep in La Palma.

DAY 8

Get up early and take the bus to the trailhead for **Cerro El Pital,** the highest point in El Salvador. Hike El Pital and return to Suchitoto for dinner and sleep.

Eastern El Salvador
DAY 9

Take the bus to San Salvador first, and from there to **San Miguel.** Check out *parque central* and the **Catedral Nuestra Señora de la Paz** with its red steeples and pretty stained glass. Spend the night in San Miguel.

DAY 10

Get up early to catch the bus to **Perquín.** Once in Perquín, take the afternoon to check out the **Museo de la Revolución Salvadoreña,** which documents the history of the country's civil war. Sleep in Perquín.

DAY 11

Get up early and take the bus to El Mozote and visit the **El Mozote memorial,** dedicated to the

victims of one of Latin America's most brutal massacres. Then walk to **Río Sapo** and spend an hour or two in the cool, clean water. Take the bus back to Perquín to sleep.

The Pacific Coast: Eastern Beaches
DAYS 12-13

Take the bus back to San Miguel and then take the bus to the beaches in **El Cuco.** Check out **Playa Esterón** for a relaxing day, or **Playa Las Flores** for a surf day. If you are feeling adventurous, take a boat trip around the **Golfo de Fonseca,** a relatively untouched area showcasing the country's natural beauty. Sleep at the beach.

Back to San Salvador
DAY 14

Take a bus back to San Salvador, head to the ruin of **Joya de Cerén,** or do last-minute shopping at the **artisanal market** before catching your flight home.

view of the crater lake from the top of Volcán Santa Ana in Parque Nacional Los Volcanes

From Cool Cloud Forests to Warm Waves

The rugged, relatively unexplored landscape of El Salvador will keep outdoor enthusiasts happy with plenty of variety and adventure, from hiking through the steep tropical forest of Parque Nacional El Imposible to diving in crater lakes near the capital or surfing the warm waves on the coast.

San Salvador

One of the best things about visiting San Salvador is the outdoor activities that can be found on the outskirts of the city.

- **Parque Nacional El Boquerón** offers easy walks around the crater, or tough hikes that go all the way down inside.

- **Puerta del Diablo** offers short but steep hikes that lead to spectacular views.

- Visit **Lago Ilopango,** where you can spend the day diving in the country's largest crater lake.

Western El Salvador

The western part of the country is a hiker's haven, with three national parks and much of the country's only remaining virgin forest.

- **Parque Nacional El Imposible** is the largest and most biologically diverse protected area in the country, with intermediate to very difficult hiking trails, excellent bird-watching, and well-maintained campsites.

- **Parque Nacional Montecristo-El Trifinio** is another hub of biodiversity, with a cool cloud forest trail that ends at the highest point in the park, where the borders of El Salvador, Honduras, and Guatemala converge.

Parque Nacional El Imposible

Surf's Up!

The rumors are true. El Salvador is a warm-water, right point haven with enough waves to keep everyone happy. The surf season here is March to October and coincides with the rainy season, when swells coming from the south can reach up to three meters high.

The most popular surf spots are in the west. **La Libertad, Playa El Tunco, Playa El Sunzal,** and **Playa El Zonte** attract many visitors; but if you are up for exploring, there are less publicized, hidden gems to be found all along the west coast. Fortunately, these are close enough to each other that you can easily bounce around between them, all in a day's surf. Most hotels provide transportation to and from the best surf spots, or if you are on a budget, it's easy to hop on the bus with your board and travel between beaches. However you choose to get there, the next wave is never more than half an hour away.

The ultimate waves in El Salvador are Punta Roca in the west, and Las Flores and Punta Mango in the east.

Playa Las Flores

- Some say **Punta Roca** is one of the best waves in Central America; some say it is *the* best. Either way, a serious surf trip to El Salvador is not complete without at least one visit to this famously fast, hollow right point break located in La Libertad.

- In the east, five minutes west by car from the fishing village of El Cuco, you will find **Playa Las Flores,** the gorgeous sandy beach with a very long, consistent right point break.

- **Punta Mango** is 15 minutes west of Las Flores, only accessible by boat or a 4WD vehicle; and don't get your hopes up, there are no mangoes in sight—it was named this because of the nearby beach called Playa Mango. This powerful right point break is best left to the experts, even when it's small, due to strong currents and shallow inside rocks.

If you are still learning, there are plenty of other waves to keep you busy:

- **La Bocana** in El Tunco is a local favorite for its left break created out of a wide river mouth.

- **Playa El Sunzal** is known for its consistency and quality, and is probably the best place to learn how to surf, but also has a fast right beach break that experienced surfers love. Easy access means it can get crowded.

- **Playa El Zonte** is the best place to learn how to stand up on a surfboard, because of its abundance of white water, but intermediate and experienced surfers will also enjoy Zonte's short but fun right-hander, set in a cute little cove with gorgeous views.

Whatever wave you find yourself riding, the surf's always up in El Salvador.

- **Parque Nacional Los Volcanes** is centrally located with three prominent volcanoes, two of which you can hike.

- **Lago Coatepeque** offers water sports, diving, and hiking.

The Pacific Coast

El Salvador's coastline offers world-class surf. Not into surfing? There are plenty of other activities to keep you busy.

- The **surfing** along El Salvador's coast draws thousands every year, and they are never disappointed with the warm water and right points. The beaches of **La Libertad** are the most popular, as well as **Playa Las Flores** and **Punta Mango** in the east.

- Hike through the forests of **Parque Nacional Walter Thilo Deininger.** Its two main nature trails both end at a spectacular mirador.

- Go **fishing** around **El Sunzal.** If you're feeling adventurous, try your hand at surf fishing.

- Hike to the stunning **Tamanique Waterfalls,** where you can jump into the pools below to cool off.

- Take a **bird-watching boat tour** through the otherworldly mangroves in **Barra de Santiago.**

Northern and Eastern El Salvador

The remote northern and eastern parts of the country offer a bevy of untrodden natural treasures to intrepid travelers.

- The **Río Palancapa waterfall trek** in Suchitoto will not disappoint adventurers who aren't afraid of getting wet.

- Far north, the hike through the cool cloud forest to the highest point in the country, **Cerro El Pital,** is a must if you crave peaceful surroundings and clean air.

- In the rugged east, ex-guerrillas can guide you from **Perquín** to the **Río Sapo,** where you can camp by the river and return the next day.

- For hard-core hikers, the granddaddy of El Salvador's volcanoes is **Volcán Chaparrastique** in San Miguel.

Art and Culture: Past and Present

El Salvador's unique culture may not be as famous as somewhere like neighboring Guatemala, but make no mistake—underneath the veneer of sun and surf, there is much to discover. A fascinating pre-Hispanic history, traditional artisanship, and a burgeoning contemporary art scene all provide plenty of opportunities to experience the other side of El Salvador.

San Salvador

- Zona Rosa in the country's capital is a great place to start. **Museo Nacional de Antropología Dr. David J. Guzmán (MUNA)** is the most comprehensive museum in the country, offering different exhibits that explore pre-Hispanic culture, art, agriculture, and religion. The nearby **Museo de Arte de**

Fernando Llort's signature style adorns old milk canisters in La Palma.

El Salvador (MARTE) showcases some of the most influential Salvadoran artists in a beautiful modern museum.

- Downtown, the **Museo de la Palabra y la Imagen** maintains exhibits that keep the historical memory of the guerrilla movement alive and also focuses on Salvadoran literature.

- Just west of the city in the suburb of Santa Tecla, the **Museo Municipal Tecleño (MUTE)** offers art shows and contemporary theater, and **Paseo El Carmen** has an excellent pedestrian fair every weekend that showcases unique local artisans, musicians, and more.

- Northwest of San Salvador, the ruin of **Joya de Cerén,** a UNESCO World Heritage Site often called the Pompeii of the Americas, provides a glimpse into the daily village life of early Mayan culture.

Western El Salvador

- Visit the indigenous town of **Nahuizalco** to see traditional **basket-weaving and furniture-making.**

- Check out the **weekend artisanal market** in **Concepción de Ataco,** where local artists gather around the *parque central* to sell their work.

- Learn about **coffee culture** in **Juayúa,** a mountain town surrounded by lush green coffee farms.

- In **Santa Ana,** visit **El Teatro Nacional,** a majestic theater that features beautiful artwork—and provides a fascinating window into El Salvador's social strata in the early 20th century.

- The ruins of **Tazumal** in Chalchuapa are an excellent way to learn about what was once a major Mayan center in Mesoamerica.

Suchitoto's main square

Northern and Eastern El Salvador

- **Suchitoto** is the cultural touchtone of this area, with **indigo workshops,** the **Casa Museo de los Recuerdos Alejandro Cotto,** and the **Centro Arte para la Paz** all offering a glimpse into the traditional art and culture of El Salvador.

- Check out the popular *sorpresas,* quirky miniature clay figures that are unique to El Salvador, in **Ilobasco** and **San Sebastián.**

- The town of **La Palma** showcases the vibrant art of **Fernando Llort.** All over town are murals in cheerful colors, giving La Palma a light-hearted feel.

San Salvador

Look for ★ to find recommended
sights, activities, dining, and lodging.

Highlights

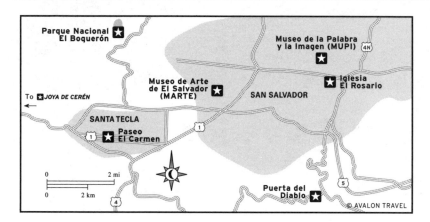

★ **Iglesia El Rosario:** Enigmatic El Rosario is one of the most beautiful and fascinating churches in Latin America (page 32).

★ **Museo de Arte de El Salvador (MARTE):** This sleek, spotless museum is home to the best Salvadoran art (page 34).

★ **Museo de la Palabra y la Imagen (MUPI):** This museum showcases the work of revolutionary writers and journalists, with a focus on the infamous Radio Venceremos, the rogue underground radio station that broadcast to the world during the civil war (page 35).

★ **Puerta del Diablo:** Stunning views, clean air, and peace and quiet make this the perfect and most accessible escape from the chaos of downtown San Salvador (page 41).

★ **Parque Nacional El Boquerón:** This park offers a cool climate year-round, walking trails around the crater of El Boquerón, and impressive views of the baby crater inside it (page 43).

★ **Joya de Cerén:** Often referred to as the Pompeii of the Americas, this pre-Columbian Mayan farming village has been frozen in time thanks to the eruption of a nearby volcano around AD 600 (page 62).

★ **Paseo El Carmen:** Pedestrian weekends are the perfect window to Salvadoran culture, where outdoor vendors sell local food, art, and crafts, and the nightlife beckons people from all walks of life to enjoy the scores of sweet cafés, bars, and restaurants (page 63).

C haotic, congested, and consistently noisy, San Salvador is El Salvador's capital and resilient urban heart. Battle hardened by civil unrest and natural disasters, the city bears the scars of its past with a fierce determination to create a better future, and it seems that perhaps finally, the tide is turning. You can see it in the world-class restaurants and homegrown cafés popping up in the affluent **Zona Rosa,** and in the yoga studios and independent boutiques on the tree-lined streets of **Colonia Escalón;** but most significantly you can see it in the city's **Centro Histórico,** where, until recently, most middle-class Salvadorans dared not go since the war ended in 1992. Today, however, the well-heeled are returning to nights out at the Teatro Nacional; bargain hunters are hitting the sprawling, informal market to shop for clothes; and brightly colored murals are turning up between the crumbling buildings and bullet-scarred walls. The young people of San Salvador are taking the first cautious steps toward reclaiming their city and building it into something they can call their own.

It's an exciting time of transition, and as a visitor, there is much to see and do. In fact, San Salvador can be the perfect base for your travels, with all of the comforts and amenities you need and many of the country's top sights within a short bus ride away, including **Parque Nacional El Boquerón,** the ruins of **San Andrés** and **Joya de Cerén,** and **Lago Ilopango.** You can complement your day trips with visits to museums and churches, both of which will give you a deeper insight into the turbulent history of the country. The **Catedral Metropolitana** and **Iglesia El Rosario** are not only beautiful but help put the role that religion played in the civil war into context. The **Museo Nacional de Antropología Dr. David J. Guzmán (MUNA)** is an excellent way to learn more about pre-Hispanic and colonial eras, while the **Museo de la Palabra y la Imagen (MUPI)** will appeal to literature lovers and history buffs alike, honoring El Salvador's revolutionary writers and journalists, with a focus on work that came out during the civil

Previous: San Salvador's Centro Histórico; Plaza Libertad. **Above:** bookshop in the Centro Histórico.

San Salvador

To ★ PASEO EL CARMEN

To ★ PARQUE NACIONAL, ★ JOYA DE CERÉN

EL BOQUERÓN,

PASEO GENERAL ESCALÓN

CALLE DEL MIRADOR

COLONIA ESCALÓN

CALLE LA MASCOTA

79 AVE NTE

MUSEO DE ARTE DE EL SALVADOR (MARTE) ★

MUSEO NACIONAL DE ANTROPOLOGÍA DR. DAVID J. GUZMÁN (MUNA) ☐

ZONA ROSA

UNIVERSIDAD CENTROAMERICANA JOSÉ SIMEÓN CAÑAS (UCA) ★

MANUEL ENRIQUE ARAUJO

LA CASA TOMADA DEL CENTRO ★

CALLE LA MASCOTA

ANTIGUO CUSCATLÁN

HOSPITAL LA DIVINA PROVIDENCIA ★

1A CALLE PONIENTE

SEE "COLONIA ESCALÓN" MAP

CALLE SAN ANTONIO ABAD

AVE LAS AMAPOLAS

COLONIA EL ROSAL

AVE

OLIMPICA

ALAMEDA FRANKLIN DELANO ROOSEVELT

COLONIA CENTROAMÉRICA

MUSEO DE ARTE POPULAR ★

BLVD DE LOS HÉROES

BLVD DE LOS HÉROES

SEE "ZONA ROSA AND ANTIGUO CUSCATLÁN" MAP

CALLE AL AEROPUERTO

CALLE MONSERRAT

BOULEVARD VENEZUELA

6A 10A CALLE

MUSEO DE LA PALABRA Y LA IMAGEN (MUPI) ☐

AVE JOSÉ GUSTAVO GUERRERO

BLVD TUTUNICHAPA

UNIVERSIDAD DE EL SALVADOR ★

COLONIA EL REFUGIO

CALLE A HUIZÚCAR

CALLE GERARDO BARRIOS

CENTRO HISTÓRICO

IGLESIA SAGRADA CORAZÓN

PALACIO NACIONAL

ALAMEDA JUAN PABLO II

DIAGONAL UNIVERSITARIA

To ★ PUERTA DEL DIABLO

AVENIDA IRAZÚ

IGLESIA CALVARIO

METROPOLITAN CATHEDRAL ★

TEATRO NACIONAL

5A. AVENIDA

8A AVENIDA SUR

IGLESIA EL ROSARIO ☐ ★

AVENIDA ESPAÑA

CALLE AVE INDEPENDENCIA

CALLE CONCEPCIÓN

SEE "DOWNTOWN SAN SALVADOR" MAP

© AVALON TRAVEL

0   500 yds
0   500 m

war. For entertainment in San Salvador, remember to look past the sprawling shopping malls and American chains and you will find restaurants and bars to suit any budget and taste, including cheap and delicious street food, artsy cafés with live music and poetry, and stylish fine dining. Finally, just a short cab ride away is **Paseo El Carmen** in the suburb of **Santa Tecla,** an essential weekend day trip, where a pedestrian walkway offers stall after stall of delicious traditional and international fare, live entertainment, and quaint cafés and pubs that come to life after dark.

HISTORY

San Salvador was founded in 1545, after two other attempts to establish the colonial capital north of the city near Suchitoto. The settlements in Suchitoto failed due to fierce resistance by the indigenous Pipil people, sending the Spanish to look for greener pastures. Motivated by the size of the land and the fertility of the soil around present-day San Salvador, they settled here. The city began where Plaza Libertad now stands and grew from there, with help from income gained from *añil* (indigo), cacao, balsam, and other profitable crops. San Salvador played a pivotal role in the years leading up to the independence of Central America. This is where the first uprisings against the Spaniards took place, in 1811 and 1814, and although the independence movement gained momentum quickly, the revolution was still in the distant future. After the uprisings, any kind of rebellion was swiftly cut down by the Spanish. In the years to follow, pockets of resistance secretly grew until September 15, 1821, when El Salvador officially became part of the Federal Republic of Central America before achieving its own independence in 1834. San Salvador has been the capital ever since.

During the second half of the 19th century, the city really began to take shape, thanks to the profits from El Salvador's newest cash crop: coffee. Architecture began to take on the neoclassic and neo-Gothic styles of Europe, and luxurious palaces, theaters, and churches began to pepper the city center. The growing splendor continued until the 1960s, when the highly industrialized nation became the third-largest coffee exporter in the world. However, natural disasters often cruelly reversed the city's growth; most famously the earthquake of 1873 that destroyed much of the city, and the eruption of Volcán San Salvador in 1917 that also caused significant damage. The 1986 earthquake caused mass destruction of the city center, resulting in the evacuation of virtually all residents and businesses, paving the way for mass migration of the nation's disadvantaged to take over the abandoned streets for informal trade.

The capital also saw its share of violence during the civil war. The historic center was the scene of many antigovernment protests and saw the murder of many protesters by national security forces. Other neighborhoods were targeted by guerrillas for being pro-government. Civilians in the capital lived under a strict curfew and in constant fear, no matter what their political stance. Weapons proliferated and the situation grew tenser until the Farabundo Martí National Liberation Front (FMLN) undertook its largest offensive in November 1989, when its guerillas stormed the city and took control of many poor neighborhoods. The Salvadoran government responded by bombing the occupied parts of the city. Many civilians were killed in the process. In 1992, the Chapultepec Peace Accords were joyously celebrated in front of the Catedral Metropolitana in the city center, but to this day many Salvadorans still have an underlying fear about being in crowded areas in the city, especially the Centro Histórico, where so much senseless violence took place. Today the city of San Salvador has a population of around 2 million, and many of these people live and work in the center of the city.

ORIENTATION

The city's three main tourist areas, the **Centro Histórico, Colonia Escalón,** and **Zona Rosa,** are all connected by the primary east-west highway, called **Alameda Roosevelt** east of **Plaza de Las Américas** and **Paseo General Escalón** west of the plaza.

Bulevar Monseñor Romero is another major east-west road connecting the city of Santa Tecla and the neighborhood of Antiguo Cuscatlán, finally merging in San Salvador with **Bulevar los Próceres,** which later turns into the road to both **Planes de los Renderos** and the **International Airport.**

The main north-south route is through El Centro and known as **Avenida España** north of **Plaza Barrios** and **Avenida Cuscatlán** south of the plaza. The other main north-south route is **Avenida Norte,** which becomes **Bulevar de los Héroes** and splits the city in two. The neighborhoods north of the Centro Histórico around Bulevar de los Héroes, Metrocentro and the Universidad de El Salvador (the national university) are considered the downtown area.

Roads in the capital are called *calles* if they run east-west, and *avenidas* if they run north-south. Road numbering starts at the downtown intersection of **Avenida España/ Avenida Cuscatlán** and **Calle Delgado/ Calle Arce.** *Avenidas* that fall west of this intersection have odd numbers, and to the east, even numbers. *Calles* have odd numbers if they are to the north of the intersection, and even numbers if they are south of the intersection.

Plaza Barrios in the Centro Histórico

SAFETY

San Salvador is safer than most people think, but as in any other large Central American city, there is a high level of crime, and it is important to take appropriate precautionary measures.

For the most part, Zona Rosa and Escalón are very safe both during the day and at night. The city center is slightly more risky, mostly because of the sheer number of people. It's much easier to get your pocket picked in the middle of all this chaos. However, the Centro Histórico is also the most interesting part of the city, so do not be deterred by potential danger. Take normal precautions, like not wearing any fancy jewelry and carrying

expensive items such as iPods, cameras, and phones, and you will find that the whole experience is a lot less intimidating than you may have anticipated.

The downtown area around the national university is generally safe during the day, but extra precaution should be taken at night. If you go to the bars around the university, it's OK to walk between the bars in the area, but take a taxi when you are leaving the strip. The area around the budget hotels just north of Metrocentro has some nightclubs that should be avoided, and again, do not walk around this area at night. If you want to go to nightclubs, many are located inside Multiplaza, a mall near Santa Tecla, and Salvadorans consider this the safest place for late-night action. The eastern part of the city should be avoided, in particular the area of Soyapango, where there is a well-known gang presence.

Because San Salvador is so densely populated, even if you are in one of the more affluent areas, poverty-stricken shantytowns

Gangs in El Salvador

If you have made it to San Salvador, or as the locals call it, Sivar, congratulations. This means you actually have a mind of your own. You have probably had to endure the well-meaning advice of friends and acquaintances who have told you to be careful here, to stay close to your hotel, and maybe even tried to convince you not to go. They are referring, of course, to the number-one reason most people are scared of San Salvador: the gangs. But there's a good chance that those people have never been to San Salvador, because if they had, they would know there are much more relevant things to talk about, like where to find the best *pupusas* (they're at Planes de los Renderos, if you're interested), the beautiful churches (El Rosario is a must), or the best salsa nights (Café la T).

The truth is that the terrifying media image of the gangs of El Salvador and the reality on the ground are strangely incongruous. If you do come across members of the *mara*, as they are called in Salvadoran slang, you are much more likely to find yourself engaged in a friendly conversation rather than a victim of violence (many gang members speak perfect English after years of living in the United States). A Salvadoran is a Salvadoran, and whether they are a member of a deadly gang or not, that good-natured hospitality seems to be imprinted in their DNA.

This is not to say that the media coverage is not true. The statistics are inarguable: The homicide rate in El Salvador is among the highest in the world, averaging around 10 murders per day. However, as a visitor, your experience here is vastly different than that of a local. You are likely never to see the seedy side of El Salvador, unless you go looking for it. Gang violence is localized, mostly in the eastern part of the city, and targeted at members of rival gangs, business owners who are being extorted, and people involved with drugs. Gang members do not want to involve tourists because that brings the international spotlight to them; and if there is one thing all Salvadorans can agree on, it's that the last thing they want is more negative attention from the media.

You might find it hard to reconcile the image of a gang member making genial small talk over beers or politely helping an elderly woman onto the bus with the reality of their criminal records, but understanding how they got there helps. Many gang members fled the civil war when they were just young boys, forced to leave their families behind and seek survival in the United States. There they faced a whole new set of problems. Seen as intruders by established Immigrant groups in Los Angeles, they found themselves victims of violence again. They banded together in self-defense to form what would eventually become the Mara Salvatrucha 13 or MS-13, one of the biggest and deadliest gangs in the world. After years outside their home country, many of these men have now been deported back to El Salvador, importing criminal tactics learned in the States to a country teeming with left over weapons and struggling to overcome widespread poverty. These conditions made it easy to recruit new members, mostly young men in poor areas with little hope for a sustainable future. Not surprisingly, the result has been disastrous and extremely difficult for the government and police force to manage.

However, under the current FMLN government, important strides have been made in mitigating the endemic crime, including the negotiation of an unprecedented truce between rival gangs MS-13 and Calle 18 in March 2012, and the allocation of peace zones, where money has been invested in creating new job opportunities for gang members. To the surprise of many, the result has been a drop in homicides. The fact is that even the most hardened gang members admit they are tired of the violence and would prefer to live in peace than continue the vicious cycle of crime.

The bottom line is that, as a visitor, you are lucky enough to probably never have to see this side of El Salvador. Those who live and work here are not so fortunate. Whether or not they will one day be able to live free from the constant fear of the *maras* remains to be seen.

---

are never far away. Unfortunately, there have been some reports of nighttime robberies on some of the less frequented side streets in Zona Rosa. The best way to stay as safe as you can is always to take a taxi at night, no matter what part of the city you are in. Like any big city, especially in Central America, your safety is not guaranteed unless you are inside a secure neighborhood or building. This is why many people love having a night out in Santa Tecla, the nearby suburb of the city, where there is a pedestrian strip lined with bars and restaurants that get very lively on the weekends. The area is well lit and convivial with a heavy (friendly) police presence; it is widely regarded as one of the safest and most fun areas for a taste of Salvadoran nightlife.

El Salvador has a strong culture of fear, unfortunately based on very real events in the past and present. Many locals will tell you it is dangerous to go somewhere or do something, based on residual anxiety from the civil war era or present-day reports of gang violence. However, it is important to note that in general, foreign visitors are not targeted here. Reports of theft or violence directed at visitors are much less frequent than in other Central American cities. Stay alert, use your common sense, and enjoy what this thriving city has to offer.

PLANNING YOUR TIME

If you have a few days to spare, that's enough to hit the highlights in San Salvador. The **Museo de Arte Popular** and **Museo de la Palabra y la Imagen (MUPI)** can be visited at the same time as they are in the same neighborhood, near the national university. **Museo Nacional de Antropología Dr. David J. Guzmán (MUNA)** and the **Museo de Arte de El Salvador (MARTE)** can also be done together in Zona Rosa; it is possible to do all of these in one day if you want. You will need half a day to explore the Centro Histórico, starting with the **Palacio Nacional, Teatro Nacional,** and the famous **Catedral Metropolitana.** Head west three blocks to check out **Iglesia Calvarío** and the nearby **Mercado Central.** Four blocks east is the fascinating **Iglesia El Rosario,** best explored in the late afternoon for perfect lighting. Give yourself a day to escape the traffic of the city and visit either the **Puerta del Diablo** or **Parque Nacional El Boquerón.** If you want to do them both, it's best to set aside two days, as they are located at opposite ends of the city.

Although hotels are scattered throughout the city, the majority of people stay in Zona Rosa or Escalón; however, there are budget options near both universities, Universidad de El Salvador downtown and the Universidad Centroamericana José Simeón Cañas (UCA) in Antiguo Cuscatlán. For backpackers it is worth checking out Joan's Hostel, right next to UCA; it's conveniently located next to a major bus stop and has plenty of budget food available.

Sights

CENTRO HISTÓRICO

Unlike most city centers, downtown San Salvador is not where you will find the seat of government or the financial center, which makes it such a charming area to explore. Full of crumbling old buildings, historic plazas, and beautiful churches, this area is a fascinating cultural window into the past. The city center has existed since the 16th century, and most of the original Spanish buildings have been destroyed by natural disasters over the years, with the exception of those built in the 19th century. Continuous seismic activity means that there are no high-rise buildings in the center; the highest point is the bell tower of the Catedral Metropolitana. The eclectic architectural styles that can be found in the center reflect the grandiose past, before the city was battered by earthquakes and civil war. The turn of the 20th century saw the construction of elegant palaces and beautiful churches in neo-Gothic and neo-classic styles, followed by art nouveau in the 1920s and 1930s and art deco in the 1940s and 1950s. However, almost all of it was seriously damaged in the earthquake of 1986. The rubble of the former splendor was abandoned, and soon after, the empty streets of the center were taken over by the thousands of Salvadorans who had been displaced by war or left homeless due to land disputes. To this day, high levels of unemployment have made the city center one of the most vibrant informal marketplaces in the country. The streets are lined with stores full of bins overflowing with secondhand clothing from the United States and independent vendors selling anything from vegetables to vitamins to pirated DVDs, all against the backdrop of the dilapidated art deco signs and the grand buildings in all their current and former glory.

Catedral Metropolitana

The most imposing building in the Centro Histórico is the **Catedral Metropolitana** (Calle Ruben Dario, in front of Plaza Barrios, tel. 2221-0003, 6am-6pm daily). This large white church with its tall bell towers and bulbous yellow and blue dome has a history of tragedy and rebirth that traces the tales of natural disasters and human struggle in San Salvador. In the 19th century this was the site of the colonial church of Santo Domingo until it was destroyed by the earthquake of 1873. In 1888 a new church was built entirely out of wood, only to burn to the ground in an accidental fire in 1956.

Construction of a new cathedral began immediately—the style was to be dramatic, with eclectic architecture using Byzantine and Roman influences. When Monseñor Óscar Romero became archbishop of El Salvador in 1977, the cathedral was still in the middle of construction, which abruptly came to a halt. Romero, a champion of human rights, redirected the money for the construction of the cathedral to help the poor and insisted on giving his sermons inside the partially constructed building.

Between 1977 and 1980 the cathedral was taken over on many occasions by people participating in antigovernment protests, and in 1979 tragedy struck when police opened fire on civilian protesters, killing 24 people on the steps of the church. In March 1980, Romero was assassinated while he was giving mass at another church, Hospital La Divina Providencia, and his funeral was held at the cathedral. Tragically, during the funeral, 44 people died in a stampede of mourners trying to escape gunshots fired by security forces from the roof of the neighboring Palacio Nacional.

After Romero's death, construction of the cathedral resumed but suffered significant damage from the earthquake in 1986. Finally, four decades after it began, the construction of the cathedral was finished in 1999.

The Catedral Metropolitana in the heart of San Salvador took four decades to complete.

The main altar features an image of Jesus donated by the Spanish king Charles V in 1546. The painting rests inside a four-column ornamental canopy surrounded by images of the prophets Moses and Elijah, and the main altar is surrounded by eight large paintings dating from 1996 by artist Andrés García Ibáñez, depicting scenes from the life of Christ. Above it all, the bright cupola stands 45 meters in height with a 24-meter radius. The last and most significant adornment was a colorful mosaic on the facade of the building, designed by revered Salvadoran artist Fernando Llort in 1992 in his signature style, titled *The Harmony of My People*. The art was meaningful because it celebrated the peace accords and was funded by the people of the parish. In January 2012 the archbishop of El Salvador ordered that the mosaic be removed, without consulting the government or the artist. Construction workers chipped away at the symbolic work of art until there was nothing left but a pile of broken tiles. No explanation was given for the destruction of the artwork.

Today, the main reason many people come to the cathedral is to pay respect to the late archbishop Óscar Romero, whose tomb is located in the basement and is open for viewing during regular church hours.

Palacio Nacional

Right next door to the Catedral Metropolitana is the beautiful **Palacio Nacional** (Calle Ruben Dario, in front of Plaza Barrios, tel. 2222-7674 or 2222-9145, 8am-4pm Mon.-Fri., $3), considered the first building of the republic, originally built in 1870. After having burned down in 1889, it was rebuilt in 1905. Designed by iconoclastic engineer José Emilio Alcaine, it was nicknamed the coffee palace because of the fact that the funds used for the construction came from the export of coffee. The palace was occupied by government offices until 1974 when it became a national historic landmark. Home to the national archives, the national palace was opened to the public in 2008, and there are occasional exhibitions.

The architectural style of the palace has neo-Gothic, neoclassic, and Renaissance influences. The front of the palace has six towering columns with statues at each end, one of Christopher Columbus and one of Queen Isabella I, donated by King Alfonso XIII in 1924. Inside are four principal rooms and more than 100 smaller ones. Each room has a distinct *mudejar* tile pattern on the floor, ornate cornices, and chandeliers. Many of the materials used were imported glassware

tomb of national martyr Archbishop Óscar Romero in the Catedral Metropolitana

interior. Today, the theater is used for opera, symphony, and theater performances as well as conferences and film premieres. The theater has three floors and 650 seats, including an exclusive presidential section. The ceiling showcases a 1977 painting of partially nude angelic women by famous Salvadoran artist Carlos Cañas, accented by a large crystal chandelier.

Iglesia Sagrado Corazón

Continue north from the Teatro Nacional and Plaza Morazán to Calle Arce, where you will find **Iglesia Sagrado Corazón** (Calle Arce 810, tel. 2222-8606, 6am-6pm daily), definitely worth a visit to see the 19th-century influences, notably the stamped laminate sheet metal from Belgium, imported European wood, and the dramatic neo-Gothic design on the facade. Construction started in 1901 and finished in 1913, after which it survived several earthquakes due to the strength of the imported materials. The interior is humble and quiet, with old, simple wooden pews, lit candles, and sun streaming in through the gorgeous stained glass windows, creating an unexpected sanctuary in the center of the city.

Palacio Nacional

from Belgium, marble imported from Italy, and timber from El Salvador.

Teatro Nacional El Salvador

The **Teatro Nacional El Salvador** (Calle Delgado and 2 Av. Norte, across from Plaza Morazán, tel. 2222-8760, lplatero@cultura. gob.sv, hours vary by show) is the oldest theater in Central America and the most important space for arts and culture in El Salvador. It was built in 1911, and the original ornate French Renaissance style was the brainchild of French architect Daniel Beylard, who was awarded the design contract for the theater in an international contest organized by the state. In 1966 it was transformed into a space primarily for film screening, with sporadic live performances, until renovation work began in 1976 under the direction of architect Ricardo Jiménez Castillo, who rallied renowned local artists to contribute to the design of the building. The facade remained the same, but romantic art nouveau touches were added to the existing Renaissance-themed

Iglesia Calvarío

The exquisitely beautiful **Iglesia Calvarío** (6 Calle Oriente, between 5 Av. and 3 Av. Sur, 6am-6pm daily) is the oldest church in San Salvador, originally built in 1660, and most recently rebuilt in the 1950s, with many of the original pieces still intact. This grand gothic church was conceived by engineer Augusto Baratta, who was heavily inspired by Italian and Spanish architecture. A beautiful stained glass dome casts natural light on the towering Italian marble columns and 19th-century religious sculptures. The central altar is made from Carrara marble and has a carved replica of Da Vinci's *The Last Supper*.

La Casa Tomada del Centro

Quickly becoming a countercultural touchstone in the middle of abandoned lots and buildings, **La Casa Tomada del Centro** (6

Av. Norte 233, near Parque San José, tel. 6109-6096, free) is an old house in the center that has been taken over by artists. Inside you will find rotating art exhibits, an eclectic collection of used books, and activities such as art classes, workshops, and lectures. It's a great place to meet young, creative Salvadorans and exchange ideas, buy books, and take (or give) a class.

★ Iglesia El Rosario

By far the most fascinating building in the Centro Histórico is **Iglesia El Rosario** (4 Calle Oriente and 6 Av. Sur, no phone, 7am-noon and 2pm-6pm daily). Sitting on the east side of Plaza Libertad, this decrepit hangar-shaped building is easy to dismiss if you don't know what lies inside, which is exactly what makes it so interesting.

Inside, thousands of different colored stained glass pieces are built into walls that curve up to become the ceiling, creating an enchanting kaleidoscope of moving light and color as the sun and clouds cross the sky. El Rosario is the brainchild of Salvadoran sculptor Rubén Martínez. At barely 30 years old in 1962, he came up with the revolutionary design for the church that would become one of the most significant artistic and architectural achievements of the country. His idea was to create a space that symbolized equality and solidarity of the Roman Catholic Church with the working class. This involved a design that would place the altar at the same level as the congregation and eliminate all private and divisive details such as columns, steps, confessionals, and chapels.

When Martínez presented his proposal to the Dominican priest in charge of the project, Father Alejandro Picador, he was intrigued by the idea—but would the conservative Archbishop of El Salvador approve such a radical design? Father Alejandro did not want to risk rejection, so in an audacious move, he traveled to Rome and went directly to Pope John XXIII himself. Amazingly, the Pope approved the design. It turned out that the young Salvadoran's ideas coincided with ideas that had just begun percolating in Rome. The Vatican had been rethinking the nature of the church and how Catholicism might become more involved with the struggles of the poor. And so Rubén Martínez set to work, living on-site for the next seven years, designing and directing construction of the first church to be a visual statement against the elitism of the Latin mass.

The design changed many times over the years, but in the end, the church has a breadth and openness similar to makeshift outdoor churches in poor areas. The half-moon shape of the church makes it earthquake resistant (it was the only one left intact after the earthquake of 1986). The different colored glass in the walls creates a beautiful atmosphere, and on the back wall the glass appears to be arranged in the shape of an eye—religious scholars take it to represent the eye of God, all-seeing but not necessarily always seen. The front of the church has an iron image of the Savior, and at the top of the church is a window that lets sunlight filter in over the congregation, which many believe represents the protection of the Holy Spirit. One of the most praised accomplishments of Iglesia El Rosario is how Martínez managed to capture the essence of the holy trinity in such a beautiful and unique way; Martínez claims, however, that none of this design was conscious and that he was merely an instrument of God. Don't miss the 14 Stations of the Cross, located on the right-hand side of the church, all made from leftover stone and iron and welded into abstract minimalist designs.

ZONA ROSA
Museo Nacional de Antropología Dr. David J. Guzmán (MUNA)

The **Museo Nacional de Antropología Dr. David J. Guzmán** (Final Av. de la Revolución, tel. 2243-3750, 9am-5pm Tues.-Sun., $3) is a perfect way to escape a sticky, smoggy afternoon in the city. This cool expansive space has five beautifully executed exhibits that chart the course of El Salvador's history and

Zona Rosa and Antiguo Cuscatlán

LA GRAN VIA

MERCADO MUNICIPAL DE ANTIGUO CUSCATLÁN

MANUEL ENRIQUE ARAUJO

To ■ PARQUE NACIONAL EL BOQUERON, Santa Tecla, and Western Beaches

AVENIDA JERUSALEM

Parque Bincentenario

MULTIPLAZA

CALLE EL ESPINO

ZONA ROSA

TICA BUS TERMINAL

MUSEO DE ARTE DE EL SALVADOR (MARTE)

DELIKAT

EL ZÓCALO

AL POMODORO

SHERATON HOTEL

ATELU

EL BOTON

ANTIGUO CUSCATLÁN

ALICANTE HOTEL Y RESTAURANTE

ÁRBOL DE FUEGO

AVENIDA RÍO AMAZONAS

MR. SOUVLAKI

MILBURRITOS

UNIVERSIDAD CENTROAMERICANA JOSÉ SIMEÓN CAÑAS (UCA)

CALLE DEL

MUSEO NACIONAL DE ANTROPOLOGÍA DR. DAVID J. GUZMÁN (MUNA)

HOTEL TERRA BELLA

RIUMO BBQ

REVOLUCIÓN

VILLA FLORENCIA

HOTEL SUITES LAS PALMAS

LOS RINCONCITOS

PRINCESS HILTON

REPUBLIK

VINALIA WINE BAR

CAMINITO

CHOCOS

CADEJO BREWING COMPANY

CALLE LOMA LINDA

CALLE LA REFORMA

MERCADO DE ARTESANÍAS

MANUEL ENRIQUE ARAUJO

JOAN'S HOSTAL

MEDITERRANEO

CHEVY'S

GENZANO DI ROMA CAFFÉ

AVENIDA ALBERT EINSTEIN

CALLE ANTIGUA A HUIZÚCAR

0
1 km

0
1 mi

AVENIDA LAS AMAPOLAS

CALLE A HUIZÚCAR

TERMINAL DE OCCIDENTE

CALLE AL AEROPUERTO

culture, starting with the pre-Hispanic era of Cuscatlán. Other exhibits focus on the colonial era and contemporary El Salvador, including information about art, agriculture, and early trade. The museum houses many fascinating artifacts dating as far back as AD 900 that have been found at various ruins in the country, most notably from the archaeological site of Cihuatán. Examples include jade jewelry, obsidian pieces, ceramics, tools, and dolls. Learn about the history of cacao or balsam, sacred indigenous sites, land issues past and present, or traditional Salvadoran song and dance. English-speaking guides are available if you ask at the front desk.

The restaurant in the museum is excellent and worth visiting even if you don't go to the museum. **Bistro San Lorenzo** (tel. 2243-7566, 10am-10pm daily, $7-16) has a sleek, contemporary design and serves up excellent *panini,* salads, and pastas. This air-conditioned space is also nice to enjoy a cup of coffee or wine after a tour of the museum.

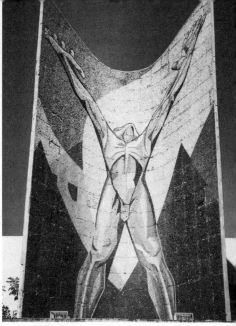

mosaic sculpture in front of the Museo de Arte de El Salvador (MARTE)

★ Museo de Arte de El Salvador (MARTE)

The **Museo de Arte de El Salvador** (Final Av. de la Revolución, tel. 2243-6099, www.marte.org.sv, 10am-6pm Tues.-Sun., $1.50, free Sun.) showcases past and present Salvadoran art, including an excellent permanent collection from Rosa Mena Valenzuela, one of El Salvador's most famous artists. Before her death in 2004, she donated her entire collection of art to the museum. Valenzuela was one of the main exponents of expressionism in El Salvador and used a unique combination of materials such as graphite, industrial paint, colored pencils, and even makeup to create gorgeous abstract paintings. Many other Salvadoran artists are featured in this large modern space. The museum focuses on contemporary art, sculpture, and collections of older paintings from the mid to late 20th century that show the subtle entry of the topic of the civil war into art, depicting rivers of blood, religious symbolism, and peasant uprisings.

There is a small shop inside the museum that carries a very nice selection of books, local crafts, and jewelry. The rooftop restaurant in the museum, **Punto Café** (tel. 2243-7606, noon-11pm Mon.-Sat., $10-20) serves excellent food and is a beautiful spot to enjoy a cup of coffee or a glass of wine after exploring the museum.

DOWNTOWN
Museo de Arte Popular

The **Museo de Arte Popular** (Av. San José 125, tel. 2274-5154, www.artepopular.org, 10am-5pm Mon.-Sat., $1) is full of surprises—literally. This cute museum houses the permanent exhibition of *sorpresas,* the famous Salvadoran miniature clay figures that come from the town of Ilobasco, 54 kilometers northeast of San Salvador. First created by artist María Dominga Herrera in the 1940s, a *sorpresa* is a tiny scene hidden in a small oval about the size of an egg. The original *sorpresas* were made to look like an egg, but now you can find ones that are in the shape of just about anything (most often fruit and vegetables). When you lift the top and look inside—surprise! There is the miniature scene, most typically depicting daily rural life, such as the harvesting of corn or the preparation of a meal. The museum also has plenty of other traditional art from around the country, including masks, sculptures, jewelry, paintings, and textiles.

★ Museo de la Palabra y la Imagen (MUPI)

Founded by Venezuelan journalist Carlos Henríquez Consalvi, a.k.a. Santiago, the brain behind **Radio Venceremos,** the itinerant underground radio station that broadcast guerrilla news and caustic political commentary during the civil war, the **Museo de la Palabra y la Imagen** (27 Av. Norte 1140, between 19 Calle and 21 Calle Poniente, tel. 2275-4870 or 2564-7005, www.museo.com. sv, 8am-noon and 2pm-5pm Mon.-Fri., 8am-noon Sat., $2)—the Museum of the Word and Image—was set up to honor the preservation of historical memory and the promotion of human rights. Inside you will find rotating exhibits dedicated to Salvadoran activists, writers, and authors such as Roque Dalton, Salarrué, and Monseñor Óscar Romero. There

is one permanent exhibit that celebrates the 1992 signing of the peace accords and tracks the history of the civil war on a mural timeline. Other exhibits include personal items such as the journals, clothing, and photographs of famous Salvadoran writers, artists, and activists. There is usually also an exhibit related to Radio Venceremos and the journalists who lost their lives in the name of freedom of information. A visit to MUPI is an excellent way to learn a little more about some of El Salvador's most important human rights advocates as well as how the civil war influenced the country's literary culture.

Attached to the museum is a small bookstore with excellent books by Salvadoran authors related to national history and culture. There is also a room where you can watch films (some have English subtitles). Films and question-and-answer sessions can also be arranged with Santiago—just call the museum to arrange it ahead of time. You can also call to arrange for an English-speaking guide if they have one available.

Capilla Divina Providencia

Capilla Divina Providencia (Final Calle Toluca and Av. Rocio, tel. 2261-1286, 8am-noon and 2pm-5pm daily, free) is the small

timeline of the civil war on permanent display in the Museo de la Palabra y la Imagen (MUPI)

chapel where Monseñor Óscar Romero was assassinted in 1980. The chapel is located inside **Hospital La Divina Providencia,** where nuns, doctors, and nurses offer economic, emotional, and medical care to the terminally ill. It was here that Romero took up residence and gave many of his stirring homilies that gave hope and direction to the poor and suffering.

Romero was appointed archbishop of El Salvador in February 1977. Many believe the Vatican chose him because of his status quo personality and conservative ways, guaranteed not to cause any problems between the church and the state; that might have been true if not for the murder of Rutilio Grande, a Jesuit priest who was Romero's good friend. On March 12, 1977, less than one month after Romero's appointment as archbishop, Grande and two other priests were driving in rural El Salvador where they were working with landless campesinos. They were pulled over by government forces and Grande, a very charismatic and outspoken human rights advocate, was shot to death. Romero was deeply moved by this, and many say Rutilio's death was the turning point in Romero's life from conservative peacekeeper to radical champion of human rights. He believed that the church had a responsibility to help the poor, and that the teachings of Jesus unequivocally espoused equal rights for all. This landed him on the government's list of most wanted socialist dissidents.

On March 24, 1980, just after Romero had finished giving his sermon, as he was standing at the middle of the altar, a shot to the chest killed him instantly. He fell to the floor, dying underneath the image of Jesus. His bloodstained robes can be seen here in the chapel, along with the typewriter he used to compose his open letter to U.S. president Jimmy Carter, pleading with him to stop sending aid money to El Salvador, as all it was doing was funding the deaths of innocent people. You can also see the modest room where Romero lived, a display of photos and other memorabilia, and his car.

ANTIGUO CUSCATLÁN
Centro Monseñor Romero

Centro Monseñor Romero (Universidad Centroamericana José Simeón Cañas, tel. 2210-6600, 8am-noon and 2pm-5pm Mon.-Fri., free) is a small museum located on the UCA campus. It pays homage to Monseñor Óscar Romero, the former Archbishop of El Salvador who was assassinated while giving mass in 1980, as well as the six Jesuit priests, their housekeeper, and her young daughter who were murdered here on campus on November 16, 1989. The murders were part of a larger military campaign that targeted priests all over El Salvador. During this time, many priests were sympathetic to the struggles of the country's poor, and many used mass as an opportunity to preach about basic human rights. The government saw this as aligned with communist ideals and subsequently took steps to get rid of those they considered the most troublesome. Inside this small museum are graphic photos of the victims and some of their personal effects as well as many of Monseñor Romero's belongings and photos. There are usually students available to give guided tours. When you go, enter the university through the pedestrian entrance, off Calle del Mediterráneo, near Joan's Hostel. Make sure you bring photo ID, as you will need it to get onto the campus.

TOURS

Most of the tour companies in San Salvador offer city tours that hit all of the major attractions. For a fascinating and comprehensive tour of the Centro Histórico, be sure to contact Antonio García Espada of **Toony Tours** (tel. 7367-8111, www.medievaltraveler. blogspot.com, $20 per hour), a professor at UCA who also works in the Palacio Nacional with the public archives. This English-language walking tour takes you to as few or as many historical sights as you would like, covering everything from the architectural style of the buildings to the history of religion and the civil war, the impact of coffee on the growth of the capital, and the series of popular

anyone interested in learning more about the history of San Salvador, this tour is essential.

Adventures El Salvador (tel. 7844-0858, www.wtf-elsalvador.com, 4 hours, Sun. only, $30 from the beaches, $25 from the city) runs another interesting tour in the city that takes you on a short run of the highlights of the Centro Histórico, including Iglesia El Rosario, Palacio Nacional, Teatro Nacional, and Catedral Metropolitana, before heading to the underground world of *lucha libre,* the gritty and dramatic free wrestling that was first popularized in Mexico in the 1940s. El Salvador soon followed the trend, and to this day it is extremely popular entertainment for regular working-class Salvadorans. Enjoy some cold beer and fried shrimp balls as you watch the masked *technicos* (the good guys) and *rudos* (the bad) battle it out in the ring. With stage names like "Father of Death" and "El Diablo," this is as much a show as it is sport, and after a few beers you just might find yourself screaming along with the rest of the crowd and becoming an unlikely fanatic. Tours are in English and involve both walking and transfer in a vehicle. Pickup and drop-off at your hotel are provided.

Wrestlers battle it out in the underground world of *lucha libre* in downtown San Salvador.

uprisings and natural disasters that inevitably shaped the heart of the city. Espada leaves no detail undiscovered or story untold. For

Entertainment

NIGHTLIFE
Bars
Zanzibar (Centro Comercial Basilea, tel. 2279-0061, www.barzanzibar.com, 5pm-2am Tues.-Fri., 3pm-2am Sat., no cover) is a popular outdoor bar in Zona Rosa that often has live music. The type of music is very diverse, running the gamut from jazz, rock, grunge, pop, to global groove. Zanzibar is part of Centro Comercial Basilea, a popular complex with shops, cafés, and restaurants. There is outdoor seating and it's a great central place to start off the night.

The brand-new **Vinalia Wine Bar** (Av. Dr. Manuel Gallardo #2-8, inside Yemaya, Santa Tecla, tel. 2223-3937, 5pm-midnight Tues.-Sat.) is stylish and sophisticated, but thankfully doesn't take itself too seriously. This is the perfect spot for good conversation with friends or a romantic date over a glass (or bottle) of wine. This intimate, candlelit second-floor space boasts a few beautiful wooden tables and a bar with stools below open windows that look out over Zona Rosa. The menu includes an eclectic international collection of wines that focus on quality over brand, served by a multilingual certified sommelier. Prices range $4-6 for a glass and $19-100 for a bottle. They also serve fresh bread, olives, cured meats, and imported cheese ($10-30). The friendly owners have achieved the perfect balance between casual and refined, and as a result Vinalia's popularity is quickly gaining momentum.

Los Rinconcitos (Bulevar Hipódromo, tel. 2298-9661, www.losrinconcitos.com, 6pm-2am Mon., 6pm-5am Tues.-Sat., no cover) is a classic bar in San Salvador. Most people will tell you Los Rinconcitos is past its prime, but it still draws crowds due to its location right on the main strip in Zona Rosa. It's a labyrinth of many bars, starting with a lounge with a pub-like atmosphere, TVs, a long wooden bar, and tall tables, all perfectly designed to have a couple of beers with friends. Once you are feeling good, you can make your way to the next room and belt out a few songs in the karaoke bar. If you dare enter the final door, things get heady with a full-on club atmosphere, complete with lots of cigarette smoke, little ventilation, throbbing *cumbia,* flashing lights, and a small dance floor that often gets crowded with very good dancers.

Republik (Calle La Reforma 243, tel. 2240-0041, 5pm-2am Tues.-Sat., no cover) is your Irish pub in Zona Rosa, complete with a massive bar with an extensive selection of booze, wooden kegs, old photos on the walls, and a stage for live music (usually '90s rock). A grand staircase leads to the second floor, which has a smoking section with more tables and cozy corners. It's the perfect place for getting rowdy with your friends or hiding out in a corner for something more intimate. There is typical pub fare available, with popular chicken burritos and mini chipotle burgers. Guinness lovers should note there is none of the dark stuff on tap; you can buy a can, which will set you back around $10.

Cadejo Brewing Company (Calle La Reforma 222, tel. 2223-3180, www.cervezacadejo.com, noon-11pm Mon.-Thurs., noon-midnight Fri., 9am-midnight Sat., 9am-3pm Sun., no cover) serves locally crafted beer on a small terrace in the heart of Zona Rosa. Try one of the excellent staples, the *wapa,* wheat American pale ale, or *roja,* a heartier red ale. Alternatively you could check to see what the seasonal brew is at the moment, or try a sampler of whatever is on tap, for just $1 a glass. This is a great spot to start off the night, sampling beer and watching people go by on the street.

Bar Leyendas (9 Calle 104, between 6 Av. and 7 Av., no phone, leyendascafebar@gmail.com, 6pm-1am Tues.-Sat., no cover) is where 20-something Salvadorans like to hang out while they wait for the work week to end. Located near the Universidad de El Salvador, it's a basic, dimly lit space with tall tables, low tables, and a very small bar. Come ready to drink like a champ and rock out to Pearl Jam. If you come on a Saturday night, it's likely to be dead, as most of the regulars have gone to the beach.

Nearby **Café La T** (Calle San Antonio Abad 2233, tel. 2225-2390, 10am-9pm Mon.-Wed., 10am-11pm Thurs.-Sat., no cover) is the long-standing favorite for university students, artists, and expat volunteers, who appreciate the fun cultural vibe. This large space has indoor and outdoor seating, colorful campesino murals on the walls, cozy old couches, and candles on the eclectic collection of tables. They often host poetry nights, have live music (rock, jazz, reggae), and every Friday night is salsa night. No matter that you have never danced salsa in your life, the crowd is friendly and you are likely to find a teacher by the end of the night.

Clandestino (Calle San Antonio Abad 2237, tel. 2566-9755, 4pm-2am Tues.-Sat., no cover) is the newest bar on this strip, located just a few doors down from Café La T, and so far it's drawing crowds. This very long space has made good use of the walls by painting them with interesting murals. There is no stage, but a small space on the floor does just as well for live music (rock, jazz, and reggae). Expect salsa after the live music is done.

In the same neighborhood is **La Arpa Irlandés** (Av. A 137, just off of Calle Antonio Abad, behind Citibank, tel. 2225-0429, 4pm-1am Mon.-Thurs., 3pm-2am Fri., noon-2am Sat., no cover), the darker, cheaper, more philosophical version of Zona Rosa's Republik. Expect to find left-leaning university students drinking until at least last call, probably

Summer Festivals in San Salvador

Fiestas Agostinas (August Festivals) are celebrated the first week of August in San Salvador. This is when San Salvador's patron saint, the Divine Savior of the World (a.k.a. Jesus Christ), is celebrated. Expect crowds, parades, fireworks, and more. Most people have at least half the week off and travel to the beaches or mountains for their yearly vacations. The religious events of the week culminate with an evening mass on August 6, celebrating the Transfiguration of Jesus.

    Las Bolas de Fuego (Balls of Fire) happens on August 31 every year in Nejapa, a small municipality just north of San Salvador, and is considered one of the best and craziest festivals in the country. The public gathers along both sides of the main street and watches as the people of Nejapa hurl flaming kerosene-soaked rag balls at each other for a couple of hours. The tradition is more than 100 years old and commemorates the eruption of the volcano El Playón in November 1658, when incandescent balls of fire flew into the air. Paramedics and police are on-site in case of injuries and fires, and after the show, a raging party ensues. Yes, this really happens. If you want to check it out, ask at your hotel to arrange transportation with a guide; it's too complicated to get there and back on your own.

    Día de Independencia (Independence Day) celebrates independence from the Spanish and is observed annually on September 15. It is a national holiday celebrated with parades, fireworks, and, of course, lots of food.

discussing topics like Latin American history, culture, and literature over multiple jugs of beer.

    Circo Bar (Pasaje Istmania 128, Colonia Escalón, tel. 2298-4911, www.barcirco.com, 7:30pm-2am Mon.-Sat.) is a somewhat exclusive bar where well-heeled 20- and 30-somethings come to see and be seen. Located in upscale Escalón, this circus-themed bar has different events every night, ranging from fashion shows to costume theme parties, live music, and drama. The space is huge, with a stage surrounded by glittering tables and chairs, low-hung glowing red lamps, and red curtains draped from the ceiling, creating a dramatic circus-tent feel. Check the website to find out what's on. Cover charge varies depending on the show.

    Also in Escalón, **Bar Bass** (79 Av. Norte and 3 Calle Poniente, tel. 2264-1924, 7pm-2am Tues.-Sat., no cover) is the newest hot spot for live music in San Salvador. This small casual-chic space showcases bands that run the gamut from pop, ska, and reggae to heavy metal and rock. Wooden tables are scattered throughout the bar along with cozy cushioned benches, and colorful murals cover the walls. Bar Bass also serves good food, including sushi, pizza, and the popular pulled-pork sandwich.

Nightclubs

Most of the nightclubs in San Salvador are quite elitist, meaning that if you go, make sure you are dressed appropriately; if not, chances are you will be turned away at the door. In general, you will need to be dressed formally to enter. For men this means dress pants, dress shoes, and a buttoned shirt. Women should wear skirts or a dress and high heels. All of the clubs seem to be cut from the same cloth, with top 40 salsa and dance music blaring from the speakers, flashing lights, overpriced drinks, and overly drunk patrons. Depending on what kind of a mood you are in, this could be fun. Most people go to the clubs in **Multiplaza** (Av. Jerusalén and Carretera Panamericana, tel. 2248-9800, www.gruporoble.com), on the way to Santa Tecla. The clubs are located on the rooftop, and there are three primary ones: **Stanza** (tel. 2243-7153, 5pm-3am Wed.-Sat.) and **NVY** (tel. 2243-2576, 5pm-5am Wed.-Sat.), both of which charge a cover and draw crowds mostly in their early to mid-20s; and **Los Alambiques** (tel. 2243-3872, 5pm-3am Wed.-Sat.), which draws a more mature crowd (late 20s to early 30s) and does not charge cover.

THEATER

El Teatro Nacional (Calle Delgado and 2 Av. Norte, tel. 2222-5731) often has plays or performances by the San Salvador Symphony on the weekends. Costs vary according to the show.

CINEMA

There are movie theaters in **Multiplaza** (Av. Jerusalén and Carretera Panamericana, tel. 2248-9800, www.cinepolis.com.sv), **La Gran Vía** (Calle Chilitupán and Carretera Panamericana, tel. 2289-2105, www.lagranvia.com.sv), and **Galerías** (Paseo Escalón 3700, tel. 2245-0800, www.galerias.com.sv) that normally show family films or action-packed thrillers in English with Spanish subtitles. Galerías mall is located in Escalón, and Multiplaza and La Gran Vía are located between Antiguo Cuscatlán and Santa Tecla off Carretera Panamericana (Pan-American Hwy.).

Shopping

MALLS

El Salvador loves malls, and the bigger the better. **Metrocentro** (Av. Sur and Bulevar de los Héroes, tel. 2257-6000, www.gruporoble.com, 10am-10pm daily) is actually Central America's biggest mall, and indeed it is easy to get lost for hours inside if you do not have a targeted plan before entering. Located downtown, near Universidad de El Salvador, Metrocentro has multiple parking lots, three floors, and about a dozen wings of shops, where you can expect to find just about anything you need. The much flashier **Galerías** (Paseo Escalón 3700, tel. 2245-0800, www.galerias.com.sv, 10am-10pm daily) in Escalón offers quality over quantity, providing a smaller number of shops with higher-end clothing and technological gadgets along with cafés.

Between San Salvador and Santa Tecla, you will find the very popular **La Gran Vía** (Calle Chilitupán and Carretera Panamericana, tel. 2273-8111, www.lagranvia.com.sv, 10am-8pm Mon.-Thurs., 10am-9pm Fri.-Sat., 10am-7pm Sun.), a strip of shops and restaurants that line an outdoor pedestrian area. La Gran Vía gets packed on weekends with Salvadorans who come to shop, sit at one of the outdoor cafés, or go to the movies.

Nearby **Multiplaza** (Av. Jerusalén and Carretera Panamericana, tel. 2248-9800, www.gruporoble.com, 10am-8pm Mon.-Sat., 10am-7pm Sun.) is an unlikely looking mall, with its brutalist cube-shaped architectural style. Inside are two floors of open spaces between the more than 200 shops. Multiplaza is probably best-known for its nightlife on the third floor, where there are various nightclubs that are very popular with Salvadorans on the weekends.

In Zona Rosa, **Basilea Centro Comercial** (Bulevar Hipódromo, Zona Rosa, tel. 2279-0833, www.ccbasilea.com) is a small, charming commercial center with an excellent artisanal shop inside called **Nahanche** (tel. 2260-1581, www.nahanche.com, 9am-7pm Mon.-Sat., 10am-6pm Sun.). Basilea is also home to **Shaw's Café** (tel. 2223-0959, www.shaws.com, 9am-7pm daily), a café that specializes in locally produced chocolate but also serves snacks and coffee; **Bookmarks** (no phone, www.bookmarks.com.sv, 9am-6pm daily), a cute little bookstore with mostly Spanish titles; a beauty salon; Zanzibar nightclub; and the popular Oskar Bistro.

MARKETS

The **Mercado Central** (between Calle Cementario and Av. 29 de Agosto, no phone, 7am-6pm daily) is a sprawling, chaotic market in the Centro Histórico. The streets are literally taken over by vendors—you'll see elderly women chopping fruit on the side of the road, men pushing around wheelbarrows full of vegetables, pirated DVDs, makeshift pharmacies, live chickens, and secondhand clothing. This is where the locals come to do their shopping, and it is as worth a visit for the cheap necessities as it is to see an unpolished urban Latin American market in full swing.

The **Mercado Ex-Cuartel** (8 Av. Sur and Calle Delgado, no phone, 8am-6pm Mon.-Sat., 8am-3pm Sun.) is the tamed-down, more tourist-friendly version of Mercado Central. Contained inside a former army barracks, this large public market houses a rather underwhelming collection of shoes, clothing, textiles, and hammocks. It's not a bad stop if you are looking for cheap handmade shoes or a local hammock.

The **Mercado Nacional de Artesanías** (Alameda Dr. Manuel Enrique Araujo, behind the international fair grounds, tel. 2224-0747, 9am-6pm daily) is a convenient place to stop if you have reached the end of your trip and realize you had so much fun sightseeing that you forgot to buy souvenirs. This is your one-stop shop for all things artisanal in El Salvador, including colorful textiles, black pottery, art, jewelry, and clothing. Although many of the goods are from El Salvador, it's worth noting that a large amount has also been imported from Guatemala, especially the shirts and handbags. Expect to pay a small premium for the convenience.

Sports and Recreation

★ PUERTA DEL DIABLO

Legend has it that the **Puerta del Diablo** (Planes de Los Renderos, daily, free, parking $1) is the result of an earthquake in the 18th century that split one massive boulder into three towering rocks, two of which have staircases carved into them and can be climbed. The hike up either rock is steep but short and takes about 15 minutes. From the top you can enjoy panoramic views of the verdant rolling hills as well as the San Salvador and San Vicente volcanoes, Lago Ilopango, and the Pacific Ocean. It's cool, the air is clean, and it's incredibly peaceful.

You would never guess its dark history, but during the war, La Puerta was used as a body dump site, the extreme cliffs exploited as a method of rapid disposal. There is nothing at the site to acknowledge this vicious past, but you can check out Joan Didion's chilling account of a visit to this site during the war in her book *Salvador*.

During the week, the site is popular for couples or close friends seeking a peaceful, private spot to escape the madness of the heavily populated city. It gets busier on the weekend, especially Sunday. At the bottom of the boulders are various *comedors* and *tiendas* selling souvenirs and other knickknacks.

To get to La Puerta del Diablo, 23 kilometers southeast of San Salvador, you need to catch bus 12 ($0.50, 40 minutes, runs every 20 minutes) to Planes de los Renderos from the east side of Mercado Central on 12 Calle Poniente. This will take you to Parque Balboa. From there, you can walk the two kilometers south or take bus 12 with the sign "Mil Cumbres" ($0.25, 5 minutes, runs every 30 minutes) to La Puerta del Diablo.

PARQUE BALBOA

Parque Balboa (8am-6pm daily, $3, $4 with vehicle) is just two kilometers north of La Puerta del Diablo and offers an expansive park with towering trees of bamboo and palms, creating the perfect cool forest getaway. The park is flat, so there is no hiking per se, but walking trails are available. There is also a basketball court, a section for skateboarding, a paved road for biking, and a few *pupuserías*.

To get here from San Salvador, take bus 12 ($0.50, 40 minutes, runs every 20 minutes) to Planes de los Renderos from the east side of

Mercado Central on 12 Calle Poniente, and get off at Parque Balboa.

BALNEARIO LOS CHORROS

Balneario Los Chorros (just west of Santa Tecla on Carretera Panamericana, 8am-5pm daily, $3) is a collection of beautiful sea-green natural pools with cool, clear water to swim in. There are even little fish that will come to nibble at your toes, if you are into that kind of thing. Surrounded by tall boulders covered in greenery and small waterfalls that feed the pools, this is truly a tropical paradise just a 10-minute drive outside of Santa Tecla. The trails on the grounds are chained shut to prevent vandalism, but if you ask one of the soldiers working at the entrance, they will gladly open them up and guide you around the lush area. There are also open-air cafés serving cheap and delicious grilled chicken and beer. Like most other natural attractions in the country, Los Chorros gets really busy on the weekends, so unless you want to be caught up in the crowds, best to go on Wednesday or Thursday.

Puerta del Diablo

To get to Los Chorros, you can take any bus going to Santa Ana, Sonsonate, or Ahuachapán (buses 201, 202, or 205, $0.50/10 minutes from Santa Tecla, $0.75/one hour from San Salvador, buses run every 10 minutes) and ask to be let off at Los Chorros.

JARDÍN BOTÁNICO LA LAGUNA

Also called Plan de La Laguna, **Jardín Botánico La Laguna** (Urbanización Industrial Plan de La Laguna, Antiguo Cuscatlán, tel. 2243-2012 or 2243-2013, jardinbotanico@jardinbotanico.org.sv, 9am-5:30pm Tues.-Sun., $1 adults, $0.60 children), a botanical garden, is an unlikely oasis in an industrial part of the city, located at the bottom of a volcanic crater that offers a cool refuge from the chaos of the city center. Meandering stone paths are flanked on both sides by lush tropical greenery, papyrus trees, groves of towering bamboo, and plenty of bougainvillea. There is also an impressive orchid garden showing off some of the species that thrive in certain parts of the country. The garden has plenty of space to chill out, with pretty bridges covering ponds full of fish and benches throughout, as well as a small cafeteria and library. All of the trees and plants are identified with signs, and there is a nursery where you can buy plants and seeds. Because of its somewhat awkward location off Carretera Panamericana, most people arrive by car. Juan Granados of **Juancito's Mango Inn** in Santa Tecla offers great tours to the Jardín Botánico La Laguna.

LAGO ILOPANGO

Lago Ilopango lies about 30 kilometers east of the city. The large, crystal-clear green crater lake is beautiful, and there are areas with hammocks and picnic tables right at the lake's edge for public use.

Lago Ilopango is great for swimming, boating, and diving (it is 76 meters deep at the center), although diving trips should be prearranged with a provider, as there are no diving offices on the lake. **El Salvador Divers** (3 Calle Poniente and 99 Av. Norte, No. 5020, Escalón, tel. 2264-0961, info@elsalvadordivers.com) does excellent trips to Lago Ilopango. Once here, you can rent a small motorized boat for $10 and get the driver to take you to the **Cerros Quemados** (Burned Hills), small volcanic islands in the center of the lake where you can walk around and enjoy the tranquility and panoramic views. Some of the small *comedors* around the lake may also have canoes that you can rent for a few dollars.

Getting here is a bit of a trek, and you must take the bus through the chaotic eastern part of the city, which is rarely frequented by tourists. Take bus 15 from Palacio Nacional (Calle 9 Poniente and 1 Av. Norte) to Apulo. The bus costs $0.40, takes about one hour, and runs every half hour.

★ PARQUE NACIONAL EL BOQUERÓN

Parque Nacional El Boquerón (Final Carretera Volcán de San Salvador, tel. 2243-7835, ext. 165, 8am-5pm daily, $1) is about a 30-minute drive west of downtown San Salvador and a beautiful respite from the heat. The park comprises three major peaks that make up Volcán San Salvador: Jabalí, Picacho, and the well-known El Boquerón, meaning "big mouth" because of its steep-walled crater. The volcano has an elevation of 1,800 meters and the crater is 5 kilometers wide and 170 meters deep.

There are various **hikes** you can do once you reach the park. The first is to the **lookout point;** this 20-minute trek is short but steep, but the spectacular view of San Salvador and the valley below make it worth it. The walk is well signed and easy to navigate. It is also possible to walk **around the crater,** through the lush vegetation and beautiful flowers, birds, and butterflies. The hike is easy, well signed, possible to do without a guide, and takes about half an hour. For more adventurous hikers, it is possible to hike all the way down **into the crater** and back up. It's a pretty trail, peppered with wild berries and flowers, notably the beautiful hydrangeas, begonias, and orchids. You can ask the locals selling fruit at the entrance of the park for a guide, and they will help you find someone who knows the crater well. A guide should charge you around $30. This is not recommended for inexperienced hikers, as it can get quite difficult in some areas, even requiring some free rappelling. This hike takes about four hours round-trip.

Parque Nacional El Boquerón

If you don't want to hike at all, there are plenty of roadside restaurants and cafés on the way up to the entrance of the park, where you can sit back and enjoy the cool climate, fresh air, and top-notch view.

To get to the park, you need to first take bus 101A or 101B to Santa Tecla ($0.20, 20 minutes up to 45 minutes with traffic, runs every 15 minutes). Ask to get off at 6 Avenida Sur, and from there you need to catch bus 103 ($0.50, 25 minutes, runs every 20 minutes) to the park. Unfortunately, the bus stops about two kilometers outside the park's entrance, and the uphill walk is not easy. A taxi from Santa Tecla should cost $10, and from San Salvador around $25.

Accommodations

Most of the city's best hotels are located in **Colonia Escalón** and **Zona Rosa.** Zona Rosa is the flashiest area, with luxury hotels, stylish restaurants, lots of nightlife, and cute cafés. This is also where you will find the city's two largest museums, the Museo de Arte (MARTE) and the Museo Nacional de Antropología Dr. David J. Guzmán (MUNA). It is walkable and concentrated, with everything you need within a few main streets. Escalón is full of quiet, tree-lined streets with excellent restaurants, malls, and hotels; keep in mind, however, that it is not within short walking distance of San Salvador's sights, although it is possible to walk to the Centro Histórico in about 40 minutes.

The **downtown** area around Metrocentro and the Universidad de El Salvador is frankly not that pretty (think heavy traffic and smog), but there are still a few hotels that offer very good value for the money. This area is a good choice if you want to be close to the university bars, the two small but interesting museums—Museo de la Palabra y la Imagen and Museo de Arte Popular—and, for what it's worth, the largest shopping mall in Central America.

Antiguo Cuscatlán is the neighborhood west of the city center, and it offers some lovely options near the Universidad Centroamericana José Simeón Cañas (UCA), where you will find the Centro Monseñor Romero and the well groomed university grounds, a nice green space to visit. This area is also close to a major bus stop, supermarkets, pharmacies, many budget restaurants and cafés, and also just a short drive to the suburb of Santa Tecla.

COLONIA ESCALÓN AND ZONA ROSA
Under $10
★ **Hostal Cumbres del Volcán** (85 Av. Norte 637, tel. 2207-3705, www.cumbresdel-volcan.com, $8-10 pp dorm, $35 d private room) is a great option for budget accommodations in the city. Located in the upscale tree-laden neighborhood of Escalón, this new hostel is close to amenities, malls, and Zona Rosa. This large, bright, breezy space has a colorful modern lounge area with a flat-screen TV, a spotless kitchen, and a terrace. There are two dormitories with fans, one of which has bunk beds ($8), the other with regular single beds ($10). Private rooms are simple, with tile floors, a double bed with colorful bedspreads, and large windows that let the light in. Private rooms also have air-conditioning and TV, and the entire hostel has hot water and Wi-Fi.

$25-50
You would never guess from the outside, but **Hostal Verona** (11 Calle Poniente 4323, tel. 2264-6035 or 2264-6036, www.hostal-verona.com, $48 s, $55 d, includes breakfast) is an unsung treasure. Unpretentious but full of charming little details, including gorgeous fresh flowers placed throughout, a lush green garden, and a cute little bar, this small, homey hostel is a great mid-range choice in Escalón. The rooms are plain and clean, with neutral

Colonia Escalón

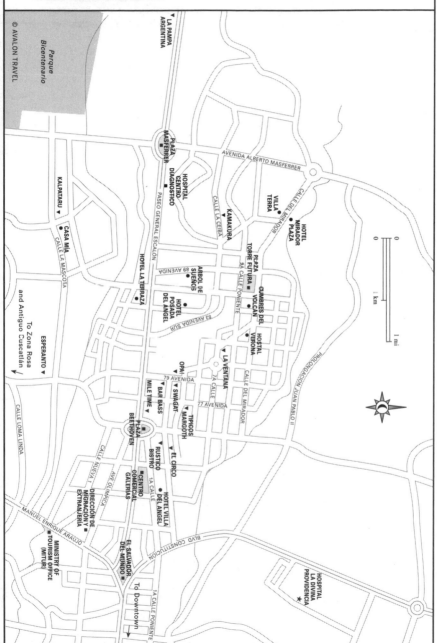

© AVALON TRAVEL

Parque Bicentenario

LA PAMPA ARGENTINA

AVENIDA ALBERTO MASFERRER

PLAZA MASFERRER

KALPATARU

CASA MÍA

CALLE LA MASCOTA

PASEO GENERAL ESCALÓN

HOSPITAL CENTRO DIAGNÓSTICO

CALLE LA CEIBA

VILLA TERRA

HOTEL MIRADOR PLAZA

CALLE DEL MIRADOR

KAMAKURA

PLAZA TORRE FUTURA

3A. CALLE PONIENTE

HOTEL LA TERRAZA

ARBOL DE SUEÑOS

89 AVENIDA

HOTEL POSADA DEL ANGEL

CUMBRES DEL VOLCÁN

HOSTAL VERONA

83 AVENIDA SUR

LA VENTANA

7A CALLE

CALLE DEL MIRADOR

PROLONGACIÓN JUAN PABLO II

0
1 km
1 mi

ESPERANTO

To Zona Rosa and Antiguo Cuscatlán

CALLE LOMA LINDA

OPA!

79 AVENIDA

SWAGAT

BAR BASS

MILE TIME

PLAZA BEETHOVEN

RUSTICO BISTRO

77 AVENIDA

TIPICOS MARGOTH

EL CHICO

CALLE NUEVA

AVE OLIMPICA

CENTRO COMERCIAL GALERIAS

HOTEL VILLA DEL ANGEL

1A CALLE

DIRECCIÓN DE MIGRACIÓN Y EXTRANJERIA

MANUEL ENRIQUE ARAUJO

MINISTRY OF TOURISM OFFICE (MITUR)

EL SALVADOR DEL MUNDO

BLVD CONSTITUCIÓN

To Downtown

7A CALLE PONIENTE

HOSPITAL LA DIVINA PROVIDENCIA

colors on the beds and walls, tile floors, gleaming baths with hot water, a minibar, TV and air-conditioning. The location is not the best, as it is right on a busy street, so you can hear the traffic; however, the rooms are on the opposite side, so it shouldn't be an issue for sleeping.

Hotel la Posada Del Angel (85 Av. Norte 321, tel. 2256-1172 or 2263-2058, www.hotel-laposadadelangel.com, $45 s or d) stands out from the rest of the mid-range hotels for its exceptional service, attention to detail, and all-around friendly vibe. A beautiful home with warm terra-cotta colors, wrought-iron furniture, and a lovely garden, this feels more like you are visiting friends or family than staying in a hotel. No request is too much for the staff and very accommodating owners, from preparing food after a late arrival to arranging taxi transportation around the city and keeping a constant flow of coffee and conversation going. The rooms are simple and clean with tile floors, beds with traditional textiles, windows to let in the light, along with TV, air-conditioning, Wi-Fi, and hot water. Breakfast is included in the price and served on the large beautiful terrace by the garden.

$50-100

The beautiful ★ **Casa Mía Boutique Hotel** (Calle La Mascota 2123, Colonia Maquilishuat, tel. 2263-9502 or 2264-3614, $68 s, $90 d) is San Salvador's hidden gem. This charming boutique hotel is set back from the street and boasts lots of tranquil outdoor space surrounded by plants, flowers, and towering shady trees. Rooms are large and airy with light colors, cool tile floors, TV, hot water, air-conditioning, Wi-Fi, and large beds with heavy wooden bed frames, some hand-painted with ornate flowers and vines and others with more modern minimalist designs. All rooms have large windows that open up to the sprawling garden and large outdoor terrace with wicker lounge furniture, where you can relax after battling the mean streets of the city. Cool off in the picturesque swimming

pool surrounded by a stone deck, lounge chairs, and umbrellas to shade you from the heat, and atmospheric soft pool lights after the sun goes down. The service is excellent as well.

La Terraza (85 Av. Sur and Calle Padres Aguilar, tel. 2565-7000, www.terraza.com.sv, $82 s, $93 d, includes breakfast) is an elegant business hotel, but you definitely do not need to be on a business trip to appreciate the beautiful details and exceptional service that this hotel offers. The lobby is large, with ornate tile floors, a large chandelier, antique chairs, and a spiral staircase creating a majestic feel. Rooms are simple and lovely with double beds in plain white bedding, complemented by subtle hues of peaches and browns on the walls. Each room has a desk, a TV, air-conditioning, and hot water. The regular rooms have windows that overlook the swimming pool, and the more expensive suites (larger, with a couch, fridge, iron, and coffeemaker) overlook the street.

It's easy to miss **Arbol de Sueños** (89 Av. Norte, tel. 2263-2545 or 2264-7200, www. arboldesuenos.com, $55 s, $65 d, includes breakfast), the artsy little gem that is overshadowed by mammoth business hotel Crown Plaza right across the street. But if you find it, you will not be disappointed. This design hotel is small and sophisticated, with modern Salvadoran art on the walls, a pretty little plant-filled terrace, and large, modern, light, and airy rooms that all have an individual touch. Rooms have air-conditioning and hot water.

Villa del Angel Hotel (71 Av. Norte 219, tel. 2223-7171, $64 s, $87 d, includes breakfast) is an excellent choice for those who want luxury hotel treatment with a moderate price tag. This brand-new boutique hotel, with its funky, fresh design and exceptional service, definitely stands out. Tucked away in a great location on a quiet tree-laden side street just around the corner from the Galerías mall, Villa del Angel offers excellent security and service. The style of the decor is contemporary, with spotless white floors and furniture complemented with avocado green and bright blue walls. Rooms have beds with beautiful, thick mattresses, dark wood paneling, flat-screen TVs, air-conditioning and hot water. The common area is full of natural light, where there is another larger TV with a collection of DVDs available. Transportation to and from the airport or bus station is provided, and excellent tours around the country are offered.

Hotel Villa Terra (Calle El Mirador 4907, tel. 2536-2000, www.hotelvillaterra.com, $74 s, $83 d, includes breakfast) is a rich red adobe-style building that opens up to a beautiful courtyard space with colorful Salvadoran pottery and paintings alongside fresh flowers and wrought-iron furniture. Rooms are also cute but not as thoughtfully decorated as the common area. Each room has two double beds on wrought-iron bedposts, rich yellow bedspreads, and brown tile floors that create a warm if simple space. TV, air-conditioning, hot water, and Wi-Fi are included.

Despite its very awkward location, right on perpetually busy Avenida de la Revolución, **Terra Bella Boutique Hotel** (Av. de la Revolución 175, tel. 2133-6900 or 2564-7762, www.hotelterrabella.com, $55 s, $70 d) is worth checking out for its stylish lobby and rooms, and its reasonable price in the flashy Zona Rosa. Furniture and art with earthy tones meet modern industrial design inside the lobby. Rooms are sleek and refined with beige and brown hues, big comfy beds, flat-screen TVs, air-conditioning, and baths with hot water, transparent glass shower doors, and vessel sinks.

Hotel Villa Florencia (Av. de la Revolución and Calle Las Palmas, tel. 2243-7164, www.hotelvillaflorencia.com, $55 s, $65 d, includes breakfast) sits right in the heart of San Benito and is a classic, comfortable mid-range stay. Rooms are small but bright with large windows bringing in natural light, light wood bed frames, and light neutral colors to match, along with tile floors, TVs, air-conditioning, Wi-Fi, and hot water. There is

a small cheerful café with plenty of windows and excellent food. The service is top notch. Although there is no swimming pool, the charming garden makes up for it, providing an oasis to enjoy a cup of coffee in the morning or a glass of wine at night.

$100-200

Hotel Mirador Plaza (Calle El Mirador and 95 Av. Norte, 4908, tel. 2244-6000, www.miradorplaza.com, $114 s, $120 d, includes breakfast) is a blend of modern and traditional design. The outside of the building sports a sleek, contemporary design with sliding glass doors that bring you into a large lobby with antique light fixtures and furniture, gleaming tile floors, modern art, and traditional Salvadoran handcrafts. The rooms are refined and simple with double beds, TVs, air-conditioning, and (sometimes) hot water. There is a small restaurant, a small gym, and a well-maintained swimming pool on the meticulously manicured grounds. Unfortunately, the staff is not as friendly or helpful as they could be, considering the room rates.

Suites Las Palmas (Bulevar Hipódromo, tel. 2250-0800, ventas@suiteslaspalmas.com.sv, $105 s, $115 d) is substantially cheaper than the other high-end hotels in the area and almost as nice. This tall sleek art deco-looking building is surrounded by palm trees and is conveniently located in the heart of Zona Rosa. Rooms are spacious and carpeted with deep red and yellow tones on the walls, lush king beds, desks, and couches. All rooms have TV, Wi-Fi, hot water, air-conditioning, and large windows, some with views of Volcán San Salvador. There is a small gym, a rooftop swimming pool with a spectacular view, laundry service, and room service. Staff are eager to please, and for the rates and location it's a good choice among the higher-end hotels in Zona Rosa.

Sheraton Presidente San Salvador (Av. de la Revolución, tel. 2283-4000, www.sheraton.com/sansalvador, $109 s, 119 d) is a grand old hotel conveniently located right next to the Museo de Arte de El Salvador (MARTE) and plenty of great restaurants and cafés. The service is excellent across the board, and all of the amenities you need are right in the hotel, including an excellent business center, a tour company, a café with snacks and coffee to go, a large outdoor swimming pool, a gym, and a spa. Wide mint-green carpeted hallways lead to rooms that are a bit dated but still manage to look fairly modern with their minimalist design and neutral colors. Large, luxurious beds are the centerpiece of the rooms, and some have outstanding views of Volcán San Salvador. All rooms have TV, Wi-Fi, air-conditioning, and hot water. An excellent breakfast buffet is included in the rates and is served on the outdoor terrace. Weekend rates ($99 s or d) are cheaper.

The **Princess Hilton** (Bulevar Hipódromo and Av. Las Magnolias, tel. 2268-4545, www.sansalvador.hilton.com, $175 s, $200 d) is definitely the most grandiose of the high-end hotels. The massive lobby is full of towering columns, ornately designed corners, and beautiful antique furniture and art. The rooms are also beautiful, with modern design, neutral colors, and large windows that offer spectacular views of the volcano. All rooms have air-conditioning, Wi-Fi, TVs, and hot water. There is an outdoor pool, a small gym, and a spa. Breakfast is included in the rates, and the restaurant also offers an exceptional lunch buffet. The staff is extremely helpful, and the hotel is conveniently located right next to Centro Comercial Basilea. Rates are considerably cheaper on weekends ($129 s or d).

The **Hotel Intercontinental Real San Salvador** (Bulevar de los Héroes and Av. Sisimiles, tel. 2221-3333, $149 s or d) is the most modern of the high-end hotels, and you can feel the difference as soon as you walk in the lobby—sleek design with distinctly Salvadoran touches such as the Fernando Llort art on the walls, modern chairs with retro designs, warm colors, and soft light all come together to create a contemporary comfortable space. Rooms are also modern, with large, flat-screen TVs, very comfortable beds with spotless white linens, large windows that bring in lots of natural light, a desk, hot water, and air-conditioning. Unfortunately, Wi-Fi costs an additional $15 for 24 hours, and breakfast will run you an additional $19. The Intercontinental has three very good restaurants, the most popular of which is Faisca do Brasil, specializing in Brazilian barbecue. Rooms are also cheaper on the weekends ($89 s or d).

DOWNTOWN
Under $10

Ximena's Guesthouse (Calle San Salvador 202, tel. 2260-2481, www.ximenasguesthouse.com, $7-10 pp dorm, $25 d) is one of the oldest hostels in the city, and although it is showing its age, it's the only budget choice if you want to stay in this central location near the Universidad de El Salvador. It's within walking distance of a strip of university bars, various fast-food restaurants, museums, and Metrocentro, Central America's largest mall. The dormitories in Ximena's have mismatched, well-worn beds, ceiling fans, and a cramped shared bath with hot water that sometimes floods. Private rooms are lacking natural light, have ceiling fans, and have small baths with hot water and cracked toilet seats. There is no restaurant, and the kitchen is not for guest use. Wi-Fi costs an additional $2. Ximena's redeeming quality is the very friendly and efficient staff, who will go out of their way to help you with directions, transportation, and any other practicalities you need help with. They do not speak English, but the owner, Lena, does, and she is also always available, either in person or by phone, to help out.

$25-50

Hotel Villa Real (Calle Sisimiles 2944, tel. 2260-1579 or 2260-1665, www.hotelvillarealelsalvador.com, $35 s, $45 d) is an excellent choice. This long-standing favorite has been

Downtown San Salvador

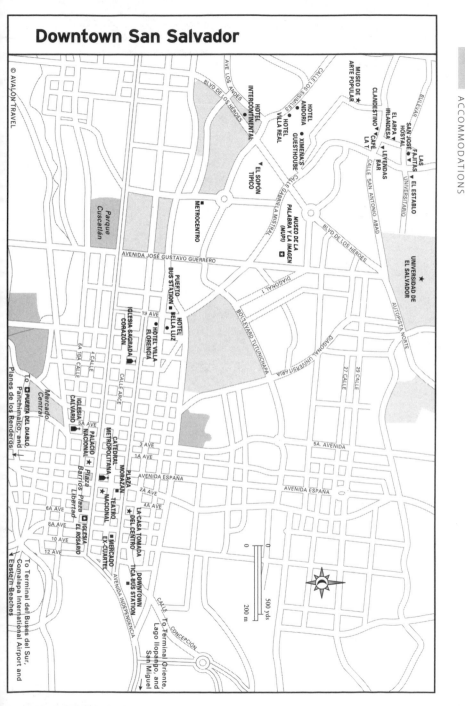

© AVALON TRAVEL

around since 1997, but you couldn't tell by looking at it. The inside of the hotel is spacious and clean with lots of natural light and common space. Colorful Salvadoran handicrafts, hanging ferns, and iron art make the common area bright and cheerful. The rooms are simple but lovely, with white tile floors, peach walls, TVs, air-conditioning, and hot water. The lobby is big and bright with couches, a vending machine, two computers, and colorful art on the walls. There is a rooftop terrace as well as a small eating area where the included breakfast is served. Free coffee available all day long is also a bonus.

The tastefully designed **Hotel Andoria** (Calle Los Sisimiles 2946, tel. 2260-8957, hotelandoria@hotmail.com, $33 s or d) is the other best option on this strip. Cheerfully painted walls, Salvadoran folk art, and antique furniture create a charming, cozy vibe. There is a spacious and bright eating area (although there is no restaurant, you can order food from one of the nearby restaurants and they will arrange delivery), a vending machine selling snacks and drinks, a coffee machine, and a microwave. The rooms are lovely, with TVs, air-conditioning, hot water, and colorful art and sliding glass doors that open up to adorable secret terraces full of plants and sitting areas.

Hostal San José (Bulevar Universitario 2212, between 39 Av. Norte and Av. Izalco, tel. 2226-4603, info@sanjosehostal.com, $30 s, $40 d) is simple, quiet hostel hidden away on a side street near Universidad de El Salvador. There is a common area with couches and chairs, a computer, and a small garden. Rooms are basic, with white tile floors, fans, double beds, private baths, and hot water. Most people don't know this hostel exists, so it is rarely crowded.

ANTIGUO CUSCATLÁN

★ **Joan's Hostel** (Calle del Mediterráneo 12, Colonia Jardines de Guadalupe, tel. 7860-7157 or 2519-0973, $13 pp dorm, $20 s, $36 d) is a small hostel with big personality, owing entirely to the vivacious and gracious owner Ana Luisa Mena, who took her family home, transformed it into a hostel, and opened its doors to travelers seeking a safe budget option in the city. The hostel retains a homey feel but with modern design—including a very cozy area for watching TV as well as a lovely lounge area with couches. There is a small kitchen and a large dining table in the common area as well as a few wrought-iron tables outside in a courtyard. There are two dormitories and two private rooms, all very basic but clean, modern, and comfortable, with fans and hot water. Located right beside UCA, Joan's is within walking distance of numerous cafés, restaurants, and bars, including very good Greek food and pizza right across the street. It's also just a short drive to Santa Tecla, where you will find some of the best nightlife in the country, and a short walk to major bus stop La Ceiba de Guadalupe.

Just down the street from Joan's Hostel you will find **Arbol de Fuego** (Av. Antiguo Cuscatlán 11c, Colonia La Sultana, tel. 2557-3601, www.arboldefuego.com, $50 s, $60 d), a little-known gem that focuses on being eco-efficient by saving energy and water and using environmentally friendly products. The rooms are lovely and bright, with colorful Salvadoran paintings and bedspreads, fresh flowers, and lots of natural light. All rooms have fans and hot water. Breakfast is included and is served in the bright eating area with a fantastic view of the volcanoes and a garden full of plants and beautiful flowers. Throw in top-notch service and Wi-Fi throughout the property, and this counts as one of the best mid-range hotels in the city.

Alicante Hotel y Restaurante (Calle Las Rosas and Av. Los Laureles, 1, Colonia La Sultana, tel. 2243-0889, www.alicante. com, $55 s, $65 d, includes breakfast) is a good choice if you are looking for something in a low-key area but still close to the city. Tucked away on a quiet side street in Antiguo Cuscatlán, Alicante offers simple, clean rooms with private baths, hot water,

TVs, air-conditioning, and Wi-Fi. The service is excellent, and there is a swimming pool and a small garden, making this hotel a comfortable refuge away from the city center, perfect for those on business or with access to a car.

CENTRO HISTÓRICO

Hotel Bella Luz (3 Calle Poniente 1010, tel. 2222-5178, $10 s, $15 d) is the cheapest option near the bus terminal, and not as bad as you might expect. This tiny hotel has a few small rooms, windowless and waiting for that last residual smell of cigarette smoke to disappear. Each one sports sponge-painted walls in primary colors, a fan, and a private bath (no hot water).

Across the street from Hotel Bella Luz, the entrance of **Hotel Villa Florencia** (3 Calle Poniente 1023, tel. 2221-1706 or 2564-2514, $15 s, $20 d) is teeming with antiques, dark wood furniture, plants, and spiral staircases with ornate iron railings. Compared to the colonial charm of the lobby, the rooms are a bit anticlimactic but still pretty. They have tile floors, fans or air-conditioning ($5 extra), TVs, and private baths (no hot water). There is no restaurant but there is a *comedor* right next door.

Food

San Salvador is not known for its restaurant scene, unless you are fond of American fast-food chains. However, as more Salvadorans return home from abroad, they are importing both business savvy and culinary skills. The options are slowly starting to expand. The best restaurants are located in Escalón and Zona Rosa, where you will find creative international fare, while cheaper, more local flavors are located around the university areas. *Comedors* are located all over the city and can range from a large cafeteria-style restaurant to someone serving meals out of the back of their truck. Of course, in a pinch, you can almost always find a *pupusa* to tide you over at any one of the endless *pupuserías* all over town.

ZONA ROSA
Barbecue

The whimsical ★ **Caminito Chocos** (Calle La Reforma, across the street from Republik Bar, tel. 2223-6807, noon-2pm and 5:30pm-10pm Mon., noon-2pm and 5:30pm-11pm Tues., noon-2pm and 5:30pm-midnight Wed., noon-2pm and 5:30pm-1am Thurs., noon-2pm and 5:30pm-2am Fri., noon-2am Sat., noon-10pm Sun., $5-15) serves Argentinean food, and does it well. This little second-floor restaurant has colorful wooden window frames that open up to an enchanting view of the twinkling lights of the city below. Caminito serves delicious chorizo, chicken, burgers, and steak, as well as the proper Argentine offerings such as *choripáns*, empanadas, and homemade *chimichurri*. Caminitos is a great place for afternoon drinks and snacks, or for a full on carnivorous feast. They also have a good selection of international beers.

French

Tucked away on a side street in San Benito, ★ **Café El Botón** (Av. La Capilla, 210, tel. 2264-9738, el.boton.ataco@gmail.com, noon-10pm Mon.-Sat., $6-12) is definitely the most colorful restaurant in San Salvador. Tables and chairs are painted in cheerful primary colors and surround a garden in the back of a charming old house converted into a restaurant. The food is French-Salvadoran fusion with local favorites being the *croque monsieur* and specialty quiches. Most dishes come with homemade organic goat cheese, made with love on owner Michel Fouillade's finca near Concepción de Ataco on Ruta de las Flores. Vegetables are also sourced locally, sustainably, and organically as much as possible. Café El Botón has a dedicated following, and the place can get packed on the weekend, especially when there is live music on Saturday night. Bands usually play *trova* and there is no cover charge. Try the sangria; you won't be disappointed.

International

★ **Delikat** (Bulevar Hipódromo 582, tel. 2124-7657, noon-3pm and 7pm-10pm Mon.-Tues., 8am-11am, noon-3pm, and 7pm-10pm Wed.-Sat., 8am-11am and noon-3pm Sun., $8-15) is a hidden gem, appreciated as much for its ambience as for its popular thin-crust pizzas. The restaurant consists of outdoor seating in a pretty garden in the back of an old house. Plants and flowers are adorned with tiny lights at night to create an intimate, cheerful space. The specialties are salads, pizza, and sandwiches, each with a respective page-long section on the menu, presenting a long list of various possible combinations using ingredients that are hard to find in El Salvador, such as arugula, fresh pesto, brie, blue cheese, and goat cheese. There is also a long wine list including a few nice malbecs, and good desserts, including the popular cheesecake in *maracuya* (passion fruit) sauce.

Located inside the Museo Nacional de Antropología Dr. David J. Guzmán (MUNA), **Bistro San Lorenzo** (Final Av. de la Revolución, tel. 2243-7566, 10am-10pm daily, $7-16) combines culture and cuisine with aplomb. This small bistro has a sleek, contemporary design and serves up excellent *panini,* salads, and pastas. It has excellent coffee, a decent selection of wine, and top-notch service. Even if you don't have a meal, the air conditioned space is perfect for a beverage after a tour of the museum.

Italian

Al Pomodoro (Av. de la Revolución and Calle Circunvalación, tel. 2243-7888, noon-3pm and 6pm-11pm daily, $10-30) is the go-to Italian restaurant in Zona Rosa. Large and beautiful with intimate lighting, exposed brick walls, colorful art, candles, and crayons and paper to doodle while you wait, it strikes the perfect balance between posh and playful. You can choose from different rooms—some are more ample and casual, perfect for group gatherings, and some are small and intimate. The pizza and pasta are consistently good, the wine selection is decent, and the service is top-notch.

Mexican

Outside on the terrace is where you want to be at **El Zocolo** (Bulevar Hipódromo 443, tel. 2243-0937, noon-2:30pm and 6pm-10pm Sun.-Thurs., noon-2:30pm and 6pm-midnight Fri., noon-11pm Sat., $10-20), enjoying the lively atmosphere and massive margaritas. Before your meal comes, you will enjoy tortilla chips and a smorgasbord of delicious salsas, ranging from mild to extremely hot. Save room for the main course because portions are big. El Zocolo is famous for its tortilla soup, which is served in a tortilla bowl and drenched in cheese. The burritos are excellent as well.

Oskar Bistro Basilea (Centro Comercial Basilea, tel. 2511-4285, contactoh@oskar-basilea.com, noon-3pm and 6pm-10pm Mon.-Sat., noon-3pm Sun., $10-30) is where discerning foodies lunch, enjoying great appetizers like salmon tartar and baked goat cheese and mains that include delicious thin-crust pizzas, *choripáns* (Argentine sandwiches made with sausage and baguette), and the signature Bistro Burger with caramelized onions, bacon, and cheese.

COLONIA ESCALÓN
Argentinean

The popular **La Pampa Argentina** (Final Paseo Escalón, tel. 2298-5817, noon-3pm and 6pm-11pm Mon.-Sat., noon-9pm Sun., $10-20) serves excellent steak in a wood cabin with an amazing view of the city. The menu is straightforward with various specials that all provide excellent value for money. Each main dish comes with a small soup and salad to start, tender high-quality meat cooked to your desired perfection, sides of potatoes and vegetables, a drink, and a dessert, all of which are good—but the real reason you are here is the steak. The wine selection is very good and the service is fast and efficient. La Pampa is always busy, especially on the weekend, so it is a good idea to make reservations.

Asian

The casual chic ★ **Swagat** (3 Calle Poniente and 79 Av. Norte, 4060, tel. 2264-3826, swagatelsalvador@gmail.com, 11am-3pm and 6pm-10pm Mon.-Wed., 11am-11pm Thurs.-Sun., $7-12) opened up recently to the delight of spice-loving foodies all over the city; and so far, El Salvador's only Indian restaurant is an undisputed success. The main color theme here is a cheerful fuchsia pink, complemented by hints of warm orange, yellow, and brown. The highlight is a Japanese table surrounded by comfy cushions and colorful drapery, creating a romantic bohemian vibe. Friendly owners will check in on you as you dine to old Hindi songs. The food is invariably authentic and tasty, but if you like your food spicy, be warned that all dishes are modified to suit the Salvadoran palate, so they are not as fiery as some might expect.

Barbecue

The modern, minimalist **HUMO BBQ ES** (79 Av. Sur, Pasaje A 29, tel. 2243-3254, 6pm-10:30pm Mon., noon-3pm and 6pm-10:30pm Tues.-Sat., 10:30am-8pm Sun., $10-20) takes barbecuing seriously. The owners traveled all over the Southern United States schooling themselves on how to prepare the perfect barbecue. The result is a combination of techniques gleaned from North Carolina, Texas, Kansas, and Memphis and a truly a memorable dining experience. Choose your own rub (coffee, sugar, garlic, or oregano, just to name a few), then your meat and cut, and then your salsa (such as vinegar and chilies, mustard, vinegar and spices, or sweet-and-spicy tomato). Slow-cooked over wood fire, the meat is invariably soft, succulent, and delicious, and it's served with equally delicious sides such as coleslaw, bean salad, and french

fries. This is one restaurant meat lovers will not want to miss.

Fusion

★ **Esperanto** (79 Av. Sur, Pasaje A 27, Colonia La Mascota, tel. 2124-7418, restaurantesperanto@gmail.com, noon-2:30pm and 7pm-11pm Mon.-Fri., 7pm-11pm Sat., $20-40) is one of the few boundary-pushing restaurants in the city. The menu here is always evolving, using local ingredients that are in season to create inventive gourmet dishes. This intimate space has a classic, clean style with dark wood chairs, white tablecloths, and modern art on the spotless walls. *Riguas* (similar to tortillas but made with sweet corn) stuffed with seafood and the pulled-pork and Cuban sandwiches are all popular favorites. Whatever you decide on, expect impeccable presentation and very attentive service. Save room for dessert—Esperanto's tiramisu and flan are melt-in-your-mouth delicious.

Greek

Opa! (79 Av. Norte, tel. 3256-9922, 11:30am-3pm and 6pm-11pm Mon.-Fri., 11:30am-3pm and 6:30pm-11:30pm Sat., $10-30) is the classier big brother to the city's only other Greek restaurant, Mr. Souvlaki. Opa! has a European flair and romantic feel to it; a clean white-and-blue motif and indoor and outdoor seating provide a candlelit atmosphere perfect for intimate dining. Specialties include the usual souvlaki, grilled meats, and homemade hummus; for a real treat try the excellent moussaka, alongside an authentic Greek salad and one of the many international beers on the menu. The homemade baklava is also delicious.

International

La Ventana (83 Av. Norte and 9 Calle Poniente, noon-midnight Mon.-Thurs., noon-1am Fri.-Sat., 8am-6pm Sun., $7-15) is laid-back, stylish, and sure of itself, drawing a slightly more sophisticated crowd than the university bars. Inside, rotating monthly art exhibitions adorn the brick walls, and a large, dark wooden bar in the center of it all has an excellent selection of international beers. Outside, there are wrought-iron tables in a lovely terrace with lots of plants. The menu includes a good selection of international dishes that focus heavily on salads, sandwiches, and pastas.

The aptly named ★ **Rústico Bistro** (3 Calle Poniente and Pasaje Los Pinos, tel. 2224-5656, noon-3pm Mon.-Tues., noon-3pm and 6pm-9:30pm Wed.-Sat., $10-20) serves the undisputed best burger in town. Enjoy bistro-style food in a rustic space with just a few wooden tables hidden in the garden. The three main burgers are the classic Rústico, Three Cheese, and California, each boasting a heavy grade-A beef patty seasoned and cooked to juicy perfection, served on homemade buns and with a side of hand-cut fries with barbecue or garlic aioli. The burgers are big enough for two, but depending on how long it has been since you've found a burger like this, you just might want to go all out. Newer varieties include the Aussie burger with chipotle mayo pineapple and bacon, and if you want to try something different, the pulled-pork sandwich with tamarind sauce gets rave reviews. Oh, did I mention the frosted Mason-jar glasses? They make it hard to resist an afternoon beer.

Japanese

★ **Kamukara** (93 Av. Norte, tel. 2263-2401, noon-2:30pm and 6pm-10pm Mon.-Sat., $20-40) has been satisfying sushi lovers since 1995, and it just keeps getting better. Stylish and elegant, it is considered the best Japanese restaurant in El Salvador—some say it's the best restaurant, period. Hidden on a side street one block from the Crown Plaza Hotel, Kamukara has outdoor seating beside a lovely garden with a fountain, and indoor seating in a room with sleek tables and deep-red walls sparsely decorated with simple Japanese art. Everything is very authentic, from the Sapporo beer and imported sake to the excellent miso soup and incredibly fresh sushi and sashimi. If you love sushi and are willing to splurge, this is where you want to go.

Salvadoran

Cafeteria-style **Típicos Margoth** (77 Av. Norte and Pasaje Itsmania, tel. 2263-3340, 7am-7pm daily, $3-6) is where you want to go to eat fast, cheap, delicious Salvadoran food. Proprietor and cook Margoth started off running a tiny *pupusería* in 1962, and the business eventually became so successful that she opened a proper restaurant—now there are four in the city, but this one is the most popular. Típicos Margoth has one side of the restaurant dedicated to *pupusas* only, and the other side is for *comida típica* (typical Salvadoran food) breakfast, lunch, and dinner items, including eggs, plantains, beans, rice, fresh cheese, and a variety of meats in typical Salvadoran sauces.

Vegetarian

The Taiwanese **Mile Time Café** (Paseo General Escalón 3943, tel. 2124-7388, 11:30am-9pm Mon.-Sat., $4-7) serves up some of the best vegetarian food in town at very reasonable prices in a casual contemporary space. Choose from a variety of authentic tasty Taiwanese dishes, including fried noodles, rice and curry, and delicious soups, all made with homemade tofu, savory sauces made from scratch, and fresh vegetables. The portions are big and complemented by an extensive selection of beverages, including bubble tea, ginger tea, and milk shakes.

Kalpataru Restaurante (Calle La Mascota 928, tel. 2263-1204, 8am-8pm Mon.-Sat., $6-12) is a small vegetarian restaurant inside a larger plaza that is dedicated to alternative health and healing. Dine to the sound of relaxing music and in a simple, tranquil outdoor space. The menus offers natural fruit and vegetable juices, vegetarian soy burgers, various soy-based dishes, soups, and salads. There is a daily lunch buffet ($10) that offers soup, salad, a drink, and a variety of main dishes, usually consisting of rice or noodles, some sort of vegetable stir-fry, and a soy-based dish. There is also a small shop beside the restaurant that sells natural products, books, and incense.

ANTIGUO CUSCATLÁN
Greek
★ **Mr. Souvlaki** (Calle del Mediterráneo Casa 26, Antiguo Cuscatlán, 11am-9:30pm Mon.-Sat., $3-6) offers affordable authentic Greek food in this cute little restaurant close to the pedestrian entrance to UCA and just across the street from Joan's Hostel. A few wooden tables and a small blue bar get packed at lunchtime and in the evening on weekends with regular customers enjoying fresh Greek salads, hummus, and the famous souvlaki, stuffed with real Greek potatoes, homemade *tzatziki,* pork, and eggplant.

Italian
Genzano DI Roma Caffé (Calle del Mediterráneo 36, Colonia Jardines de Guadalupe, tel. 2243-2153, 10am-9pm Mon.-Thurs., 10am-10pm Fri.-Sat., $4-9) is an Italian café with thin-crust pizzas, calzones, *paninis,* and pasta. The ambience is more café than restaurant, with white walls, tile floors, and uniform wooden tables in a brightly lit space, but the food is good and draws crowds for lunch. There is also a fridge full of ready-made desserts to go; the biscotti and tiramisu are both excellent.

Mexican
Chevy's (Calle del Mediterráneo 41, tel. 2243-2234, noon-3pm and 5:30pm-10pm Mon.-Fri., noon-10pm Sat., $2-5) serves cheap Mexican food and an especially tasty tortilla soup. Red tile floors, wooden tables, and murals of the countryside on the walls all create a colorful, very authentic experience.

Milburritos (Calle del Mediterráneo, Centro Comercial Plaza de Sol, tel. 2278-5252, 11am-10pm Mon.-Thurs., 11am-11pm Fri.-Sat., 11am-10pm Sun., $3-6) serves up fast, filling burritos, soup, and quesadillas with fresh ingredients, along with tasty salsas and healthy options such as burrito

bowls and salads with your choice of brown or white rice.

DOWNTOWN
Mexican
Los Tacos de Paco (Calle Andes 2931, tel. 2260-1347, noon-3pm and 5pm-10pm daily, $3-6) hosts a popular poetry slam every Wednesday night, and the tacos are great too. Tables sit in front of a stage and beside a garden, where you can peruse used books while you wait for your food; that won't be long because Paco serves up food furiously fast, making it a great pit stop if you are in a rush.

Las Fajitas (39 Av. Norte and Bulevar Universitario, tel. 2225-3570, 11am-2:30pm and 5pm-10:30pm daily, $5-15) serves up fast, tasty Mexican food in this small, air-conditioned restaurant with flat-screen TVs and an open-concept kitchen.

Pub Fare
★ **El Establo** (39 Av. Norte and Bulevar Universitario, tel. 2226-0606, restaurante. elestablo@gmail.com, noon-midnight daily, $5-10) is where many Salvadorans go for after-work drinks; with its casual, easygoing vibe, it's easy to stay all night, and many do. This is where 30-somethings come to unwind after work, enjoying the air-conditioning, flat-screen TVs often showing sports, unpretentious wooden tables, and friendly service. The highlight of El Establo is its extensive menu of *bocas,* bite-size snacks. There is a full page dedicated to these tasty little treats, such as *ceviche,* garlic mushrooms, or jalapeño poppers. If you order a pint of beer, you get a *boca* for just $1 extra.

Salvadoran
For pricier *comida típica,* check out **El Sopón Típico** (Urbanización Florida, Av. Las Palmeras, Bulevar de los Héroes, 130, tel. 2260-2671, 11am-9pm Mon.-Sat., 11am-8pm Sun., $10-20), where an extensive menu offers Salvadoran favorites such as fried yuca with pork, grilled meats that include rabbit

and iguana, ceviche, and as the name suggests, a good selection of soups served in big traditional clay bowls—including the two most popular *comida típica* soups in El Salvador, *mariscada,* a creamy seafood soup with prawns and lobster, and *sopa gallina india,* a free-range chicken soup that is usually only available on the weekend.

Information and Services

VISITOR INFORMATION

The **Ministerio de Turismo (MiTur)** (Ministry of Tourism, Edificio Carbonel 1, between Alameda Dr. Manuel Enrique Araujo and Pasaje Carbonel, tel. 2241-3200, 8am-4pm Mon.-Fri.) has an office in Zona Rosa. Although the staff are extremely helpful, there is no information available in English, nor English-speaking staff. Most hotels provide very good information about city tours and things to do around San Salvador.

VISAS AND IMMIGRATION

As part of the CA-4 agreement among El Salvador, Guatemala, Nicaragua, and Honduras, travelers are granted a 90-day visa for all four countries. If your 90 days run out while you are in El Salvador, you need to leave the CA-4 area (most people go to Mexico) and reenter after 72 hours. Alternatively, you can go to the **Dirección General de Migración y Extranjería** (Department of Immigration, Av. Olímpica and Alameda Enrique Araujo, tel. 2213-7778, 8am-4pm Mon.-Fri.) and apply for a visa extension. The cost is $25 as long as you go before the day it expires; after that it increases to $50, or potentially the maximum fee of $114, depending on how late you are. Technically, it can only be done one time.

MAPS

The **Ministerio de Turismo (MiTur)** (Ministry of Tourism, Edificio Carbonel 1, between Alameda Dr. Manuel Enrique Araujo and Pasaje Carbonel, tel. 2241-3200, 8am-4pm Mon.-Fri.) has a good selection of free tourist maps for all parts of the country, including a detailed city map. The **Museo de la**

Historia Militar-Cuartel El Zapote (Calle Los Viveros, Barrio San Jacinto, tel. 2250-0000, 9am-noon and 2pm-5pm Tues.-Sun.) has a very interesting outdoor topographical map of the country.

POST OFFICE AND COURIERS

Correos de El Salvador (15 Calle Poniente and Diagonal Universitaria Norte, Centro Gobierno, tel. 2527-7600, 8am-7pm Mon.-Fri., 8am-noon Sat.) is located in the center of the city. There is another office located on the second floor of Metrocentro with the same hours. There are also numerous **Fed Ex** offices; the main one is located in Escalón (Av. Las Magnolias 130, tel. 2250-8800, 8am-6pm Mon.-Fri., 8am-noon Sat.).

TELECOMMUNICATIONS
Telephone

You will be lucky to find a payphone when you need one in San Salvador. In the age of mobile phones, they are practically obsolete. You can make phone calls at your hotel, but they are likely to charge an exorbitant rate. If you plan on making phone calls during your time in the city, it may be worth the small investment in a cell phone. You can buy a cheap one for about $20 and then purchase prepaid phone cards to load it up and make calls. If you already have an unlocked cell phone, you can just buy a SIM card and use it in your phone. Because of the high numbers of Salvadorans making calls to the United States, you can get very cheap plans for calls to North America.

Internet Access

Although San Salvador is well connected with

Wi-Fi in many hotels, restaurants and cafés, finding Internet cafés is not so easy. The area around UCA (Calle del Mediterráneo) has many Internet cafés, but in other tourist areas, including Escalón and Zona Rosa, you will likely have to use the business centers inside hotels for Internet access, printing, scanning, or photocopying.

MONEY
Banks and ATMs

ATMs for most international systems (Plus, Cirrus, Visa and MasterCard) can be found all over the city.

Major banks include Scotiabank and Banco Citibank de El Salvador, both of which can be found throughout the city. Branches of **Scotiabank** can be found at 1158 Calle Ruben Daro (tel. 2250-1111, 9am-4pm Mon.-Fri., 9am-noon Sat.) in the Centro Histórico, at Bulevar de los Héroes and Calle Sisimiles (tel. 2250-1111, 9am-4pm Mon.-Fri., 9am-noon Sat.), and near El Salvador del Mundo (65 Av. Norte and Bulevar Constitución, tel. 2250-1111, 9am-4pm Mon.-Fri., 9am-noon Sat.) The main branch of **Banco Citibank de El Salvador** (tel. 2212-4103, 9am-4pm Mon.-Fri., 9am-noon Sat.) can be found on Avenida Cuscatlán.

Money Transfers

Western Union offices are a dime a dozen in San Salvador, as many Salvadorans rely on remittances from the United States. A few of the principal offices are at **HSBC** on Paseo General Escalón (tel. 2245-2688, 9am-4pm Mon.-Fri., 9am-noon Sat.) and at Alameda Roosevelt and 49 Avenida Norte (tel. 2260-3300, 9am-4pm Mon.-Fri., 9am-noon Sat.). MoneyGram is also popular and can be found throughout the country in various banks and supermarkets.

HEALTH AND EMERGENCIES

There are plenty of inexpensive clinics throughout the city where you can go for basic problems or blood work. Ask your hotel to recommend someone in the area. Pharmacists can also be very helpful in diagnosing simple issues and offering appropriate medicine. Salvadorans are famously concerned about their health, and as a result there are almost as many pharmacies as *pupuserías* around town. They carry a wide range of antibiotics and other medication that you would normally need a prescription for in your home country, which is very convenient if you know exactly what you need. The downside is that they are not cheap. A round of good antibiotics can cost you up to $60 for a name brand, so always ask for the significantly cheaper generic brands. **Farmacia San Nicolás** is a ubiquitous and excellent pharmacy, open 24 hours; surprisingly it has a wide selection of homeopathic remedies in addition to conventional medicine.

For emergencies or more serious health issues, it is worth going to one of the better hospitals in San Salvador. **Hospital de Diagnostico** (Urbanización la Esperanza Segunda Diagonal 429, tel. 2226-5111, www. hospitaldiagnostico.com.sv, atencioncliente@hdiagnostico.com.sv) is considered the best hospital in town, and prices reflect this. **Hospital de la Mujer** (Calle Juan José Cañas and 81 Av. Sur, tel. 2265-1212 or 2279-1440, www.hospital-mujer.com) is another excellent hospital that specializes in women's health. Both of these hospitals have English-speaking doctors available.

If you find yourself in an emergency situation in San Salvador, you will almost certainly be immediately assisted by whomever happens to be in the vicinity at the time. If you have access to a phone, dial 911 for help. If you are robbed or assaulted, go to the nearest police station and file a report. If you are robbed, chances are next to nil that you will recover your belongings, but they may make the effort to find the person responsible for the crime.

Transportation

GETTING THERE AND AWAY

Air

The **Aeropuerto Internacional Comalapa** (SAL, tel. 2366-9455, www.cepa.gob.sv/aies) is located 44 kilometers southeast of San Salvador and just 33 kilometers from the beaches of La Libertad. A common misconception is that it is easier to get to the beaches through San Salvador; in reality it makes much more sense to go straight from the airport to the beach. A taxi from the airport to get to La Libertad should cost around $20 and to San Salvador around $30.

To get to San Salvador on the local bus, you can catch bus 138 ($0.70, one hour), which runs every 15 minutes and takes you to the city center. Walk across the parking lot in front of the airport terminal and through the empty building on the other side to reach the highway, where you will find the bus stop.

If your flight arrives before 5:30pm and you are looking for budget transportation, you can take the **Acacya Shuttle** (tel. 2339-9282 airport, tel. 2271-4937 in town). They have shared taxis that leave the airport at 9am, 1pm, and 5:30pm daily. The cost is $5, it takes around 40 minutes, and they will drop you off at their office in the city center (19 Av. Norte and 3 Calle Poniente). If you want to use the service that runs from San Salvador to the airport, the taxis leave from the Taxis Acacya stand (Alameda Juan Pablo II and 19a Av. Norte, tel. 2222-2158), behind the Puerto bus station, at 6am, 7am, 10am, and 2pm daily.

Major airline offices in San Salvador include:

- **American Airlines:** Edificio la Centroamericana, Alameda Roosevelt, tel. 2298-0777

- **Copa Airlines:** World Trade Center, 89 Av. Norte and Calle del Mirador, Escalón, tel. 2209-2672

- **Delta Airlines:** World Trade Center, 89 Av. Norte and Calle del Mirador, tel. 2275-9292

- **TACA:** Galerias Escalón, 3700 Paseo General Escalón, main level, tel. 2267-8222

- **United Airlines:** Km. 42, Carretera Comalapa, tel. 2366-9455

International Buses

There are several options for buses running through Central America. Most leave very early in the morning. Make sure you book your tickets at least one day in advance and bring your passport to the office when you buy your ticket.

Transporte del Sol (Av. de la Revolución 159-A, Colonia San Benito, tel. 2243-1345 or 2243-8897, www.busesdelsol.com) has buses that go to Guatemala (7am and 4pm daily, $25) and Nicaragua (6am daily, $50).

There are two offices for the popular **Tica Bus** (Bulevar Hipódromo, Local 301, tel. 2243-9764; Hotel San Carlos, Calle Concepción 121, tel. 2222-4808, www.tica-bus.com). They have buses that run all over Central America; check the website for schedules and prices.

King Quality (Bulevar Hipódromo, Pasaje 1, tel. 2241-8787, www.kingqualityca.com) is a luxury line that offers direct buses to Guatemala, Honduras, Nicaragua, and Costa Rica. See the website for prices and schedules.

Domestic Buses

There are three main bus terminals in San Salvador.

Terminal de Occidente

Terminal de Occidente (Bulevar Venezuela, near 49 Av. Sur, no phone) is the most orderly of the three, and serves all western destinations in the country. The main tourist destinations from this terminal include:

- Ahuachapán: bus 202 ($1, 2.25 hours, every 15 minutes)

- Joya de Cerén: buses 108 or 40 ($0.65, 1.75 hours, every 15 minutes)

- La Libertad: bus 102 ($0.60, 1 hour, every 10 minutes)

- Metapán: buses 201A or 19 ($2.50, 2 hours, every 30 minutes)

- Santa Ana: bus 201 ($1.35 *especial,* $0.80 normal, 1.25 hours, every 10 minutes)

- Sonsonate: buses 16, 17, or 205 ($1, 1.5 hours, every 5 minutes)

From Sonsonate you can catch connecting buses to Ruta de las Flores, Los Cóbanos, and Barra de Santiago.

Terminal Oriente
The loud and chaotic **Terminal Oriente** (Alameda Juan Pablo II, no phone) serves all major eastern destinations. The main tourist routes are:

- Chalatenango: bus 125 ($0.90, 2 hours, every 10 minutes)

- El Poy (Honduran border): bus 119 ($1.75, 3 hours, every 30 minutes)

- Ilobasco: buses 112 or 181 ($0.75, 1.5 hours, every hour)

- La Palma: bus 119 ($1.70, 2.75 hours, every 30 minutes)

- La Unión: buses 304 or 446 ($3.25, 4 hours, every 30 minutes)

- San Miguel: bus 301 ($2.50-5, 2-4 hours, every 10 minutes)

- Suchitoto: bus 129 ($0.70, 2 hours, every 15 minutes)

Terminal del Sur
The **Terminal del Sur** (Autopista a Comalapa, no phone) serves the south and southeastern locations. Its main destinations include:

- Costa del Sol: bus 495 ($1.25, 2.5 hours, every 10 minutes)

- Puerto el Triunfo: bus 185 ($1.60, 2 hours, departures at 9am, 11am, 12:30pm, 1:30pm, and 2pm daily)

- Usulután via Jiquilisco: bus 302 ($1.70, 2.5 hours, every 10 minutes)

Rental Cars and Motorcycles
Renting a car can be a great way to see the country, but keep in mind that it might be more hassle than it's worth for getting around the city. San Salvador's many one-way streets, insane traffic, and unpredictable drivers might make it difficult to navigate on your own. Parking is difficult, and in certain areas at certain times, break-ins are a legitimate concern. Consider using a taxi to get around the city center and a car for all your other travel.

The most reputable rental car company in San Salvador is **National** (www.nationalelsalvador.com). They have three offices, including two in the city. One is inside Hotel Princess Hilton (Av. Las Magnolias and Bulevar Hipódromo, tel. 2367-8014), and the other is in Edificio Sunset Plaza (Calle La Mascota and Av. Jerusalén, tel. 2367-8015). There is also an office at the airport (tel. 2367-8015). Second choices include **Avis** (43 Av. Sur 127, tel. 2261-1212, www.avis.com) and **Budget** (Calle Mirador and 85 Av. Norte 648, tel. 2263-9777 or 2264-3888, www.budget.com.sv). Budget also has an airport location (tel. 2339-2828, aerobudget@intercom.com.sv).

Many people prefer renting from independent companies in El Salvador. It's usually cheaper and more reliable. You can contact Ricardo Aramis Artiga Cabezas of **Ri-Cars** (83 Av. Sur, Pasaje a Casa 11, Escalón, tel. 7925-3301 or 2566-6121, riar_005@hotmail. com) to rent a car or a motorcycle for $20 per day, including insurance.

GETTING AROUND
Local Buses

Buses around San Salvador are cheap and frequent. Most trips cost between $0.25 and $0.50. The most important route you will need is most likely bus 30B, which runs from Metrocentro on Bulevar de los Héroes across the city to Zona Rosa and vice versa. Many other buses can be taken in front of Metrocentro, including bus 34, which goes through Zona Rosa and then to Terminal de Occidente. Buses 101A and 101B run between San Salvador and Santa Tecla. Other major bus stops include Plaza Salvador del Mundo (also called Plaza de las Américas) at Alameda Roosevelt and Bulevar Constitución; and La Ceiba de Guadalupe (Km. 6.5, Carretera Santa Tecla, Antiguo Cuscatlán). La Ceiba de Guadalupe can be especially useful if you are staying at Joan's Hostel near UCA. The bus stop is within walking distance of the hostel, and almost all of the principal lines pass by here. It is essentially a de facto bus terminal, and catching transportation here can save you the trip to the terminals in the city.

Taxis

Taxis are all over the place in the city, and any trip within San Salvador should cost $5-10. Generally, you will not have to call for a taxi—just flag one down on the street. Taxis do not have meters, so you need to agree on a price before you get into the car. In general, drivers are fair and haggling will not be very productive. Prices go up marginally late at night. **Taxis Acacya** (tel. 2271-4937) is a reputable company.

Vicinity of San Salvador

PANCHIMALCO

This cool, tiny mountain town, just 15 kilometers southeast of San Salvador, is considered one of the last indigenous strongholds in El Salvador. Panchimalco is where the Pipil people fled during the Spanish takeover of San Salvador during the 16th century. Here they settled with the preexisting Mayan population, and to this day they have preserved much of their indigenous heritage. This is one of the few villages in the country where you will see women wearing traditional clothing and also where you will find the oldest surviving colonial church in El Salvador. The tiny **Iglesia Santa Cruz de Panchimalco** (town center, 7am-7pm daily), with its classic baroque-style facade, was built in 1725 and retains much of its original materials and design. The inner nave is supported by 16 wooden columns on stone bases that separate the nave from the aisles. The main altar retains its original gold finish, and if you look closely, you will see the image of the Holy Cross of Rome dating back to 1792. The church is considered one of the highlights of Panchimalco.

Although the history, cool climate, and delicious *pupusas* make Panchimalco a worthwhile day trip any time of year, its real draw is the popular **Festival de las Flores y Palmas,** which takes place the first Sunday of May. The original meaning of the celebration was to commemorate the beginning of the rainy season, but today the festival honors two Roman Catholic saints, the Virgen del Rosario and the Virgen de la Concepción. If you come early in the day, you will find the women of Panchimalco meticulously stripping palm fronds of their leaves and then skewering them with gorgeous colorful flower blossoms, creating huge flower-laden fronds that they will then carry throughout the town. The procession begins in the afternoon around 2pm and starts with the dance of the Moors and Christians, an unlikely vestige of a tradition brought over by the Spaniards that celebrates a Spanish victory over Muslim invaders during the Middle Ages. After the men perform the dance, women dressed in traditional clothing carry a large altar with the Virgin Mary on top through town. The rest of the day can be spent exploring the town, checking out the artisans and food vendors selling *comida típica*, and sampling *chicha* (a fermented drink made of corn and *dulce de panela*).

Panchimalco is also known for its local art and culture, in particular the portraits you will probably see around the city of children with massive eyes. The **Casa Taller Encuentro** (Calle Antigua Barrio San Esteban 18-B, tel. 2280-6958 or 7760-3180, www.artpanchimalco.com, 8am-5pm Mon.-Sat., 1pm-5pm Sun., free) is a great place to check out if you are interested in seeing the work of local artists. This lovely home has a small art gallery showcasing local work, a garden with sculptures, and a sitting area. The Casa Taller Encuentro focuses on preserving the heritage of Panchimalco through involving youth in workshops and classes from making art to learning the indigenous Nahuatl language. You could explore Panchimalco on your own, or take a guided tour with **Adventures El Salvador** (tel. 7844-0858, www.wtf-elsalvador.com) to visit local artists or take a class in traditional textile weaving.

Getting There

Bus 17, 17A, and 17B all go to Panchimalco from Avenida 29 de Agosto on the south side of Mercado Central in the Centro Histórico. The cost is $0.35, the trip takes about one hour, and buses run every half hour.

If you are driving, take the road toward Planes de Los Renderos until you reach the turnoff for Panchimalco; it is clearly signed. The drive takes about half an hour.

SAN ANDRÉS RUINS

Head west of the city 32 kilometers to find the **San Andrés Ruins** (Km. 32, Carretera Panamericana, tel. 2319-3220, 9am-4pm Tues.-Sun., $3 foreigners, $1 Central Americans), originally founded by a community of farmers in 900 BC and but abandoned in AD 250 because of the catastrophic eruption of Volcán Ilopango. It was eventually reoccupied from AD 600 to 900, when it became the powerful Mayan administrative capital that ruled over the Zapotitán Valley and the Valley of the Hammocks. The site is expansive, grassy, and peaceful, with a very good museum that includes some English information as well as ceramic artifacts, a photo exhibit about the history of the region, and galleries with both pre-Hispanic and colonial-era exhibits. So far, only a few of the principal ceremonial areas have been excavated, but aerial photos suggest that the site contains up to 1,200 homes. The main and most impressive structure is the Acropolis pyramid, which is surrounded by smaller neighboring pyramids that were likely used for ceremonial purposes.

Incense burners and sacrificial tools, such as stingray spines for bloodletting, have been discovered at the site, and excavated ceramics suggest that the city was an important trade center with links to communities in what is now Mexico, Guatemala, Belize, and Honduras. San Andrés was abandoned during the Classic Maya Collapse toward the end of 900 AD, and the settlement remained residential until the Spanish conquest, when it became a center for coffee growing and indigo production. The whole site was buried by volcanic matter during the 1658 eruption of Volcán Playón and not rediscovered until the late 19th century. In addition to the ruins, there is an indigo factory that you can see; it was left nearly perfectly intact from the ashes of the eruption.

Getting There

Take bus 201 to Santa Ana or bus 202 to Ahuachapán and ask to be let off at the San

Andrés ruins. The cost is $ 1.50 and should take about one hour. Buses run every 10 minutes.

If you are driving, take Carretera Panamericana (CA1) toward Los Chorros, and continue as if going to Santa Ana. The entrance is on the right at Km. 35 and is clearly signed. The drive takes about 45 minutes.

★ JOYA DE CERÉN

Nearby the San Andrés ruins is **Joya de Cerén** (Km. 35, Carretera Panamericana, tel. 2401-5782, 9am-4pm Tues.-Sun., $3 foreigners, $1 Central Americans), the most fascinating site in El Salvador and the only one of its kind in all of Mesoamerica. All other archaeological sites provide insight into the lives of the elite; Joya de Cerén, on the other hand, has provided detailed information about the activities of regular run-of-the-mill Mesoamerican farmers, making it a unique example of daily village life in the area. Often referred to as the Pompeii of the Americas, Joya de Cerén was abandoned right before the eruption of Laguna Caldera around AD 600 blanketed the simple farming village in seven meters of volcanic ash. Although a warning earthquake apparently gave residents time to flee, their personal belongings stayed exactly as they were, perfectly preserved in the ash, from garden tools and bean-filled pots to sleeping mats and religious items, essentially freezing the agricultural village in time. The site was later resettled by Pipiles, oblivious to the preserved village under the earth. It was not until 1976 that one of the adobe homes was discovered by a bulldozer during the construction of grain storage silos. Excavation began under the direction of American archaeologist Payson D. Sheets in 1978 and 1980, but was interrupted by the civil war. Work resumed in 1988 and has been ongoing since then. Today, Joya de Cerén is a UNESCO World Heritage Site where you can see the well-protected ruins from a platform above them. The ruins include a temezcal (sauna), simple adobe huts, and a communal kitchen. There is a small air-conditioned museum with information about the site, and free tours can be arranged. Tour guides speak enough English to get the main points across.

Getting There

Take buses 108 or 40 to San Juan Opico (there should be one leaving every 15 minutes) and ask to be let off at Joya de Cerén. It costs $0.65 and takes about 1.75 hours.

Joya de Cerén

If you are driving, take Carretera Panamericana (CA1) toward Los Chorros, and continue as if going to Santa Ana. Just before Km. 29, take the right exit marked "Este Panamericana CA1A." Follow the signs to Joya de Cerén, coming to a traffic stop and carefully going straight through. You will now be on the road to San Juan Opico. Joya de Cerén is six kilometers down from the turnoff (a few kilometers short of Opico). The site is located at Km. 35 on the left side of the road. The drive takes about an hour.

SANTA TECLA

Located at the southern foot of the San Salvador volcano, just 17 kilometers west of San Salvador, the suburb of Santa Tecla is wildly popular with Salvadorans but still relatively untapped by foreign tourists—only because most of them still haven't heard of it.

★ Paseo El Carmen

The main draw in Santa Tecla is **Paseo El Carmen** (2pm-11pm Fri.-Sun.), a street full of restaurants, bars, and shops that turns into a pedestrian area every weekend. From Friday evening until Sunday night Paseo El Carmen fills up with independent vendors selling local goods such as artisanal chocolate, coffee, indigo-dyed clothing, handmade jewelry, and art. In addition to this, there are various food stalls set up selling typical Salvadoran food, sweets, and drinks, and the Plaza de la Música (a plaza located in the center of Paseo El Carmen) almost always has live music or drumming. The afternoons and evenings around Paseo El Carmen are family friendly and a wonderful way to pass the day if you are around the city. After dark, the bars and restaurants also fill up and the nightlife goes until 2am. Paseo El Carmen has a friendly police presence and a safe, festive vibe, making it one of the most popular places for nightlife in the country. Bars offer live music, salsa dancing, and DJs. The best way to pass the time is at one of the outdoor tables on the street, making new friends and watching the people go by.

If you have some time to spend in Santa Tecla, other attractions worth checking out include the **Museo Municipal Tecleño (MUTE)** (7 Av. Sur 1-4, tel. 2534-9633, info@mutesv.org, 9am-5pm daily, free), at the far east end of Paseo El Carmen. This large mint-green neoclassical building was originally built as a prison in 1902. The building was designed with four main cells to hold up to 15 prisoners each, however, records show that

Paseo El Carmen in Santa Tecla

each cell held closer to 40 inmates at a time. These four large rooms now serve as excellent galleries for rotating art shows. The museum is a fantastic cultural space where a variety of independent work is regularly showcased, including films, contemporary Latin American art, poetry, and photography. The museum also often hosts lectures and theater productions. There is also a large open-air space in the back where there is a funky, relatively unknown café.

An architectural relic of the 19th century, **Iglesia El Carmen** sits at the west end of Paseo El Carmen. Although it is not possible to enter (the 2001 earthquake damaged it enough to make it unsafe), the grand neo-Gothic style still makes the facade worth visiting. The church was constructed between 1856 and 1914 and used brick and *talpetate* (material made from volcanic ash) to achieve the impressive facade.

Accommodations

Typically, most people don't stay overnight in Santa Tecla; however, with the recent opening of an excellent hostel right beside Paseo El Carmen, and the unique cultural vibe that continues to grow in the area, it's becoming more of a popular base. It's very close to El Boquerón, Balneario Los Chorros, and the Jardín Botánico, and is a great launching point for exploring the western part of the country. Both El Tunco and Lago Coatepeque are just a 30-minute drive from Santa Tecla. If you plan on having a night out on Paseo El Carmen, it's nice not to have to worry about getting a taxi back to San Salvador. Plus, if you spend the night on the weekend, you can get up the next day and enjoy the pedestrian fair during daylight hours.

Hotel Tecleño (1 Calle Oriente, tel. 2228-6482, $12 s or d) is located right on Paseo El Carmen and is the cheapest option. Although this place doubles as a motel, which means it can be rented out by the hour (used by people who are not using the bed for sleeping), the rooms are just fine for anyone looking for budget accommodations for a night. They are small but clean, with white tile floors, comfortable beds, a small TV, a fan, and a weathered but private bath with a cold shower.

★ **Juancito's Mango Inn** (2 Av. Norte 2-8, in front of the Alcaldía, tel. 7069-6252, $15 pp dorm, $40 d) just made Santa Tecla a whole lot better. Run by Juan, a charismatic Salvadoran, and Jenny, his equally lovely *gringa* wife, this little hostel is bright and cozy, and the first of its kind in the neighborhood. Conveniently located right off Paseo El Carmen in the heart of Santa Tecla, you'll be connected to the nearby cafés, bars, restaurants, gift shops, and the food and artisanal fair each weekend. The baths are newly remodeled, and the rooms are impeccably clean and full of beautiful local crafts. All rooms have brand-new beds, hot water, and fans. There is a kitchen for guest use, a patio and common area, a rooftop deck with hammocks, Wi-Fi, a movie library, and quick access to major bus routes, including to El Tunco, and tour services to nearby destinations such as El Boquerón, Los Chorros, downtown San Salvador, and the Jardín Botánico.

Café Hotel El Patio del Don Moncho (1 Av. Norte 2-5, Santa Tecla, tel. 2288-4766, $30 d) also offers decent private rooms on a quiet side street. Rooms are small and simple, with TVs, air-conditioning, and Wi-Fi. Comfortable beds are covered in colorful textiles, and each room has a private bath (which the hotel claims have hot water, but it is lukewarm at best). Located in a secure, enclosed space with an outdoor lounge area surrounded by trees and plants, Don Moncho offers a quiet, charming place that is just around the corner from Paseo El Carmen.

Food and Nightlife

Paseo El Carmen is full of restaurants and bars, and it can be fun just to stroll the strip and decide which vibe appeals to you most. Most establishments have tables and chairs set up on the sidewalk or on the street, making it feel like a giant block party, so it doesn't make much of a difference where you go if you are looking to have a few drinks and meet people.

However, some places do stand out in terms of food or nightlife.

Yemayá (Av. Manuel Gallardo 2-8, across from Iglesia El Carmen, tel. 2288-4095, noon-3pm and 6pm-11pm Tues.-Thurs., noon-3pm and 6pm-midnight Fri. Jan.-Nov., noon-3pm and 6pm-11pm Tues.-Thurs., noon-3pm and 6pm-midnight Fri., noon-5pm Sun. Dec., $7-14) takes El Salvador's first confident steps into the realm of hipster health in a space that is more Brooklyn, New York, than the suburbs of San Salvador. Off the main strip, Yemayá invites you in with local graffiti art adorning the facade and a front bar that is effortlessly cool with its vintage couches, a small stage for live music, and a gorgeous back garden with minimalist contemporary furniture design. The tagline here is "food from the earth," and Yemayá makes good on this promise, offering wholesome, healthy dishes that include raw and vegan options. Fresh smoothies are made with your choice of almond, coconut, or soy milk. This is also the only restaurant in the country offering the elusive quinoa grain. The patio in the garden (which is transformed into a yoga space 10am-11:30am Sat.) is a great place to enjoy breakfast or lunch; in the evening the small cozy bar inside serves up locally brewed draft beer as well as a long list of other libations. There is live music most weekends with no cover charge. Expect to hear flamenco, jazz, alternative rock, or reggae.

Cafetería Tin (1 Calle Oriente, no phone, 6:30am-9pm daily, $7-15) is the best and longest standing spot on the strip for local food and desserts. This large cheery restaurant has colorful textiles on tables and fresh flowers all around. Weekend crowds betray its well-earned popularity. Cafetería Tin has daily buffet breakfast, lunch, and dinner offering up delicious salads, grilled meats, vegetarian dishes, pasta, *pupusas,* and divine desserts. It's worth stopping by for one of their massive fruit smoothies or a cup of freshly brewed coffee.

Bambas Restaurante & Bar (1 Calle Oriente, between 1 Av. and 3 Av. Norte, tel. 2229-8276, bambas_paseoelcarmen@yahoo. com, 4pm-2am Wed.-Sun., $6-12) is a typical taste of local Salvadoran nightlife—a large space with plenty of tables and a small dance floor that gets crammed. The food here is OK (meat, pasta, sandwiches), but the real reason people come to Bambas is for the party. Offerings include karaoke, live bands, crowded salsa nights, and the famously wild Wednesday and Thursday "ladies nights," when $5 at the door will get women into two hours of open bar for rum- and vodka-based drinks.

La Brujula (1 Calle Oriente, between 5 Av. and 2 Av. Norte, tel. 2228-2231, 5pm-2am Thurs.-Sun., $5-10) is the new hot spot on the strip, attracting a good mix of locals and expats. The front part of the bar is right in front of the street and has a contemporary style, with gleaming white bar stools set up around a well-stocked bar attended by a friendly bartender. This is where the drinking and socializing takes place. If you continue to the back, there are more intimate spaces with tables for dining and talking. The food is tasty and portions are big; popular dishes include pizza and pasta. La Brujula sometimes has live music on the weekend and does not charge cover.

The charming **Lima Limón Tropical Bistro** (1 Calle Oriente 3-6, Local 4, tel. 7069-6252 or 2566-5787, 4pm-midnight Wed.-Sat., $5-10) is small but full of personality. Run by the very friendly Salvadoran-American couple Juan Miguel Granados and Jenny Johnson, Lima Limón offers a menu and vibe that are unique to the strip. Tasty dishes include tamarind ribs, Jamaican chicken with chipotle, and a towering turkey club sandwich. They also serve up one of the best steaks in the country, a large portion of grade-A meat served with a sweet balsamic wine sauce, mashed potatoes, and salad. On weekends they often have drink specials and DJs, and the famous Sunday fundays are not to be missed if you are into electronic music—on the last Sunday of every month, starting in the early afternoon, local DJs set up outside on the street, and Saturday night's party continues until everybody is finally ready to go home. There is no cover.

Café Caracol (1 Calle Oriente 3-A, tel. 7730-6502, caracolcoffee@gmail.com, 5pm-midnight Tues.-Sat., $6-12) is a tiny little café with hands-down the best coffee on the strip. One of the only places with both high-quality coffee and an espresso machine, Café Caracol creates beautiful cappuccinos, lattes, and strong americanos. They also serve a variety of gourmet loose tea and a fine chai latte. This intimate, stylish space also serves French-inspired cuisine that includes crepes, thin-crust pizza, fondue, and a variety of desserts. This is the perfect place for a date or after-dinner drinks.

Thekla Pub and Grill (1 Calle Oriente 3-8, tel. 2229-4450 or 7862-5357, theklapub@gmail.com, 5:30pm-2am Tues.-Sat., $6-12) is just a few doors down from Café Caracol and hard to miss. This large, conspicuously green Irish pub delivers in true Celtic style with more than 40 types of beer to choose from. The menu is full of delicious deep-fried comfort food such as nachos and cheese-laden french fries, burgers, and grilled meats. It's dimly lit, with dark wood furniture and lots of cozy nooks to hide away and drink in. There is live rock music every night Thursday to Saturday. Expect to hear cover bands covering music from the '70s, '80s, and '90s. There is no cover.

Nearby **Jaggers** (1 Calle Oriente and 5 Av. Norte, tel. 2563-5075, jagger503@gmail.com, 5pm-2am Tues.-Sat.) is Thekla's more sordid younger sibling, with rock-bottom prices on cocktails and shots, encouraging heavy drinking, dancing, and delving into conversations with complete strangers. There are live bands and DJs on the weekends, no cover charge, and every Thursday is "ladies night," which means women get free drinks all night long.

Getting There

To get to Santa Tecla from San Salvador, take buses 101A or 101B ($0.40, 15 minutes, buses run every 15 minutes).

A taxi between San Salvador and Santa Tecla should cost $7-13, depending on where you are coming from and the time of day (it might cost more late at night). If you stay at one of the hotels in Antiguo Cuscatlán, near UCA, you will be conveniently close to Santa Tecla; expect to pay around $6-7 for a taxi.

Western El Salvador

Look for ★ to find recommended sights, activities, dining, and lodging.

Highlights

★ **Siete Cascadas Tour:** Hike through coffee plantations and tropical forest as you pass by beautiful waterfalls on this popular Juayúa excursion (page 77).

★ **Weekend Artisanal Market in Concepción de Ataco:** Stroll the cobblestone streets of this charming mountain town while tasting local food and exploring the unique art of Ataco's finest artisans (page 84).

★ **Aguas Termales near Ahuachapán:** Give your travel-weary body a rejuvenating soak in these therapeutic thermal waters. These are more than just thermal pools—the diverse expanse of land has many trails, miradors, thermal mud, plus a restaurant and bar. Watch the sun go down with a cool drink in a hot pool (page 89).

★ **Volcán Santa Ana:** Hikers are rewarded with amazing views of crater lakes and volcanoes (page 96).

★ **Piedra Sellada:** Hike a scenic four-kilometer route to this massive rock etched with ancient Mayan writing and drawings. Around the corner there is an icy river where you can go for a swim, surrounded by flat sun-drenched rocks perfect for relaxing before continuing on through Parque Nacional El Imposible (page 100).

A 40-kilometer winding road framed with wild flowers and punctuated by charming towns, Ruta de Las Flores is El Salvador's perennial favorite. Beginning in Sonsonate and ending in the colonial town of Ahuachapán, the route includes the

five towns in between, each with its own distinct appeal.

Coming from Sonsonate, the first stop on **Ruta de Las Flores** is **Nahuizalco,** a small town with strong indigenous heritage where the streets are lined with handcrafted baskets and furniture and the only night market in the country serves up traditional Mayan food. **Salcoatitán,** the tiny town in between Nahuizalco and Juayúa, offers a picturesque *parque central* full of vendors selling yuca and the famous Salvadoran quesadillas (a dense, sweet cake made with rice flour and cheese).

Just three kilometers down the road, you enter **Juayúa,** with its traditional charm and modern conveniences. This friendly mountain town is a long-standing backpacker favorite. Surrounded by volcanoes and coffee farms, the hills have beautiful hiking trails teeming with brilliantly colored butterflies, wildflowers, and waterfalls.

Apaneca, the highest town in El Salvador, offers a cool climate to enjoy canopy tours and hiking or cycling to the nearby crater lakes. Finally, **Concepción de Ataco** is quickly turning into a trendy weekend getaway where the streets come alive with an artisanal market, live music, and an eclectic mix of excellent restaurants.

As you travel between the towns, stunning views of coffee plantations, jade-green volcanoes, and the flowers that have sprung out of their rich volcanic soil make the entire route a visual delight. Cooler temperatures and cute cafés are the trademarks of this area, enticing the masses from congested San Salvador every weekend for leisurely breakfasts or mid-afternoon coffee and dessert in one of the route's many picturesque gardens. This is the perfect region to exert or indulge yourself; and most people do a little of both.

Nearby **Santa Ana** is the fourth-largest city in the country and is quickly becoming

Previous: coffee fields in Apaneca; Concepción de Ataco. **Above:** Juayúa's food fair.

Western El Salvador

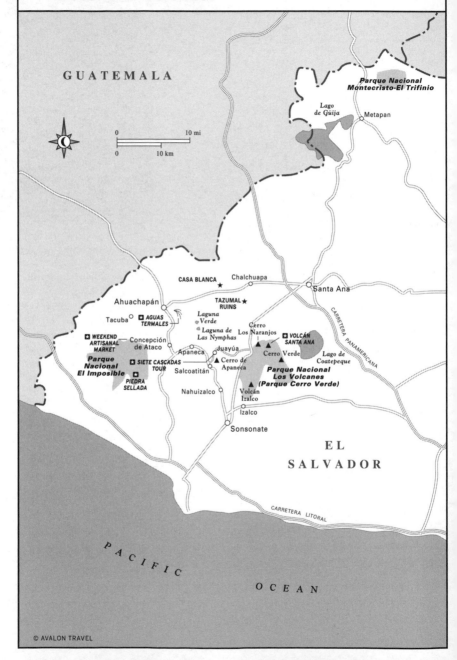

GUATEMALA

Parque Nacional
Montecristo-El Trifinio

Lago
de Güija

Metapan

0 ——— 10 mi
0 ——— 10 km

CASA BLANCA ★   Chalchuapa

Santa Ana

TAZUMAL ★
RUINS

Ahuachapán

Laguna
Verde

Tacuba ○   ⊕ AGUAS
TERMALES

Laguna de
Las Nymphas

Cerro
Los Naranjos

⊕ VOLCÁN
SANTA ANA

⊕ WEEKEND
ARTISANAL
MARKET

Concepción
de Ataco

Apaneca   Juayúa

▲ Cerro de
Apaneca

Cerro Verde ▲

Lago de
Coatepeque

CARRETERA PANAMERICANA

Parque
Nacional
El Imposible

⊕ SIETE CASCADAS
TOUR

Salcoatitán

Parque Nacional
Los Volcanes
(Parque Cerro Verde)

⊕
PIEDRA
SELLADA

Nahuizalco

Volcán
Izalco ▲

Izalco

Sonsonate

EL
SALVADOR

CARRETERA LITORAL

P A C I F I C

O C E A N

© AVALON TRAVEL

a popular stopover for travelers; many even use it as a base for exploring the western part of the country. The center is full of beautiful colonial architecture including the famous **Catedral de Santa Ana,** a striking neo-Gothic-style church that sits in the *parque central.* Volcano hiking is just a quick day trip away, and the nearby ruins of **Tazumal** are just a 30-minute bus ride from the center of the city. Farther south, **Parque Nacional El Imposible** offers extreme hiking with spectacular views of the Pacific coastline and Guatemala, ancient rock art, cool rivers, and dozens of endangered species of plants and animals.

PLANNING YOUR TIME

Four to five days is a good amount of time to really enjoy this area. Flowers are in bloom between November and February, making this the best time of the year to visit the region. The best way to explore **Ruta de Las Flores** is to make **Juayúa** your base and do day trips from there. It's a good idea to arrive on Friday, as the towns on the route don't come alive until the weekend. One day in Juayúa and one day in **Ataco** make for a great weekend. On Monday there will be nothing going on, so it's a perfect time to head out on a hike in Juayúa and check out restaurants between Apaneca and Ataco, or end the day in the hot therapeutic **Aguas Termales** near Ahuachapán. Allow yourself two days to explore **Parque Nacional El Imposible.**

Buses run frequently from San Salvador to both Ahuachapán and Sonsonate, the main transportation hub for travel around the region. Sonsonate's large, bustling bus terminal provides transportation to everywhere in Western El Salvador, and also has many *comedors* inside the terminal serving up tasty, cheap food. From Sonsonate, buses leave daily for Ruta de Las Flores and Cara Sucia (to go to Barra de Santiago or El Parque Imposible). Ruta de Las Flores buses run frequently, however if you are planning on heading to Barra de Santiago or El Parque Imposible, it is necessary to arrive on time for one of the two daily departures. Moving between the towns on Ruta de Las Flores is straightforward, as there are buses that run the length of the route every half an hour from 5am to 6pm daily. These buses leave from the entrances of the towns, or alternatively can be waved down at any point on the route. There is also a bus that travels daily between Juayúa and Santa Ana, passing through Los Naranjos, a misty mountain town with beautiful views and a few roadside cafés. Finally, if you are at one of the western beaches and want to head directly to Ruta de Las Flores, this can easily be done without having to backtrack to San Salvador. Just walk up to the Carretera Litoral (coastal highway), and wait for one of the two daily buses coming from San Salvador to Sonsonate.

Sonsonate

The only reason to pass through hot, sticky, and crowded Sonsonate is to catch a bus going somewhere else. Sixty-four kilometers west of San Salvador, Sonsonate's large bus station is the transportation hub for the region, and chances are you will have to stop here. This is also the largest city before you get to Ruta de Las Flores, and known for its high crime rates, so it's best to pass through fairly quickly. If you happen to miss a bus and need to spend the night in Sonsonate, there are a couple of safe, comfortable options.

ACCOMMODATIONS AND FOOD

Plaza Hotel (9 Calle Oriente, between 8 Av. and 10 Av. Norte, tel. 2451-6626, hotel-plaza_sonsonate@yahoo.com, $30 s, $35 d) is a quick cab ride from the bus station. This feels like an American budget hotel, with long carpeted hallways that lead into clean basic rooms with mini refrigerators, air-conditioning, cable TV, and hot water. There is an indoor bar and a large common area with tile floors and wicker chairs alongside an outdoor pool, which is a bonus in Sonsonate, where the heat can get intense.

Across the street from Plaza Hotel, you will find the excellent *comedor* **La Estancia de la Abuela Café** (9 Calle Poniente, in front of Plaza Hotel, tel. 2451-1667, 6:45am-7pm daily, $2-3) serving up delicious home-cooked meals and desserts inside a beautiful colonial home with outdoor seating beside the garden. Main dishes change every day and include options such as cheese crepes, potato lasagna, pizza and grilled meats, and fresh desserts such as tiramisu, cheesecake, and bread pudding.

On the outskirts of town you will find **Hotel Agape** (Km. 63, Carretera San Salvador, tel. 2429-8759, www.hotelagape.com.sv, $30 s, $35 d), which is part of the larger gated community of Agape, a safe area established and financed by social worker and priest Flavian Mucci. The money you spend here goes toward financing his work with single mothers, youth at risk, and orphans. In fact, one of the largest orphanages in the country can be found at Agape (not seen from the hotel or restaurant but on the same property). The rooms are simple and clean, with air-conditioning, although they lack natural light. The grounds are pretty, with lots of green space, flowers and plants, and a swimming pool. The hotel includes a restaurant that serves tasty Salvadoran food as well as pasta and a good selection of meat, including chorizo, steak, and rabbit. There is also a small supermarket.

The nearby **Chicken Steak** (Bulevar Las Palmeras and Carretera San Salvador, in front of the Shell Gas Station, tel. 2451-7670, 10am-10pm daily, $7-12) is easy to overlook if you don't already know that it is one of the best restaurants in town serving, you guessed it, chicken and steak. A small weathered orange sign hangs in front of the restaurant, which is hidden among banks and gas stations on an otherwise uninteresting street. Inside there is a lovely large courtyard with a barbecue slow-cooking whole chicken that is served with homemade *chimichurri,* fresh salad and fried yuca.

INFORMATION AND SERVICES

There is a **Scotiabank** (Carretera San Salvador and Bulevar Las Palmeras, tel. 2451-0161, 8am-4pm Mon.-Fri., 8am-noon Sat.). Around *parque central* you can find other ATMs, including an HSBC. Also beside the park is the grocery store **Dispensa Don Juan.** There is a post office (1 Av. Norte between 1 Calle and 3 Calle Poniente), and Internet cafés can be found all around the city center. There is also a Metrocentro mall where you will find ATMs and a supermarket.

GETTING THERE

From San Salvador, take bus 205 from Terminal de Occidente (Bulevar Venezuela). There are two buses; the *directo* costs $0.70 and takes about 1.5 hours. This bus leaves the terminal about every five minutes from 4:20am to 8pm daily. The other option is the *especial,* which is a little faster and usually air conditioned. This one costs $1 and takes 1.25 hours. The *especial* leaves every 15 minutes from 5:30am to 7pm daily.

To leave Sonsonate, the bus terminal has buses heading to all of Western El Salvador as well as to San Salvador. The bus terminal is located two kilometers east of the city center.

GETTING AROUND

Sonsonate's *parque central* is the transportation hub in the city. Buses pass by for all parts of the city. There is also a taxi stand that is always well stocked with drivers. It is recommended to travel in taxis when traveling around at night. To travel from *parque central* to the bus station, take bus 53C or a taxi. A taxi should cost around $4. Buses leaving Sonsonate for San Salvador leave from a different station, located directly across the street from the entrance of the bus terminal.

Nahuizalco

Nine kilometers uphill from Sonsonate is the former indigenous capital Nahuizalco, a small, undeveloped town noted for its hand-made furniture, handwoven baskets, and long-running night market. Nahuizalco maintains a strong indigenous culture, and this is one of the few places in the country you might still find elderly people wearing traditional clothing or women weaving baskets out of tule, a dried water plant. The central plaza is flanked by a small but informative Pipil museum on one side and the bustling daily market on the other. A few hours would be well spent here exploring the shops full of local handicrafts, including jewelry, handwoven baskets, and wooden furniture, or visiting the churches that date back to colonial times. El Salvador's only night market is a great way to finish off the day, sampling traditional Mayan food made from scratch. Nahuizalco does not have anything in the way of accommodations, but **Hotel Anahúac** (1 Calle Poniente and 5 Av. Norte, Juayúa, tel. 2469-2401, hotelanahuac@tikal.dk) in Juayúa offers transportation to and from the night market.

SIGHTS

Nahuat-Pipil Community Museum (across from *parque central,* tel. 7389-5904, 9am-5pm daily, $1) is a small but informative museum outlining the history of indigenous culture in Nahuizalco and the region. The museum includes a fascinating collection of photos taken by a Swiss photographer and anthropologist who chronicled the daily lives of the Pipil people in El Salvador in the 19th century. There are also replicas of artifacts along with handicrafts. The staff is well informed and very helpful, but they do not speak English, and all of the curatorial signs are in Spanish.

SHOPPING

The **Nahuizalco Night Market** (located on the west side of *parque central,* in front of the *alcadía,* 5pm-9pm daily) runs every night of the week, but the best time to go is on the weekend, when all the vendors are out. Traditionally the market ran without electricity, and the food stalls were lit by the soft glow of candles only. Today, there are lights, but some vendors still use candles to showcase their food, creating a peaceful community atmosphere. Dishes include traditional Mayan fare such as chicken in pumpkin-seed sauce, rabbit tacos made with freshly ground corn tortillas, tamales, crab, tripe, endless varieties of freshly baked sweet bread, and traditional drinks such as hot chocolate (made with local cacao) and *atol* (a sweet warm drink made from corn). There is also plenty of *comida típica* (typical Salvadoran food) for the less adventurous (beans and rice, grilled chicken, and *pupusas*).

CEDART (Final 3 Av. Norte, tel. 2453-1244, 9am-5pm daily) is a lovely little shop on the same street as the night market, a couple of doors down from the museum and *alcadía.* Here you will find jewelry, brightly colored wall hangings, baskets, and art, all made by local artists. If you are lucky you may even catch one of the local women weaving together a basket out of tule.

TOURS

Nahuizalco Tours (contact via the Nahuat-Pipil Community Museum, tel. 7389-5904) offers two-hour walking tours that visit the Nahuizalco market and local artisanal workshops. The tours take around two hours, cost $5, and are available on demand. They also guide hikes to the nearby **La Cascada Golonderia,** a pristine towering waterfall that rushes through a moss- and fern-covered canyon that leads to a swimming pool. The hike is moderate and takes about two hours. It takes you through coffee fincas and forest, offering views of the surrounding mountains.

GETTING THERE AND AROUND

Bus 249 runs every 15 minutes from Sonsonate ($0.45) or any other town along La Ruta de Las Flores, and will stop at the entrance to Nahuizalco. It's about a one-kilometer walk into town, where you are able to explore the town on foot.

SALCOATITÁN

Six kilometers north of Nahuizalco is the tiny and often overlooked Salcoatitán, worth a quick visit if only for the excellent Los Patiós restaurant and a stroll around the quiet, picturesque town, with a crumbling colonial church, quiet tree-lined streets with colorful houses, and a large *parque central* surrounded by vendors selling delicious yuca and sweets.

★ **Los Patiós** (Calle Principal, 2 blocks east of Salcoatitán, tel. 2401-8590, 9am-6pm Sat.-Sun., $6-12) is a must for foodies, serving up gourmet *comida típica* in a tranquil outdoor setting on two small patios surrounded by a garden and with a great view of the mountains. Only open on weekends, Los Patiós offers a small but excellent menu using lots of fresh local ingredients. Try the *ofeteles,* the specialty that Salvadorans come here for; it's a kind of gnocchi, wrapped in savory *tenquique* mushrooms, indigenous to this area, and served in a cream sauce. The owner of the Los Patiós is also an artist, and there is a small gallery housing her sculpture work next to the restaurant.

Bus 249 runs every 15 minutes, costs $0.45, and stops in Salcoatitán.

Juayúa

High up in the Apaneca Sierra, nestled in a valley surrounded by lush green coffee fincas and a ring of volcanoes, lies Juayúa, or the "River of Purple Orchids" in Nahuatl. Just three kilometers from Salcoatitán, Juayúa is a peaceful, slow town where life takes place on the cobblestone streets. In the thick farms that surround the town, you will find excellent hiking trails that are teeming with waterfalls and brilliant indigo butterflies. There is a large and shady *parque central,* full of flowers and benches, surrounded by street vendors and flanked by the gorgeous Iglesia Santa Lucia. A small but well-stocked market, a bank, and a diverse selection of restaurants and hostels make this a perfect base for exploring the other towns along the route. Every weekend, Juayúa hosts a long-running food and artisanal festival that creates a vibrant family-friendly mood in and around the town center. During the week, things quiet down, but there is still plenty to do, including hikes, coffee tours, or just taking a few days to recharge at one of Juayua's charming, homey hostels.

SIGHTS

Iglesia Santa Lucia (6am-6pm Wed.-Mon.), also known as Iglesia Cristo Negro, sits on the west side of *parque central.* The white and red church was built in the neobaroque style in 1956, but the statue of the black Christ predates the church by around 400 years. Made by the same Spanish sculptor who made the black Christ in Esquipulas, Guatemala, this one was carried to El Salvador by a group of Dominican priests who were fleeing a malaria outbreak in Guatemala. According to local legend, they started their journey with the icon in Acajutla, proceeding through various towns before reaching Juayúa, where they found Maya and Pipil fighting over control of the town. The priests liked Juayúa and decided to settle the conflict between the two indigenous groups by usurping power for themselves and attempting to convert them all to Christianity. They placed the Black Christ on an altar in what was the spiritual center of Juayúa for the Pipil people and soon converted the indigenous place of worship into a church. Today, the inside of the church

Juayúa

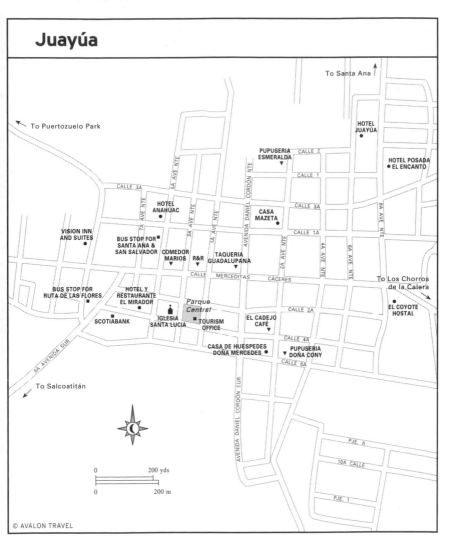

boasts towering columns, a wooden ceiling, and stained glass windows, and the famed black Christ sits at the center of it all, above a marble altar.

ENTERTAINMENT AND EVENTS
Nightlife

There is pretty much one place to go if you are looking for nightlife in Juayúa: **El Cadejo Café** (Calle Monseñor Romero, tel. 7536-9334 or 7528-6848, 11am-2am Thurs.-Sat., 11am-10pm or later Sun.). This hip little bar is a great spot to enjoy a nightcap and homemade dessert and chat with the locals or other travelers. Co-owners Roca (who will keep the drinks flowing and conversation going) and Alejandro (who serves up one of the best espresso coffees in the country) have created a warm, chic space that will make you feel like you are hanging out with friends (chances are, by the end of the night, you will be). There is free live music most Saturday nights, spanning reggae to jazz to folk.

Festivals

Every New Year between January 6 and 15, thousands of Salvadorans make the pilgrimage to Juayúa to celebrate **Festival Cristo Negro.** The streets bustle for two weeks with music, food, and general levity.

SHOPPING

The **Feria Gastronómica** (around *parque central,* 11am-5pm Sat.-Sun.) draws people from all over the country. Food vendors set up stalls on the north side of the *parque central,* where you will find no shortage of grilled meat and seafood, tamales, traditional soups, *refrescos* such as *horchata* (a sweet drink made out of sesame, peanuts, and rice), and tamarind juice, and a variety of sweets. On the south side of the park you will find artisans selling handcrafted jewelry and souvenirs as well as textiles and clothing imported from Guatemala. There is also lots of cheap trinkets such as earrings and sunglasses. There is much better shopping to be found in El Salvador, but the crowds that the fair draws make it worth a visit, if only to wander around and take in the festive atmosphere.

RECREATION AND TOURS
Hiking

Hiking tours to Los Chorros de la Calera and Siete Cascadas can be organized through **Hotel Anahúac** (1 Calle Poniente and 5 Av. Norte, tel. 2469-2401, hotelanahuac@tikal.dk) and **Casa Mazeta** (1 Calle Poniente 22, tel. 2406-3403, http://casamazeta.com). The walk to Los Chorros de la Calera can also be arranged for free with the local police.

Los Chorros de la Calera

A two-kilometer round-trip walk east from the center of town, Los Chorros de la Calera is a fairly easy hike and takes about two hours. A dirt road takes you past homes and small communities living among coffee farms, and eventually ends up at a descending path that opens up to the beautiful waterfalls bursting out from behind a rock wall and rushing down into an artificial pool, where ferns and moss cover the rock and wildflowers peek out from all corners. This hike can easily be done on your own; just follow Calle Los Chorros all the way to the end. However, if you pay $1 for a guide, you can hike up through the coffee plants instead of along the dirt path, which can get very dusty and present

El Cadejo Café offers the best coffee, cocktails, and conversation along Ruta de Las Flores.

A hiker free rappels down a waterfall on the Siete Cascadas hike in Juayúa.

private park on a coffee farm. Guided hikes around the farm are available, as is horseback riding and bike tours. **Hikes** in the park range 1-3 hours and cost $7-10. You can also hike from the park to Apaneca through coffee farms, where you will have views of the volcanoes and towns below; this takes 2.5 hours and costs $7.50. **Horseback riding tours** take 1-3 hours and cost $20-35, depending on the route and duration. The tours go on different paths up the hills around Juayúa. **Bike tours** are $25 per hour, and the route is determined according to your ability.

There are also beautiful tents ($35 d) and cabins ($65 d) if you want to sleep on the farm. The tents are large and have real beds inside, with a shared outdoor washroom with hot water. The cabins are spacious, with huge beds, lots of sunlight, and large colorful murals on the walls. They include a common area with hammocks and fireplaces. There is an on-site restaurant that prepares food if ordered in advance. You must make reservations in advance if you want to stay, eat, or do any of the activities on the farm, and often during the week there is no one managing things at the farm, so it is best to plan well ahead.

Coffee Tour

A visit to western El Salvador is not complete without deepening your understanding of how the golden grain becomes a cup coffee. Local coffee grower and aficionado Cesar Magaña Arevelo of **Hotel Anahúac** (1 Calle Poniente and 5 Av. Norte, tel. 2469-2401, hotelanahuac@tikal.dk) takes you to **La Majada Coffee Cooperative,** where he will guide you through the entire process, passionately explaining what makes a cup of coffee great as opposed to just keeping you awake. Join in on taste testing, learn about the history of the "coffee republic," and finally understand the difference among dark, medium, and light roast varieties. Finish off with a cup of intensely aromatic freshly roasted coffee. The tour of the facility takes around 2 hours and costs $10 pp; you must pay the day before, and there is a minimum of two people

problems for people with any kind of respiratory issue or allergies. Also, there have been reports of robberies along this route in recent months, so if you do decide to go alone, be sure to leave any valuables (including your camera) at your hotel.

★ Siete Cascadas Tour

The Siete Cascadas Tour is one of the best hikes in the country. It's a challenging eight-kilometer round-trip hike through lush forest and coffee fincas, interspersed with waterfalls of varying heights; you can free rappel down a waterfall and enjoy lunch with a spectacular view. This hike also includes an invigorating swim at the end in **Los Chorros de la Calera.** You have to hire a guide to do this hike; the cost is $20 and it takes about four hours.

Portezuelo Park

About seven kilometers north of Juayúa is the beautiful **Portezuelo Park** (tel. 2245-2614, www.akwaterra.com, 8am-6pm daily, $3), a required. If you are in Juayúa already, go to Hotel Anahúac to pay, or you can pay via phone using a credit card.

ACCOMMODATIONS
Under $10

A long-standing favorite for travelers of all stripes, **Hotel Anahúac** (1 Calle Poniente and 5 Av. Norte, tel. 2469-2401, www.hotelanahuac.com, $9 pp dorm, $17 s, $25 d private room) has an artsy, boutique hotel feel to it. Dormitories and private rooms have walls adorned with local art, fans (though you will not need them), and showers with wonderfully hot water. They all surround a peaceful garden with inviting hammocks, visiting birds, and colorful flowers. There is a very small kitchen for use, and a few tables located around the garden where guests can enjoy the highly recommended Anahúac breakfast ($3-5). Be sure to try the aromatic export-quality coffee straight from the family farm, guaranteed to kick-start any weary traveler before heading out on one of Anahúac's very professionally run tours.

Three blocks east of Hotel Anahúac on 1A Calle Poniente, another backpacker-friendly hostel, **Casa Mazeta** (1A Calle Poniente 22, tel. 2406-3403, www.casamazeta.com, $9 pp dorm, $17 s, $25 d), strikes a great balance between feeling spacious and cozy, with a large common area that includes the comforts of home such as a TV, a well-stocked DVD collection, a big kitchen, and a seemingly bottomless pot of coffee brewing. The rooms are also large, with fans and plenty of storage space for backpacks and gear. A beautiful garden with hammocks, sitting areas, and sculptures makes for a lovely place to while away an afternoon (or a few) trying to decide where to go next. There is also a charming private room hidden away in the back of the garden. The very friendly bilingual owner, Darren Clarke, is extremely helpful and always ready to answer questions or even show travelers around town.

About a 15-minute walk up the hill north from the center of town, **Hotel Juayúa** (at the end of 6 Av. Norte, Barrio La Esmeralda, tel. 2469-2109, www.hoteljuayua.com, $35 d shared cabin, $50 d suite) is a quiet, offbeat option with a spectacular view of the surrounding mountains, a small swimming pool, and a large open lawn and garden, creating lots of green space. There are only three rooms, two of which share an old cabin, one room on top (opening up to an incredible view of the seven surrounding volcanoes) and the

beans at a coffee cooperative near Juayúa

other below. They have funky wooden art and private baths with hot water. If you stay in the shared cabin, be aware that you will hear your neighbors through the thin, rickety wooden ceiling/floor. The bigger, more expensive suite is a hidden gem, located in its own house beside the other rooms, with a large open-concept space decorated with Asian rugs, Salvadoran art, wicker and wood from Nahuizalco, and big windows opening up to the unrivaled view outside. There is Wi-Fi, and all the rooms have fans. The owner, Alfredo, is a friendly guy and offers informal tours around the area. The prices for the rooms are negotiable.

$10-25

Five rooms are hidden inside the lovely hostel **Casa de Huespedes Doña Mercedes** (2 Av. Sur and 6 Calle Oriente, tel. 2452-2287, $10 pp dorm, $20 d), conveniently located across the street from the most popular *pupusería* in town and around the corner from the best bar. Pink walls, fake flowers, and comfy couches will make you feel like you are visiting a grandmother's house (in a good way). Spotless and peaceful, the common area also includes a sunny little courtyard with ferns, geraniums, aloe plants, and more. The rooms have lots of windows, TVs with cable, fans, hot water, and for an additional fee, Wi-Fi. There is a small kitchen that guests can use and very affordable laundry service ($2.50 per load).

Clean and quiet **El Coyote** (8 Av. Sur 1-5, tel. 2407-5493, $15 d) offers basic rooms with ceiling fans that are sparsely decorated with dressers, wall mirrors, and well-worn mattresses. Three simple rooms with one shared bath are located in the back of single mom Sonia's home. The rooms all face the backyard of the house, where there is a couch to lounge in and lots of plants. It might be a good option for two people looking for a cheap private room.

Aside from its proximity to the bus stop and its lovely rooftop view of the mountains, there is no other reason to stay at **El Mirador** (4 Calle Poniente 4-4, tel. 2452-2432, $20-50). The hotel houses 40 mostly windowless rooms with fans that have all seen much better days. Stained walls and old bedspreads betray the hotel's age, and a lack of light creates a bit of a depressing vibe. El Mirador is the first hotel you will see walking north from where the buses stop, so if you arrive after dark and are exhausted, it might be an easy option for one night.

The friendly family-run **Hotel Posada El Encanto** (road toward San José de la Majada, tel. 2452-2187, info@hotelelencanto.com, $30-50) is a bit off the beaten track, on the road that leaves Juayúa toward Santa Ana. It offers lovely new rooms with TVs, hot water, fans, lots of natural light, pretty tiling on the floors and walls, and fantastic views of the surrounding mountains. It might be better suited to traveling families, however, as the unofficial curfew (they lock the doors at 9pm) coupled with the street noise make for early nights and mornings. The place is clean and comfortable; with a small dining area and a garden. A modest breakfast is included in the rates. There is also a swimming pool across the street that guests can use.

$50-100

Vision Inn and Suites (9 Av. Norte, Calle Merceditas Cáceres Poniente and 1 Calle Poniente, Barrio San José, tel. 2469-2968 or 2469-2969, vision.inn.and.suites@gmail.com, $85 s, $110 d) is the nicest hotel in Juayúa, though it might be hard to tell from the uninspired facade. Sitting on the western edge of town, this glaringly white, utilitarian-looking building could easily be overlooked as something other than a higher-end hotel. Like many of the more expensive hotels in El Salvador, it has a cavernous feel, with lots of big, characterless rooms intended for events such as conferences and a small windowless dance bar in the basement; however, the rooms make up for the otherwise bland space. They are big, bright, and modern with sleek, minimalist design and sliding glass doors that open to individual terraces with unrivaled views of the volcanoes that surround Juayúa. The rooms have air-conditioning,

Wi-Fi, jetted bathtubs, flat-screen TVs, and room service.

FOOD

Serving up delicious salads, soups, and sandwiches alongside signature cocktails and artisanal beers, ★ **El Cadejo Café** (Calle Monseñor Romero, tel. 7536-9334 or 7528-6848, 11am-2am Thurs.-Sat., 11am-10pm or later Sun., $6-12) is the perfect way to end a day in Juayúa. Life-size portrait photographs, planters made of recycled plastic with greenery and lights peeking out of them, and a small but lovely open-air space full of plants make this the most atmospheric place in town. The menu has several vegetarian and vegan options, including homemade pasta, excellent sandwiches, fabulous organic coffee, and sublime key lime pie.

The Canadian-trained chef serves savory seasonal food at the popular **R & R** (Calle Merceditas Cáceres 1-2, tel. 2452-2083, 10:30am-9pm daily, $5-10), where an intimate space is enhanced with plants, flowers, colorful murals of local scenery on the walls, and candlelit dinners. Cooking with fresh local ingredients means that there may be variation in the same plate on subsequent visits, but most people don't seem to mind. The steaks are excellent (there is even one with coffee-infused salsa), as is the vegetarian lasagna. All entrées are served with a small salad.

Taqueria Guadalupana (Calle Merceditas Cáceres and Av. Daniel Cordón, tel. 2452-2195, 10:30am-9:30pm Tues.-Sun., $2-5) is hard to miss. Most nights there is loud music blaring, colorful streamers hanging from the ceiling, and a crowd of hungry locals. Tortilla soups, burritos, and tacos are the mainstays here, and although the food is not outstanding, it's the only place you will find Mexican on La Ruta de Las Flores; it's good for fast, cheap fare.

The tiny **Mario Comedor** (Calle Merceditas Cáceres, beside ANDA office, just west of Superselectos, tel. 2469-2990, 7am-9am and 11:30am-2pm daily, $1-3) will not disappoint if you are looking for cheap *comida típica*. This local favorite serves up excellent *comida a la vista* for breakfast and lunch at rock bottom prices. The *comedor* does not have a sign and is hidden behind a peeling red and white wall beside the ANDA office. Inside, a few wooden tables and a tiny kitchen make up the no-frills restaurant. Typical plates include *pollo encebollado, sopa de res,* and grilled meat. All dishes come with a healthy portion of salad, rice, and tortillas.

The most popular *pupusería* in town, **Pupusería Doña Cony** (2 Av. Sur and 6 Calle Oriente, tel. 2452-2931, 4pm-10pm daily, $1-4) is busy every night. This no-frills *pupusería* has bright lights, a TV in the corner, and tables with colorful tablecloths. You will find the very best traditional fare, *refrescos,* coffee, and hot chocolate.

Taking a modern twist on the *pupusa,* **Pupusería Esmeralda** (La Urbanización Esmeralda, tel. 2452-2931, 5pm-10pm daily, $1-4) is a cute little gem, with light purple and yellow brick walls and cafeteria-style tables both inside and outside. You will find giant *pupusas* with more adventurous fillings such as *ayote* (a kind of squash) and spinach.

INFORMATION AND SERVICES

There is a **Scotiabank** at the entrance of town with one of the few ATMs where you can often take out more than the usual $200 limit. There is a **tourist office** (1 Av. and 2 Calle, turismo@alcaldiadejuayua.gob.sv, 8am-5pm Tues.-Sun.) on the east side of *parque central* with English-speaking staff on weekends only. Internet cafés, pharmacies, and a supermarket can all be found on the main street, Calle Merceditas Cáceres.

GETTING THERE

From the Sonsonate bus terminal, or from any other town along La Ruta de Las Flores, bus 249 costs $0.45, runs every 15 minutes, and stops in Juayúa. There are daily buses that leave Santa Ana and go directly to Juayúa; bus 238 leaves from Santa Ana's main terminal daily at 6:45am, 9:50am, 12:30pm, 2:30pm, 4pm, and 5:35pm. It takes one hour and costs $0.80.

Apaneca

Ten kilometers west of Juayúa is Apaneca, home to Laguna Verde and its sister lake, Laguna de Las Ninfas. There are various options for visiting the *lagunas*, including walking, cycling, or driving an all-terrain buggy.

Laguna Verde, so named because of the emerald-green hue of the water (not to mention the blanket of cypress trees that surrounds it), is the bigger of the two and has more activity around it; it's a nice spot to stop and enjoy some *pupusas* or chat with the locals as you admire the lake. Laguna de Las Ninfas is smaller and less frequented by tourists, but the views of volcanoes and coffee farms and fresh, clean air on the way up make it worth a visit. It's an incredibly peaceful place; once there, the only sounds you will hear are the birds above and the lake grass swaying in the breeze below.

The actual town of Apaneca is very mellow, with a slow and quiet *parque central* where vendors set up tables with sweets, handcrafted jewelry, and coffee on the weekends. The highest town in the country, Apaneca is appreciated for its cool, gentle breezes and sunshine.

RECREATION AND TOURS
Laguna de Las Ninfas and Laguna Verde
Hiking

It is possible to hike to both *lagunas*. Both hikes take around two hours and are not very difficult. The walk to **Laguna de Las Ninfas** is a four-kilometer round-trip and follows a dirt path with great expansive views of volcanoes and coffee plantations. The walk to Laguna Verde is a five-kilometer round-trip on the road, so expect to have cars passing by occasionally. Along the way you will walk past the small communities along the road to the *laguna*, making it an interesting walk, but it

is the less scenic of the two hikes. Guides for these hikes can be provided for $5 pp by the *alcadía*, which is located just west of *parque central*. It is possible to do the hikes on your own; the trailheads can be found opposite the entrance to Apaneca, where you will see signs.

Biking

There is also the option of biking to the lakes. The route to Laguna de Las Ninfas is very difficult—a steady incline up the rocky dirt path. The route to Laguna Verde is a little easier because of the paved road, but it is still quite an intense incline. Both routes take about three hours and can be arranged by **Hostal Il Piamonte** (2 Av. Sur, 4, Barrio San Pedro, tel. 7739-5830) or **Akwaterra Tours** (tel. 2265-1111, www.akwaterra.com). Prices depend on the tour. A new local company called **Bici Tours Providencia Divina Apaneca** (ask at the tourist kiosk at *parque central*, tel. 7656-2182, ulicesperez@hotmail.com) offers guided bicycle tours to Laguna Verde for $5 or bicycle tours of Apaneca for $3. They also offer cycling on more difficult trails through the surrounding villages for $30.

All-Terrain Buggy Rides

The final and most fun option is to join an all-terrain buggy tour with **Apaneca Aventura Buggy Tours** (Calle Los Platanares, on the corner across from the municipal court, tel. 2614-7034, 9am, 11:30am, and 2:30pm Mon.-Sat., $50 pp, $70 for 2 people), which will take you to both lakes, stopping along the way to enjoy the views. This tour takes about two hours. It is also possible to drive to the thermal waters in Ahuachapán. The total trip takes six hours and costs $115 for two people, which includes entrance to the thermal waters.

Zip-Lining

With **Apaneca Canopy Tour** (Av. 15 de

Abril and Calle Central, tel. 2433-0554, www.elsalvador.canopy.com, 9:30am, 11:30am, and 3pm Mon.-Sat., $30 pp), you'll spend two hours soaring over coffee plantations and lush vegetation on cables of 12 varying heights. It's a great way to see the flora and fauna of the region—possibly even eagles and toucans.

Tours

Owner Massimo Tinetti of **Hostal Il Piamonte** (2 Av. Sur 4, San Pedro, tel. 7739-5830) offers the only hiking or cycling tours with an English- and Italian-speaking guide to the lakes. Tours take about three hours and cost $5-10 pp. He also provides transportation to the nearby Cascada de Don Juan ($7 pp) and Aguas Termales de Santa Teresa (minimum group size 7 people, $15 pp) near Ahuachapán.

ACCOMMODATIONS

A life-size Darth Vader will greet you at the door of **Hotel Il Piamonte** (2 Av. Sur 4, tel. 7739-5830, $8 pp dorm, $15 private room), where the Italian owner offers the best budget rooms in Apaneca in tandem with a small but well-stocked action-figure museum. The hostel is the owner's home, and as a result it has a very cozy feel. Thankfully the action-figure theme does not continue inside the guest rooms, which are very clean, quiet, and infused with natural light. Rooms have fans and private baths. There is a very small restaurant ($4-8) in the hostel serving up Italian food on the weekends, and owner Massimo is available for tours in and around Apaneca.

Tucked away in the backyard of the owner's home, **Hostal Rural Las Orquideas** (Av. Central Sur 4, tel. 2433-0061, $15 pp) has very basic small rooms with private baths, hot water, and fans. The rooms share a patio with hammocks that face the small orchid garden. Breakfast is available for $2.50.

The quaint and colorful **Hostal Colonial** (1 Av. Sur and 6 Calle Poniente, tel. 2433-0662 or 7948-9277, hostalcolonial_apaneca@gmail.com, $30 d) is a favorite among locals. It offers nine private rooms that all face a lovely garden. The rooms have colorful murals painted on the walls, cable TV, fans, and small windows to let the light in.

The newest hostel in Apaneca is **Solvang** (Av. 15 de Abril, tel. 7025-5862, $40 d with 2 beds). On a corner in the center of town, this brand-new house has a modern large kitchen that is sleekly designed with brand-new appliances, a big common area with couches, chairs, and a dining table, and a small terrace that looks out over the cobblestone street. Private rooms with fans, shared baths, and hot water are also clean and new with white tile floors and big windows.

Las Cabañas de Apaneca (Km. 90.5, Carretera Sonsonate, tel. 2433-0500 or 2433-0400, info@cabanasapaneca.com, $30 s, $41 d, breakfast included) offer *cabañas* set in a lovely large garden with brightly colored mosaic sculptures and secret stone pathways. Some of the rooms are dark and uninspired, but some are beautiful and bright, with windows facing the green scenery outside, so if you decide to stay here, ask to be shown a few different rooms before choosing. All have private baths with hot water, fans, and Wi-Fi.

The most beautiful rooms along La Ruta de Las Flores are at **Santa Leticia** (Km. 86.5, Carretera Ataco-Apaneca, tel. 2433-0351 or 2433-0357, www.hotelsantaleticia.com, $68 d). Just east of Apaneca on the left side, a dirt road takes you down to this sprawling property, where tucked away in the back you will find wooden *cabañas*, painted muted yellow and green with stained glass windows, fans, and handmade furniture. They are set around a charming courtyard, which is quiet and far removed from the traffic of the main road. Each has a hammock and its own little sitting area, and there is a lovely swimming pool with solar heating. The restaurant has very good Salvadoran food as well as comforting cheese lasagna. There is also a $5 tour that will take you to see some Mayan ruins that were recently discovered in the area.

FOOD

There are not many options for food in Apaneca. On the north side of *parque central* there are *comedors* that serve excellent cheap *comida típica*, coffee, and hot chocolate (7am-7pm daily, $2-4). **Las Cabañas Apaneca** (Km. 91, Carretera Sonsonate, tel. 2433-0400, info@cabanasapaneca.com, 8am-5pm Mon.-Fri., 7am-7pm Sat.-Sun., $5-12) has good Salvadoran food and is open during the week.

If you are looking for something special on the weekend, **Café Café Apaneca** (Av. 15 de Abril Norte and Calle Francisco Menéndez, in front of the Casa de Cultura, tel. 2263-2413, rcuadra@cafecafe.com.sv, 11:30am-10pm Sat., 11:30am-4:30pm Sun., $10-20) is the only higher-end restaurant in Apaneca. The Peruvian-trained chef Richard Siwady de Cuadra serves stylish meals that focus on seafood and meat, with a Peruvian twist. This large space has a barnlike feel, with high ceilings and wooden rafters, and tables scattered throughout the room. This is a great place to enjoy a quality meal after a day of hiking, ziplining, or buggy tours, and then cozy up at the big wooden bar with a tumbler of cognac. Try the *gratinado de mariscos*—fresh shrimp and fish au gratin, smothered in cheese and baked to perfection.

GETTING THERE

From Sonsonate, Ahuachapán, or anywhere along La Ruta de Las Flores, bus 249 runs every 15 minutes and stops in Apaneca.

BETWEEN APANECA AND ATACO

On the stretch between Apaneca and Ataco, you will find some of the most popular restaurants and nicest hotels in the area.

Set far back above the main road on a large expanse of land, **Finca Los Andes** (Km. 92.5, Carretera Ataco-Apaneca, tel. 2433-0429 or 7736-8923, $30 d) offers secluded small cabins surrounded by the finca's coffee plants and flower gardens. The *cabañas* are simple but attractive, with local handcrafted furniture, fans, hot water, and front porches. There is no restaurant, but each *cabaña* has its own barbecue, and wood is provided.

★ **Jardín de Celeste** (Km. 94, Carretera Ataco-Apaneca, tel. 2433-0281, www.el-jardindeceleste.com, 6am-6pm daily, $6-14) is certainly the most ethereal place to enjoy an excellent meal or divine dessert. The restaurant is located just off of the main road, in the middle of a shady garden with sculptures, flowers, and chirping birds. The menu boasts high-quality Salvadoran food as well as excellent salads, soups, and pasta dishes. Owner Jill Lacina makes all of her signature desserts, such as coconut flan and tiramisu, from scratch with fresh ingredients, and you can taste the difference. Try the delicious hot pineapple tea, a welcome change from the ubiquitous Ruta coffee. You can even linger all evening and spend the night in one of the charming cabins nestled in the greenery behind the restaurant ($30 pp).

Just a little farther east down the road you will find **Las Flores de Eloísa** (Km. 94, Carretera Sonsonate, tel. 2433-0281, www.el-jardindeceleste.com, 6am-6pm daily, $3-6), owned by the same family and very similar to Jardín de Celeste but smaller and more casual. The menu has the same delicious desserts but less formal mains such as soups and excellent sandwiches made with quality cheese in a sandwich maker; the cheese and asparagus sandwich is especially popular. There are also *cabañas* ($27-40 d) where you can sleep.

Continue east from Las Flores de Eloísa and you will find the quirky **Entre Nubes** (Km. 94, Carretera Ataco-Apaneca, tel. 7922-8592, cafeentrenubes@gmail.com, 9am-5:30pm Mon.-Fri., 8am-6:30pm Sat.-Sun., $4-8), where owner Jorge García has also created an interesting place to stop and relax for a while. The ground is covered in sawdust, making a soft floor to wander around and soak in the atmosphere. A large garden with walking paths sits behind the restaurant, and handwritten jokes hanging all over the place will keep you happily distracted if you are dining alone. The food is significantly cheaper than at Jardín de Celeste and also very good, focusing on Salvadoran dishes as well as pizzas, soups, and salads. Jorge will happily fix you up with a bottomless cup of coffee, and the homemade desserts are not to be missed, especially the amazingly fresh and irresistible chocolate cake. Try the *horchata* here; it is maybe the best you will find in the country.

Finally, **Alicante Montaña Hotel** (Km. 93.5, Carretera Sonsonate, tel. 2433-0175 or 2433-0572, www.alicanteapaneca.com, $71 d, $150 *cabaña,* includes breakfast) is a good option for large groups or families. It's located on beautiful sprawling grounds that include a swimming pool, a small gym with a massage room and excellent sauna, and an enclosed collection of rare imported animals that may delight or disturb you, depending on how you see things. Wooden *cabañas* with room for four people have TVs, hot water, fans, and fireplaces. There are also smaller rooms available with two beds, fans, and no fireplace. There is a massive restaurant that serves *comida típica,* popular with locals for events such as weddings and parties.

If you want to visit any of these places, you can hop on bus 249, which runs every 15 minutes, and just advise the bus driver, who will let you off wherever you like.

Concepción de Ataco

Cobblestone streets, creative cuisine, and colorful murals make this cool little town a hot spot on the route. Just eight kilometers west of Apaneca, Ataco is known for its restaurants and cafés, and it has an excellent weekend artisanal market with unique local arts and crafts. Brightly painted murals adorn the walls of the town's buildings, and arts and crafts can be found in shops on every corner. There is a friendly community vibe here. It's a really fun spot to spend the weekend wandering in and out of art shops, cafés, and restaurants. The weekend market is smaller than the one in Juayúa but offers more exotic fare, such as grilled iguana and lizard, and local treats such as wild honey and sweet bread. On Friday and Saturday evenings, street lamps light up the town, and the sounds of live music float out of the restaurants and bars.

Recently, some artifacts have been found in and around Ataco, including vestiges of pre-Hispanic ceramics as well as stone sculptures such as jaguar heads; it is an exciting time of discovery, and the archaeological potential of Ataco continues to grow. Unfortunately, none of these discoveries are officially on display. However, they are kept in the office of the *alcaldía* right beside *parque central,* and if it is open, you can ask to have a look.

★ WEEKEND ARTISANAL MARKET

The **Weekend Artisanal Market** (around *parque central,* 11am-8pm Sat.-Sun.) in Ataco is not to be missed. This small market has live music, artisans, and samplings of local food and culture. You can try grilled iguana or lizard, check out the uniquely Salvadoran crafts such as clothing dyed with indigo and jewelry made from local stones and shells, or check out local art in one of the galleries across from the park.

OTHER SHOPPING

Diconte and Axul (*parque central,* with the murals out front, tel. 2633-5030, 9am-6pm daily) was the first established artisanal shop in Ataco, and it remains the best. If there is one place to do your shopping in town, this is it. The house dates to 1910 and sells high-quality handicrafts from all corners of the country. The outside of the building is covered in murals of cats, the favorite artistic subject in Ataco, and inside, the five-room shop presents a rainbow of vibrant color, including art, woodwork, textiles, pottery, and clothing. In the back you will find men weaving tapestries on traditional looms, and also a little café in the shade serving desserts and coffee.

Concepción de Ataco

Tingere Teñidos Naturales (in front of *parque central,* local 5, tel. 2450-5760, info@ tingere.com, 10am-6pm Wed.-Thurs. and Sun., 10am-9pm Fri.-Sat.) is a lovely little boutique shop that sells wall hangings, purses, clothing, and more all made with natural fibers and dyes. Owners Grazzia and Sandra have been making natural dyes for the last eight years, using local plants such as avocadoes, rosemary, coconut, and indigo, and are proud to sell eco-friendly products that are beautiful and 100 percent natural.

RECREATION
Hiking

About a 15-minute walk up through coffee fincas is **Mirador de La Cruz,** with a massive white cross, that looks out over the town of Ataco. This is an easy hike, and possible to do on your own; just turn left at the bottom of Calle Los Naranjitos, beside Iglesia Calvario, and follow the path.

Coffee Farm Tours

Quinta El Carmen, which is located just

outside the entrance to Ataco (Km. 97, Carretera Ahuachapán, tel. 2298-4188 or 2450-5146, www.elcarmenestate.com) is a beautiful coffee farm that was established by the Morán family in 1930. The family-run business continues to produce one of the most popular coffees in the country, called Café Ataco, and also offers coffee tours that guide you through the farm, explaining the entire process from bean to brew. Tours cost $5 and take 1.5 hours.

ENTERTAINMENT AND EVENTS
Nightlife

There are two main places to go for live music and general levity. **El Arky Café** (2 Calle Oriente, beside La Placita, tel. 7551-2681, elarky_ataco@hotmail.com, 5pm-2am Fri.-Sat.) has live rock music every Saturday night (no cover). At **Portland Bar and Grill** (2 Calle Central and 1 Av. Sur 1, tel. 2450-5798, noon-10pm Fri., noon-11pm Sat., 9am-3pm Sun.), live bands play every weekend, and there is no cover.

Festivals

Ataco celebrates one of the most beautiful festivals in El Salvador. **Los Farolitos** is a festival of lights that celebrates the birth of the Virgin Mary. Every September 7, as soon as night falls, hundreds of people take to the streets carrying pretty lanterns in a parade of light. There is also lots of music, food, and revelry later in the evening.

ACCOMMODATIONS
$10-25

By far the best budget choice in Ataco is **Segen Hotel** (3 Calle Ataco, one block behind *parque central*, tel. 2405-0832, Sun.-Fri. $10 dorm, Sat. $15 dorm, $30 private room any night). Segen offers dormitories as well as simple private rooms with TVs, hot water, fans, and Wi-Fi. There is a small common space with a little bar and tables, but no areas to relax outside the rooms. The rooms all face a cute little courtyard with a fountain and some green space with flowers. Very helpful owner Eduardo speaks English, and if he is around, he can advise you on what to do around the area. He is also able to organize tours in and around Ataco.

The only other budget hotel is **Meson de San Fernando** (1 Calle Poniente 14, tel. 7871-2126, $10 dorm, $20 d). The rooms are clean, though a little dark and damp, and don't have fans, air-conditioning, or hot water; they're set along a garden with a sitting area to eat and a small playground for little ones. Fernando and his wife prepare *comida típica* ($3-5), but there is not a proper restaurant per se.

$25-50

The lovely **Villa Santo Domingo** (Calle Central Poniente Francisco Lorca, tel. 2450-5442, $30 d) has 12 rooms that surround a quiet, pretty garden. High ceilings, stone floors, exposed brick walls, and pretty tiled sinks in the baths give the rooms a boutique look. All of the rooms face a courtyard with lots of plants hanging around the periphery and a few tables where breakfast can be provided for the additional cost of $2.50. The rooms have TVs, hot water, fans, and Wi-Fi.

Hostal El Portal (Calle Principal, beside the church, no phone, $30 private room) has three big, bright, very well maintained rooms that sit beside a peaceful garden. The rooms have excellent hot water, fans, comfortable beds and local handcrafted furniture adds a decorative touch.

Raíces Hostal (Av. Central and 6 Calle Poniente 1, tel. 2512-4331, www.raicesataco. com, $25 s, $30 d) is a new hostel, with clean, basic rooms, TVs with cable, fans, private baths, and hot water. There is no common space or restaurant in the hostel.

The staff is a bit aloof at **El Balcón de Ataco** (8 Calle Oriente, a.k.a. Calle "El Naranjito," tel. 2450-5171, $35 s, $65 d) but the views are unrivaled. It's a bit of a hike (about 15 minutes) up the hill on the south end of town to get here, making it a perfect place to stay to get away from it all. There are beautiful, simple rooms with private baths and hot water, fans, pretty tile floors, and huge windows that let in the light and provide a fantastic view of the town below. There is no Wi-Fi and no restaurant.

$50-100

El Pueblito de Don Luis (10 Av. Norte and 1 Calle Oriente, tel. 2450-5904, www.hotelpueblito.com, $85 for 2 double beds, includes breakfast) is the nicest place to stay in Ataco. Tucked away in a very quiet corner of town, enclosed by a tall wraparound adobe wall, you will find cute light-orange, yellow, and green houses nestled behind a beautiful garden bursting with plants and colorful flowers. Each large house has about four rooms located on the first floor. The rooms are big, with windows that let the sunshine flow in, multicolored locally made bedspreads, TVs, air-conditioning, hot water, and Wi-Fi. Each room has its own little space on the terrace with wooden rocking chairs to kick back and relax in.

FOOD

The tiny little **KaféKali** (next door to the *alcadía* on the west side of *parque central,* tel. 2100-2234, 7am-5pm daily, $3-6) is a great place to sit on the weekend and watch the festivities in the park. You will find tasty *comida típica,* crepes, desserts, coffee, and hot chocolate. Plus, this is the only place in Ataco that is open from 7am during the week, serving up budget breakfasts and fresh coffee.

Café El Carburo (5 Calle Poniente, in front of *parque central,* near Iglesia Ave María, tel. 7412-4576 or 2406-8370, cafecarburoataco@gmail.com, noon-10:30pm Thurs.-Sun., $4-10) is a small, rustic space serving up fantastic food from a constantly rotating menu created by inspired chef Christian Hess. Expect international fare with Salvadoran twists using fresh, local food. Some of his favorite dishes include rabbit stewed in a white wine and thyme cream sauce served with roasted potatoes and vegetables or roasted chicken over mashed herb polenta. The menu is always changing, so you never know what you may get, but you can be sure it will be delicious.

A good place to escape the barrage of crafts and commotion is **The House of Coffee** (Av. Centro Sur 13, tel. 2450-5353, 11am-5:30pm Mon.-Thurs., 11am-8pm Fri., 11am-9pm Sat., 8am-9pm Sun., $4-8), a modern café with espresso machines, comfy leather chairs and couches, wooden tables alongside a rack of magazines, and a lovely open-air space where you can sit and enjoy not only coffee and dessert but casual meals such as salads and sandwiches.

As the name suggests, **Portland Bar and Grill** (2 Calle Central and 1 Av. Sur 1, tel. 2450-5798, noon-10pm Fri., noon-11pm Sat., 9am-3pm Sun., $4-10) is an American-style pub, known more for its nightlife than its food, but it does serve decent pub fare such as chicken wings, nachos, and burgers and fries. True to Yankee culture, there is a long well-stocked bar with amiable bartenders happy to keep you topped up and entertained with casual conversation. There are also two flat-screen TVs, making it a popular spot for those looking to enjoy a cold beer and catch a sporting event on cable.

The excellent ★ **Piccolo Giardino Ristorante & Taverna** (1 Calle Poniente and 5 Av. Norte, tel. 7600-2986, noon-10pm Thurs.-Sun., $6-12) is especially pretty for dinner, where a torch-lit path will guide you to this hidden gem, an outdoor restaurant beside a garden infused with the scent of orchids. You will find savory thin-crust pizza baked in a wood-burning pizza oven as well as homemade pasta, calzones, and grilled meat, freshly ground hot chocolate, and generously poured glasses of wine.

The perfect mix of modern and rustic, the trendy ★ **Tayúa** (2 Av. Norte and 5 Calle Oriente, tel. 2450-5755, tayuacafe@gmail.com, noon-11pm Fri.-Sat., noon-6pm Sun., $8-15) offers thin-crust artisanal pizzas, salads made with organic greens direct from the restaurant's garden, and delicious sandwiches made with homemade bread and imported cheese, all against the backdrop of a beautiful breezy space with cozy nooks to kick back and lounge in. Tayúa really comes to life on Friday and Saturday nights when many people from around La Ruta come to enjoy the relaxed vibe and excellent food. Antique furniture, candlelit tables, and large wooden windows that open up to the cobblestone street create a space unlike any other in town. Young, hip owners Louis and Veronica set a welcoming vibe by personally greeting customers and chatting with the regulars.

La Raclette (5 Calle Poniente and 2 Av. Norte, tel. 2450-5836, 10am-9pm daily, $7-15) serves tasty cheese fondue as well as sandwiches and pastas accentuated with imported gouda and blue cheese. Pricier items such as grilled meats and seafood options are also available. Most of the tables are outside on the terrace that overlooks *parque central,* making it a great spot to visit for a meal or even just a drink on the weekend.

El Brasero (Av. Central, across from La Placita, tel. 2415-9985, 11am-8pm Wed.-Fri. and Sun., 11am-10pm Sat., $10-15) serves Chilean inspired dishes that focus on *asado* (barbecued meat). There are a couple of tables on the main floor, but you will find a much nicer atmosphere upstairs, where there is a small terrace overlooking Avenida Central. The food is excellent and includes steak, chicken, pork, and seafood (served with baked potatoes, fresh salad, or grilled vegetables) as well as vegetarian options such as a lovely vegetable gratin. Choose from a selection of Chilean wines as well as fresh fruit juices and smoothies. As an added bonus, the staff are very friendly and attentive, and the headwaiter speaks English.

Casa Guimerá (2 Av. Sur, near Iglesia Calvario, tel. 2406-6312, noon-3pm and 6pm-9pm daily, $10-20) is a small, intimate space with dark wood tables, decorative antiques, and a lovely hidden terrace out back. This Spanish restaurant serves excellent grilled meats, pastas, and wine, making it the perfect place for a special occasion or a date.

INFORMATION AND SERVICES

The main street has a Scotiabank ATM, various pharmacies, a couple of Internet cafés, and a post office. This is also where you will find the central market.

GETTING THERE

Bus 249 runs every 15 minutes and stops at the entrance of Ataco and goes north to Ahuachapán ($0.35, 15 minutes) and south to Apaneca ($0.25, 10 minutes), Juayúa ($0.45, 30 minutes), and Sonsonate ($0.80, one hour).

Ahuachapán

The last town on Ruta de Las Flores, Ahuachapán is 11 kilometers north of Ataco. This pretty colonial town sits on the edge of the country, just minutes from the Guatemalan border. There is not much to do in town, other than wander and enjoy the large, shady *parque central* (with public Wi-Fi) and the pretty whitewashed church that sits right beside Plaza Concordia, a lovely pedestrian area.

Three kilometers outside town on the way to Apaneca, there are active hot springs that drive the city's electric power plant, which provides a portion of the country's electricity. It is not possible to visit the plant, but these same hot springs create one of the highlights of Ruta de Las Flores, the Aguas Termales, a collection of hot therapeutic pools. Most hotels along the Ruta offer transportation to and from the pools, so there is no need to stay in Ahuachapán if you would like to visit them; if you do decide to spend a night in Ahuachapán, however, there are a couple of excellent options.

RECREATION

★ Aguas Termales

The main reason many people come to Ahuachapán is to visit the nearby hot springs pools, located about three kilometers outside the town on the way to Ataco. There are two *aguas termales* right next to each other; which one you choose depends on what kind of experience you want.

The older **Aguas Termales de Santa Teresa** (tel. 2423-8041, www.termalesdesantateresa.com, 9am-6pm daily, $10 pp) is a gorgeously designed coffee finca where the river from the hot springs flows into seven hot pools of varying temperatures, from very hot to tepid. Each pool is surrounded by beautiful plants and lounge chairs, and there are rooms where you can spend the night ($70-100 d). The rooms are quite plush, with air-conditioning, flat-screen TVs, lots of natural light, and one room even has its own private little hot pool. There is no restaurant here, so it's best to bring your own groceries if you plan staying for a while.

Nearby **Aguas Termales de Alicante Ahuachapán** (tel. 2417-6492, noon-5pm daily, $10 pp) is much larger and has plenty of green space to wander and relax in. One large pool has magnificent views of the surrounding mountains and a deck space with lounge areas. Below are three smaller pools of varying temperatures in a shaded area with a bar and restaurant. The land has a couple of beautiful miradors and plenty of areas for walking and enjoying the views. Owner Eduardo Méndez is a young entrepreneur and very flexible with the hours of operation. If you would like to visit at night, you can call him and arrange for the pools to be open. Méndez is also the owner of **Segen Hotel** (tel. 2459-5832, segenhostel@hotmail.com) in nearby Ataco, which can arrange transportation from Ataco to Termales de Alicante.

The pools are hard to get to on your own, and there is no direct bus. You can take bus 249 and ask the driver to let you out at the *aguas termales,* but from the highway it is a hot, dusty four-kilometer walk, by the end of which you will feel like swimming in cold water, not hot. Most of the hotels and hostels along Ruta de Las Flores can arrange transportation to and from the pools, usually at a cost of around $30.

ACCOMMODATIONS

Hotel de La Casa Mamapan (2 Av. Sur and Plaza Concordia, in front of *parque central,* tel. 2413-2507, www.lacasademamapan.com, backpacker prices negotiable, $40 d) is a hidden gem, full of natural light, eclectic knick-knacks, and lots of character. Ten rooms with private baths, hot water, air-conditioning, and TVs with cable are tucked away in this colonial treasure just off of Plaza Concordia. Local art, light fixtures made out of wine bottles, a sunny courtyard, and a small restaurant with tall wooden stools and tables create a funky yet traditional ambience in the common areas, and the rooms are simple, clean, and quiet, with access to Wi-Fi throughout the house.

Another excellent option is **Casa Blanca Hotel** (2 Av. Norte and Calle Barrios 1-5, tel. 2443-1505, casablancaahuachapan@hotmail.com, $30 s, $40 d), a gorgeous historic home with wrought-iron gates, high ceilings, massive wooden doors, and tile floors. The rooms surround a garden with plenty of plants and a small restaurant ($3-7) serving *comida típica.* Each spacious room has big windows and high ceilings, dark wood furniture, TV, Wi-Fi, air-conditioning, and hot water.

FOOD

The cute little **Mixtas** (2 Av. Sur and 1 Calle Poniente, no phone, 8am-9pm daily, $3-5) serves up cheap breakfast, sandwiches, burritos, and hamburgers in an American-style diner with brightly colored booths, very friendly service, and delicious milk shakes. As the name suggests, they specialize in *mixtas,* which are pitas stuffed with meat, cheese, salsa, and vegetables.

La Estancia (1 Av. Sur between Calle Barrios and 1 Calle Oriente, 7am-6pm Mon.-Sat., $2-7) serves up delicious *comida a la vista* in a large open air house that gets busy for both lunch and dinner. Choose from typical meat dishes, steamed vegetables, salads, and rice.

GETTING THERE AND AROUND

From San Salvador, take bus 202 ($1, 2.5 hours, runs every 15 minutes) from Terminal de Occidente.

Plaza Concordia and Parque Menéndez, the *parque central,* are five blocks apart and are connected by the busy Avenida Menéndez, which runs north-south and is full of banks, pharmacies, and clothing shops.

Santa Ana

More and more travelers are choosing Santa Ana, with its colonial architecture and weekend nightlife, over the capital for a taste of El Salvador's urban culture. About 35 kilometers east of Ahuachapán, Santa Ana is full of beautiful crumbling buildings, tree-lined streets, and low multicolored house fronts that open up into exquisite Old World homes and flourishing gardens. At the center of it all is a large shady central plaza, surrounded by striking buildings to explore, such as El Teatro Nacional and the Catedral de Santa Ana, unique restaurants, and one of the country's best hostels. Even though the city is big, the attitude is humble, giving it a small-town vibe. Situated among green hills and near three of the country's most prominent volcanoes, there is no lack of excursions to keep you busy. Day trips that can be done from the city include Lago Coatepeque, Parque Nacional Los Volcanes, and the ruins of Tazumal and Casa Blanca, both in the nearby town of Chalchuapa.

SIGHTS
Catedral de Santa Ana

The grand neo-Gothic **Catedral de Santa Ana** (tel. 2441-0278, diocesissta.ana@integra.com.sv) sits on the east side of *parque central* and commands well-deserved attention. The original church was finished in 1576 but was partially burned when struck by lightning in the 19th century. Since then the church has gone through various restoration projects over the years and is now protected by the 1954 Hague Convention for the Protection of Cultural Property. The facade is covered in impressive intricate design with various arches and tall bell towers the shape of sharpened pencils. The inside has towering light pink and gray columns and a beautiful marble altar, where you will find the statue of the cathedral's namesake patron, Saint Anne. Legend has it that when the Spanish priests carried the statue into the city, they set it down and were unable to pick it up again; so there it stayed, and now it sits above the altar inside the church. Saint Anne is the patron saint of childbirth, and today women come to the cathedral to pray in the days leading up to bearing their children.

El Teatro Nacional

On the north side of the park is **El Teatro Nacional** (tel. 2441-2193, teatrosantaana@cultura.gob.sv, 9am-5pm Tues.-Sat., $1.50). Built in 1910 with taxes collected from the coffee industry, the theater showcases majestic staircases, ornate doors, and beautiful artwork by the Italian artist who was commissioned to paint the walls and ceilings of the theater. While he was working in Santa Ana, he fell in love with a married Salvadoran woman; many of his paintings depict the taboo affair. The theater also provides a fascinating window into the social strata of El

Map of Santa Ana showing streets and landmarks including: IGLESIA CALVARIO, THE CORNER, VILLA MORENA, E-CENTER INTERNET CAFÉ, Parque Menéndez, OFICINA MUNICIPAL DE TURISMO, TEATRO NACIONAL, CATEDRAL DE SANTA ANA, HOTEL SAHARA, PALACIO MUNICIPAL DE SANTA ANA, Parque Libertad, TALI TUNAL, MERCADO CENTRAL, CENTRO DE ARTES OCCIDENTE, MUSEO REGIONAL DE OCCIDENTE, MUSEO DE ANATOMÍA HUMANA DE UNASA, CASA VERDE, SANTA ANA POST OFFICE, CAFÉ EXPRESIONES CULTURALES, IGLESIA CARMEN, Parque Colón, EX-ESCUELA DE ARTES Y OFICIOS, MERCADO COLÓN, TERMINAL FRANCISCO LARA PINEDA, CAFÉ TEJAS, To Metapán, LA TABERNA EL CAPITAN, TERMINAL DE LA VENCEDORA, To San Salvador bus stop, Chalchuapa, Sonsonate, and Ahuachapán, PUERTOBUS STATION, CENTRO MÉDICO DE SANTA ANA, LOVERS STEAKHOUSE, QUATTRO ESTACIONES/CASA FROLAZ, LAS PALMERAS, To Hotel Tolteka, Lago Coatepeque, Parque Nacional Los Volcanes, and San Salvador.

300 yds / 300 m

© AVALON TRAVEL

Salvador in the early 20th century. You will see the separate rooms for men and women and the different areas according to social status (the poor were only allowed standing room on the second floor in a dark, cramped space without ventilation). Today, the theater is used for concerts and community events. Check with the front office to see what the schedule is. There are free guided tours available.

ENTERTAINMENT AND EVENTS
Nightlife

You will need to take a taxi to get to **Trench Town Rock** (Km. 65, Carretera Panamericana, beside the turnoff to Chalchuapa, tel. 7261-9030, noon-midnight Tues.-Sat.), the reggae bar that has earned its name as one of the best options for nightlife in the country. This outdoor space is illuminated colorful lights, art, and people. There is live music on some weekends, usually ska or reggae, and the cover charge ($3-10) depends on the band. If you are lucky, you may the catch the popular local group the Blue Beat Makers performing. When there is no live music, the sweet sounds of reggae records (yes, there is actually a record player) and friendly staff create a warm vibe. There is some food available ($3-7); make sure to try the excellent pizza or famous baked potatoes.

For nightlife in the city center, **Villa Morena** (2 Calle Poniente, between Parque Isidro Menéndez and Parque Libertad, www. paseovillamorena.blogspot.com) is a street that has recently been developed for tourism. Friday through Sunday the street is closed off to traffic between 5pm and 2am, and impeccably dressed waiters bring tables and chairs out into the street, where locals gather for dinner and drinks. The service is invariably excellent in all of these places, but unfortunately none of the restaurants stand out for the food.

Santa Ana's crumbling colonial buildings and narrow streets create a romantic, Old World feel.

Festivals

Every year during the last two weeks of July, Santa Ana celebrates **Fiestas Julias.** The city gets busy, especially during the last weekend of the month; there are street parades, masses, live music, rodeos, and fairground rides and entertainment. This is considered one of the best festivals in the country.

ACCOMMODATIONS

Überhelpful owner Carlos Batarse of ★ **Casa Verde** (7 Calle Poniente, between 8 Av. and 10 Av. Sur 25, tel. 7840-4896, $10 dorm, $16 s, from $23 d) is a legend in Salvadoran hospitality. Casa Verde has foreseen every possible need of the weary traveler—right down to an electronic foot massager, medicine for whatever ails you, free coffee, and a fridge full of beer. Dorm rooms provide each occupant with their own storage space for luggage, individual lamps and fans, and shared baths with hot water. Private rooms are equally lovely with comfortable beds, storage space for luggage, fans, and private baths with hot water.

They all surround a swimming pool and large common area with pretty flowering plants, hammocks, and large wooden tables for group meals. Two fully stocked kitchens, a barbecue, a rooftop terrace, a small lounge with a TV and DVDs, and all the travel information you need make this an easy place to stay; some stay here for weeks at a time. Throw in a complimentary ride to the bus station when you are on your way back to San Salvador; and it's official: Casa Verde delivers like no other hostel in El Salvador, and likely in all of Central America.

Casa Frolaz (29 Calle Poniente and 10 Av. Sur 42, tel. 2440-1564, $10 pp dorm, $20 d) is the other lovely budget option for accommodations in Santa Ana. If you are looking for something quaint and quiet, this is the perfect place. Extremely hospitable brothers Francisco and Bruno Olano Rodríguez offer dorm beds on the second floor of a beautiful old house on the periphery of town. The rooms are large, with beautiful tile floors, fans, private baths with hot water, and local art on the walls. There is a lovely terrace, a common room with lots of light and plants, and the excellent restaurant Quattro Estaciones on the first floor.

At first glance, the entrance of the colonial-style **Hotel Sahara** (3 Calle Poniente, between Av. Sur and Av. José Matías Delgado, tel. 2447-8865 or 2447-0456, hotel_sahara@ yahoo.com, $44 s, $54 d) can seem a bit dark and gloomy, but once you climb the majestic staircase to the open-air second floor, with lots of plants complementing the varying shades of green on the walls, the place really comes alive. The rooms are very clean and quiet, with hot water, air-conditioning, Wi-Fi, and cable TV. There is a restaurant (9am-9pm daily, $5-10) on the first floor serving seafood, pasta, and sandwiches.

Hotel Tolteka Plaza (Km. 62, Carretera Internacional, Av. Independencia Sur, tel. 2487-1000, toltekaventa@gmail.com, $53 s or d) is about a $4 cab ride outside the city center. Fifty rooms surround a lovely swimming pool and central courtyard. The rooms all have cable TV, hot water, and air-conditioning. Spotless rooms and great service make this a wonderful place to relax if you are just passing through and not interested in being in the heart of the city.

FOOD

Tali Tunal (7 Av. Norte between Calle Libertad and Calle Oriente, No.1-B, tel. 2441-2297, 9am-5pm Tues.-Sun., $1.50-4) is truly a hidden gem for vegetarians or anyone else looking for healthy, budget food. Three blocks east of the cathedral in a quiet residential neighborhood, Edwin and Carmen Maldonado have transformed their sunny, plant-filled courtyard into a modest restaurant where you will find the only vegetarian burger in the region, along with large fresh salads that include shredded beets, carrots, celery, radishes, and other seasonal vegetables all topped with a homemade creamy sesame dressing. The menu changes daily and includes soups, soy-based dishes, and other rotating vegetarian entrées. The veggie burger

is always available; just ask. Homemade whole-wheat bread and baked goods are also available, as well as breakfast fare such as whole-wheat pancakes and fruit salad. In the front of the restaurant is a small shop that sells medicinal herbs and other natural health products that are difficult to find in pharmacies.

Just down the street from Casa Verde is **Café Expresiones Culturales** (11 Calle Poniente between 6 Av. and 8 Av. Sur, tel. 2440-1410, 6:30am-9pm Mon.-Sat., 8am-6pm Sun., $5-10), a curious café that serves pastas, salads, and a long list of specialty chicken dishes. The café has exposed brick walls, a small sitting area outside with wrought-iron tables, and an awning made out of leaves to provide shade. There are also tables inside as well as a random book collection, wall hangings depicting scenes from pre-Hispanic history, and a very small stage for occasional live music (no cover) at lunchtime or in the evening. There is no alcohol or smoking permitted at the café.

★ **Quattro Estaciones** (29 Calle Poniente 42, between 8 Av. and 10 Av. Sur, tel. 2440-1564, www.quattroestaciones.blogspot. com, noon-9pm Mon.-Thurs., noon-11pm Fri.-Sat., $6-17) is definitely the most polished place in town, where sleek style meets an antique atmosphere on the bottom floor of the house that is Casa Frolaz. Rotating art exhibitions, smooth dark wood tables, and sliding doors that open up to a small garden make this a great place for a weekend dinner. The kitchen takes a different spin on meat dishes, offering plates such as Caribbean chicken served in a coconut-orange-pineapple sauce. Finish your meal with one of the popular baked pears. The bonus of staying at Casa Frolaz is that after a big meal, your bed is just a short staircase away.

Las Palmeras (corner of Av. Independencia Sur and 27 Calle Oriente, tel. 2455-3778, 5pm-10pm daily, $4-12) serves *pupusas* cooked on a *comal,* a concave, smooth, flat griddle crafted from Salvadoran black clay. A big outdoor restaurant with multicolored lights and murals on the walls makes for a lovely place to sample some of these delicious *pupusas*, filled with atypical ingredients such as carrots, garlic, and jalapeño and *loroco*, a local plant.

Lover's Steakhouse (21 Calle Oriente, between Av. Independencia and 3 Av. Sur, tel. 2440-5717, www.loverssteakhouse.com, 5pm-10pm daily, $7-12) is a longtime favorite for locals and visitors alike. This large restaurant has a lovely little courtyard lit up with colored lights and local art hanging on the walls. The floor is also covered with pottery and handwoven crafts to create a warm, intimate feeling. Lover's serves up very generous portions of steak and seafood at reasonable prices.

Café Téjas (2 Av. Sur 52, between Calle José Mariano Méndez and 13 Calle Poniente, tel. 2447-6505 or 7799-6088, 8:30am-6pm Mon.-Sat., $5-10) is Santa Ana's hidden gem. Tucked away on a side street near the exit from town, this family home has a small shop where antiques are set among imported clothing, local crafts and art, and some other eclectic merchandise such as kitchenware, sunglasses, and jewelry. This is a charming setup, but the main attraction is definitely out back, where there is a small idyllic garden with lush greenery crawling over the tall walls and a few small tables that make for a perfect spot to escape the heat of the city and enjoy a cup of iced coffee, homemade ice cream, or one of the famous chorizo sandwiches. Run by young Canadian-Salvadoran couple Ameera Dennis and Roberto Basagoitia, they set a tone that you won't find anywhere else in town, with a fine selection of reggae music, fusion plates such as yuca *poutine*, and fresh salads and soups. Everything is made from scratch and always with fresh, local ingredients.

The Corner (6 Av. Norte and 2 Calle Poniente, tel. 2407-5962, 6pm-midnight Tues.-Sat., $3-7) is small but full of good stuff. This little gem specializes in European beers, and the chef makes simple dishes like sandwiches and pizzas come to life with delicious homemade sauces and quality ingredients. The Corner is a great place to grab a beer and a bite.

INFORMATION AND SERVICES

There is a **tourist office** (Av. Independencia 2, in front of *parque central*, tel. 2402-4576, 8am-noon and 1pm-5pm Mon.-Sat., 8am-noon Sun.) in the *alcaldía*; there is also a DHL office in the same building. You can find many banks near *parque central*, including **Scotiabank** (Av. Fray Felipe de Jesús Moraga, tel. 2250-1111, 8am-4:30pm Mon.-Fri., 8am-noon Sat.) and **Banco Hipotecario** (2 Av. Norte and 2 Calle Poniente, behind the *alcaldía*, tel. 2441-1272, 8:30am-4:30pm Mon.-Fri., 8:30am-12:30pm Sat.), where you will also find a Western Union office. Nearby you will find **Banco Proamerica** (2 Calle Poniente and 4 Av., tel. 2513-5000, 8am-6pm Mon.-Sat., 8am-noon Sun.), with a MoneyGram office inside the bank. There is an office of **TACA Airlines** (Plaza Florida, 2nd Fl., local 210, tel. 7786-1572 or 7850-2353, 8am-5:30pm Mon.-Fri., 8am-noon Sat.) and an office of **TICA Bus** (Plaza Florida, 2nd Fl., tel. 2448-2387, 7:30am-6pm daily).

GETTING THERE AND AROUND

From San Salvador, take bus 201 ($0.90, 1.25 hours, every 15 minutes). If you are driving to Santa Ana, head 64 kilometers northwest of San Salvador on Carretera Panamericana (Pan-American Hwy.).

Avenida Independencia runs north-south from Parque Libertad, while Calle Libertad runs east-west. Most tourist sights are located right at the center of town around Parque Libertad, within walking distance of all hotels.

AROUND SANTA ANA
Tropical Organic Farm El Salvador

Tropical Organic Farm El Salvador offers volunteers the chance to work and live on an organic farm. Owners Mauricio and Gloria have set up their own little piece of paradise on this farm nearby Santa Ana, on the way to San Andrés ruins. You can choose what kind of work you do, from farming to construction to teaching the local children. An important part of their vision is to educate and involve the surrounding communities in their projects and the benefits they bring. There is a space for yoga and meditation, very basic dorms with shared baths, and three organic vegetarian meals a day, all for $8 pp. To get to the farm, call Mauricio (tel. 7544-8953 or 7224-4869) and he will arrange to pick you up near the San Andrés ruins.

Lago Coatepeque

Located between Santa Ana and Parque Nacional Los Volcanes, 56 kilometers west of San Salvador, Lago Coatepeque is a shimmering emerald green national treasure. The 26-square-kilometer crater lake was formed through a series of eruptions that took place thousands of years ago, and the volcanoes Izalco, Santa Ana, and Cerro Verde (not responsible for its birth, but gorgeous nonetheless) stand proudly behind it, creating a magnificent backdrop. Unfortunately for visitors, most of the land around the lake has been bought up by Salvadorans to build private homes, so it's very difficult to find public areas to swim and sunbathe. If you want to enjoy the lake, you will need to go to one of the restaurants and use their piers. Food on the lake is not cheap, with a plate of fish costing roughly $15 at any of the hotels right at the lake's edge. Up above, where the road starts to descend toward the lake, there is a series of cheaper restaurants that all serve seafood and offer the best views and photo opportunities. If you just want to see the lake and take some photos, this is your best bet.

Recreation, Accommodations, and Food

If you are interested in doing some hiking around the lake, an excellent option is through **Los Pinos Coffee Cooperative** (Km. 55.5, Carretera Cerro Verde, tel. 2434-0038, $10 for up to 5 people), a beautiful coffee finca that sits high up on the eastern edge of the lake and is very easy to get to from Santa Ana. This is one of the best ways to access the lake for the day, without having to stay at a hotel or go to a restaurant. The excellent guided hike takes about two hours and begins at the top of the mountain ridge surrounding the lake, and slowly descends along coffee fincas and primary forest until you reach the water's edge. This interpretative trail is dotted with beautiful lookout points, providing excellent views of the

Lago Coatepeque

sparkling lake and volcanoes. At the bottom is a private dock and plenty of grassy space to picnic, swim, and sunbathe.

The only budget lodging option on the lake is **Amacuilco** (formerly El 3er Mundo Hostal, tel. 2441-6329 or 7822-4051, $8 pp dorm, $20 d), a large property that sits on the edge of the lake. There are rustic dorms and a cozy lounge area with a bar and a large grassy lawn that leads to the lake and a pier. Private rooms are also very basic, with well-worn beds, colorful bedspreads, and eclectic art on the walls. All rooms have fans. It's a perfect place to relax for a while or take out some of the kayaks and bicycles available for rental. Spanish lessons are also available for $120 per week, which includes 18 hours of classes, a dorm bed, and food. The food here is average, but much cheaper than everywhere else—you can get a small pizza for $4.

Next door to the hostel is the restaurant **Las Palmeras** (tel. 7248-5727, 7am-9pm daily, $10-20), definitely the flashiest place on the lake, serving up fresh, pricey seafood on the large dock with a thatched roof to provide shade.

A few doors down, **Rancho Alegre** (tel. 2441-6071, ranchoalegre@hotmail.com, $40 d) is a popular restaurant and hotel with a massive dock that gets packed on the weekend. The ambiance is a bit less sophisticated than Las Palmeras, but the food is just as good. It offers several rooms near the dock that are simple and clean, with TVs, air-conditioning, Wi-Fi, and private baths with hot water. Here you will also find the office for **Waterquest** (tel. 7160-8361, 8am-5pm Fri.-Sun., noon-4pm Mon.-Thurs.), which offers certified PADI diving in the lake (2 hours, $90) as well as Jet Ski rentals ($70 per hour) and boat rentals ($40 per hour).

Getting There

Lago Coatepeque is 12 kilometers from Santa Ana. To get to the lake, take buses 220 or 242 from Terminal Pineda in Santa Ana. They leave every 30 minutes, and the last one returns from the lake at 5pm.

Parque Nacional Los Volcanes (Parque Cerro Verde)

Parque Nacional Los Volcanes (tel. 7227-5466 or 2222-8000, 9am-5pm Tues.-Sun., $3), commonly known as **Parque Cerro Verde**, includes three prominent volcanoes that create the country's most poetic portrait. They are of distinct ages rarely seen so close together. Volcán Izalco is the youngest volcano in Central America; Cerro Verde is considered middle aged, formed around 25,000 years ago; and Santa Ana is one of the region's oldest volcanoes.

Cerro Verde

Cerro Verde (2,030 meters) is the lowest of the three volcanoes and offers easy trails that can be explored in less than an hour. The humid air, abundant greenery, and multicolored birds make this a lovely walk for those looking to explore the park without too much physical exertion. A 45-minute walk around the old crater can be done with park guides and is free, but a voluntary tip of $1-5 per group is a nice gesture and enough to get an appreciative smile and thank-you from any of the young men and women that are park guides.

Volcán Izalco

Volcán Izalco (1,910 meters), the youngest of the three volcanoes and the most striking in appearance, is also the most difficult to climb because of the steep ascent. Once named the "lighthouse of the Pacific" because of its constant eruptions, today the dark, perfect cone of Izalco is inactive, last erupting in 1966. It is possible to climb the steep, gravel-laden volcano, but it is necessary to take a guide. Guides leave the parking lot of the park at 11am daily. The hike takes about four hours and costs $1.

★ Volcán Santa Ana

Volcán Santa Ana (2,365 meters) is the most popular hike in the park for good reason. The view from the top of El Salvador's largest volcano looks down on its striking green crater lake on one side and gorgeous Lago

Coatepeque on the other. Unlike its younger neighbor Izalco, Santa Ana has been around long enough to have vegetation. As a result, the climb up leads through coffee plantations and cool forested areas where you will see a variety of birds and flora and fauna, including lots of agave plants and various species of hummingbirds, woodpeckers, jays, and emerald toucanets..

Although Santa Ana is taller than Izalco, the hike up is easier because it is not as steep. The hike takes around four hours and costs $5-8 pp, depending on how many people are in the group (3 people minimum). Guides for this hike leave the parking lot at 11am daily.

Getting There

To get to Parque Nacional Los Volcanes (Parque Cerro Verde) from Santa Ana, take bus 248 from La Vencedora bus terminal (1 block west of Parque Colón, tel. 2440-8453). The bus takes 1.75 hours and costs $0.85. If you want to climb either Volcán Santa Ana or Volcán Izalco, you must catch the 7am bus so that you arrive in time for the 11am start time for the hikes. From San Salvador, take bus 205 from Terminal de Occidente, leaving no later than 6:30am; tell the driver you would like to get off at El Congo Bridge, where you will need

to catch bus 248, which should pass by around 8:30am. The last bus leaves the park at 4pm. It is possible to get back to San Salvador from Santa Ana the same day, though by the time you get back, it will be dark.

If you are driving, the park is 67 kilometers from San Salvador via Sonsonate.

Tazumal

About a 30-minute bus ride west from Santa Ana in the town of Chalchuapa is the archaeological site **Tazumal** (Final 11 Av. Sur and Calle El Canton, Chalchuapa, tel. 2444-0010, 9am-4pm Tues.-Sun., $3). It is estimated that most of the Mayan city was constructed between AD 400 and 600, and it was a well-organized city by the time the Spanish arrived. The ruins were discovered and studied in the 1940s by American archaeologist Stanley H. Boggs, and today there is a small museum at the entrance of the site named after him. He identified more than a dozen structures made of stone and clay, including a collection of pyramids, a ball court, and a water drainage system.

Today, the biggest pyramid (23 meters tall) is fully excavated and has been refurbished. Around the ruins is forested area with walking paths and picnic tables, which provides a

Mayan ruins at Tazumal

peaceful, unique place to have a picnic. Inside the museum, you can see excavated ritual objects such as Mayan pottery, jade tools, and jewelry, with explanations in English. In front of the museum is an Olmec statue that predates the pyramids by 800 years, indicating that there was a link between El Salvador and other Central American Mayan communities, namely in Veracruz, Mexico.

Casa Blanca (Km. 74.5, between Chalchuapa and Santa Ana, tel. 2408-4295, 9am-4pm Tues.-Sun., $3) is only five minutes on foot from Tazumal and is a small piece of what was once a much larger complex that existed sometime between 250 BC and AD 250. The site is very small but contains three pre-Hispanic pyramids, a small museum, and a free indigo-dyeing workshop.

Getting There

Chalchuapa is 18 kilometers from Santa Ana. Bus 218 leaves Santa Ana for Chalchuapa from 9 Calle Poniente, between 8 Avenida and 10 Avenida Sur (very close to Casa Verde), approximately every 15 minutes starting at 5am until 7pm, and costs $0.40.

If you are driving, head west on Carretera Panamericana (Pan-American Hwy.) to Las Chinamas International Border exit (just a few kilometers from Santa Ana), which will take you to Chalchuapa. There are signs indicating where the ruins are located.

NORTH OF SANTA ANA
Parque Nacional Montecristo-El Trifinio

Thirty-two kilometers north of Santa Ana is the town of Metapán, and 20 kilometers farther north of Metapán is the largest cloud forest in Central America: **Parque Nacional Montecristo-El Trifinio** (tel. 2233-6276, www.marn.gob.sv, 7am-3pm daily year-round, El Trifinio 7am-3pm daily Dec.-Feb., $6 pp) is the most pristine region of El Salvador, where 1,973 glorious hectares of primary forest boasts one of most biodiverse areas in the country. The forest includes more than 3,000 species of plants and

Parque Nacional Montecristo-El Trifinio

animals, including more than 200 species of orchids, quetzals, toucans, wild pigs, and pumas. Towering pine, oak, and cypress trees, some centuries old, create a leafy awning that provides shade for ferns, lichens, and moss to thrive. The result is a flourishing eco-paradise that is unrivaled in the rest of the country.

The cool, clean air makes for incredible hiking, and there are several trails and miradors. The most difficult hike is an 18-kilometer trail up to El Trifinio, the highest point of the park at 2,418 meters elevation—it's the lookout point where El Salvador, Honduras, and Guatemala all meet, and it offers beautiful views of the neighboring countries. The hike takes about three hours and takes you from the park's lowest elevation at 700 meters through subtropical forest, farther up through transitional forest, pine forest, cypress plantations, and finally the misty cloud forest.

Montecristo cloud forest is one of the most endangered ecosystems in the world. Because of this, the hiking trail up to El Trifinio is closed from March until November every year, when wildlife is left in peace to reproduce.

There is a campsite in the park. Camping is free, and tents are available to rent ($5). Local Spanish guides can lead you on the hike to El Trifinio ($5).

Getting There

Unfortunately, getting to the park is very difficult unless you do it as part of an organized tour. There are no buses that travel to the park, and if you want to go on your own, you will need a 4WD vehicle (the road is clearly marked from Metapán). You can usually find a ride in a pickup from the park turnoff in Metapán, however the cost will be at least $85 for a drop-off and pickup. **El Salvador Turismo** (Av. Masferrer Norte 139, Centro Comercial El Amante, tel. 2510-7640) is an excellent tour company that often organizes tours to the park ($25 pp). This includes transportation, entry to the park, and the El Trifinio hike. The tours leave from their office at 6am and return to San Salvador around 6pm. Call to see if they have one scheduled during your visit.

Parque Nacional El Imposible

Just southwest of Ruta de Las Flores is El Salvador's largest national park, **Parque Nacional El Imposible** (tel. 2411-5484, www.salvanatura.org, open daily, $6 pp). The park is a haven for hikers and nature lovers, offering pristine rivers, archaeological sites, well-maintained campsites, and challenging terrain.

Parque Imposible's 4,000 hectares of protected tropical mountain forest are home to an array of wildlife, including wild boars, *tigrillos,* and more than 285 species of birds. You are more likely to see wildlife if you spend the night in the park, as many of the animals are nocturnal, but day hikes will take you past towering ceiba trees and local plants with educational signs, plenty of butterflies and birds, and maybe even some smaller creatures like armadillos. It has been years since the last puma prints were detected, but it's possible that this majestic animal also still roams the forest.

The steep topography of the park offers extreme hikes and incredible views that reach all the way to the Pacific coast and Guatemala's edge. Multiple rivers rush down the slopes of the park, creating waterfalls and swimming pools throughout and finally emptying out into the Barra de Santiago. The park was named El Imposible because of the steep, vertical gorge between two mountains that used to claim the lives of people and pack mules traversing the forest on their way to the Pacific port in the early 20th century. In 1968 the government finally built a bridge at El Imposible Pass, adorned with a plaque that reads "The year 1968: no longer is it impossible."

The park is administered by **SalvaNatura** (tel. 2279-1515, www.salvanatura.org), El Salvador's excellent independent conservation organization. The main entrance to the park is on the southeast side through the tiny community of San Miguelito in the town of San Benito. This is a true rural tourism project, with the park entrance fee going toward maintaining the park, and the $10 hiking fee going directly to your guide. There are 12 guides who have been professionally trained and are very knowledgeable about the flora and fauna as well as the history of the park.

The best time of the year to visit the park is November to April, when the weather is warm and dry.

RECREATION AND TOURS
Hiking

You must have a guide to explore the park;

visitors are not allowed to hike alone. The $10 hiking fee is per group. You do not need to book a guide in advance—just tell the park ranger when you pay your entry fee that you would like a guide.

Los Engaches

A seven-kilometer round-trip hike will bring you to Los Engaches, a beautiful shady part of the park with swimming pools and lots of grassy areas for sunbathing or picnics. If you want, you can continue from here another kilometer to **Mirador El Mulo,** a mirador that looks out over the forest and river.

★ Piedra Sellada

An eight-kilometer round-trip hike takes you to Piedra Sellada, where you will find fascinating petroglyphs on massive boulders in the middle of the forest beside the Río Venado Canyon. They date back to AD 600-900 and contain more than 100 pictures of geometric patterns, butterflies, and birds. You can swim in the cool, crystal clear, and clean river and relax on the sun-warmed rocks before heading back. This hike takes about two hours and is intermediate in difficulty.

Cerro El León

The most challenging hike in the park is to Cerro El León, a very steep, eight-kilometer round-trip through primary forest that opens up to spectacular views of the park and the Pacific coast. You will need at least four hours to complete this hike.

Tours

Another option for exploring the park is the backdoor route through Tacuba, just west of Ahuachapán. **El Imposible Tours** (Av. Cuscatlán near Calle 10, Tacuba, tel. 2417-4268, www.imposibletours.com) offers hikes that enter the park unofficially (not at the main entrance) and some that explore the periphery. These tours are for those seeking a more rugged and adventurous experience. Guides will take you through difficult terrain on the famous waterfall tour, a seven-hour hike through the thick of the forest, jumping off waterfalls and swimming in pristine pools. El Imposible Tours also offer bike tours that go all the way from El Imposible to Barra de Santiago; the 20-kilometer route takes a day.

It is best to organize your tour a few days in advance, and to be very clear about what you expect from your tour, as there can be

Parque Nacional El Imposible

discrepancies around the level of difficulty as well as the actual route.

ACCOMMODATIONS AND FOOD
Inside the Park

Camping is available inside the park for $1. Sometimes the guides rent out tents ($5), but it is preferable to bring your own. There is one large campsite, with elevated platforms to set up tents, as well as cooking areas and restrooms.

A small *cabaña* right beside the entrance to the park, **Cabaña Guaquito** (tel. 7916-9419, cguaquito@gmail.com, $10 d) is basic but newly constructed, clean, and quiet, with one outside bath.

Farther down from the park's entrance is the lovely **Hostal El Imposible** (tel. 2405-6505 or 7885-7438, hostalelimposible@gmail.com, $25 pp), initiated by SalvaNatura and since handed over to the community of San Miguelito. It is actually a series of *cabañas* built on a hill, interspersed with stone pathways surrounded by plants and flowers. The *cabañas* have hot water and fans, and there's Wi-Fi in the restaurant area.

Hostal El Imposible's restaurant ($4-6) has very good food using fresh local ingredients. There is also a *comedor* closer to the park's entrance, serving up economical *comida típica*. If you are camping, make sure you bring all the food you will need, as there are no markets in San Miguelito.

Tacuba

Tacuba is a cute little village 14 kilometers west of Ahuachapán that is a popular backdoor to the park. Surrounded by mountains and volcanoes, Tacuba sits on the northern side of the park. There is not much to see in this tiny town other than the crumbling remnants of the town church, destroyed by an earthquake in 1773. It sits in the center of the village and only the front facade remains; the rest is overgrown with grass and trees.

The well-known **Mama y Papa's** (Av. Cuscatlán, near Calle 10, Tacuba, tel. 2417-4268, $8 pp dorm, $15 d) is a home that has been turned into a hostel, giving the place a homestay kind of feel. Although the dorms are comfortable, with fans and lots of space, insomniac roosters outside the windows will keep light sleepers awake most of the night. The kitchen may be used for the cost of $1, although the women who work here, along with Mama, are usually cooking, so it might feel a bit awkward; you are probably better off ordering from their menu, as the food is excellent. El Imposible Tours is based at Mama y Papa's.

The other budget option in town in is **Hostal Miraflores** (7 Calle Oriente, tel. 2417-4746, $10 d). This cute little hostel sits kitty-corner to *parque central* has economical rooms, a small garden, and a colorful little restaurant with daily prepared lunch and vegetarian options. There is no hot water, but rooms have fans. The kitchen has a tile bar to enjoy a cup of coffee and watch Tacuba go by. Hiking tours to El Imposible can also be organized here.

For something a little nicer, 11 spacious rooms with private baths and air-conditioning sit around a beautiful breezy garden and a swimming pool at the lovely **Las Cabañas** (3 Av. Norte and 1 Calle Poniente, tel. 2417-4332, $35 d, including 3 meals), which is tucked away on a quiet street. The very attentive staff and lovely food will not disappoint.

GETTING THERE
Getting to Parque Nacional El Imposible

From Sonsonate, take bus 259 ($0.80, 1.75 hours, every 10 minutes 4:30am-7:30pm) going to Cara Sucia. Ask to be let off at Sectora San Benito. From here, two buses pass by every day, one at 11:30am and one at 2:30pm; the cost is $0.50 and the ride takes about 15 minutes. You get dropped off at the main entrance to the park.

If you miss the buses, you can hitch a ride with one of the pickups heading up the hill toward the park. A sure bet is Freddy Molina (tel. 7325-3401), who charges $15 per trip. Best to call him ahead of time.

The same bus that brings you to the park takes you back to the main road. It leaves from the entrance of the park around noon and 3pm. Again, alternatively it is possible to catch a ride with a pickup truck.

If you are driving, the park's entrance is 68 kilometers west of Sonsonate. From Sonsonate, head five kilometers toward Acajutla South. At "Kilo 5" is the intersection of CA2 Coast Highway. Turn right and drive to Km. 116, where you turn right onto a dirt road and continue about 16 kilometers to the park.

Getting to Tacuba

From Ahuachapán by bus, take bus 264 (40 minutes, every 30 minutes).

Driving from Ahuachapán, look for Parque Concordia and the white church there, where you'll see a sign directing you onto the road for Tacuba. The drive from Ahuachapán takes about 30 minutes.

The Pacific Coast

Look for ★ to find recommended
sights, activities, dining, and lodging.

Highlights

★ **Hiking in Parque Nacional Walter Thilo Deininger:** Choose from two trails that take you through beautiful subtropical and dry forest, natural swimming pools, caves, and a spectacular mirador (page 109).

★ **Surfing at Playa El Tunco:** Surf La Bocana, El Salvador's most popular break for locals and tourists alike. This intermediate to advanced wave is the most consistent spot to surf in the country, with conditions that are often described as perfect, including year-round warm water, a grinding left, and an understated right (page 111).

★ **Hiking to Tamanique Waterfalls:** Hike through lush greenery, cornfields, and rivers to get to the gorgeous waterfalls of Tamanique, where you can jump into the clear, cool water in the pools below (page 112).

★ **Fishing Around Playa El Sunzal:** Choose from a variety of tried and tested catching methods with fishing aficionado Roberto Figueroa in El Sunzal (page 118).

★ **Marine Life Boat Tour:** Take a boat tour through protected waters and look for dolphins, huge manta rays, turtles, and beautiful birds. If it's the right time of year, take in the majestic humpback whales as they migrate (page 123).

★ **Bird-Watching in Barra de Santiago:** Help boost rural tourism and have a great time doing it by enjoying a boat tour through the surreal mangroves, spotting some of the colorful birds who call this peaceful estuary home (page 124).

The secret is out. For years, the beaches of El Salvador's coast were strictly the terrain of fearless surfers, some who came in the 1970s and dug the waves so much they never left, even while a civil war raged on. But today, the war is over, the

waves are still sweet, and more and more curious travelers are showing up to check out what coastal El Salvador has to offer. They are discovering that the coast is not just for surfers. Yes, there are world-class waves all along the coast line, but these beaches are interspersed with quaint fishing villages and large coral reefs, white sand beaches perfect for relaxing and swimming, mangroves teeming with colorful birds, beautiful bays, volcanic gulfs, and otherworldly estuaries.

Most people head straight for the **west coast,** a surfer's paradise that stretches from La Libertad, conveniently located just a 30-minute drive from Aeropuerto Internacional Comalapa, to Mizata, a much remoter western beach. This coastline consists of rocky dark-sand beaches with hot temperatures, strong currents, and rolling, bold waves. The heart of the action is in **Playa El Tunco,** a popular beach town with a string of beachfront hotels and bars that draw crowds every weekend to enjoy the sun, surf, and sociable evenings. El Tunco has the most variety in accommodations and restaurants, and it boasts the best nightlife outside of San Salvador. Right next door, **Playa**

El Sunzal doesn't party. Here you will find great surfing for beginners and experienced surfers alike. Next stop is **Playa El Zonte,** a magical little beach where the rocky shore and crashing waves are set against the beautiful backdrop of towering cliffs and tropical birds. Keep heading west and you will hit **Playa Mizata,** a remote getaway with capricious waves that capture the hearts of adventurous surfers searching for solitude. In the small fishing village of **Los Cóbanos,** simple seafood shacks line the white-sand beach, and the craggy shoreline opens up to the largest coral reef in Central America. Finally, **Barra de Santiago** boasts the most unique of landscapes due to its location between a

---

Previous: Playa El Zonte; mangroves in Barra de Santiago. **Above:** surfing at La Libertad.

The Pacific Coast

mangrove-filled estuary and the roaring Pacific Ocean.

On the other side, the **east coast** offers expansive white-sand beaches, unexplored islands and bays, and when the conditions are right, some of the best surfing in the country. Heading east from San Salvador, the first and arguably most beautiful beach in the country is **Costa del Sol,** where a long stretch of pearl gray coast is flanked by the **Jaltepeque Estuary,** a prime location for fishing and birding, or simply relaxing on the beach with a cocktail in hand. Next up is **Isla Montecristo,** where untouched beaches, mangroves, and cashew plantations make a perfect destination for those seeking peace and solitude in a rustic setting. Next, **Bahía de Jiquilisco** is Central America's largest remaining mangrove forest and coastal estuary,

providing critical habitat for birds and the most endangered turtle species in the world, the beautiful hawksbill. Farther on, **Playas El Cuco, Las Flores,** and **Esterón** offer excellent surf and beautiful beaches. If you make it to where the ocean's shore meets the country's edge, the islands in the **Golfo de Fonseca** offer raw natural beauty for intrepid travelers who seek off-the-beaten-path adventure.

PLANNING YOUR TIME

Two weeks is enough time to enjoy the coast of El Salvador, but realistically most people usually only have about a week. Unless you are doing a targeted surf trip, it is not easy to get both coasts in one week. It's better to choose one, and most people choose the west, as it is more developed for tourism and easier to get to from the airport or San Salvador.

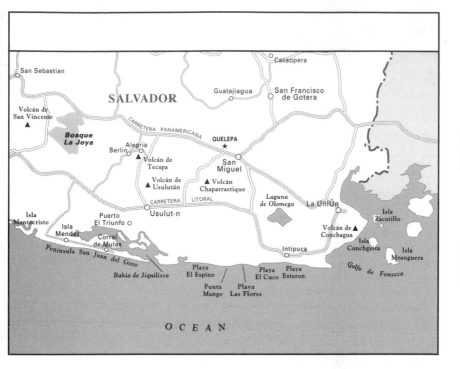

Traveling the **west coast** is easy. There are buses that run along the Carretera Litoral (coastal highway) frequently, and you can flag one down at any point. Whether you are surfing or not will influence how much time you want to spend here; in general, a week should be enough time to see all the beaches on this side of the country.

Your time on the **east coast** also depends on whether you are surfing or not. One or two days in **Playa El Cuco** and vicinity should be enough, but many people end up staying longer (or wishing they could). **Bahía de Jiquilisco** and **Isla Montecristo** take a bit more time to reach, but one day and one night

in each place is enough to do a tour, take in the natural beauty, and move on. If you plan to go to the **Golfo de Fonseca,** you will need two days. There is only one boat that leaves the islands for the mainland each day, very early in the morning, so unless you hire a private boat, you will have to spend the night on **Isla Meanguera.**

You can learn to surf at any time of year, but November to February offers ideal conditions for beginners. The waves are smaller and there are consistent offshore winds. Peak surfing season is March to October, so expect the more popular surf resorts to be fully booked most of the time.

Western Beaches

The western beaches of El Salvador are quickly becoming a beacon of surf, sun, and socializing for visitors of all stripes. Surfers flock to the strip of beaches along this side of the country, each of which offers unique breaks of varying difficulty. The famous Punta Roca in La Libertad is a favorite for experienced surfers, and nearby Playa Sunzal and Playa El Zonte are both great spots to learn. But you don't have to be a surfer to enjoy these beaches. The west coast is also attracting backpackers and travelers looking to relax on beaches that are still relatively undeveloped; there are plenty of great places just to kick back in a hammock and be mesmerized by the waves, practice yoga, sunbathe, and enjoy the fresh seafood and social atmosphere.

Playa El Tunco is the most developed for tourism and boasts an eclectic mix of locals and visitors, including surfers, artists, tourists, and urbanites coming to party for the weekend before heading back to the daily grind in smoggy San Salvador. If you are looking for action, this is where you will find it. Other beaches such as Los Cóbanos and Barra de Santiago offer secluded getaways where you will get a taste of the local culture.

The western beaches are easy to get to, easy to travel between, and the number of hotels, English-speaking guides, and tourism amenities are increasing every day.

LA LIBERTAD

Just 32 kilometers southwest of San Salvador and 25 minutes from Aeropuerto Internacional Comalapa, the port town of La Libertad is the gateway to the western beaches of El Salvador, and exactly where you want to be if you are looking for fresh, cheap seafood. The *malecón* along the waterfront has recently been revamped with the objective of improving its once less-than-savory reputation, and so far it seems to be working. A long pier juts out to the sea and is surrounded by colorful fishing boats that bring in their fresh catch every day. On the western side of the pier you will find the Complejo Turistico, a freshly painted boardwalk with higher-end bars with live music, fancy cocktails, and fresh seafood. The other side of the pier also serves plenty of fresh seafood, ceviche, and beer for the more budget-minded. The less-manicured town center is teeming with *pupuserías,* blaring reggaeton, pharmacies, and small shops. The crowded central market seems to spill out onto every street corner, where colorfully clad women peddle equally colorful fruits and vegetables.

La Libertad draws local and international surfers to its world-class Punta Roca waves on a daily basis. For everyone else, the chaos and heat do not make this unpolished port town a prime destination. Most people visit simply to use the ATM, enjoy fresh seafood on the *malecón*, or pick up food at the market before heading to one of the prettier beaches farther west.

Recreation
Surfing
Surfers come to La Libertad to surf **Punta Roca** at the small beach called Playa La Paz, and most come in to surf and then leave. The waves here are for experienced surfers only, and it is one of the two places along the west coast that is considered a local surf spot (the other is La Bocana in El Tunco). This long hollow barrel can reach up to five meters but does get shallow during low tide. The beach is very rocky, so surf this wave with caution, or wear surf shoes.

Located at the entrance to Playa La Paz, **Hospital de Tablas** (tel. 7944-3632, 7am-4pm daily) is the only surfboard repair shop along the coast. It also sells boards and offers surf classes ($10 per hour), and you can also rent boards (10 for the day).

★ Hiking in Parque Nacional Walter Thilo Deininger

Parque Nacional Walter Thilo Deininger (just east of La Libertad at Playa San Diego, tel. 2345-5684, 7am-4pm daily, $3) is one of the largest forest reserves in the country and is often overlooked, which is a shame, especially if you are interested in learning more about the flora, fauna, and history of the area. This dry forest is home to 25 different species of mammals, 27 species of reptiles, and 115 species of native and migratory birds, many of them endangered. The best time to spot wildlife is when the park's rivers are dry, by the end of December until the beginning of April. During this time, you may spot iguanas, ocelots, or the local *tepezcuintle*, a large rodent similar to a guinea pig.

There are two main nature trails you can do in the park. Explore on your own, or go with a local guide, who will provide information about the landscape, history, and biodiversity of the area. The easier trail is a three-kilometer round-trip hike that takes you past a cool pool that you can swim in and a cave. If you want something challenging, you can do the eight-kilometer round-trip that goes up into the surrounding mountains. Both of the trails end at a beautiful mirador with a stunning view of the Pacific Ocean. The first hike is easy to do upon arrival, however it's best to call ahead to arrange a guide if you are interested in doing the more challenging trail. Other interesting highlights on the guided hikes include vestiges of Pipil structures dating back to approximately AD 700, likely used for rituals involving water, and a cave where a unique type of bacterium has been discovered. Research is currently underway to develop it into an antibiotic.

While the best time to visit the park to see wildlife is December to April, the best time for swimming and seeing the lush greenery and rushing rivers is May to November.

To get to the park, take bus 80 from La Libertad and ask to be let out at the park. It runs every 30 minutes and costs $0.25.

Accommodations and Food

For surfers with their hearts set on finding budget accommodations next to the best waves in the country, there are cheap hotels and homes with rooms for rent along the *malecón,* but none that I would recommend. These kinds of places have garnered bad press in the past, mostly due to security issues. Things have definitely improved in the last few years with the installation of security cameras along the *malecón,* and most hotels now employ 24-hour security guards. If you are willing to spend a bit more money, there are two perfectly safe and suitable options in La Libertad.

$50-100

Surfers who do decide to stay in La Libertad usually stay at **La Terraza Surf Hotel** (Malecón Turístico 2-7, Edificio AST, 3rd Fl., tel. 2346-2381, info@laterrazaelsalvador. com, $85 d), which is located right on the *malecón* and run by the international company Adventure Sports Tours (www.astadventures.com); guests are usually people who have booked tours through them, but it is possible to rent rooms if you are not part of a tour group. The rooms are on the second level, with a fantastic view of the ocean. Rooms are simple, clean, and bright, with retro floral print sheets on the beds, beige and salmon colored walls with surf art, brown tile floors, air-conditioning, and sliding glass doors that bring in the breeze from the ocean. There is a restaurant with the same great view, with passable food, but it's a great place to have some drinks after a day of surfing.

The other best bet for lodging is **Hotel Pacific Sunrise** (Carretera Litoral and Calle El Obispo, tel. 2526-7000, www.hoteleselsalvador.com, $59 d, includes breakfast). Part of a wider chain of hotels in El Salvador, what Pacific Sunrise lacks in character it makes up for in comfort. This large hotel has 30 air-conditioned rooms with neatly made double beds, private baths, spotless tile floors, and if you are on the second floor, lovely views of the ocean. They all surround a pool and lounge area, with a small restaurant, Wi-Fi, and excellent service.

Sueños Pacíficos (Playa el Cocal, Hacienda Santa Emilia, Lots 1-4, beside Río Comasagua, tel. 7112-0662, suenospacificos@ gmail.com), an eco-farm located near Playa La Paz in La Libertad, should be running by the time you read this book, with six oceanfront rooms with solar power and sustainable amenities. Sueños Pacíficos aims to combine conventional tourism with small-scale community tourism that directly involves the traveler with the locals. They will offer hands-on opportunities to learn new skills such as organic farming, permaculture, and natural building. They also plan to offer workshops in yoga and massage therapy. In addition to the oceanfront rooms, Sueños Pacíficos will have volunteer housing made entirely out of cob and rammed earth. If this isn't enough to get you excited, the farm is also located just steps from one of the best surf breaks in the country.

Information and Services

The **Ministry of Tourism** (Km. 34, Carretera Litoral, right at the entrance of town, tel. 2346-1898) has an office in La Libertad with visitor information about the western beaches. **El Faro Centro Comercial** is located right at the entrance to La Libertad on Carretera Litoral. This shopping complex has a grocery store and an ATM.

Getting There

From San Salvador, take bus 102 ($0.60, 1 hour, runs every 15 minutes) from the southern terminal. From Sonsonate, you can take bus 287 ($1.50, 3 hours, 5:55am and 3:30pm daily). If you are driving from San Salvador, follow the CA4 highway for 45 minutes southwest to La Libertad.

PLAYA SAN BLAS

Just west of La Libertad is San Blas, a pretty, peaceful beach lined with private homes and a few quiet hotels. San Blas is a good swimming beach with pearl-gray sand and not many travelers. It is also very close to Punta Roca, and Punta Roca Hotel is a popular choice for surfers who want a quiet place to stay that is close to the surf break. San Blas is a good choice if you are looking for a very low-key secluded beach with not much to do. It's a perfect getaway with few restaurants and amenities—think romantic weekend away.

Accommodations and Food

Punta Roca Hotel (Playa Cocal, San Blas, tel. 2335-3261 or 7213-2178, www.puntaroca. com.sv, $60 d) is easy to find, with plenty of signage on Carretera Litoral and on the road to the beach, just a five-minute drive from the Punta Roca break. This tranquil and popular surf hotel is a good alternative for those who are looking for a quiet, relaxed place to stay, away from the crowds and parties in El Tunco. Lovely large rooms with tile floors, colorful art of ocean scenes, sofas, rocking chairs, TVs, air-conditioning, double beds, and private baths with hot water are set among the garden, right in front of the beach. There is a swimming pool and an excellent restaurant. Rooms can be rented on a nightly basis, but they also offer popular surf packages that include meals and daily transportation to Punta Roca and other surf spots. Check their website for details.

SABAS Beach Resort (Km. 39, Carretera Litoral, tel. 7670-5768, www.sa-basbeachresort.com, $78 s or d) is a remote getaway for those looking for a quiet vacation. The resort is a two-story peach-colored building with art deco style—it looks more like Miami's South Beach than El Salvador—but for those looking for a secure American-style hotel, SABAS is a good choice. The service is excellent, and the restaurant serves very good food. Rooms are spacious, breezy, and brand-new, with dark wood bed frames, mint green walls, white tile floors, and sliding glass doors that open to a terrace with an ocean view. All rooms have air-conditioning, TVs, and modern private baths.

Getting There

Buses 192 or 192B ($0.25, 15 minutes) run frequently from La Libertad to San Blas.

PLAYA EL TUNCO

About two kilometers west of San Blas, El Tunco is the most popular beach on the west coast and the perfect place to catch the vibe of El Salvador's international surf scene. A beautiful rock formation is the inspiration for the name of the beach—*el tunco* means "pig," and the large rock that sits in the water is shaped like one. The famous El Tunco rock creates the river mouth that is La Bocana, one of the busiest surf spots in the country, drawing crowds who will captivate you with their grace and agility riding currents that can reach up to three meters high. Surf lessons are widely available here, as well as beachfront yoga classes and hikes to nearby waterfalls. A variety of restaurants and nightlife draws foreigners and Salvadorans alike to bustling bars with live music and open-mike nights, and there is a wide range of accommodations available, from cheap surf hostels to beautiful beachfront hotels.

Shopping

The main pathway to the beach is lined with shops selling sun hats, bathing suits, beachwear, sunscreen, and jewelry. For higher-quality clothing and bathing suits along with surfboards and other surf gear, check out **Papaya's Surf Shop** (tel. 2389-6185, 9am-6pm daily), right on the corner of the two main streets.

Xaltenco El Salvador (beside Hotel Tunco Lodge, tel. 2389-6322, www.toururales.com, 8am-5pm daily) sells handicrafts from local artisans as well as soaps, local coconut oil, and shoes. Check out the art from Artesanias El Pedregal, local artists who specialize in found and recycled art such as lanterns made from seashells, painted rocks, and hand-sewn bags.

Recreation
★ Surfing

La Bocana is the locals' favorite break, and one of the most consistent waves in the country; with a grinding left and an underestimated right, these hollow waves often hit perfection. Expect to find wave hunters from the city being quite territorial on weekends. It's best to surf La Bocana during the week when things quiet down. La Bocana is for experienced surfers only.

Surf classes can be arranged by any of

surf lesson at Playa El Tunco

the hotels in El Tunco, but the only certified surf instructor in El Tunco is **Marcelo Castellanos** at **Puro Surf El Salvador** (tel. 7737-4759, info@purosurf.com.sv). This professional surfer and national champion can be found at **Club Tecleño,** located on the beach. It's the first surf club you will see leaving El Tunco on the way to El Sunzal. Marcelo charges $40 per hour for high-quality surf lessons. For all other instructors, the going rate is $10 per hour. It is also possible to rent surfboards at almost all of the hotels; the rate is usually $10 for the day.

★ Hiking to Tamanique Waterfalls

The hike to Tamanique Waterfalls is an excellent intermediate hike. The four-hour round-trip includes walking past cornfields, through lush rainforest, scrambling up and down large rocks, jumping over rivers, and finally past a series of waterfalls where you can jump into the cool pools below. The hike ends at a large pristine pool fed by a gorgeous waterfall and surrounded by large smooth rocks perfect for relaxing in the sun.

Hikers cool off after the trek to the Tamanique Waterfalls near El Tunco.

If you would like to support community development in the town of Tamanique, you can contact **TouRurales** (next to Hotel Tunco Lodge, tel. 2389-6322, 8am-5pm daily, $20 pp for up to 4 people, $15 pp for a group of 5 or more). This excellent company supports sustainable tourism and provides transportation to and from Tamanique, where they organize local guides to take you on the hike.

The hike can also be done with Baltazar Monroy of **Eternal Summer Tours** (tel. 7842-8886, baltazar_monroy@yahoo.es, $20 pp for up to 4 people, $15 pp for a group of 5 or more), which includes transportation to and from Tamanique and a bilingual guide. If you are willing to take the bus, **Tamanique Cascadas Tour** (tel. 7226-2534, $7 pp) is a fun local outfit that takes groups on the bus to Tamanique and also does guided hikes.

Alternatively, you can just show up in Tamanique on your own. There is never a shortage of entrepreneurial boys hanging out, happy to guide you for a few bucks. To get to Tamanique, take bus 187A ($0.50, 45 minutes, runs every half hour) from the Tamanique Desvío on the Carretera Litoral. Bring a hat, water, and sunscreen—it gets hot.

Tours

Many people offer tours to **San Salvador** from El Tunco, but your best bet for a bilingual guide who offers unique tours you will not find anywhere else is **El Salvador Adventures** (tel. 7844-0858, www.wtf-el-salvador.com). Go to San Salvador to take a tour of a local brewery and finish with the best burger in the city, or head to an underground parking lot in downtown San Salvador to experience the heated excitement of *lucha libre,* the Mexican-inspired free wrestling that involves colorful masks, dramatic characters, and plenty of beer. El Salvador Adventures also offers more traditional tours through **Ruta de Las Flores,** where you will visit artisanal villages, waterfalls in Juayúa, and the ruins of Tazumal, San Andrés, or Joya de Cerén. Check the website for details, or find out more at **Gekko Trails Explorer** (tel. 7249-6263, www.gekkotrailsexplorer.com, 10am-5pm daily), located on the main road near Mopelia Hotel.

Yoga

Ashtanga yoga classes are offered by experienced teacher **Suni Apter** of **Essy Retreats** (tel. 7682-3237, www.essyretreats.com, $5 pp) three times a week at either **La Guitarra** or **El Tunco Veloz.** Apter also offers excellent therapeutic massages and personal training. See her website for class schedules and details.

Entertainment
Nightlife

El Tunco is notorious for its nightlife, and Salvadorans flock to this beach every weekend to enjoy the sun, surf, and party. The beachfront bars are the most popular and usually have live music on Friday and Saturday nights. **La Guitarra** (tel. 2389-6398, www.surfingeltunco.com, 5pm-2am Fri.-Sat.) is right in front of El Tunco rock, which is lit up after dark, creating an amazing view of the rock formation and ocean at night. La Guitarra brings the best bands in the country to its stage every weekend and does not charge cover. Expect to hear jazz, funk, soul, reggae, and ska. If La Guitarra is not your thing, you can check out **D'Rocas** (tel. 2389-6126, rocasunzal@hotmail.com, 5pm-2am Fri.-Sat.), which is right next door. D'Rocas has a cover charge of $3 and also often has live dance music. There are two floors with a towering balcony where you can have a drink with a bird's eye view of the action on the dance floor below. Both La Guitarra and D'Rocas have seating available outside where you can enjoy the ocean breeze and view.

Farther west, down the beach, things get a little headier, where the pummeling reggaeton and flashing lights of **La Bocana** (tel. 2389-6134, www.baryrestaurantelabocana.com, 7pm-2am Fri.-Sat., no cover) and **Erika's** (tel. 7890-1923, 7pm-2am Fri.-Sat., no cover) compete for the attention of dancers.

For action farther away from the beach, be sure to check out **Surfo's the Bar** (tel. 7666-4745 or 7854-8839, ivan_patino72@yahoo.com, 9am-midnight Fri.-Sat.). Minimart and travel agency by day, international watering hole by night, this space may not be big, but the vibe is always right. Stock up on snacks, buy a bus ticket, grab a beer, and make some friends—it can all be done here. Affable owner and local musician Patiño will keep you moving with premium selections of funk, soul, house, and hip-hop, plus he has the coldest beer in town. There is no cover.

Right next door to Surfo's is **Jaguar Bar and Restaurant** (tel. 2389-6159, barjaguar@gmail.com, 8am-10pm Sun.-Thurs., 8am-2am Fri.-Sat.), a casual bar that usually plays a good selection of reggae and serves up colorful cocktails on the lovely street-side patio. There is an outdoor open-mike night every Tuesday (no cover) starting at 8pm, which always draws a crowd. Get there early if you want a table.

Right across the street from Jaguar, **The Lab** (tel. 7817-3383, 5pm-2am daily, $5-10) definitely has an experimental vibe to it. White tables sit under black lights and fluorescent psychedelic art and electronic music keeps the crowd moving. The Lab has a variety of tasty infused vodkas, from jalapeño to strawberry. Their other shtick is meat on a stick, which is also very good. There is no cover.

Accommodations
Under $10

The most popular budget hostel in town is **La Sombra Hostel** (located on the second dirt road on the left side after entering El Tunco from the Carretera Litoral, no phone, www.surflibre.com, $7 pp dorm, $18 s with fan, $20 s with a/c, $25 d with fan, $30 d with a/c). Boasting a very laid-back vibe with amiable management, a swimming pool, Wi-Fi, and a small kitchen, La Sombra is also just a short walk to the beach, and it is almost always full. Simple rooms with tile floors and clean white walls are complemented with surf art and colorful bedspreads. The dorms are small and very basic, but at $7 it's the cheapest bed you will find in El Tunco.

$10-25

A little farther down the road from La Sombra Hostel, you will find the equally laid-back but more intimate **Casa Makoi** (tel. 2389-6360, catherine.b1@gmx.ch, $10 pp dorm, $15-20 d with fan, $35-45 d with a/c). Hidden behind a sliding wooden gate are a garden and a colorful mural covering the front of a lovely three-story house, where you will find a small dorm and private rooms. The rooms are basic but clean and new. The private rooms on the top floor have a great private terrace and windows that open up to the palms and birds. Casa Makoi is a favorite for those interested in more long-term stays (ask about weekly and monthly discounts), although it works just as well for a short visit. There is a very small kitchen on the second floor and a cute café on the first floor serving breakfast, freshly baked bread, sweet treats, and coffee fresh from the in-house espresso machine.

★ **Hotel Mopelia** (Calle Principal, near the entrance to El Tunco, tel. 2389-6265, produitblanc@hotmail.com, $10 s with fan, $15 d with fan, shared bath; $25 s with a/c, $35 d with a/c, private baths) is an excellent budget choice. This hotel offers a long, peaceful piece of land where stepping-stones lead you to colorful *cabañas* set amid papaya and palm trees; you're close enough to the beach for the waves to lull you to sleep. The rooms are basic, with concrete floors, double beds, shelves, and a small side table. There is a swimming pool and a very good restaurant with the best selection of beer in El Tunco. Wi-Fi is available, but only in the restaurant area.

Although centrally located on the main street, **Papaya's Lodge** (tel. 2389-6027, www.papayalodge.com, $8 pp dorm, $25 d with fan) is a bit inconspicuous due to its large wooden gates that hide the inside of the hostel. Once inside, you are greeted by a swimming pool, spacious lounging areas with hammocks,

a small kitchen, and a TV area. Owned by longtime surfer and laid-back El Tunco local "Papaya," the lodge was the first place to open its doors to traveling surfers back in the 1990s. He has since rebuilt the hostel, which now boasts two floors with wraparound terraces and plenty of lodging options. Rooms are simple, keeping with the bright color theme, with yellow and green walls, surf art, and striped bedspreads. Surfboard rental and surf lessons are also available.

Tunco Lodge (tel. 2389-6318, www.tuncolodge.com, $10 pp dorm with fan, $12 pp dorm with a/c, $30 d with fan, $40 d with a/c) sits on the street that runs perpendicular to the main road, heading away from the beach. This is a very competitive backpacker place because of the little extras, like the option of air-conditioning in dorms for just a few dollars more, Wi-Fi, computers, a kitchen, a shady lounge area with a TV and DVDs, and a swank swimming pool where the parties can occasionally get wild. There are rooms for different budgets, from dorms with fans to brand-new private rooms with air-conditioning. They are all hidden away in its own little complex, close enough to the action but still a nice little refuge. You can arrange transportation, tours, and surf lessons here; just ask at the front desk.

Zuzu's Hangout Guesthouse (turn left at the end of the road that runs perpendicular to Calle Principal, heading away from the beach, tel. 2389-6239 or 7468-9898, www.zuzusplayaeltunco.com, $10 pp dorm, $25 d with fan) is cute enough but never really took off due to its location. Close to the main road, far away from the beach, in a quiet residential part of town, Zuzu's is a good place to check if you are in El Tunco on a busy weekend and everywhere else is full. It is the one place where you can almost always find a room. There is a great lounge area with throw pillows and hammocks that overlooks the river, and rooms are small but cute with seashell themes. There is also a TV area and a small kitchen for guest use.

$25-50

Beside the river, on the road that runs perpendicular to Calle Principal, heading away from the beach, you will find **Posada Luna** (tel. 2389-6147 or 7721-3420, www.lunasurfingelsalvador.com, $35 d with fan, $45 d with a/c), a quiet little hostel offering basic private rooms, a cute lounge area beside the river, and a swimming pool.

Set on a quiet side street away from the bustle of El Tunco, but still close to the beach, **Hotel Pupa** (first left coming into El Tunco from Carretera Litoral, tel. 7529-1414, hotelpupa@gmail.com, $25 d with fan, $30 d with a/c) is a hidden gem. Pupa offers private rooms in a quiet, laid-back environment with friendly, helpful owners who are always nearby to answer questions or perhaps even invite you on one of their informal tours around the country. A cheerful yellow and green house with a terra-cotta roof sits in among the trees and flowers and large beautiful hammocks, perfect for postsurf naps. This all surrounds a courtyard with a small swimming pool and a kitchen. The rooms are spacious, with pretty tile floors, big windows letting in lots of light, and private baths.

Hotel La Bocanita (Calle Principal, near the entrance to El Tunco, tel. 7211-9519, $20 d with fan, $30 d with a/c shared bath; $40 d with fan, $50 d with a/c private bath) is a nice new addition to El Tunco's mid-range options, offering brand-new air-conditioned rooms around a courtyard full of plants and a big swimming pool. Rooms are basic, with chocolate brown and orange tones, couches, and tile floors. The rooms on the second level have a terrace that overlooks the pool.

★ **La Guitarra** (corner of Calle Principal and the path to the beach, tel. 2389-6398, www.surfingeltunco.com, $28 s, $50 d) is the most comfortable mid-range stay in El Tunco, offering amenities such as a swimming pool, Wi-Fi, and a kitchen for guests to use. It is a local favorite, and designed to appeal to long-term stays (ask about long-term discounts). Each room has two big beds with tie-dyed bedspreads, ceiling fans, cool tile floors, exposed brick walls, and private baths. Sliding glass doors open up to cute individual terraces and hammocks that faces a tranquil green space with a stone pathway that takes you out to the restaurant and beach, or to the main road. La Guitarra also has a popular bar, with live (loud) music on the weekend. Unless you are planning on taking part in the revelry, or you're an exceptionally deep sleeper, it's best not to plan a stay here on Friday and Saturday nights.

$50-100

On the same road as budget hostels La Sombra and Casa Makoi, **Eco del Mar** (no phone, www.ecosurfelsalvador.com, $50 d with fan, $60 d with a/c) is a lovely if not-so-aptly-named hostel (although it's beautiful, there is nothing about it that makes it specifically eco-friendly). Popular with those looking for a comfortable mid-range option, Eco del Mar has stylish rooms in a modern yet organic-looking building, with terraces built out of local wood logs. The rooms are clean, new, and full of neutral colors, with sleek white walls adorned with simple art in primary colors. Each room has a kitchenette, including a tiny dark-wood bar. There is a swimming pool, hammocks on the terraces, and a small restaurant, but you need to order food in advance so the staff can arrange for someone to come in and cook.

El Tunco's only boutique hotel, **Tekuani Kal** (Calle Principal, tel. 2389-6388, www.tekuanikal.com, $86 d, includes breakfast) offers simple, elegant rooms with low platform beds covered in brightly embroidered Guatemalan textiles, TVs, air-conditioning, and a great view of the sea. The grounds are peppered with indigenous sculptures, sleekly designed waterfalls, and an infinity pool. Although the property design is gorgeous, the carpeted rooms are quite worn and do not do the rest of the hotel justice. At the time of publication renovations were underway, so hopefully the rooms are looking a little fresher by now.

Beachfront hotel **Roca Sunzal** (tel. 2389-6126, rocasunzal@hotmail.com, $75 d) offers lovely rooms around a swimming pool and restaurant, all facing the famous El Tunco rock formation that the town is named after. The rooms are simple and spacious, with air-conditioning, TVs, cool tile floors, and big double beds with floral bedspreads, but the real draw here is the location and the view. It's possible to walk from your hotel room straight onto the beach. The restaurant is a perfect place for evening drinks as you watch El Tunco's famous sunset. Be warned that if you stay here on the weekend, you will hear the live music from La Guitarra next door until about 1am.

Food

Tucked away in a pretty backyard garden, the casually refined ★ **Tunco Veloz Pizzeria** (Calle Principal, in front of Tekuani Kal Hotel, tel. 2319-8611, tuncoveloz@gmail.com, 4pm-10pm Tues.-Sun., $5-10) is the perfect spot to start a night out, or to make a night of it—enjoying a slow, intimate meal away from the chaos and crowds. Serving up delicious thin-crust pizza with homemade dough and local ingredients alongside infused oils and a decent wine selection, this hidden gem is not to be missed. The menu also boasts tasty pastas, soups, and salads.

The rustic and cozy ★ **Mopelia** (Calle Principal, tel. 2389-6265, produitblanc@hotmail.com, 9am-11am and 5pm-10pm daily, $3-7) has the most extensive beer selection in town (the owner is Belgian; what would you expect?). Combine this lengthy list of libations with hearty home cooked meals like excellent pastas, the best steak in El Tunco, meatballs, pork chops, and if you still have room for dessert, proper Belgian waffles—it's no wonder this place is so popular with hungry surfers and locals alike. Lounge areas with throw cushions, Wi-Fi, a Ping-Pong table (including a pretty serious Ping-Pong competition every Monday night starting at 8pm), and an excellent selection of music all come together to create a great atmosphere.

On the same property as Mopelia, the Asian-inspired **Take a Wok** (Calle Principal, tel. 6007-5539, 4pm-10pm Mon.-Thurs., 4pm-11pm Fri., noon-11pm Sat., noon-10pm Sun., $3-7) fills a much needed niche with its popular fast-food open kitchen. Staff furiously work over hot woks as they prepare rice or noodles, combined with your choice of protein and vegetables, and unique homemade sauces like coconut curry and ginger guava. Portions are big and economical, and freshly brewed iced teas with ginger, basil, and honey are delicious too.

★ **Soya Nutribar** (Calle Principal, near Mopelia, tel. 7887-1596, 8am-5pm daily, $3-5) is the perfect solution to a weekend of excess in El Tunco. This tiny little juice and salad bar offers fresh vegetable juices, fruit smoothies, and other chlorophyll-infused elixirs to get your blood cleansed and energy levels back up for more surfing and socializing. They also serve excellent salads and other treats such as gluten-free granola, chocolate energy balls, and local honey.

Centrally located on the main street, **Jaguar Bar and Restaurant** (tel. 2389-6159, barjaguar@gmail.com, 8am-10pm Sun.-Thurs., 8am-2am Fri.-Sat., $4-10) is a good stop for pub food. Jaguar is popular for its massive smoothies, steaks, nachos, big salads, and hearty fish-and-chips. It's one of the only restaurants with Wi-Fi and outdoor seating, ideal for people-watching while you check your email.

Right across the street from Jaguar is the most tastefully designed place in town, **Loroco Bistro** (tel. 7725-5744, hours vary, hit or miss). This outdoor bistro is designed with local wood from Ruta de Las Flores, with trunks serving as both tables and chairs. Owner Carlos Cardona Sasso tries to bring a bit of culture to this surf town, with occasional art exhibits and guest lectures about Salvadoran culture and history. The sign that hangs out front is also wooden and painted with the signature colorful designs of local artist Renacho Melgar. The food aims to use local ingredients to create international fare, offering dishes such as pulled-pork sandwiches, black bean burgers, and potato salad.

Esquina la Comadre (tel. 7261-3873, 8am-11pm Mon.-Sat., $3-8) is the long-standing El Tunco favorite for budget food. Cheap breakfasts and burritos are the mainstays in this small family-run restaurant, located on the corner of the two main roads in town. This is a popular gathering spot for lunch after a morning surf session. **Taco Guanaco** (tel. 7730-5933, 7:30am-11pm daily, $3-10) is the other budget favorite. As you walk on the main pathway that leads to the beach, look up and you will see the sign on the left side. Serving reasonable portions at reasonable prices, Taco Guanaco specializes in burritos, seafood plates, grilled meat, and pasta. There are a couple of tables right on the pathway, but the majority are upstairs, where a small second level overlooks the pedestrian traffic. The brand-new **Coyote Cojo** (left side of the pathway to the beach, no phone, 9am-5pm daily, $3-6) is known for its popular sandwiches and an extensive breakfast menu, including eggs prepared any way you can think of, such as egg quesadillas, eggs benedict, and bagels with eggs.

Dale! Dale! Café (tel. 2389-6126, 6am-5pm Mon.-Thurs., 6am-9pm Fri.-Sat., 6am-8pm Sun., $3-5) is a popular pit stop for surfers seeking a caffeine hit. Located on the right side of the main path toward the beach, Dale! Dale! Café has an espresso machine and offers lattés and cappuccinos alongside specialty teas, great breakfast options like fruit, yogurt, and granola, and healthy lunches that include salads, hummus and pita, and sandwiches. There is a nice shady seating area out back with a great view of the river and beach. They also have Wi-Fi.

La Cuma Burgers and Grill (tel. 2389-6126, 7am-10pm daily, $6-14) is right next door to Dale! Dale! Café, and as its name suggests, serves burgers and does them right. High-quality beef is served on homemade bread and with toppings that come together to make a burger you will keep coming back for.

Try *La Niña,* with Sriracha aioli, grilled pineapple, and onion rings *la local* with jalapeño garlic mayo, cheddar cheese, bacon, grilled onions, red bell pepper, and mushrooms. La Cuma also serve great pasta, grilled meat, and seafood. The seating is beside the river so there is more of a breeze than most other places, and there is Wi-Fi.

La Bocana (at the end of the main pathway to the beach, left side, tel. 2389-6134, www.baryrestaurantelabocana.com, 7am-10pm daily, $5-15) serves decent food with a great view. This is a local favorite for seafood, ceviche, and beer. The second floor looks out over the ocean and catches a lovely breeze. If you are craving pasta, La Bocana serves tasty, generous pasta plates for $5.

Information and Services

On the main road, you can find **Gekko Trails Explorer** (tel. 7249-6263, www.gekkotrailsexplorer.com, 10am-5pm daily), an excellent tour company that can arrange package tours and provide shuttle transportation from El Salvador to Honduras, Nicaragua, and Guatemala.

Surfo's Travel Agency (tel. 7666-4745 or 7854-8839, ivan_patino72@yahoo.com, 9am-10pm daily) is also located on the main street in El Tunco, closer to the main path toward the beach. This is where you can book international bus tickets, private shuttles, and taxis. Owner Ivan Patiño speaks English and can help you out with any questions you may have about getting around El Salvador or out of the country to neighboring Guatemala or Honduras.

Xaltenco El Salvador (beside Hotel Tunco Lodge, tel. 2389-6322, 8am-5pm daily) is the only Internet café in El Tunco. Services include Internet access, international calls, printing, scanning, and photocopies. There is no supermarket in El Tunco, just small *tiendas* with the basics. The closest grocery store is in La Libertad.

Dr. Luis May (Calle Principal, close to the entrance of El Tunco, tel. 7887-1596) has an office inside **Soya Nutribar** and provides excellent consultations ($25 per session) for alternative health treatments.

Getting There and Around

Buses 80, 192, 102A, and 187A (30 minutes, $0.25) all run from La Libertad to El Tunco.

You can rent a car in El Tunco, but it will cost you significantly more than it would in San Salvador. The going rate for car rental in El Tunco is $40-50 per day, as opposed to $25 per day in San Salvador. Beware of locals offering to rent their cars; they sometimes break down, so you could be left stranded and likely not get your money back. Ronaldiño of **360 Rentals** (tel. 7648-1477) provides reliable car rentals. You can ask for him at **Xaltenco El Salvador.**

PLAYA EL SUNZAL

Just a seven-minute walk west along the beach from El Tunco is El Sunzal, where one of the most consistent and powerful waves in the country keeps serious surfers content. There is one high-end hotel here, but the other options are strictly for surfers who are looking for a secluded budget option close to the popular point break.

Recreation

Surfing

Sunzal is famous for its surf, and all of the hotels here offer surf lessons and surfboard rentals. This fun, long right-hander seems to pick up every bit of swell in the water, making it a favorite break. This is a great beginner to intermediate and longboarding wave. Rides of over 150 meters are not uncommon.

Eternal Summers Tours (tel. 7842-8886, baltazar_monroy@yahoo.es), run by Baltazar Monroy, manager of Sunzal Point Hostel, can arrange surf tours.

★ Fishing

La Libertad Fishing Co. (tel. 7887-0666, esfishinco@gmail.com, prices vary by tour) offers expert fishing instruction on offshore and inshore fishing trips around Sunzal. Head out to sea on a seven-meter *panga* with a 115-hp engine to fish for jack, tuna, red snapper, grouper, mahimahi, barracuda, roosterfish, snook, and mackerel. Your guide, Roberto Figueroa of Hostal Los Almendros, is bilingual, and his passion for fishing is infectious. The area around Sunzal is rocky, but those who are adventurous enough can also try their hand at surf fishing. Take your catch back to the beautiful hostel, where the kitchen will cook it for you (in Thai curry if you want) and enjoy it with a cold beer and an unrivaled view of the sunset over the Pacific Ocean.

Cacao Farm Tour

Learn about the history of cacao in El Salvador on a tour of a local cacao farm with Roberto Figueroa of Hostal Los Almendros (tel. 7887-0666, chocotoursv@gmail.com, about 4 hours, $200, up to 10 people). This tour will take you to the indigenous town of Izalco, where you will learn how cacao is grown and how it goes from seed to chocolate. Finish with a chocolate-making session by the beach and then savor the sweet fruits of your labor.

Accommodations

Three budget surf hostels sit beside each other in the shade of mango trees right beside the beach. **Surfers Inn Hostel** (tel. 2355-7049 or 7925-4232, surfersinnantonio@hotmail.com, $10 d private room), a friendly, family-run hostel with small, simple, but clean cinder block rooms with fans, hammocks, and a very small, very basic kitchen.

Right across the way from Surfers Inn Hostel is **Guesthouse El Balsamo** (tel. 7404-8117 or 2389-6140, guesthouse@elbalsamo.com, $5 pp dorm, $25 d with fan), where the dorm is a great deal. Four bunk beds are inside a cheerfully painted green and orange brick room, with a shared bath, floor fans, and a common lounge area. The private rooms are spacious and new, with lots of light, plants, shiny black tile floors, and space to store your surfboards. There is no kitchen, but some burners are set up outside the dorm for basic cooking. El Balsamo also has a half pipe for skateboarding as well as cool little wooden bar set up on a platform in the shade.

Sunzal Point Hostel (tel. 7237-9869, sunzalpoint@sunzalpoint.com, $7 pp dorm, $18 d) has been around the longest and is an established favorite for serious surfers on a budget. It is located right in front of the other hostels, closer to the beach. Nestled between mango and tamarind trees, just steps from the beach, Sunzal Point has one dorm with eight beds (most of which are quite well worn) and one private room with the same setup as the dorm (basic, worn bed, surf art on the wall, one fan). Rooms can get crowded and hot during the day, but they open up to a shaded common area with hammocks. There are two common showers and toilets, an outdoor volleyball court, and a small not-so-clean or well-stocked kitchen. Manager Baltazar Monroy also runs **Eternal Summers Tours** (tel. 7842-8886, baltazar_monroy@yahoo.es) and can arrange surf tours and hiking trips.

★ **Hostal Los Almendros** (tel. 7887-0666, hostal.losalmendros@gmail.com, $25 s, $35 d) is the hidden gem of this part of the coast. This large beachfront house, with plenty of outdoor terrace space, hammocks, and lounge chairs, is just steps away from the Sunzal surf break. Rooms are spacious and simple, with cool tile floors, fans, and private baths. The vibe here is friendly and mellow, and the extremely helpful bilingual owner Roberto Figueroa also runs excellent fishing trips, and cacao tours. Thai food is available at the restaurant. You can add three meals a day to your stay for an additional $15.

★ **Casa de Mar Hotel and Villas** (Km. 43, Carretera Litoral, tel. 2389-6284, www.casademarhotel.com, $153 s, 189 d) is one of the best boutique hotels in the country and a popular place for all-inclusive surf tours, but you don't have to be a surfer to appreciate this beautiful hotel for both its superior service and beautiful rooms with ocean views. Two-story wooden *cabañas* are set above the beach, nestled between flowers and palm trees with a spectacular view—surfers can practically check the lineup from bed when they wake up in the morning. The rooms are impeccable, with large windows that let in sunlight and the sound of the palms swaying in the ocean breeze. Double beds with a simple design of white and red sheets, plants, sofas, and chairs with floral-print throw pillows all come together to create the perfect blend of tropical style and boutique chic. All rooms have air-conditioning, TVs, modern baths with hot water, and nice little touches like hooks in the shower to hang wet bathing suits. There is a swimming pool and a bar as well as one of the finest restaurants along the coast, Café Sunzal. Tours, surf classes, massages, and yoga classes can all be arranged here; just ask at the front desk.

Food

Sharky's (tel. 7959-3458, sharkyssunzal@gmail.com, 9am-9pm daily, $4-8) is the only budget restaurant in Sunzal, and sits right across from Sunzal Point Hostel. This casual outdoor restaurant, on a patio underneath a thatched roof, serves up a hearty breakfast burrito and lots of other great breakfast options as well as burgers, quesadillas, and other yummy pub fare.

Los Almendros (tel. 7887-0666, hostal.losalmendros@gmail.com, noon-2pm and 5pm-7pm daily, $8-10) is the only place in the country serving up Thai-influenced tropical curry made with freshly pressed coconut milk straight from the trees in front of the restaurant. Daily plates vary, but beef, chicken, fish, and vegetarian options are usually always available. This friendly, informal restaurant is a part of the Hostal Los Almendros and offers a simple outdoor seating area and beautiful ocean views. Hours are flexible; if you show up and the chef is here, you can eat.

Café Sunzal (Km. 43, Carretera Litoral, tel. 2355-7137, www.casademar.com, 11am-5:30pm Sun.-Thurs., 11am-9:30pm Fri.-Sat., $7-15) is Casa de Mar's adjunct restaurant and offers some of the best food on the coast. A large wooden deck built into a cliff overlooking the ocean offers a sweet breeze and choice views of surfers doing their thing. This is a gorgeous place to have a meal or just stop by for a drink. The seafood is your best bet. Try the fish fillet with sesame seeds and honey-roasted almonds, or island-style fish with coconut curry.

Getting There

Buses 80, 192, 102A, and 187A ($0.25, 35 minutes) all travel from La Libertad to Sunzal. If you are coming from El Tunco, it's faster to walk along the beach, but don't walk between beaches at night; it can be dangerous.

PLAYA EL ZONTE

A relaxed community vibe appeals to surfers and nonsurfers alike in El Zonte, about 15 kilometers west of El Sunzal. It's the perfect place to while away a few days in a hammock, or to take surf lessons with some of the most highly recommended teachers in the country (although at slightly higher prices than at El Tunco). A handful of restaurants and hostels line the beach, and every evening there is a certain magic in the air as the locals and tourists gather at the shore to admire surfers ride the gorgeous sunset crests. Everything shuts down here by 9pm or earlier, unless one of the local bars decides to stay open (this usually depends on the number of people harassing the bartender).

Sports and Recreation

Surfing

El Zonte is one of the best spots in El Salvador to learn how to stand up on a surfboard. The waves here are very forgiving. Classes cost more here than in El Tunco, but they are less crowded, and the teaching style is better suited to beginners, meaning students start off by practicing in the white water instead of immediately being taken out to tackle intimidating waves. Surf lessons are offered at all the hotels in El Zonte, but the teachers at **Esencia Nativa** (tel. 7737-8879, www.esenci-anativa.com, $20 per hour) come highly recommended. You can also rent surfboards at Esencia Nativa for $10 per day.

Intermediate surfers will love Zonte's hollow, fast right-hander with clean sections. Just past the point on Zonte there is also a good left-hander that offers a welcome change to the ubiquitous right points.

Yoga

Alexandra Pacheco of **Yoga Group El Zonte** leads yoga classes five days a week in El Zonte: 9:30am Monday and Thursday at **Casa de Frida** (west side of the river, tel. 7561-0315), and 8:30am Tuesday, Wednesday, and Friday at **Olas Permanentes** (west side of the river, tel. 7432-7560).

Tours

For guided trips to Parque Nacional Los Volcanes (Cerro Verde), informal surf tours, cultural tours to the ruins of Tazumal, San Andrés, and Joya de Cerén, or a fun day trip to Ruta de Las Flores, contact the lovely Luis Rivas of **Zonte Spanish S'cool and Tours** (tel. 7297-6003). He speaks English and also offers highly recommended Spanish classes. Ask for him at Esencia Nativa.

Accommodations

Under $10

Esencia Nativa (tel. 7737-8879, www. esencianativa.com, $8 pp dorm, $20 d) sits in the heart of El Zonte, with a perfect view of the palm-lined river and the rocky shoreline that leads to the breaking waves. A simple *palapa* with a huge mural of indigenous art on its facade creates the restaurant area, which sits beside a swimming pool surrounded by flowers, green space, and pretty mosaic stepping-stones that lead you around the property. There is lots of chill-out space with hammocks and loungers, all put together with sleek, organic design that blends beautifully with the landscape. Sociable owner Alex Novoa is one of the best surf instructors in the country, and his staff are among the hardest working, serving up top-notch food from the open-concept kitchen and bar. Esencia Nativa offers one large dormitory with wooden bunk beds, fans, and one shared bath, as well as cute private rooms with double beds, fans, surf art, and private baths. There is also an indoor lounge area with a TV and DVDs, a small shop with beach essentials (sunscreen, bikinis), surfboards for rent, transportation, and surf tours provided. Just ask Alex for details.

Canegue Hostal (tel. 7598-6913, $3 camping, $7 pp dorm, $20 d) is a small two-story house set back from the beach with a sprawling property where it is possible to camp or rent hammocks. The dorm is small and simple with four beds, one floor fan, and a colorful mural on the wall. There are two simple but cute private rooms on the top floor, with double beds, private baths, and storage space. Both open up to a large terrace with hammocks and tables and chairs. One more private room is hidden behind the house in an adorable little casita with its own tiny porch and hammock. All rooms have fans. Quirky owner Zancudo is well known for surfing El Zonte's bold waves on a boogie board as well as hosting some of El Zonte's impromptu parties.

$10-25

On the west side of the river is **La Casa de Frida** (tel. 7561-0315, www.lacasadefrida.com, $25 d), a popular spot for day trippers, but also an excellent deal for those who want to stay the night. Rooms are spacious, each with two double beds, fans, exposed brick walls, tile floors, big windows, and private baths. Outside, a relaxing green space with hammocks and a few tables right on the beach make for a great place to spend a lazy afternoon. The restaurant serves good food, and the new management is very friendly and accommodating.

Horizonte Surf Resort (tel. 7737-5239, horizontesurfresort.com, $10 pp dorm, $20 budget s, $40 d, discounts for longer stays) is across the street from Esencia Nativa and is known for the colorful parrots and large iguanas that hang around the swimming pool. The grassy grounds are well manicured and relaxing, with a shady lounge area with a flat-screen TV, a small basic kitchen, and a restaurant. The double rooms have cinderblock

walls with modern art, sliding mirrored glass doors encasing the baths, and tiny floor fans, creating a strange blend of utilitarian and chic style. There is also a great third-story terrace space with hammocks, a small swimming pool, and expansive view of the ocean. The budget single rooms are very small and stuffy, with floor fans and no windows; you would be better off going for the dorms, which sit on the second-level terrace, with fans, overlooking the ocean and catching a great breeze. There is Wi-Fi in the lounge area only.

$25-50

El Salvador Surf House (tel. 7297-1633, $25 pp with fan, $30 pp with a/c, $70 3rd Fl. suite with a/c, private bath, and patio overlooking the ocean) is a bit farther away from the beach than the other hotels, but what American owner Dan Roberts lacks in location he more than makes up for with atmosphere. Entering town from Carretera Litoral, take the first left down a dirt road; it's the first house on the right side. Th. house boasts a beautiful wide-open air space with hammocks for lounging, a small but well-stocked kitchen, and a gorgeous swimming pool that is lit up at night and has stylish waterfalls flowing into it. The rooms are simple but new and attractive, with double beds, towels, and private baths. Roberts is an experienced surfer who has been living in El Zonte for years and can provide customized surf tours for groups or facilitate long-term stays. This is the perfect place for a group of surfers looking for a private house with a fun host.

Surf hostel **Olas Permanentes** (tel. 7432-7560, www.olaspermanentes.com, $40 d) is located on the west side of the river, just a few doors down from Casa de Frida, and has a great shady lounge space with comfy sofas and chairs, sea shell mobiles swaying in the breeze, wooden tables, and surf art. There is a good restaurant with thatched-roof shade. The rooms are simple and spacious, with air-conditioning, wallpaper with aquatic designs, cool tile floors, and private baths with seashell mirrors. Surf tours, classes, and board rentals are offered.

$50-100

El Dorado (first hotel west of the river, tel. 7226-6166, www.surfeldorado.com, $92 d) is the swankiest place to stay in El Zonte. Run by a French Canadian surfer, El Dorado is a popular vacation spot for French Canadian surfers. Geared toward surfers, there is a short but powerful left break right in front of the hotel, with outdoor showers and plenty of hammocks and lounge chairs for relaxing between sessions and keeping an eye on the waves and the lineup. The rooms are lovely, all set on the second floors of wooden *cabañas* with thatched roofs, with minimalist organic design including low wooden platform beds, fans, and private baths (also with wooden floors and some with open air showers). There is a swimming pool that is beautifully lit up at night as well as a hip little bar that gets busy during the high season and serves cocktails made with local fruits, and a popular Long Island iced tea made with Zacapa rum. The restaurant serves fusion food with Thai, French, and Italian influences on Salvadoran staples.

Information and Services

There are no services in this tiny beach town. You will not find Wi-Fi, but some places have a USB device that you can rent for about $2 an hour that provides an Internet connection.

Getting There

From La Libertad (or anywhere between La Libertad and El Zonte), take buses 192 or 192B ($0.25, 1 hour); buses run every 15 minutes.

PLAYA MIZATA

Continue west along the winding road, popping in and out of a series of tunnels, and the views get more and more impressive. The road hugs the coastline, and jaw-dropping views of the roaring Pacific on one side are complemented by the vibrant green cattle fields and expansive palm-laden land on the other. About 30 kilometers from El Zonte, Mizata is the last surf town on the west coast, a remote

paradise where there is not much else to do but ride the famously unpredictable right point wave. Mizata is a favorite for surfers looking for a tranquil, secluded vibe.

Mizata Point Resort (tel. 7977-4994, www.mizatapointresort.com, $65 d) is a beautiful remote resort with a sprinkling of lovely *cabañas* facing the sea. A small pool sits right in front of the ocean with a view of the towering cliffs and crashing waves. The rooms are simple, with queen beds below surf murals, air-conditioning, hot water, TVs, and a terrace facing the ocean. There is a large open-air restaurant that serves seafood and other snacks. Surf lessons and surfboard rentals can be arranged.

The aptly named **The Last Resort** (tel. 2347-9041 or 7243-0401, www.mizataresort. com, $10 pp dorm, not including breakfast; $50 s, $65 d, includes breakfast) sits at the end of the road in Mizata. This newly constructed hotel has air-conditioned rooms with crisp white walls adorned with massive surf photos. A beautiful pool is flanked by a shady restaurant that offers salads, burgers, sandwiches, and seafood. They can also arrange transportation to El Tunco.

Getting There

Getting to Mizata from La Libertad is very difficult, requiring various bus changes and a total travel time of about three hours. It is worth hiring private transportation for the trip. Alternatively, take bus 281 ($1.45, approx. 1 hour) from Sonsonate; it leaves 10 times daily.

If you are driving, when you arrive at Km. 86 on the Carretera Litoral, you will see a sign that says "Mizata." Take the small dirt road beside the restaurant Mama Con. When you get to a fork in the road, follow the left road, which leads to the point.

LOS CÓBANOS

West from Mizata, the coast gets more remote and rural. Los Cóbanos is a small fishing village about 80 kilometers from San Salvador.

This remote beach is a protected marine area with the largest coral reef in Central America just off its craggy shores. Los Cóbanos is a popular diving spot, and also a great destination to see humpback whales during their migration in November-December. Otherwise, this beach is perfect for those looking for a quiet, secluded getaway and a taste of the rural coast of El Salvador.

Sports and Recreation
Diving
Los Cóbanos offers excellent diving around the coral reef and at the sites of two sunken ships, where you can see moray eels, angelfish, eagle manta rays, green turtles, and lobsters. The best time to visit is December to May; January and February are the prime months for visibility. Diving trips can be arranged through **Los Cóbanos Village Lodge** (tel. 2264-0961, www.loscobanosvillagelodge.com, $65 per person).

★ Marine Life Boat Tour
Los Cóbanos is home to the Salvadoran NGO **Fundarrecife,** an organization that works to protect and preserve the coral reef and the area around it. They work with **Los Cóbanos Tours** (tel. 2417-6825 or 2420-5615, loscobanstours@yahoo.com) to help educate travelers about the ecology of the area and how they are working to protect it. They offer excellent **Marine Life Boat Tours** (3 hours, $35 pp, minimum 5 people), where you explore the marine life in this beautiful protected area, including dolphins, manta rays, turtles, and birds. If you go between November and January, chances are high you will also see the majestic humpback whales as they migrate.

Other Tours
Los Cóbanos Tours (tel. 2417-6825 or 2420-5615, loscobanstours@yahoo.com) also offers excellent artisanal fishing trips (3 hours, $34 pp, minimum 5 people), turtle releases (Sept.-Dec., 2 hours, $12 pp, minimum 2 people), and snorkeling around the coral reef and two sunken ships (3 hours, $12 pp, minimum 2 people).

Accommodations
Casa Garrobo (Playa del Amor, tel. 2469-2401, www.casagarrobo.com, $15 pp dorm, $40 d) is a cute, secluded hostel on the beautiful Playa del Amor, a white-sand beach with a rocky shore. Rooms are large and simple, with double beds, private baths (no hot water), and

fishing boats anchored off Los Cóbanos

fans. The dorm is also large, with two sets of bunk beds, ceiling fans, and one shared bath. There is a large shady common area where fresh seafood and breakfast is served (breakfast is included in the rates for double rooms). Between the rooms and the beach is a small swimming pool with lounge chairs and hammocks. This is the perfect place to relax for a few days, away from the crowds.

Nearby **Los Cóbanos Village Lodge** (tel. 2264-0961, www.loscobanosvillagelodge.com, $59 d with fan, $79 d with a/c) is the other option, and many consider it to be overpriced for what is offered. Cute second-floor rooms with seashell curtains open up to terraces with ocean views. The rooms are big, with large beds, tile floors, a small sitting area with cozy chairs, TVs, ceiling fans or air-conditioning, and hot water. Below is a restaurant and a swimming pool. Diving and fishing trips can also be arranged.

Getting There

From Sonsonate, take bus 257 ($0.50, 45 minutes), which stops right in Playa Los Cóbanos. It leaves the bus terminal in Sonsonate every half hour.

If you are driving, from San Salvador, take CA8 highway to the Carretera Litoral (CA2). Take a left at the Club Salinitas turn. From here, it's about eight kilometers to Los Cóbanos.

BARRA DE SANTIAGO

On the southwestern edge of the western department of Ahuachapán lies the surrealistically beautiful Barra de Santiago (or as the locals call it, "La Barra"), a sandbar flanked by the Pacific Ocean on one side and a mangrove-filled estuary on the other. The remoteness of La Barra is both its biggest draw and its greatest deterrent. Many travelers overlook it due to the fact that it is off the beaten track, but those who make the journey find that it has a magical allure, and is definitely not just another beach on the backpacker trail.

Sports and Recreation
★ Bird-Watching

The mangroves here are teeming with birds, and a boat tour through the estuary is the best way to see them. If you speak Spanish, local bird aficionado **Juan Pérez** (tel. 7366-4768, perez-2022@hotmail.com) can guide you on a peaceful **bird-watching boat tour** ($50 for 2 people, 8-10 hours) through the surreal scenery of the mangroves. The shores of the estuary create a cool, shady haven for birds like the American pygmy kingfisher, the yellow crowned night heron, and the mangrove yellow warbler. Pérez also offers excellent artisanal fishing trips and bicycle rentals. Ask for him at the local NGO Asociación de Mujeres de Barra de Santiago (AMBAS), located on the main street.

If you need an English-speaking guide, contact **Green Trips El Salvador** (tel. 7943-5230, greentripselsalvador@gmail.com), where English-speaking Benjamin Rivera (who works in partnership with Pérez) arranges excellent boat tours in La Barra for a significantly higher price ($270 a day for 2 people, 8-10 hours).

Surfing

Although not one of the country's most popular surf spots, this sandy beach break could be a good spot for absolute beginners. For those interested in lessons, contact local guide **Julio César Avilés** (tel. 7783-4765, or look for him at Capricho Guesthouse), who gives lessons for $10 per hour.

Accommodations
Under $10

Mercendero Don Antonio (tel. 7427-9316) is on the right side of the main road coming in to La Barra. This is the office of AMBAS, where a rustic restaurant sits right beside the estuary, providing a beautiful place to have dinner (bring your mosquito repellent). Owner Antonio and his wife also rent out a very basic second-story terrace where they will bring a mattress for you to sleep on in the open air, with the sound of the waves crashing in the distance. They charge $8 for this, or you can sleep in a hammock for free, as long as you have a few meals at their restaurant, or even better, buy fresh fish in the morning and ask to have them prepare it for you. There is access to clean baths beside the restaurant. This is a good investment in community development.

Rancho Familiar Santiago Apostol (tel. 2455-1773 or 7413-8412, $30 for 5 people) is the first place you will see on the left side coming in via the main road. Here you will find simple *cabañas,* each with five single beds, a fan, and a bath. The rooms get pretty hot at night, but the grounds are quite nice, with a swimming pool and lots of green space. You can hear the traffic from the road in front of the hotel, but the bonus is that the back gate opens to a short path that takes you straight to the beach. There is no restaurant, but the woman who sells food on the street corner will take your order and bring food to you.

$25-50

There are two proper hotels on the Barra, one of them the very expensive luxury eco-resort La Cocotera Resort and Ecolodge, and the other cheaper but still not budget Capricho Guesthouse. They are right next door to each other, about three kilometers west of the center of town.

Capricho Guesthouse (tel. 2260-2481, www.ximenasguesthouse.com, $40 d) has clean, basic rooms with air-conditioning and private baths. There are hammocks that line the shared porch alongside lounge chairs, so you can kick back and relax with an ocean view. The restaurant serves decent (though like the rooms, a bit overpriced) food.

La Cocotera Resort and Ecolodge (tel. 2245-3691 or 7359-5238, www.lacocoteraresort.com) has a small house on the property that is available for rent. This house is an excellent mid-range option, with the same stylish rooms and king beds of La Cocotera, each with air-conditioning. There's a terrace overlooking the estuary, a kitchen for

guest use, and a swimming pool. The entire house sleeps eight and can be rented for $190, or alternatively rent one of the second-story rooms for $75 d. There is a dormitory on the first floor with single beds ($25), also with air-conditioning.

$100-200

La Cocotera Resort and Ecolodge (tel. 2245-3691 or 7359-5238, www.lacocoteraresort.com, $100-200 depending on the season, check the website for details), three kilometers west of the town center, is an absolutely gorgeous place on a large expanse of land with incredible views of the ocean and estuary, coconut and palm trees, and flowers. It offers five beautiful individually designed rooms, with Salvadoran art on the walls and sliding glass doors that open to either the ocean or the estuary, both with exquisite views. Everything is eco-friendly, from the solar heating and saltwater pool to the biodegradable soap and shampoo. Meals are included in the rates.

Food

The seafood shacks in front of the beach in the center of town all sell very good seafood for reasonable prices.

SieteMares (Av. Jaragua and Calle Shasca, tel. 7855-5491, 4pm-9pm daily, $1-3), the best *pupusería* in town, is hard to miss: It's a big white building in the center of town. The inside is full of white plastic tables and chairs beside bright blue walls and plenty of windows, creating a cross breeze to counteract the heat from the furious *pupusa* making. They serve delicious seafood *pupusas* as well as the more traditional choices, as well as excellent *refrescos* such as fresh pineapple and tamarind juice.

If you are staying at Capricho or La Cocotera, you can walk 15 minutes to the edge of the peninsula, where you will find **Julita's** (Final de la Bocanada de la Barra, tel. 6129-7280, 8am-6pm or later daily, $7-12), a little shack that sits at the edge of the estuary beside the ocean. On a day with perfect weather conditions, you can see the entire mountain range of Parque Imposible, as well as Volcán Santa Ana. Fresher and cheaper seafood can be found in town, but it might be worth a visit simply for the novelty of the location.

Getting There

From San Salvador, take bus 205 ($0.80, 1.5 hours, runs every 10 minutes) from Terminal de Occidente to Sonsonate. From the bus terminal in Sonsonate, there are two daily buses to Barra de Santiago. Bus 285 ($1, 1.25 hours) leaves at 10am and 4:30pm daily; returning to Sonsonate, the bus leaves the beach at 4:30am and noon daily.

If you are driving, head west along the Carretera Litoral (CA2) to Km. 98.5. Just before the Río El Naranjo bridge, turn left at the sign and follow the dirt road until you reach Barra de Santiago.

Eastern Beaches

The eastern beaches of El Salvador (with the exception of Costa del Sol) are still unexplored and generally lack tourism infrastructure, but as more and more travelers are deciding to visit the east coast, this is slowly changing. The majority of travelers who hit the eastern shores are there for one reason: the waves. Playa Las Flores and nearby Punta Mango are two of the best surf spots in the country, boasting not only world-class surf but also some of the country's best resorts. The surrounding beaches are starting to develop as destinations for those seeking secluded beach getaways. Playa Esterón, east of Las Flores, is quickly gaining popularity for surfers and nonsurfers alike. Close enough to the surf spots, but also with a pristine beach suitable for sunbathing and swimming, this beach has a wider appeal than nearby Las Flores. Also in the east, Isla Montecristo and Golfo de Fonseca are undeveloped and raw, enticing those looking for a more challenging and nontouristy coastal adventure, while Bahía de Jiquilisco offers either community tourism or relaxing resorts.

COSTA DEL SOL

This is the longest stretch of perfect pearl-gray sand beach in the country; and most of it is privately owned. Its accessibility—just a 45-minute drive from the capital—makes Costa del Sol the preferred weekend getaway for San Salvador's upper crust. Most of the paved Bulevar Costa del Sol is lined with tropical-colored adobe walls that enclose beautiful beachfront vacation homes. There are also hotels on the Pacific side of this peninsula, offering tranquil places to relax for the day or spend the night. Costa del Sol is a great day trip for deep-sea fishing, or just to relax on the beach, in a safe, secluded environment.

Recreation

Serious fishers will want to check out Javier Vairo of **Hipocampos Tours** (tel. 7797-1116, hipocampostours@gmail.com). He is passionate about fishing, and by the time you are done with this tour, you will be too. This **deep-sea fishing trip** (8 hours, $130 pp) takes you more than 100 kilometers offshore—in a boat equipped with GPS, radio communication, a stereo, a compass, and a sonar fish finder—where you can try your luck catching mahimahi, sailfish, albacore tuna, marlin, and more.

Aqua Fun (Km. 75, Bulevar Costa del Sol, tel. 7064-6207, info@aquafundelsol.com, 8am-5pm Wed.-Sun.) offers boat trips in the estuary (prices and duration vary by destination) as well as deep-sea fishing trips. Fishing trips cost $500 for up to five people, last the entire day, and include food and beer. You can also rent Jet Skis ($75 per hour).

Fishing is popular around Costa del Sol.

Accommodations

$10-25

Mini Hotel Mila (tel. 2355-7400 or 2338-2074, $10 s, $15 d) is a decent budget hotel located in the small village in the middle of the peninsula. Small cement-block rooms with peach-colored walls, plastic tables, fans, and private cold-water baths are a pretty good deal. The outdoor area is quite cute, with hammocks and a swimming pool. A second-floor restaurant has a great breezy terrace, also with hammocks.

$50-100

Hotel Izalco Cabaña Club (Km. 65.5, Bulevar Costa del Sol, tel. 2524-5406, www. hotelizalco.com, $65 d, includes breakfast with room service) has the most flair out of all the mid-range hotels and surprisingly is the cheapest. The rooms are set around the swimming pool and restaurant area, which also has a cute little bar with colorful cushions on top of tree trunks for seats. The common area has

lots of lounges, chairs, and hammocks underneath the palms, and it is all just steps away from the beach. The rooms are spotless and new with a funky 1970s vibe, beige and brown tones covering the walls and floors, retro designs on the bedspreads, a simple dining table (breakfast can be served in your room), TV, and air-conditioning.

The **Comfort Inn Bahía Dorada** (Km. 75.5, Bulevar Costa de Sol, tel. 2325-7500, $70 pp, includes 3 meals) has all the trappings of a decent mid-range North American hotel. From outside it is a tall, nondescript concrete building; inside there is a lobby with worn leather couches, tile floors, and a front desk with very attentive staff. Small elevators take you to the upper floors where interminable hallways open to pleasant rooms with carpeted floors, generic art, flat-screen TVs, air-conditioning, and a small terrace with a great view. Outside, there is a colorful courtyard with a dining area beside two swimming pools, and the beach is just a short walk away.

Just a short drive farther down past the Comfort Inn is the well-known **Hotel Bahía del Sol** (Km. 78.5, Bulevar Costa del Sol, tel. 2506-4444, $70 pp, includes 3 meals and unlimited alcoholic drinks), which is usually defined as upscale, but is definitely not. However, it is very popular because of the package rate that includes unlimited booze. The hotel comprises small individual buildings, each painted a different cheerful color and each with a simple sitting room with tile floors, wicker furniture, a TV, air-conditioning, a bedroom with unappealing well-worn blankets, and a bath. The "luxury" suites ($100-150) are the much nicer rooms, but still not the definition of luxury. They have larger bedrooms and newer bedspreads, and a lovely common area with couches, a kitchen, and a small jetted tub in the back. You can choose from rooms with either a view of the ocean (although they're not oceanfront) or of the estuary. There is a swimming pool and a lovely dock with a restaurant that looks over the marina. This hotel hosts a popular international fishing competition every year in the first week of November. Teams can enter one of several categories, including blue or black marlin, tuna, or mahimahi fishing. Group fishing trips can also be arranged.

$100-200

Pacific Paradise Hotel (Km. 75, Bulevar Costa del Sol, tel. 2338-0156, $150 d, includes 3 meals and 2 snacks) has sprawling grounds with a large, very clean swimming pool, shaded tables, and beachfront access. Ask for one of the newer rooms, which have clean tile floors, air-conditioning, big double beds with crisp white sheets and colorful pillows, and tropical-style wicker couches and chairs beside large windows that let in the light and have great oceanfront views. The grounds are large and pretty, with tables with individual awnings right in front of the beach, where dinner is served. If you are traveling with kids, it is good to know they also have licensed lifeguards on duty every day for both pool and ocean swimming.

Tortuga Village (Km. 66.5, Bulevar Costa del Sol, tel. 2564-1777 or 2564-1778, www.tortuga-village.com, $165 d) is without a doubt the most beautiful hotel on the coast. Unfortunately, the owners do not have full-time managers here, so you are left to fend for yourself as far as service goes. One of the managers from the restaurant next door will check you in and out, and aside from that, you will be left completely alone. If you are looking for a remote getaway without any disturbances, it just might do. A few bungalows built out of gorgeous teak rise up from stilts that sit in the white sand, with thatched roofs and amazing views. Each *cabaña* has a double bed with crisp white sheets, a TV, air-conditioning, and a view of the ocean. They all sit around a swimming pool with lounging chairs built right into it, and it is all just steps away from the beach, a truly idyllic setting. The beach area has wooden lounging chairs and beds with white cotton awnings, where you can nap in the shade or get a massage, offered with virgin coconut oil and aromatherapy.

There is no hotel restaurant, but one of the best seafood restaurants in the country has set up on the same property: **La Ola Betos's** (tel. 2338-2210, 9am-7pm daily, $10-15) serves cocktails, beer, and large portions of delicious fresh seafood on the beach. They also serve excellent *comida típica* (typical Salvadoran food) breakfasts.

Getting There

From San Salvador's Terminal del Sur, take bus 495 ($1.10, 2.5 hours, runs every 30 minutes). If you are driving from San Salvador, follow the Carretera Litoral (CA2) east to Km. 43 and look for the detour south toward Costa del Sol.

ISLA MONTECRISTO

Where the Río Lempa meets the Pacific Ocean, in the region called Bajo Lempa, this little island (it's actually a peninsula) is a remote getaway with untouched gray sand beaches, mangroves, and a progressive, friendly community. You can walk the length of the island in about 30 minutes, through mangrove forest that eventually opens up to an untouched beach where you can spend a few hours swimming and sunbathing. All tourism activities on the island are organized by the community, who have yet to see many foreigners come to visit, but they are expertly preparing the area for tourism through boat trips, walking tours, and visits to the beach with packed lunches. The island is exceptionally clean compared to the rest of the country, and the local community is interested in sustainable, community-based tourism. Quiet and sparsely populated, this is a wonderful place to visit to feel like you are far away from civilization—it's pretty much guaranteed you will be the only visitor here. This is best done as an overnight trip.

Accommodations

Very basic *cabañas* are available at **Hostal Montecristo** (right in front of where the *lancha* lets you off, tel. 7470-9745, $25 d). Each wooden *cabaña* has a bed and a fan, and a small porch with a hammock overlooking the river. From here you can arrange boat trips around the island and walking tours to a cashew plantation and onward to the other side of the island. They run a small restaurant serving fresh daily plates with some vegetarian options.

Getting There

From San Salvador, take bus 302 from Terminal del Sur toward Usulután ($1.70, 2.5 hours, runs every 30 minutes) and tell the driver to let you off at San Nicolás Lempa near the Texaco station. Buses leave from there for the 13-kilometer trip to La Pita daily at 5am and 2pm, and return at 5:30am and 3pm. The journey takes 40 minutes and costs $0.70. From La Pita, you can catch a *lancha* to the island. It only takes about 10 minutes and should cost around $25; however, the cost varies depending on how many people there are. Alternatively, you can call ahead to the hostel on the island and arrange for a pickup from Geovanny Reyes (tel. 7470-9745).

BAHÍA DE JIQUILISCO

Called Xiriualtique (Bay of Stars) by the local indigenous people because of the way its tranquil waters reflected the stars at night, Bahía de Jiquilisco consists of more than 27 islands that are undeveloped, peaceful, and teeming with biodiversity. In recent years it has also been discovered as one of the most important turtle nesting areas in the world. This complex of inlets, intertidal wetlands, and beaches has untouched natural beauty and provides critical habitat for shellfish, crabs, migratory birds, and a variety of fish.

The people who live on these islands were forced from their coastal towns during the civil war and returned in the 1990s to rebuild homes in the largest remaining mangrove forest in Central America. The islands are now homes to these communities, and to this day they depend on the mangroves for survival, as the trees protect them from inclement weather, and crabbing and fishing help them make their living. The area consists of the mainland Península San Juan del Gozo, the mangroves, and various small islands that dot the bay.

The bay is an interesting destination for nature lovers and environmentalists, with boat tours through the mangroves, fishing, bird-watching, and amazing volunteer programs that allow visitors to have hands-on experience in saving the hawksbill turtle population. There have been recent proposals for the

The shores of Isla Montecristo are remote and pristine.

development of the area, which would mean the arrival of large high-end resorts. This could potentially displace many of the communities on the bay and undoubtedly affect the natural habitat. By supporting local tour groups and conservation efforts, you can help convince the government of El Salvador that tourism can work in tandem with environmental efforts, instead of against them.

The **Península San Juan del Gozo** is the mainland side of the bay and where you will arrive by road. The peninsula has two main towns, **Isla Méndez** and **Corral de Mulas,** both of which are launching points for exploring the bay by boat. Local community group **Adesco** (tel. 7727-3453) works out of Isla Méndez and can provide boat tours through the mangroves ($35, approx. 2 hours). Another excellent option for getting around the bay is to arrange a boat with one of the hotels. Hotel y Restaurante Solisal is highly recommended.

Recreation

To organize activities around the bay, your best bet is to go through one of the hotels. **Hotel y Restaurante Solisal** (Península San Juan del Gozo, tel. 2243-2590 or 7890-2638, www.hotelsolisal.com) provides excellent bilingual service. They can arrange different tours around the bay, including kayaking ($5 per hour), horseback riding on the beach ($15 per hour), fishing in the bay or the ocean (price vary by duration and destination), and boat trips to the other islands and beaches ($50-100).

If you are interested in releasing baby turtles or any kind of volunteer opportunities working with Hawksbill turtles in the bay, the **Eastern Pacific Hawksbill Initiative** (ICAPO, Caserío La Pirraya, Isla San Sebastián, tel. 7697-1551, www.hawksbill.org) is an excellent organization that is spearheading the turtle preservation project here. If you speak Spanish and are interested in low-impact tourism such as fishing or birdwatching tours, ICAPO can help connect you with excellent local guides. Alternatively you can contact **Green Trips** (tel. 7943-5230, greentripselsalvador@gmail.com), based in San Salvador, a company that provides top-notch birding tours ($200-300 per day) with bilingual guides.

For more adventure tourism around the bay, contact **Suchitoto Adventure Outfitters** (Calle San Martín, 4B Plaza Central, tel. 7921-4216, www.suchitotoadventureoutfitters.com) for excellent kayaking trips (full-day trip $150 pp, minimum 3 people, includes lunch).

Accommodations
$10-25

Hostal Pirryata (La Isla Pirryata, tel. 7555-3149) is a basic hostel with wooden *cabañas* starting at $20 d. Each has two double beds, a fan, and not much else; but you are not here for the rooms. The pier takes you out to a large deck with a five-star view of the bay with the beautiful backdrop of the eastern volcanoes of Usulután and San Vicente. Here you will find two more *cabañas,* which sit on stilts. They have the same rustic setup but with windows that open up to that incredible view. There are shared composting toilets and showers. The hostel is partnered with ICAPO and can arrange boat tours, fishing and birding trips, and turtle releases. For those who want a more involved turtle volunteer program, this is also the hostel where you stay and eat; the food at the hostel's restaurant is excellent.

★ **Hotel y Restaurante Solisal** (Península de San Juan del Gozo, tel. 2243-2590 or 7890-2638, www.hotelsolisal.com, $40 d) has simple wooden *cabañas* right on the water with a gorgeous view of the estuary and volcanoes, a swimming pool, hammocks, and large grassy grounds. Rooms are simple, with private baths and air-conditioning. There is also a restaurant serving excellent food. Kayaks are available for rent and boat trips around the bay can be arranged. The bilingual owner is extremely helpful.

Puerto Barillas (tel. 2263-3620 or 2675-1135, www.puertobarillas.com, treehouse $118 for up to 6 people, two-story apartment $238 for up to 8 people) offers sprawling grounds and beautiful apartments for groups. Set right on the bay, this hotel with exceptional service doubles as a marina, complete with immigration officials available to process your documents if you are arriving by water from another country. The treehouse and two-story apartments, set back from the bay deep in the lush greenery of coconut palms and towering bamboo, have simple organic design and are gorgeous. Rooms are painted in neutral greens, brown, and beige to complement the trees and plants outside. Each apartment also has a well-stocked kitchen, a TV, air-conditioning, a barbecue, and a large terrace with sliding glass doors. The grounds also boast a swimming pool, a small shady restaurant with a view of the bay, a convenience store, horses (horseback riding tours also available), and a wild monkey sanctuary. Excellent boat tours to the different islands can also be arranged; just ask at the front desk (prices vary depending on destination). Bring mosquito repellent; you will need it here.

Food

A series of four floating restaurants serve up seafood and snacks at **Restaurantes Flotantes** (in front of Corral de Mulas, tel. 2434-2613 or 7714-3792, 8am-5pm daily, $4-10). Hard to miss, these electric-blue restaurants are a development project launched with the help of the NGO Action Aid. Set in the middle of the estuary, you can only arrive by boat. A boat from Corral de Mulas should cost approximately $10 round-trip. The food at all four restaurants is the same, and it's all good, so it doesn't really matter which one you choose.

Hostal Pirryata (La Isla Pirryata, tel. 7555-3149, 8am-5pm daily, $4-6) has a restaurant in the back of the hostel, but feel free to ask them to pull a table out to the dock, where you can dine with a jaw-dropping view of the bay and the volcanoes. Here, the local women serve up excellent wholesome food. Just ask what the plate of the day is: If you are lucky, it will be freshly caught fish, served alongside a *chirmol* (tomato salsa) with fresh herbs, rice,

and delicious tortillas. At $5 a plate, this is one of the best deals in the country.

Getting There

From San Salvador, take bus 302 from Terminal del Sur toward Usulután ($1.70, 2.5 hours, runs every 30 minutes). In Usulután, from 4 Calle Oriente or the small de facto bus lot east of town, across the street from Despensa de Don Juan supermarket, catch bus 363 ($0.50, 1 hour, runs every 10 minutes 4:30am-5:30pm) to Puerto El Triunfo. From El Triunfo, take the boat to Isla Méndez. Alternatively you can hitch a ride with the *pickacheros* at the Puente de Oro bridge at the Río Lempa; they leave every half an hour or so until 5pm. The ride should cost $1.

PLAYAS EL CUCO, ESTERÓN, AND LAS FLORES

Playa El Cuco proper does not offer much for visitors other than seafood and beer in one of the many shacks that line the beach. The real draw of El Cuco is the two beaches on either side of this tiny fishing village. Just west is Playa Las Flores, a gorgeous gray-sand beach with towering rock cliffs and one of the best surf breaks in the country. Just east of El Cuco is the beautiful and remote Playa Esterón.

Playa El Cuco

If you do decide to stay in El Cuco, the best bet is **Azul Surf Club** (1.5 kilometers east of El Cuco, tel. 2612-6820 or 7132-2175, www.azulsurfclub.com, $75 s, $85 d). Hotel Azul provides exceptional service for surfer and nonsurfers alike in a hidden tropical paradise just minutes from the fishing village of El Cuco. No request is too onerous for the attentive staff, and owner Lissette Pérez will go out of her way to make your stay memorable, from making sure surfers catch the waves when the conditions are ideal to providing special gluten-free or vegetarian meals in the restaurant. The rooms are simple but lovely with strong air-conditioning, hot water, and flat-screen TVs. A large terrace faces the palms

Turtles in El Salvador

"Real men don't eat turtle eggs" reads the back of the T-shirt of the man standing in front of me. The slogan is showing up more and more often, and this campaign is slowly gaining momentum in El Salvador, a country where in the recent past it was common to hear men order a side of turtle eggs to go with their beer. The belief that the eggs have aphrodisiac powers is entrenched in machismo culture and has contributed to the sharp decline in natural turtle populations over the years. Although the exact origin of the belief is difficult to pinpoint, many people say it has to do with the fact that turtles mate for 4-6 hours at a time. Some men believe that eating the eggs might imbue them with similar powers of endurance. Science says this is impossible. The nutritional and energy content of a turtle egg is half that of a chicken egg, and there is no proof that turtle eggs have any aphrodisiac attributes; but cultural habits can be hard to break, and the placebo effect is very powerful.

Up until 2009 it was common to find turtle eggs listed on the menus of many restaurants in El Salvador. It is now officially illegal, but turtle eggs are still sold on the black market, and if you ask in some restaurants, sadly, they may just oblige. Due to the demand for turtle eggs, many people trying to boost their income will scour the beach looking for eggs so that they can sell them. Some hotels along the coast will buy the eggs at a marginally higher price than the market pays, so that the turtles can be saved, and tourists can have the experience of releasing the babies once they hatch. If you ask just about any hotel along the Salvadoran coast about releasing baby turtles, they can arrange it for you. However good their intentions may be, the fact is not all of these turtles are being released properly, and the reason has to do with the timing of the release. Right after turtles hatch, they absorb a yolk sac that provides them with just enough energy to make it from their nest on the beach to the ocean. If the release does not happen within these first few days after hatching, their chances of survival drop dramatically. Considering that only 1 out of every 1,000 hatchlings will make it to adulthood, these vulnerable little creatures need all the help they can get.

There are four types of turtles found in El Salvador: olive ridley, green, leatherback, and hawksbill. Of these, hawksbills are the most threatened, and are in fact the most threatened turtle species in the world. Part of this is due to the poaching of their beautiful shells for jewelry, eyewear frames, and other ornamental objects. You will know the hawksbill shell by its distinctive translucent dark and light brown design.

and flowers of the lovely grounds, and a pool with a swim-up bar makes the perfect way to end a day of surfing. Most people who stay here do surf packages; details can be found on the website. Azul also runs a nonprofit project that helps provide education to local children.

Playa Esterón

Just east of El Cuco is Playa Esterón, a clean, wide white-sand beach good for swimming, with an active turtle nesting area and a great hotel called **La Tortuga Verde Hotel** (10 kilometers east of Playa Cuco, tel. 7774-4855, www.latortugaverde.com, $10 pp dorm, $35 d). To get to Playa Esterón, you can take a taxi in El Cuco (free of charge because the hotel covers the cost), about 10 kilometers farther east, to the beautiful and somewhat remote

hotel, where a long piece of beachfront property, complete with a swimming pool, yoga *shala,* and a coconut nursery dares you to try not to relax. A stone pathway leads to the lovely dorm, built of stone and wood, with screens instead of walls, creating a great cross breeze. Dorm rooms have double beds, brand-new floor fans, and ambient lighting. Private rooms are simple but pretty with beach decorations such as conch shells, fans, and tropical art. They have screened in porches with hammocks, lounging chairs, and free drinking water. American owner Tom has been living and surfing in El Salvador for many years and is an excellent source of information about surfing, border crossings, and any other practicalities. He can arrange border crossings into Nicaragua by boat. La Tortuga

A child releases a baby turtle along the Salvadoran coast.

Fortunately, there are organizations working to curb the illegal market and to conserve the threatened turtle populations. **Eastern Pacific Hawksbill Initiative (ICAPO)** (Caserío La Pirraya, Isla San Sebastián, tel. 7697-1551, www.hawksbill.org) has recently discovered that Bahía de Jiquilisco is one of two areas in the world where a significant population of hawksbill turtles has been found, and local communities are now working hard to protect this endangered species.

If you are interested in releasing baby turtles, and want to be sure that you get an experience that is ecologically sound and in the best interest of the turtles, you should contact ICAPO. They can also give you hands-on volunteer opportunities helping to protect the hawksbill turtle in Bahía de Jiquilisco, and remember: Real men don't eat turtle eggs (rumor has it they taste vile anyway).

Verde is the perfect place to kick back and do sweet nothing, but there is also plenty to do if you are seeking a little adventure. Boat rides to the nearby islands of Fonseca, trips to Volcán Conchagua, and other activities can easily be arranged. Surfers can also often catch an early morning ride to Las Flores with Tom.

Playa Las Flores

West of El Cuco is Playa Las Flores, one of the most revered surf spots in the country, offering world-class waves. Las Flores is a very fast, machine-like right that can run up to 300 meters long. Less experienced surfers may be able to enjoy surfing Las Flores when the waves are moderate, but when the swell is big at low tide, Las Flores is a freight train suitable for experienced surfers only. Nearby **Punta Mango**

(accessible only by boat or 4WD vehicle), with the fastest, strongest waves in the area, is a powerful point break that is for experienced surfers only. This right point breaks over sand or large smooth rocks, depending on the tide. At its best, it is a double overhead open barrel from start to finish, and because of its relative isolation, less crowded than the other popular surf spots in the country.

Playa Las Flores is for surfers, and all of the hotels here are geared toward surf tours.

Accommodations

At the far west end of the beach are two budget options. **Hotel Clemen** (tel. 7442-4472, $25 s, $35 d) and **Hotel Natalie** (tel. 7724-0153, $25 s, $30 d) are essentially the same setup, with small cinderblock rooms with nothing more than a bed and a floor fan. The rooms are located right on the beach, and budget surfers looking for no-frills accommodations head here. Hotel Clemen also has a small restaurant serving very good food.

Heading west from El Cuco, the first hotel you will see on the road to Las Flores is **Vista Las Olas Surf Resort** (Calle Conchagüita, tel. 7215-2951 or 2619-9053, www.vistalasolas.com, $96 s, $130 d, includes breakfast), a beautiful brand-new whitewashed home with beachfront rooms. Lounge chairs sit beside a small infinity pool that looks out to the ocean, and right behind the pool is an indoor icy-cold (you will want it around here) restaurant and lounge area with a large flat-screen TV and couches. The rooms are beautiful, boasting a fresh organic style with lots of windows letting in the natural warmth and air-conditioning to keep you cool. Tweed furniture and dark, gleaming wood bed frames and ceiling fans are complemented by muted orange, brown, and green walls decorated with modern art. The restaurant serves excellent seafood and boasts a quiet, intimate vibe. Relax in the outdoor jetted pool after a day of surfing as you gaze at the stars and hear the crash of the waves.

Next up is **Hotel Miraflores** (Calle Conchagüita, 500 meters from El Cuco, tel. 2252-7822, www.elhotelmiraflores.com, $60 d), long a popular choice for surfers looking for a comfortable mid-range option. Miraflores has a casual atmosphere, with friendly staff, lots of green space with hammocks, and an outdoor restaurant with a fabulous views of the waves. The rooms are simple and clean, though a little cramped for two people. They have muted brown walls, cool tile floors, TVs, and air-conditioning. To get to the beach from the hotel, you need to walk down a beautiful staircase that zigzags to the shore, offering inspiring views of the waves rolling in. It's not so bad on the way down but can be challenging returning after a surfing session. Reward yourself with a massage and meal from the restaurant, offering seafood, burgers, and salads, or alternatively take the short walk into town to eat at one of the cheaper seafood restaurants that line El Cuco. Miraflores offers great tours around the area, like kayaking and stand-up paddleboarding in Bahía de Jiquilisco. They also offer transportation to and from the nearby surf spot Punta Mango.

One of the best hotels in the country is ★ **Las Flores Surf Resort** (Calle Conchagüita, tel. 2684-4444, ventas@lasfloresresort.com, $100-150 d depending on the season), which is generally booked as a package deal through **Wavehunters** (www.wavehunters.com). It is possible to make a booking independently, but whether or not you can get a room will depend on luck; during the high season, the place gets packed with repeat clients. The rooms here are gorgeous, integrating sleek, modern design into the natural environment. Marked by muted colors, clean lines, and organic material such a wood, wicker, and marble, all the suites have large windows and some have small decks with views of the ocean. The grounds are just as pretty, with a swimming pool, an outdoor restaurant, and the surf break just a short walk away. Personalized packages can include yoga classes, boat trips, surf lessons, and cultural tours.

Getting There

Getting to Playas El Cuco, Esterón, and Las Flores is straightforward, though a little time-consuming. From San Salvador, take bus 301 ($1.25-5, depending on the bus, 2-5 hours, runs every 15 minutes) to San Miguel from Terminal de Oriente (Alameda Juan Pablo II). From San Miguel, take bus 320 ($1, 1.5 hours, runs every half hour). Once in El Cuco, you can take a taxi to Playa Esterón. It costs $5, but if you stay at La Tortuga Verde, they will cover the cost when you arrive. To get to Las Flores, you will need to walk 2-3 kilometers west of El Cuco, or take a taxi that should cost $2-4 depending, on where you are staying.

PLAYA MACULIS

This relatively unknown beach is the antithesis to the sprawling homes and hotels of Costa del Sol. Playa Maculis is a gorgeous untouched beach with beige sand and gentle waves, making it perfect for swimming, sunbathing, and relaxing.

There is only one place to stay on the beach, a house that can be rented: The charming **Los Caracoles** (Km. 175, Carretera Litoral, tel. 2335-1200 or 7786-9949, $250 for the house, sleeps up to 8 people) is a four-bedroom house right on the beach. Bedrooms are simple but pretty, with sliding glass doors, comfortable beds with mosquito nets, and private baths. It has air-conditioning, a fully equipped open-air kitchen, a beautiful living room with a concrete floor inlaid with shells, and a large wooden deck with a round plunge pool and lounge chairs that face the beach, which you will have all to yourself.

Getting to Playa Maculis is very difficult on public transportation. If you plan to go, contact the owners of Los Carocoles to arrange transportation.

LA UNIÓN

The sweltering, less-than-savory port town of La Unión is definitely not a destination in its own right, but since it is the gateway town to the Golfo de Fonseca, you may end up needing to spend a night there if you miss the *lancha*.

The only appropriate lodging option in town is the **Comfort Inn La Unión** (Km. 2.8, Calle a Playitas, Carretera Panamericana, tel. 2665-6565, www.comfortinn.com, $69 s, $81 d). This upscale business hotel is a very comfortable stay, with all the amenities you need, including a small business center with Internet access, a gym, a swimming pool, and a bar. The location is beautiful, overlooking the gulf and the San Vicente and Usulután volcanoes, and the restaurant is the perfect place to enjoy it, with massive windows offering the perfect vista. The rooms are sleek and spotless with modern design, including flat-screen TVs, air-conditioning, and Wi-Fi. The hotel is located near the dock where you take the *lancha* to the islands.

To get to La Unión, take bus 324 ($1, 1.25 hours, runs every 15 minutes) from San Miguel.

GOLFO DE FONSECA

If you have made it to the Golfo de Fonseca, you have reached the country's eastern edge, where a collection of small islands are shared among Honduras, Nicaragua, and El Salvador. From the sweaty, unrefined port town of La Unión, you can catch a boat to the islands.

Isla Meanguera is the most developed island and the one most travelers visit. The City of Small Jade, as it was originally named, was a Lenca settlement, and there are still vestiges of those indigenous people around the island. This island has almost no tourism infrastructure aside from a beautiful hotel with unparalleled views of the gulf.

Hotel La Joya del Golfo (tel. 2648-0072, www.hotellajoyadelgolfo.com, $79 s or d) is an elegant whitewashed hotel that sits gracefully at the edge of the water, with a beautiful dock and an excellent restaurant. The rooms are gorgeous, with queen beds and towering antique wooden bedposts, cool tile floors, and sliding glass doors that lead to little porches with postcard-perfect views. All rooms have cable TV, Wi-Fi, air-conditioning, and pretty private baths with both bathtubs and showers. They also offer guided walking tours, fishing trips, and kayaks that are free for guests to use.

The only other option for sleeping on the island is with one of the *lancha* drivers, José Vicente Osorio (tel. 2648-0083; ask for him at the dock when you arrive) who rents a room in his house for $20. The room is right by the water's edge, also with spectacular views of the gulf and neighboring islands Conchagüita and Zacatillo. It's incredibly peaceful. The room has a fan, one single bed, and a private bath. You can sleep with the window open and be lulled to sleep by the lapping of the waves against the dock.

On the other side of the island is a pretty beach, **Playa el Majahual.** It's about a 40-minute walk from the hotel or a $20 *lancha* ride. There is one family that lives on the beach and will allow you to set up a tent and camp. You can ask the family to cook you freshly caught fish, but bring anything else you may want, because this really is a stranded-on-a-remote-island experience—the only thing you can buy here is coconut water and soda. If you want food prepared, it's best to call ahead (Ismail, tel. 7434-4814).

Trips to Isla Meanguera can be done on your own, but if you would like to go with a tour company, **La Ruta del Zapamiche** (tel. 2228-1525, www.larutadelzapamiche.com), based in Santa Tecla, does a great overnight tour to the island; prices depend on the kind of tour and the number of people.

Getting There

Public *lanchas* heading to Isla Meanguera leave from the dock in La Unión daily at around 10:30am. The time varies, so it's best to be there about 10am or even earlier to make sure you catch the boat, because there is only one trip per day. The boat ride costs $3 and takes about 45 minutes. If you decide to stay at Hotel La Joya del Golfo, contact them beforehand and they can arrange a pickup from the dock once you arrive. Coming back from the island to La Unión, there is only one trip per day; it leaves at 5:30am. The length of the island can be walked in about an hour.

Northern and Eastern El Salvador

Look for ★ to find recommended sights, activities, dining, and lodging.

Highlights

© AVALON TRAVEL

★ **Río Palancapa Waterfall Trek:** This trek in Suchitoto provides lots of slippery aerial adventure for those who like a little adrenaline with their hiking (page 144).

★ **Cerro El Pital:** Follow the cool cloud forest of towering pines and wildflowers to the highest point in El Salvador, where the temperature dips low enough for you to enjoy hot chocolate by a fire (page 155).

★ **Museo de la Revolución Salvadoreña:** Learn about El Salvador's civil war from ex-guerrillas who run this museum housing old FMLN radio equipment, solidarity posters, weapons, newspaper articles, photographs, and testimonials from survivors of the armed conflict (page 166).

★ **El Mozote Memorial:** The tiny town of El Mozote is the site of the largest known massacre in Central America, made all the more poignant because of the testimonial of sole survivor Rufina Amaya Mírquez, who witnessed it all. This is a must-see for those who want to pay their respects to the civilians who lost their lives during the civil war (page 167).

★ **Cueva del Espíritu Santo:** It may be a bit off the beaten track, but the journey is a small price to pay for the opportunity to take in some of Mesoamerica's oldest known prehistoric rock art on the walls of this mysterious cave in the town of Corinto (page 173).

Northern and eastern El Salvador remain largely untrodden, especially the eastern parts of the country, where heavy fighting took place during the civil war. These remote areas may take a little more effort to get to, but they are the gateway to authentic Salvadoran culture, uncorrupted by tourism and relatively unfazed by American influence.

Just 45 kilometers northeast of San Salvador, the cobblestone streets of **Suchitoto** offer a quiet, quaint getaway where time seems to stand still. Set against the backdrop of spectacular **Lago Suchitlán,** this balmy colonial town offers boutique hotels, bird-watching, world-class art, and waterfalls. Nearby **Volcán Guazapa** and **Cinquera** are your first stops for civil war tourism, with hikes and horseback riding through former guerrilla camps, and firsthand accounts of what life was like for people in these communities during the armed conflict. The archaeological site of **Cihuatán** is the largest pre-Hispanic ruins in El Salvador, with new discoveries about its inhabitants continually being made.

Just north of Suchitoto is the whimsical **La Palma,** with brightly painted murals all over town. La Palma makes a wonderful day trip and is also the gateway to the cool cloud forests of El Salvador's highlands, where cozy cabins are nestled between expansive fields of fruits, flowers, and vegetables.

Continue east to **Alegría,** where the fresh air and friendly locals make for a relaxing retreat. More adventurous travelers can keep going into the "Wild East," where hiking trails, waterfalls, rivers, and mountains are as abundant as the stories that were created around them. The green pine forests of Morazán (the department where **Perquín** and **El Mozote** are located) were known as the guerrilla red zone during the civil war, and it was here that the rebels constantly escaped army attacks by hiding in the mountains and thick forests throughout the region. Today, these same outdoor hideaways serve as uncharted territory for adventurous history buffs and nature lovers alike. The Museo de la Revolución Salvadoreña in Perquín and the

Previous: Suchitoto; boats on Lago Suchitlán. **Above:** hiking up Volcán Guazapa.

Northern and Eastern El Salvador

© AVALON TRAVEL

PACIFIC OCEAN

Playa Costa Del Sol

Isla Montecristo

Bahía de Jiquilisco

COMALAPA INTERNATIONAL AIRPORT

Parque Nacional Walter Thilo Deininger

Santa Tecla

Panchimalco

SAN SALVADOR

Volcán San Salvador

Lago de Coatepeque

Lago de Ilopango

Cerro de Guazapa

Aguilares

Suchitoto

Lago Suchitlán

RÍO PALANCAPA WATERFALL TREK

Cojutepeque

Cinquera

Ilobasco

San Sebastián

Chalatenango

San Ignacio

La Palma

Río Chiquito

CERRO EL PITAL

EL NORTE

CARRETERA TRONCAL

CARRETERA PANAMERICAN

CARRETERA LITORAL

EL SALVADOR

Bosque La Joya

Volcán de San Vicente

Berlín

Volcán de Tecapa

Alegría

Santiago de María

Volcán de Usulután

El Triunfo

Usulután

San Miguel

Volcán Chaparrastique

Guatajiagua

San Francisco de Gotera

Cacaopera

Corinto

Río Torola

ESPÍRITU SANTO

CUEVA DEL

EL MOZOTE MEMORIAL

Jocoaitique

Perquín

Cerro Pericón

MUSEO DE LA REVOLUCIÓN SALVADOREÑA

Arambala

Meanguera

San Fernando

Río Negro

Llano el Muerto and Bañadero del Diablo

HONDURAS

Laguna de Olomega

La Unión

Volcán de Conchagua

Isla Zacatillo

Isla Conchaguita

Isla Meanguera

20 km

20 mi

El Mozote Memorial officially document the brutal history of the region, while conversations with local people reveal more personal and painful memories.

Eastern El Salvador's ancient history is often overshadowed by this recent past, but it is no less arresting in its own right. East of **San Miguel** in the towns of **Corinto** and **Cacaopera,** numerous caves with prehistoric rock art and petroglyphs reveal a fascinating glimpse into the ancient cultures of Mesoamerica. **Cueva del Espíritu Santo** is one of the most important archaeological sites in Central America, where 8,000-year-old cave paintings await the intrepid traveler—and the best part is that it is just far enough off the beaten path that you will likely have this archaeological marvel all to yourself.

PLANNING YOUR TIME

This part of the country should be split into two parts. A few days is a good amount of time to explore **Northern El Salvador,** using **Suchitoto** as a base. Give yourself two days for Suchitoto and the vicinity: one day in the town and one day outside in **Cinquera** or the archaeological site of **Cihuatán.** Suchitoto is the center of this region, and to reach most other nearby destinations, it is necessary to backtrack a little to the town of Aguilares. A fast and frequent bus leaves Suchitoto daily. Alternatively, you can take the ferry across Lago Suchitlán to the town of San Francisco Lempa, where frequent buses leave

for the business and transportation hub of Chalatenango. However you get here, two days is enough time to leisurely enjoy the highlands and **La Palma.**

Eastern El Salvador takes a bit more time and planning. In the east, the transportation hub is **San Miguel,** with several buses running directly to **Perquín** daily, where there are the best options for accommodations. A few days should be set aside to explore this area. From Perquín it is easy to make day trips to **El Mozote** and **Río Sapo.** The indigenous town of **Cacaopera** and the rock art in **Corinto** are a bit more of a long haul. If you get an early start, it is possible to visit them both in one day, stopping in Cacaopera first and then continuing on to Corinto. Most people then end up spending the night in Corinto. It all depends on the buses and how long you want to stay at the sights. If you are staying in Perquín, you can catch buses going to both towns from the small town of San Francisco de Gotera, which is about a 45-minute bus ride from Perquín. Otherwise, you can catch buses from the terminal in San Miguel.

Alegría can be done as a trip on its own, preferably on the weekend, when vendors set up in the *parque central.* One day is enough time to hike to the lake and enjoy strolling around the small town. The trip from San Salvador to Alegría is straightforward, with buses leaving frequently from Terminal Oriente. Alegría could also be a stopover on your way to or back from Perquín.

Suchitoto

Sprinkled with boutique hotels, NGOs and art galleries inside charming old colonial homes, Suchitoto is El Salvador's burgeoning cultural touchstone. Despite the predictions from trailblazing travelers looking for the next hot spot, Suchitoto has yet to be overrun by tourists, and the relative lack of travelers only adds to its charm. Pretty and progressive, full of cute cafés and terra-cotta roofs, Suchitoto

draws people mostly for a few days of relaxation; some take on volunteer projects and stay for a few months. One of the few towns in the region that was able to avoid total destruction during the war, Suchitoto's cobblestone streets and crumbling homes present the El Salvador of yesteryear, and the people who live here share a peaceful warmth of character that makes it easy to pass a few languid days hanging around the town square, chatting with locals.

Set against the beautiful backdrop of **Lago Suchitlán,** the largest artificial lake in the country, Suchitoto also offers excellent birdwatching opportunities and boat tours. The surrounding area provides great day trips, including the archaeological site of **Cihuatán,** the largest ruins in El Salvador; **Volcán Guazapa,** where you can hike through former guerrilla camps; and **Cinquera,** the tiny ex-FMLN stronghold that now has a wonderful eco-park run by ex-guerrillas who provide guided hikes through the subtropical rainforest.

SIGHTS
Iglesia Santa Lucia

Constructed in 1857, **Iglesia Santa Lucia** (1 Av. Norte, on the east side of *parque central,* tel. 2335-1049, 7am-7pm daily) is impossible to miss. Standing where one of El Salvador's first religious sites was built around AD 1000, when Suchitoto was a Mayan town, Santa Lucia's whitewashed neoclassical facade has six towering columns and two bell towers that are put to good use. The interior of the church is lined with hollow wooden pillars and an arched ceiling, showing a baroque style with rococo influence. Today, the church is the iconic image that is most associated with colonial El Salvador. Throughout the day, the bells can be heard chiming, and at any given time you are likely to find at least a few people sitting inside. A well-attended mass takes place at 6pm every evening.

Casa Museo de los Recuerdos Alejandro Cotto

Suchitoto's most famous patron of the arts, filmmaker Alejandro Cotto was also one of the leading forces behind saving the town of Suchitoto from total destruction during the civil war. Legend has it that one time, Cotto was warned by a friend in San Salvador that the military was coming to attack the town. Cotto was advised to get out as soon as possible, but instead he cleverly called in all the international ambassadors he could find for a dinner party at his home, averting the attack and single-handedly preserving the town. The truth is, according to the aging Cotto (now in his 90s), it wasn't one specific phone call or dinner party but rather a sequence of strategic moves that saved Suchitoto.

Today, his home doubles as a museum. A visit to **Casa Museo de los Recuerdos Alejandro Cotto** (Final Av. 15 Septiembre, beside the turnoff to Puerto San Juan, no phone, hours vary, donation) shows just how well-connected and respected he was, and the idea that he could have so much influence over a country begins to look plausible. On display are a lifetime of collectibles from around the world, including incredible art created by famous Mexican artist Ignacio Barrios, antique furniture (including former Cuban dictator Fulgencio Batista's sofa), a collection of photos (including personally autographed photos from King Carlos of Spain as well as Pope John Paul II), a small chapel full of statues of saints, and an entire room dedicated to his diplomatic awards. The grounds are beautiful, with a large garden that leads out to a top-notch view of the lake. Whether or not the museum is open is unpredictable; just knock on the door and try your luck.

Centro Arte para la Paz

Centro Arte para la Paz (2 Calle Poniente 5, tel. 2335-1080, www.capsuchitoto.org, 9am-6pm daily, free) is located in an old Dominican convent, which operated from 1917 until 1980, when the civil war forced the nuns to abandon their posts. The convent is now open again and functions as a nonprofit community center and museum where local kids come to learn art, music, dancing, and more. The old building has a huge courtyard surrounded by beautiful high-ceilinged rooms where you might hear the sounds of children giggling and learning how to play the piano, or the gentle voice of a yoga teacher leading a class. The museum has a very good film that covers civil war history in the area (about one hour long, ask for a screening), way. The souvenirs and food available are nothing special, but the view is lovely, and it is a great spot to have a cold drink and pass an hour or two.

Lago Suchitlán is popular for boat tours, which can be arranged at the port. A 45-minute tour including a visit to the lovely **Isla de Ermitaño,** which offers silence, solitude, and gorgeous views of the lake, costs $25. An hour-long tour with a visit to **La Isla de las Pájaros,** which, as the name suggests, is teeming with waterbirds, costs $30. There is also a ferry that crosses the lake several times throughout the day to the neighboring town San Francisco Lempa ($4). From there it is possible to catch a bus to the transportation hub of Chalatenango, where it is possible to take a bus to the highlands.

SPORTS AND RECREATION
Cascada Los Tercios

Cascada Los Tercios is a 1.5-kilometer walk south of town and easy to do on your own. This unique 10-meter-tall wall of hexagonal-shaped basalt rock was formed by volcanic activity. Basalt, also found on the surface of the moon, is packed with tiny quartz crystals that sparkle in the sun, creating a rather otherworldly effect. This is an excellent spot to relax for a while and cool off under the rushing waterfall, which is active June to November, but even when the waterfall is dry, it's worth a visit to admire the distinctive geometric rocks.

To get to Los Tercios, walk south on the road in front of Iglesia Santa Lucia until it intersects with the main road at the entrance of town. Turn left and follow the dirt road for about half an hour until you see a sign on the left side. Enter through the gate and continue down the hill to the waterfall. Usually there are no safety concerns doing the walk on your own, but things can change within a matter of weeks, so ask around beforehand. If you do not want to walk alone, the local tourist police will take travelers, usually only once a day, and the service must be requested the day

Cascada Los Tercios

and the center also often has art exhibits or film screenings. If you are interested in volunteer opportunities in the area, a good contact is Peggy O'Neil, who works at the center and has been in Suchitoto since 1987. She can coordinate volunteer opportunities and is very well connected with nonprofit organizations in the area.

Lago Suchitlán

This 135-square-kilometer lake—the largest artificial lake in the country—is a birdwatchers' haven and a spectacular backdrop to Suchitoto. Embalse Cerrón Grande, as the lake is formally called, was built in 1973, on top of what was once known as Valley of the Almonds; it now provides electricity to nearly 500,000 people in El Salvador.

Located on the edge of Lago Suchitlán is **Puerto Turístico San Juan** (tel. 2335-1782, turismosuchitoto@gmail.com, $0.50), a collection of vendors and eateries. It is about half an hour's walk north of the center of Suchitoto, offering spectacular views on the before. They will wait for you at the waterfall and escort you back to town.

★ Río Palancapa Waterfall Trek

The Río Palancapa Waterfall Trek is the most exciting excursion you can take in Suchitoto. Join adventure tour guide René Barbón of **Suchitoto Adventure Outfitters** (Calle San Martín 4B, Plaza Central, tel. 7921-4216, www.suchitotoadventureoutfitters.com) on a three-hour hike ($15 pp, minimum 3 people) along the Río Palancapa, trekking through cornfields, forest, and finally zigzagging across the river, jumping from rock to rock, until you reach a beautiful 25-meter waterfall in a remote location. Take some time to swim and relax under the rushing water before moving on to the really fun part. The next two waterfalls are jumpable, one at 7 meters (called the "baby jump") and one at 11 meters (the jump-at-your-own-risk one). Don't worry, if suddenly fear gets the better of you, there is a walking route that will take you down instead. Either way, it's a great trek, and the expert tour guides know the terrain like the backs of their hands, pointing out birds, flora, and fauna on the way. Don't forget to bring sunscreen, a hat, a bathing suit, and a change of clothes.

Volcán Guazapa

Eleven kilometers southeast of Suchitoto is the peaceful inactive volcano with the silhouette of a reclining woman, Volcán Guazapa. This was a guerrilla stronghold during the war—in no small part as a result of the construction of Lago Suchitlán. When the dam was built in 1973, the fertile valley that the lake submerged put many farmers out of work. Frustrated and disenfranchised, many of them joined the FMLN and moved to Guazapa, an extremely strategic location, as it was very close to San Salvador. This is where many attacks on the capital were planned and then carried out, with the guerrillas quickly retreating back to the safety of Guazapa. They knew the volcano well, giving them a crucial advantage over the military, who frequently bombed the area.

Today, ex-guerrillas give guided hikes up the volcano passing by bomb craters, *tatús* (underground bomb shelters), and guerrilla camps. Tours include a history of the volcano, the people who lived on it, and how the civil war affected them. Tours of Guazapa can be done on horseback or walking and take 3-4 hours. The trail is not difficult but can get hot, so bring sunscreen, water, and a hat. Tours (in Spanish only) can be arranged through **EcoTurismo La Mora** (tel. 2323-6874 or 2335-1782, www.ecoturismolamora.es.tl, $15 for 1-3 people) or **Guazapa Tours** (tel. 2352-5363 or 2313-4388, www.guazapatours.com, $25 for 1-3 people).

Bird-Watching

Suchitoto is gaining popularity as a birders paradise. **Lago Suchitlán** is a stopover for migratory birds of all colors, shapes, and sizes. A small sampling of some the birds you can expect to see here include the cinnamon hummingbird, orange-fronted parakeet, streak-backed oriole, and great egret. Bird-watching is good year-round, but the very best months are September to April. In October and November the southern hawk migration happens, and also in November there is a weekend-long birding marathon organized by local NGO SalvaNatura.

Birding tours are common here because of the knowledgeable local guides, wide variety of birds, and great hotels and restaurants. A boat tour will guarantee some great bird spotting, especially around **Isla de las Pájaros,** but it is also possible to spot some birds on guided walking tours around the lake, or even from the terrace of your hotel. Robert Broz of **El Gringo Tours** (Calle Francisco Morazán 27, tel. 2327-2351, www.elgringosuchitoto.com) offers excellent bird-watching tours around Suchitoto, including a two-hour boat birding tour on the lake ($35 pp, minimum 3 people) and 5- to 10-hour birding tours to Volcán Guazapa and Cinquera (half-day $125 pp, minimum 3 people; full-day $200 pp, minimum 3 people).

Spanish Language School
Want to escape the throngs of travelers learning Spanish in neighboring Guatemala? **Pajaro Flor Spanish School** (4 Calle Poniente 22, tel. 2327-2366 or 7230-7812, www.pajaroflor.com, $8 per hour) is the perfect alternative. This beautiful 200-year-old mansion has an outdoor classroom that looks over the lake, along with great teachers and homestay options.

SHOPPING
Casa de la Abuela (1 Av. Norte and 2 Calle Oriente, tel. 2335-1227, 7:30am-7:30pm daily) sits on the corner of the north side of Iglesia Santa Lucia. This beautiful century-old home was converted into a shop in 2005 and now has an excellent selection of Salvadoran handicrafts, including artwork from La Palma, textiles from San Sebastián, pottery from Guatajiagua, locally crafted jewelry, indigo-dyed clothing, local honey, and other knick-knacks as well as a small selection of Spanish books. The house also has a café serving food and drinks, with excellent coffee and average food. Casa de la Abuela also offers tours around the area; the price depends on the tour and the number of people.

Galería de Pascal (4 Calle Poniente, across from the police station, tel. 2335-1200, 10am-6pm Mon.-Fri., 10am-7pm Sat., 9am-6pm Sun.) is an art gallery and gift shop located in a beautiful old home with soft-blue walls, large breezy rooms, and a garden out back. The gallery, which displays domestic and international art, also has a gift shop with high end Salvadoran crafts, including textiles from San Sebastián, art from La Palma, clothing, natural soaps and shampoos, and jewelry.

ENTERTAINMENT
Nightlife
Suchitoto is not known for its nightlife. The town pretty much shuts down after 9pm,

but if you feel like having a nightcap with some revolutionaries, **Bar El Necio** (Calle 5 Noviembre 2A, 10 meters from *parque central*, tel. 7452-3059, bar.elnecio@gmail.com, 4pm-2am Wed.-Sun.) is where you want to go. This inconspicuous century-old home is run by ex-combatants and is a long-running institution in Suchitoto. Inside, the walls are covered in old FMLN solidarity posters, photos of Che Guevara, and other collectible socialist propaganda. This is a simple, quiet place that almost always has at least a couple of ex-guerrillas hanging out at the bar, drinking rum and shooting the breeze. It's the perfect way to cap a day of civil war history, by having a few drinks and hearing some personal stories. These guys may not warm up to you right away, but if you buy them a round or two and politely ask some questions, you just might find yourself talking politics all night.

Festivals
The **Permanent International Festival of Arts and Culture** is held in Suchitoto every year throughout the entire month of February. The festival includes theater, art exhibits, and dance performances by Salvadoran and international artists. The performances take place in various venues throughout the town. The **Guazapa Mountain Festival** is held every January 12-16 and celebrates the Chapultepec Peace Accords. Ex-guerrillas and community members gather in Guazapa to share music and memories. The party on the 16th is said to go all night. The **Festival of Corn** is celebrated either the first or second Sunday of August. It is held in honor of the annual corn harvest and Suchitoto celebrates with a parade and plenty of corn-based snacks and drinks.

Religious Holidays
Semana Santa is celebrated the week before Easter and is marked by a silent procession, a dramatic reenactment of the Stations of the Cross, and *alfombras,* murals made out of colored sand that cover the streets. **Día de los Muertos** is celebrated on November 2 and

is a good time to visit Suchitoto's cemeteries, where you will find candlelit vigils, beautiful flower arrangements, and families paying homage to their deceased loved ones. **Santa Lucia,** the patron saint of Suchitoto, is celebrated with a week of activities that end on her birthday, December 13. The week is full of food, music, masses, and processions.

ACCOMMODATIONS
Under $10

Hotel Blanca Luna (Calle Poniente and 5 Av. Sur 7, tel. 2335-1661, $7 pp) is a longtime basic Bohemian favorite. Private rooms, each with two beds, a fan, and a small TV, are a bit rough around the edges, but for the price, you can't go wrong. Tile floors, peeling wall paint, colorful mismatched bedsheets, and a private bath with a makeshift door made out of a shower curtain create backpacker ambience. There is a very cute common area, eclectically decorated with whimsical dolls, statues, and paintings as well as lots of plants; it has a tiny kitchen space. The rooms on the second level open up to a lovely little terrace, and the location is great, close to the town center.

Simple, clean, and quiet, **Hostal El Rinconcito El Gringo** (Calle Francisco Morazán 27, 1.5 blocks west of the *alcaldía*, tel. 2327-2351, www.elgringosuchitoto.com, $7 pp dorm, $12 private room for 1 person, $18 for 2) is a great budget option, especially for backpackers who do not speak Spanish. Transplanted Californian Robert Broz (nicknamed "El Gringo") offers lodging and advice for those seeking some guidance in and around Suchitoto. There are two basic private rooms with fans and double beds with new mattresses, and one dormitory with fans. All rooms have shared baths, one for the two private rooms and one for the dorm. The private rooms also share a common area with cool tile floors, a hammock, a rocking chair, and a computer area. There is Wi-Fi, a small but sufficient kitchen available for guests to use, and a great restaurant upstairs serving Tex-Mex food.

$10-25

The best thing about the budget **Hostal Vista Al Lago** (Calle 6 Poniente and Final Av. 2, 18B, tel. 2335-1357 or 7889-3076, $10 pp dorm, $25 d private room) is, as the name suggests, the view. Six small rooms with fans are inside what used to be an art school, with residual student murals cheering up the walls. The hostel has a summer-camp kind of feel, complete with dim lighting and an open ceiling design, which means you can hear what is going on in the next room. There is one shared outdoor bath best described as rustic. The highlight is the outdoor sitting area, with one of the best views in town, where there is a wooden table with board games and books, and hammocks to lounge in. The hostel now also offers nicer private rooms with private baths that sit right on the edge of the property, offering incredible, affordable views.

Hostal Sánchez (4 Calle Poniente, 7, tel. 7120-6841, $10 s, $15 d) is the newest budget option in town, and quite a good one. Two large, clean rooms are on the second floor of this family home. One has a large double bed and the other has two single beds. They are both spacious and clean, with tile floors, big windows, colorful bedspreads, large windows, fans, private baths, and a terrace.

Located at the bottom of a quiet hill and with a great view of the lake, **Hostal Villa Barranca** (on the north side of Parque San Martín, tel. 2335-1408 or 2269-3687, www.villabalanza.com, $20 d with fan, $25 d with a/c) offers the best mid-range deal to be found in Suchitoto. This lovely house has a common area and kitchen on the first floor, including Wi-Fi and a flat-screen TV. Freshly painted yellow walls, local art, lounging furniture, and clean tile floors create a very comfortable atmosphere. Follow the stairs to the second floor, where there are two private rooms with fans, private baths with hot water, charming murals of birds and vines, and spotless tile floors. The rooms open up to a wraparound terrace with hammocks, offering a spectacular view of the lake. Behind the house are three more rooms with private baths and air-conditioning that face a cute courtyard with wrought-iron tables and chairs, a coconut tree, and a meditation room. Villa Balanza Restaurante is on-site and will serve you food in the courtyard if you ask. This is a quiet refuge and a great deal; the only potential drawback is the short but steep hill that must be climbed to get into the center of Suchitoto.

$25-50

El Corte del Chef (2 Av. Norte 29, tel. 2335-1276, $35 d) offers two simple rooms in the back of the restaurant around a cute, colorful courtyard with an artsy vibe. Each room has a double bed, a fan, and a private bath. There is a small rooftop terrace with tables and plants and a great view of the lake; it's perfect for decompressing with a glass of wine and a custom-made meal after a day of touring or hiking.

The simple colonial-style hotel **Posada Alta Vista** (Av. 15 de Septiembre 8, tel. 2335-1645, www.posadaaltavista.com, $29 s, $35 d) has eight rooms on the second floor that open up to a wraparound terrace that looks out onto one of the main streets in Suchitoto (but don't worry about traffic noise—there isn't any). Each room has air-conditioning, a private bath with hot water, and a TV. The style is simple, with clean tile floors, a bedside table, and two double beds. There is a parking lot and a large rooftop terrace that offers great views of the church and the mountains of Guazapa, but unfortunately it has no shade or furniture.

$50-100

Modern comfort and Old World style meet at **Hotel Las Puertas** (2 Av. Norte and Av. 15 de Septiembre, facing *parque central,* tel. 2393-9200, www.laspuertassuchitoto.com, $85 d). The definition of colonial, this striking white hotel, with its perfect arcaded facade, faces Iglesia Santa Lucia. Past the cozy restaurant and bar, a staircase leads to the second floor, where wicker furniture and plenty of plants create a lovely lounge area outside the guest rooms. The large, breezy rooms are simple and

elegant, each with two double beds on dark wooden frames with towering bedposts from which crisp white mosquito nets hang. Large windows let the sunlight filter in, and white and mint-green sheets create a simple, clean look. The rooms have air-conditioning, and cool tile floors lead out to a terrace that overlooks the park and the church, a perfect place to watch the sun go down.

★ **Los Almendros de San Lorenzo** (4 Calle Poniente, beside the police station, tel. 2335-1200, www.hotelsalvador.com, $89 d, $115 suite, $141 suite with 2 floors and jetted tub) is considered one of the top hotels in the country, and it is easy to see why. This beautiful 200-year-old mansion was converted into a boutique hotel with panache by French owner Pascal Lebailly, and every little detail lends itself to a classy getaway. Upon entering the hotel, you find a courtyard full of lush green plants, beautiful antiques from around the world, and a terrace adorned with incredible high-end Salvadoran art on the walls. A gorgeous little library with large windows lets the sunlight stream in to show off the antique furniture, ornate rugs, and book collection. A second courtyard boasts a swimming pool, lounge chairs, and a restaurant enclosed in glass, with icy-cool air-conditioning to keep you comfortable while you dine on some of the best food in town. There are various guest rooms to choose from, including the regular colonial-style rooms that boast ornate ceilings and antique furniture with air-conditioning, private baths, and flat-screen TVs. There are also two beautiful suites, also with air-conditioning, private baths, and flat-screen TVs, one of which has a jetted tub and two floors; both are extremely spacious, with large windows, dramatic drapery, local touches such as furniture upholstered with indigo dyed fabric, and international flair, such as a faux zebra-skin rug.

The beautiful rooms of **La Posada Suchitlan** (Final 4 Calle Poniente, tel. 2335-1064, www.laposada.com.sv, $100 d) are hidden away in a quiet corner of town, ensconced in colorful gardens surrounded by grand

Salvadoran antiques and famously gorgeous views of the lake. Rich yellow adobe cabins with terra-cotta roofs open up into big, breezy rooms with two double beds accented by simple neutral colors, air-conditioning, TVs (enclosed in a tall, heavy wooden cabinet), and individual terraces with unrivaled views of the lake and surrounding mountains.

El Tejado Restaurant and Hotel (3 Av. Norte 58, tel. 2335-1769, www.eltejadosuchitoto.com, $60 s, $75 d) is a popular choice, not only for the beautiful grounds and rooms but also for the excellent service. A large swimming pool overlooks the lake, creating the perfect place to escape the Suchitoto heat and still feel like you are appreciating the sights. Light orange and yellow *cabañas* are simple, accentuated with wooden ceilings, pretty tile floors, wrought-iron light fixtures, art, and colorful Salvadoran textiles covering the beds. All *cabañas* have fans and private baths, and the double rooms have amazing views of the lake.

FOOD

Serving up tasty, generous portions of Tex-Mex fare, **El Rinconcito del Gringo** (Calle Francisco Morazán 27, 1.5 blocks west of the *alcaldía,* tel. 2327-2351 or 2335-1371, www.elgringosuchitoto.com, 8am-8pm daily, $3-7) is a Suchitoto favorite. Delicious tacos, tortilla soup, quesadillas, and super burritos big enough for two all come with freshly made *chirmol* (salsa) and tortilla chips. The smoothies are massive and frosty, the perfect intervention for the intense Suchitoto heat. An added bonus is that if you want some advice about what to do around Suchitoto, there's no better dinner conversation than El Gringo's tips about the region.

Located right in front of the main square, ★ **La Lupita del Portal** (*parque central,* tel. 2335-1429, 7:30am-9:30pm Thurs.-Tues., $4-10) is the perfect place to enjoy evening drinks as you watch the sun go down and the people go by. Lupita's serves delicious sandwiches with homemade baguette bread and a proper salad with greens, seasonal vegetables, and homemade dressing. If you are in the mood for something traditional, go for the famous *pupusas,* or the delicious *gallo en chicha* (rooster marinated in moonshine with *panela* and spices), the house specialty. If you are interested in the local moonshine, just ask and the owners will provide a shot on the house. Lupita's is open early and is also a lovely breakfast option, serving *desayuno típico* (typical breakfast, consisting of eggs, beans, tortillas, plantain, and fresh cheese) as well as fruit, yogurt, and granola, along with the best coffee in town. The service is great too.

Restaurante El Harlequín (3 Av. Norte 26, tel. 2335-1009 or 2325-5890, harlequincafe@hotmail.com, 10am-10pm daily, $4-15) is definitely the cutest restaurant in town, hidden in a courtyard with a flourishing garden, wrought-iron tables with wine bottle candleholders, and exposed brick walls with beautiful local paintings. Harlequín is the only place in Suchitoto that is open until 10pm, with live *trova* music on the weekends, drawing crowds from San Salvador. They serve excellent pastas, seafood, and smoked rabbit dishes. The *pasta de hierbas* is the pièce de résistance, a delicious, incredibly rich cream pasta with fresh cheese and savory herbs. They make good mojitos too, also served up with a barrage of fresh herbs in your glass.

On the road to Lago Suchitlán, **La Fonda El Mirador** (Av. 15 Septiembre 85, tel. 2335-1126, 11am-7pm daily, $5-10), with its simple white and black facade, has been around since 1995. This fern-laden open-air restaurant, with dining tables made out of old wooden doors and windows, offers popular seafood plates alongside perfect views of the lake. Top choices include the red snapper, which comes with your choice of homemade salsas made with local fruits such as tamarind and *mamey* (think a cross between a mango and a papaya), and unexpectedly, a delicious deep-fried ice cream. Tables are arranged on a beautiful patio beside a shady garden. The restaurant gets busy on the weekends.

El Corte de Chef (2 Av. Norte 9, tel. 2335-1276, 11am-7pm Mon.-Sat., $3-7) is a sweet new addition to Suchitoto, not only because of the colorful courtyard with cheerful melon-painted walls, local art, and flowers, but also the daily lunch specials for $3. Plates include a meat of the day (usually chicken, fried fish, or beef) alongside a bed of rice, fresh salad, and a *refresco.*

Villa Balanza Restaurante Hotel (next to Parque San Martín, tel. 2335-1408, noon-9pm daily, $5-15) is famously known for the interesting sculpture above the entrance, *la balanza* (the scale), weighing a bomb against a thick stack of tortillas. Inside, a large restaurant has picnic-style tables covered in colorful Salvadoran tablecloths. The restaurant serves very good *comida típica* (typical Salvadoran food), including *sopa de gallina,* grilled meats, and, of course, *pupusas.* Every day they offer a lunch special and are well-known for the traditional *dulces,* mostly candied fruits and nuts.

★ **Los Almendros de San Lorenzo** (4 Calle Poniente, beside the police station, tel. 2335-1200, www.hotelsalvador.com, 7am-8:30pm daily, $7-20) is easily the best restaurant in Suchitoto. Enclosed in glass with views of the gardens and the hotel pool, this tastefully designed space boasts polished wooden floors and ceiling, neutral brown and orange table settings, and wonderfully cool air-conditioning. The menu is unique in El Salvador, using local ingredients to prepare delicious meals with French inspiration. The most popular dish is *pollo San Lorenzo,* grilled chicken with bacon, onions, and pesto sauce, served with potatoes au gratin and steamed vegetables. Los Almendros also serves excellent pasta such as cheese lasagna, ravioli, and linguini with your choice of sauces, including a divine carbonara, lemon and butter, or homemade pesto. They also have a good selection of wine, as well as large creamy and cold smoothies, made with avocadoes and local fruits.

Reservations must be made in advance to dine at **La Casa de Escultor** (6 Calle Oriente and 3 Av. Norte, tel. 2335-1711, www.miguel-martino.com, $17), where transplanted Argentine artist and *asado* aficionado Miguel Martino runs his art gallery, showcasing amazing wood sculpture made out of fallen trees and destroyed trunks. When requested, Martino cleans up the clutter and gets out the cutlery, welcoming groups of eight or more for dinner, which involves succulent imported meat slow-cooked over a wood fire, roasted vegetables and potatoes, and, of course, being hosted by an Argentine, a fine selection of red wine.

Guazapa Café (Km. 43.3, Carretera San Martín-Suchitoto, near the Texaco station, tel. 2335-1823, 10am-8pm Tues.-Sun., $5-10) is located two kilometers south of the center of Suchitoto but is worth the journey, especially since you are likely to spend a couple of hours relaxing in the beautiful garden and chatting with the charming owner, former guerrilla Kenia Ramírez. This outdoor café has makeshift wooden tables and tree-trunk chairs, and a small civil war museum to browse while you wait for your food. Guazapa's specialty is grilled meats, and you can expect large portions served in the traditional style with sides of corn on the cob, potatoes or rice, and tortillas served with a delicious spicy salsa. Guazapa Café also serves some vegetarian dishes, including quesadillas and salads. Finish off with a strong espresso, or alternatively, a nap in one of the comfortable hammocks strewn in the shade of terracotta roofs and surrounded by large leafy plants and flowers.

INFORMATION AND SERVICES

Centro Amigos Turísticos (CAT, southwest side of *parque central,* tel. 2335-1835, cat.suchitoto@gmail.com, 9am-5pm daily) should be your first stop for visitor information in Suchitoto. Extremely friendly staff (who speak Spanish only) will provide you with brochures, maps, tour guides, and more. It's also one of the only places in town with icy cool air-conditioning blasting, making it easy to stay and chat for a while.

There are no banks in Suchitoto, however

there is a **Scotiabank ATM** on the south side of *parque central.*

For any health issues, take advantage of the excellent **Clinica Orden de Malta** (4 Calle Poniente 8, no phone, 7am-noon and 12:30pm-3pm Mon.-Fri.), where there are good consultations for $2 and medication is free. **Hospital Nacional Suchitoto** (Av. José María Peña Fernández, tel. 2335-1062, 24 hours, daily) is located just a few minutes by car outside town and has a 24-hour emergency room.

GETTING THERE

From San Salvador, take bus 129 ($0.80, 1.75 hours, every 15 minutes) from Terminal de Oriente. Buses stop within walking distance of *parque central.*

If you're driving from San Salvador, follow Carretera Panamericana (Pan-American Hwy.) past Lago Ilopango until you see the sign for San Martín. Take the San Martín exit and follow it to *parque central,* where you will find signs directing you to Suchitoto. The drive takes about one hour.

Around Suchitoto

CINQUERA

An 18-kilometer rocky road heading southwest of Suchitoto leads to Cinquera, a tiny town nestled in a lush valley surrounded by forested hills. Historically, the town of Cinquera was very left-leaning, and as a result was completely decimated and abandoned during the war. Many people joined the guerrilla movement and ended up living in what is now known as **Área Natural Protegida Montaña de Cinquera** (Montaña de Cinquera Ecological Park), a mountain thriving with beautiful subtropical forest, administered by the **Asociación de Reconstrucción y Desarrollo Municipal (ARDM)** (Municipal Association for Reconstruction and Development). Today, ex-guerrillas guide hikes in Spanish through the forest, most of which is now replanted, that take you past bomb shelters, graves, and a makeshift hospital and kitchen, explaining what daily life was like hiding on the mountain during the war. The park is one of the few forests in El Salvador that is fiercely protected by the people who administer it. They are mostly ex-guerrillas, and they stand firmly by their mandate of protecting the land that protected them. The hike takes about 1.5 hours, is not very difficult, and the majority of it is in the shade. It ends with a swim in a small pool underneath a waterfall.

The town of Cinquera is also worth exploring to see the *parque central,* which is a peaceful, shady square with a monument made from the tail of a downed military helicopter surrounded by machine guns, a stark reminder of the war. Nearby, the monument is the **Memorial to the Fallen of Cinquera,** displaying the names of those killed during the war. There is also a very small museum that traces the history of the town (all signage is in Spanish).

Most people here are very open to talking about the war, and one person in particular who is worth seeking out is **Pablo Alvarenga,** a former guerrilla and flawless public speaker. He can be tracked down through **ARDM** (tel. 2389-5732, ardmcqr@yahoo.es), which has an office across the street from the *parque central.* You can also get directions to the Montaña de Cinquera park here.

If you need a translator for the trek through the park, a tour of the town, or a chat with Pablo Alvarenga, both **El Gringo Tours** (Calle Francisco Morazán 27, Suchitoto, 1.5 blocks west of the *alcaldía,* tel. 2327-2351, www.elgringosuchitoto.com) and **Suchitoto Adventure Outfitters** (Calle San Martín 4B, Suchitoto, tel. 7921-4216) in Suchitoto offer very good tour guides and translators.

If you are unable to make the afternoon bus

back to Suchitoto, there is an excellent option for spending the night in Cinquera: **Hostal y Restaurante El Bosque** (tel. 2389-5765, ardmcqr@yahoo.es, $10 pp) is located three blocks uphill from the *parque central,* where you will find newly constructed brick rooms with tile floors, fans, brand-new beds, hot water, and a terrace that meets the edge of the forest, providing a wonderful view and an orchestra of cicadas. This is a truly peaceful place and definitely recommended for anyone looking to disconnect for a night or two. There is also a restaurant (8am-7pm daily, $3-5) in the hostel, serving very economical *comida típica* breakfasts and set lunches and dinners, usually chicken, rice, and salad.

Getting There

Bus 482 leaves Suchitoto twice daily, at 9am and 1:30pm ($0.70, 45 minutes). The same bus returns to Suchitoto at 12:30pm and 5am daily.

If you are driving from Suchitoto, the turn-off for Cinquera is at the south end of town and is clearly marked. A 4WD vehicle is recommended, especially during the rainy season.

CIHUATÁN

After the Mayan civilization mysteriously collapsed in the western part of El Salvador sometime between AD 900 and 1200, a new city—most likely built by descendants of the Aztec and Toltec people from the central region of Mexico—was founded. The archaeological site of **Cihuatán** (4 kilometers north of Aguilares, Carreterra Troncal del Norte, tel. 2235-9453, 9am-4pm Tues.-Sun., $3) was the first and the largest pre-Hispanic settlement found in the country. Archaeologist Antonio Sol began excavation in 1929 and found the main pyramid, a small temple, and a *temezcal* (sauna). The news immediately made its way around the world, attracting attention to the site. Archaeologists continue to work on unearthing the mystery around both the day-to-day life of its inhabitants (who numbered up to 25,000 during its peak) as well as its eventual destruction and collapse sometime between 1150 and 1200.

It is believed that Cihuatán was the capital of a realm that most likely controlled the western half of what is now El Salvador. For 150 years, Cihuatán operated as a bustling commercial center. This is the only site in El Salvador where the *jiquilite* plant has been found, indicating that the people of Cihuatán were involved in the production and trade of indigo. Sometime between 1150 and 1200,

Unexploded bombs stand guard in front of a tiny church in Cinquera.

Cihuatán was destroyed by unknown enemy invaders; the city was burned to the ground. Found among its charred debris were obsidian points of arrows and lances, indicating that there was a battle between the residents and the invaders. Because the city was burned and never reoccupied, all the remnants of the site are buried under the burned debris, preserving evidence about daily life in this ancient city.

Today, the site is still being discovered, and is full of grassy mounds and stone rubble, exposing several partially excavated pyramids (one of which you can climb), a defensive wall, two ball courts, and a lookout point with a perfect view of Guazapa. There is a small museum with some artifacts and information in English.

Getting There

From Suchitoto, take bus 163 ($0.60, 45 minutes, runs every 40 minutes) to Aguilares. From Aguilares, you can transfer to buses 119, 124, 125, or 141 (one of these buses arrives about every 5 minutes, takes about 5 minutes, and all should cost $0.25). Ask the bus driver to drop you off at *las ruinas*. From where the bus drops you off, you then must walk about one kilometer to get to the entrance to the site. From San Salvador, take bus 119, 124, 125, or 141 ($0.60, about 1 hour, runs every 30 minutes) from Terminal de Oriente. Ask to be dropped off at *las ruinas*.

If you are driving from Suchitoto, take the road to Aguilares heading north for 20 kilometers, then take the Carretera Troncal del Norte toward San Salvador and continue about two kilometers until you reach the entrance to the site, which is well marked on both sides of the road. Continue one kilometer down the tree-lined unpaved road to the parking lot. If you are driving from San Salvador, take the Carretera Troncal del Norte toward Aguilares and continue for about 36 kilometers until you see the entrance to the site just past Aguilares.

ILOBASCO AND SAN SEBASTIÁN

A scenic drive through the Cinquera mountains 61 kilometers southeast of Suchitoto will take you to one of the oldest ceramic craft centers in Central America: the artisanal towns of Ilobasco and San Sebastián. Production in the village of **Ilobasco** is said to have started in the 18th century after the discovery of high-quality clay in the area, and it continues today. The main street in this bustling town is full of small shops selling ceramics of all kinds. The most popular ones are called *miniaturas,* tiny detailed figurines that are hidden inside *sorpresas,* ceramic vessels that are usually shaped like an egg or fruit. These quirky little crafts are unique to El Salvador, and the miniature figures usually depict scenes from rural life, such as a woman making pottery or men planting corn. You can also find the adult versions of *sorpresas,* called *picaros,* which are scenes of couples locked in erotic embrace. Be sure to check out **MOJE Casa Artesanal** (4 Av. Norte, Pasaje El Campo 11, tel. 2384-4770 or 2332-0659, www.mojecasaartesanal.com, 10am-5pm daily), where you will find the absolute best selection of traditional ceramics, made by local youth.

South of Ilobasco is **San Sebastián,** another artisanal town where old men spend their days weaving traditional textiles on antique wooden looms. It's fascinating to watch, and it is a great place to buy colorful hammocks, tablecloths, and bedspreads that are made right before your eyes. The markup between here and San Salvador is quite high, and if you buy here, you cut out the intermediary, providing direct income to the men who remain dedicated to this dying art.

Getting There

From Suchitoto, take bus 129 to San Salvador and ask to be let off in San Martín. From there, you need to transfer to bus 111 for Ilobasco ($0.75, 1 hour, runs every hour), and bus 110 for San Sebastián ($1, 1.25 hours, runs every hour). Alternatively, if you want to go to Ilobasco, you can catch bus 482 ($1.50, 2 hours) that leaves Suchitoto at 9am and 1:30pm daily in front of the central market. It continues on to Ilobasco after stopping in Cinquera.

It is much easier and worthwhile to take a guided tour of the villages, as your tour guide will know the best workshops and stores to check out. **El Gringo Tours** (Calle Francisco Morazán 27, Suchitoto, tel. 2327-2351 or 7860-9435, www.elgringosuchitoto.com) does excellent English-language tours through the artisanal route, connecting well with the locals and offering a fun, casual, and very informative trip. Tours generally take a few hours, and the cost varies depending on how many stops you would like to make.

La Palma and Vicinity

The tiny mountain town of La Palma is famed for its distinctive art, popularized by Salvadoran artist Fernando Llort. Llort, along with a group of other young artists, moved to La Palma, 84 kilometers north of San Salvador, during the social turmoil of the 1970s. They liked the relative tranquility of the cool mountain town and made it home. Llort opened an art school and taught many of the local campesinos struggling to make ends meet how to create in his unique style. There are murals all over town painted in cheerful primary colors, giving the town a lighthearted, whimsical feel. The art of La Palma has become a trademark of Salvadoran culture, depicting rural life, social struggle, and religious symbolism. La Palma is a peaceful town, with little traffic, sunny days, and crisp nights. Wander around the town and admire the storefront murals, stop for coffee, and buy some art. Whatever you do, La Palma is a perfect destination for a day trip or to use as a base for exploring the nearby highlands of Miramundo and El Pital.

SIGHTS

The tiny **Museo de Fernando Llort** (Barrio San Antonio, no phone, 8am-4pm Mon.-Sat., 8am-noon Sun., free) is worth a visit if you are interested in learning more about the life and work of Fernando Llort. The small one-room display showcases his art as well as the work of some of his students, alongside placards (in Spanish only) that describe the meaning and origin of his style and give a biography of his life.

Right around the corner from the museum is **Cooperativa Semilla de Dios** (3 Calle Poniente and 5 Av. Norte, no phone, 9am-5pm daily, free), La Palma's first art gallery, founded by Fernando Llort. Here you will find high-quality painted woodcrafts for purchase and also be able to go back to the craft shops to see the men and women working.

SHOPPING

There are shops selling art in the Fernando Llort style throughout La Palma, but the best place to browse is the **Placita de Artesanías** (2 Av. Norte, no phone, 9am-5pm daily), which is located right next door to the visitor information office and has a collection of vendors selling a wide selection of La Palma's art and crafts.

ACCOMMODATIONS
Under $10
Casa Hotel (Km. 84, Carretera Troncal del Norte, on the left side of the entrance to La Palma, tel. 2373-2334, $7 pp) is the only budget option in La Palma, and it's a good one. Inside a family home, this adorable space offers a few private rooms located at the bottom of a plant-laden staircase that also opens up to a common area. La Palma style art decorates the doorways and the rooms are simple

but pretty, with colorful bedspreads and white brick walls. Rooms have two beds, fans, private bath, and hot water. There is no restaurant or kitchen here, but the lodging is right next door to a *pupusería*. The only downside is that there is no Wi-Fi.

$10-25

Right across the street from Casa Hotel is **Hotel La Palma** (Km. 84, Carretera Troncal del Norte, on the right side of the entrance to La Palma, tel. 2335-9012 or 2305-8483, www. hotellapalma.com.sv, $20 s, 35 d), the oldest hotel in town; in fact, it is the second-oldest hotel in the country. La Palma opened its doors in 1941, and owner Salvador Zepeda Carrillo kept his hotel open through the civil war. During that time, his only clients were guerrillas and military officers, and the hotel was often taken over by one group or the other, leaving Carrillo to simply keep the rooms clean and the kitchen running. "There was a lot of fighting that took place within these walls," he says. "But it is also the place where the peace talks finally started." Today, the hotel is very peaceful, offering spacious, air-conditioned rooms with terraces facing the lovely grounds. The rooms are nice enough, with windows letting in fresh air, pretty views of the river, and trademark La Palma murals on nearly all the walls. However, the mattresses feel like they might be the same ones the warring factions slept on many years ago, and many of the rooms have the residual scent of fumigation. The novelty of staying here might be worth more than the actual experience. The restaurant serves up good *comida típica,* and owner Carrillo provides a side of great conversation.

Paso del Pital (Km. 84, Carretera Troncal del Norte, tel. 2305-9344, $20 s, $30 d) may have less character than the other La Palma hotels, but it is clean and comfortable, offering simple, spacious rooms with large windows, fans, private baths, hot water, Wi-Fi, and cable TV.

A colorful doorfront in La Palma is designed in the classic Fernando Llort style.

FOOD

Dining options in La Palma are limited, but there are a few decent *comedors* in town. The best is **Parrillada Sochi y Comida a la Vista** (Calle Barrios and Calle San Antonio 79, tel. 2305-9006, 11:30am-2pm and 5:30pm-10pm daily, $1-4), an excellent little *comedor* with a great variety of meat, vegetables, and salads. This is a no-frills family-run business with a few tables and a TV in the corner.

If you are looking for something with a little (not much) more atmosphere, **Restaurante la Teja** (tel. 7681-1223, 8am-9pm daily, $3-7) is a glorified food court right beside the *alcaldía* in the center of town, offering a shaded seating area with wooden tables and a collection of small restaurants selling options such as *pupusas,* burritos, grilled meat, soups, and pizza. This is the only place in town that sometimes has live music at night.

INFORMATION AND SERVICES

Centro de Amigos del Turista (2 Av. Norte, in front of *parque central*, tel. 2335-9076, cat. lapalma.corsatur@gmail.com, 9am-12:30pm and 1:10pm-5pm daily) is an excellent resource for information about the area. There is a **Banco Cuscatlán** (Calle Barrios and 1 Calle Poniente), and an Internet café, **Ciber Pinto** (Calle de Espina 83, no phone, 8am-8pm daily).

GETTING THERE

From San Salvador, bus 119 ($1.70, 3 hours) runs every half hour from Terminal de Oriente to El Poy, stopping in La Palma. If you are coming from Suchitoto, wait outside the central market for bus 163 to Aguilares ($0.60, 45 minutes, runs every 40 minutes), and from there you can transfer to bus 119, which passes by every half hour and should cost $1. Alternatively, you can take the ferry across the lake ($4, 1 hour, ferry leaves when full) to San Francisco de Lempa, where you can take bus 542 ($0.75, 45 minutes, 6am, 7:30am, noon, and 2:45pm daily) to Chalatenango, where you can take bus 125 ($0.50, 20 minutes, runs every hour) to the intersection called El Amayo and then transfer to bus 119 ($1, 1 hour, runs every hour) to La Palma. This second route is very time-consuming and not worth the effort unless you have your heart set on taking the ferry.

If you are driving from San Salvador, drive north along the Troncal del Norte (4N) toward Apopa and Aguilares. The route is 85 kilometers and takes about two hours, the last part of which is uphill and winding.

Highlands Around La Palma

If you have made it to La Palma, why not continue north for some hiking through the cool cloud forests of El Salvador's highlands? **Cerro El Pital** and **Miramundo** are close enough to hike during the day and be back in La Palma for the night.

HIKING

The trailheads for the hikes in the highlands are in **Río Chiquito,** a tiny town 11 kilometers northeast of La Palma.

★ Cerro El Pital

The hike to Cerro El Pital is one of the best hikes in the country, and it is easy to do on your own. The trailhead starts in Río Chiquito, and from there it's a four-kilometer hike through gorgeous cloud forest bursting with wildflowers, ferns, and birds. The trail takes about 1.5 hours and is not difficult. It's a steady but manageable climb, with just a small section of steeper inclination. The trail ends at a gate where you pay $2 to get into Cerro El Pital, the highest point in El Salvador at 2,730 meters; it is privately owned by four brothers. Once inside, follow the dirt road for about five minutes until you see the wide expanse of rolling green lawn peppered with benches and trees. This is the summit. Located around the lawn are three restaurants, each owned by one of the brothers, and each with its own accompanying rustic cabins. The cabins ($10-20) are very basic, with beds and nothing more, outdoor baths and no hot water. The restaurants do not have names, are all good, and all serve the same type of food—*sopa de gallina, pupusas,* grilled meat and fish, coffee, and hot chocolate.

For those who seek a bit more hiking and adventure, ask someone in one of the restaurants to guide you to **Piedra Rajada,** about a 30-minute round-trip walk through lush forest that leads to a massive split rock. There is a makeshift bridge made out of a fallen tree and suspended over a steep 20-meter drop that leads to the rock, where you can sit and enjoy the view of El Salvador and neighboring Honduras. If you decide to cross the tree bridge, be careful if it has rained recently, as it can get quite slippery.

For extreme hikers, there are trails that start in **San Ignacio,** a small town just outside La Palma, and go all the way to El Pital, which involves a full day of hiking or more (there are campsites at the top). Experienced guides who can arrange this are **Tomás Vázquez** (tel. 7264-3234 or 2305-8421) or **Arnoldo Días** (tel. 7551-5526, denono9@yahoo.com).

Miramundo

The hike to Miramundo starts in Río Chiquito. It's about an hour's walk along a dirt road lined with towering pine forest on either side. This hike is easier than the hike to El Pital, as it is a slow, gradual climb with no steep inclines at any point on the trail.

Once you arrive, you will enjoy a cool cloud forest area with dramatic views of just about all of El Salvador. Here, between the expansive fields of cabbage and the tall pine forests, are hiking trails peppered with cozy mountain lodges obsessed with karaoke and fireplaces.

ACCOMMODATIONS

Most of the hotels in the highlands are located in Miramundo, but one of the top hotels in the area is on the way to Cerro El Pital.

On the Way to Cerro El Pital
El Pital Highland Cabañas y Restaurant
(12 kilometers from San Ignacio, on the way to Cerro El Pital, tel. 2259-0602 or 7739-0123, www.elpital.com.sv, $86 s, $125 d, includes breakfast) is set in the pine forest, where temperatures can sometimes drop to freezing. Luckily all of the rooms here are equipped with fireplaces. The rooms are quite simple, but the *cabañas,* which sleep up to eight, are beautifully designed with a simple but modern open-concept design inside, with a fully equipped kitchen, fans, baths with hot water, and massive windows that look out to the forest. The grounds are tastefully designed with

towering pines in the cool cloud forest on the way to Cerro El Pital, the highest point in El Salvador

attention to detail, including gorgeous fresh flowers in the restaurant, antiques scattered around the hotel, and a collection of boots with flowers planted in them, giving the place a unique boutique feel.

Miramundo

Once you reach Miramundo, the first place on the right side is the **Hostal Miramundo** (tel. 2219-6251, www.hostalmiramundo.com, $56 d), with large grassy grounds amid the towering pines, with picnic tables and hammocks. Log cabins are clean and simple, with large windows as well as terraces, fans, TVs, private baths, and hot water.

Right next door to Hostal Miramundo is **La Posada del Cielo** (tel. 2289-2843 or 7598-4102, www.hotelaposadadelcielo.com, $60 d), with lots of lovely common space, including a great little mirador, a log cabin restaurant with karaoke on the weekends, and lots of hammocks among the pines. The rooms, however, are a bit dark and damp, with dark wood, carpeted floors, fans, and old sofas; it's not as good a value as other accommodations in town.

About one kilometer down the road is **Hotel de Montaña Buena Vista** (tel. 2301-6513, 7013-1377, or 7347-7743, $30 s, $50 d), where, as the name suggests, there is a phenomenal view of most of El Salvador. There are short trails on the grounds, a small restaurant, and a few rooms, each with a fireplace, double bed, fan, and private bath (no hot water).

On the opposite side of the road from Hotel de Montaña Buena Vista is the pathway that leads to ★ **Cabañas y Restaurante Allá Arriba** (tel. 7925-6154, www.alla-arriba.com, $50 cabin for 2 people), the newest and nicest place in the area, where sprawling grounds are nestled behind the cabbage fields and pine forest. Allá Arriba has 10 lovely bungalows surrounded by pines, flowers, and fruit trees. They are newly constructed with rustic style and modern comfort, including terraces, furniture for lounging, big windows, fans, hot water, and excellent service. The restaurant here serves local food, including organic fruits and vegetables and free-range chicken and eggs. There are wooden platforms built onto the sloping hill beside the hotel, with views of the farmland. These platforms are for tents, and it costs $4 to camp. There is a kitchen and shared baths (no hot water) available for those who choose to camp.

San Ignacio

Hotel Posada del Reyes (tel. 2335-9318 or 7553-1865, $15 d) is a good option if you plan on sleeping in San Ignacio. Clean rooms with tile floors, two double beds, large windows letting in lots of light, fans, TVs, and hot water are a great deal. There is a large common space outside full of plants and flowers. There's no restaurant, but you'll find a good *pupusería* right next door.

Río Chiquito

It is also possible to sleep in Río Chiquito and have easy access to the trailheads. **Lecho de Flores** (50 meters from the turnoff to El Pital, tel. 2313-5470 or 2359-0782, www.elpitallechodeflores.com, $30 s, $60 d) is a lovely hostel in Río Chiquito, set in a beautiful flower garden and right beside the little river that this small town is named after. Cozy wooden A-frame *cabañas* have pretty touches like fresh flowers in antique milk cans, two beds with colorful blankets, and a terrace with views of the cabbage fields. Lecho de Flores includes a tour of your choice in the cost of the room, and if you do not want to stay in the area, they also offer great day-trip packages, which include transportation to and from the highlands, a hike, a meal, and afternoon coffee and quesadillas. Check the website for details.

GETTING THERE

To get to Río Chiquito, first you need to get to San Ignacio, a small town just outside of La Palma. Buses leave from La Palma for San Ignacio regularly, starting at 6:30am ($0.25, 30 minutes, run every hour). From San Ignacio, bus 509 ($0.90, 1 hour) runs to Río Chiquito at 7am, 9:30am, 12:30pm, 2:30pm, and 4:30pm daily, and returns at the same times.

Alegría

The aptly named Alegría (which translates as "happiness") is a welcome respite from the heat, especially if you have been traveling the more sweltering eastern parts of the country. Set in the highlands and sitting on the side of Volcán Tecapa, Alegría is the flower capital of the country, with hundreds of *viveros* (plant nurseries) emitting the sweet smell of roses, sunflowers, orchids, and various other tropical blossoms. This quaint little town with a cool climate and friendly locals is surrounded by coffee plantations and is home to Laguna de Alegría, a beautiful emerald-green sulfurous lake about two kilometers southwest of town, said to have medicinal properties. There is not much else to do in Alegría, but you just might find that the fresh local food, clean mountain air, and equally clean streets may draw you in for a few days. Don't miss the weekend market, when vendors set up around Parque Alegría, selling local food, drinks, plants, and flowers.

Just seven kilometers southwest of Alegría is **Berlín,** a slightly more developed town known for its colorful old aluminum houses that were built with materials brought from Belgium at the beginning of the 20th century. Berlín was colonized in the 19th century by German and Italian immigrants, entrepreneurs looking to cash in on the coffee boom. It's a pretty town to walk around, if only to admire the grand old homes, one of which is the very popular Casa Mía Hotel, a great place to enjoy a cup of coffee even if you're not staying there.

RECREATION

The hike to **Laguna de Alegría** is an easy walk along a slightly inclined dirt road. The walk is very easy to do on your own, takes you past some small communities and coffee plantations, and takes about an hour each way. The strikingly green sulfurous lake sits in a crater and is especially beautiful on a very sunny day, when the deep emerald-green water sparkles in the light. On weekdays you are likely to have the lake to yourself, but it becomes a popular destination on the weekend. Most locals will tell you not to swim in the lake, as it is not deep and the bottom consists of thick, slippery mud. They recommend instead that you wade in deep enough to gather some of the clay, which is said to have healing properties for skin conditions such as eczema and psoriasis. If you decide to swim, the only deep part is in the very center of the lake, and the water is very cold, but there are plenty of big warm rocks to lie on and dry off in the sun. It costs $0.25 to enter, and once you're inside there are no restaurants, so bring a snack.

SHOPPING

The **Weekend Market** (*parque central,* Alegría, 9am-5pm Sat.-Sun.) takes place in the *parque central* every weekend. Local vendors set up with local goodies such as *nuegados* (deep fried yuca covered in either honey or *panela*), *chicha,* hot chocolate, coffee, quesadillas, and *pupusas.* Many people also bring in flowers and plants from their *viveros* to sell.

ACCOMMODATIONS
Under $10

The most economical choice in town is at **Casa de Misioneros Paulinos** (Calle Enrique Araujo, Alegría, tel. 7491-5934 or 2628-1180, www.padrespaulinosca.com, $6 pp dorm), where a large courtyard is flanked by very basic dormitories with shared baths. There is no restaurant, but across the street you will find a few vendors selling sandwiches and hamburgers.

$10-25

The charming **Casa de Huespedes La Palma** (in front of *parque central,* Alegría, tel. 2628-1012, $10 pp) is a great budget choice. Steps away from the plaza, the front door of this pretty home opens up into a courtyard that is bursting with greenery, flowers, old photos, and knickknacks. Each room has two single beds, fan, private bath, Wi-Fi, hot water, and a little common space with a hammock. This is a very comfortable stay, and you can't beat the location.

Entre Piedras Guesthouse and Café (across the street from *parque central,* Alegría, no phone, www.hostalentrepiedra.com, $20 d) is an old family home turned hostel that offers cozy rooms with wooden panel walls, comfy double beds with cute little side tables with lamps for reading, fans, TVs, hot water, and private baths. The best part of Entre Piedras is the sleek little coffee bar where you can enjoy local coffee, artisanal chocolate, wine, and beer, with a bird's-eye view of the central plaza. There is also a restaurant out back serving sandwiches, salads, soups, and other casual fare ($4-10).

Casa Mía Hotel in Berlín serves some of the best coffee in the country inside a beautiful old home.

★ **Casa Mía Hotel** (2 Av. Norte 10, Berlín, tel. 2643-0608 or 2663-2027, www.berlincasamia.com, $20 pp) is another old family home, converted into one of the loveliest hotels in El Salvador. The high ceilings, beautiful tile floors, and various antiques, including old telephones, record players, and typewriters, make the common areas fascinating to relax in, and the rooms, though simple, are tastefully designed with comfortable beds, colorful wooden panel walls, large windows, fans, and private baths with very hot water. Casa Mía is also home to a cute little café that serves some of the best coffee in the country, complete with coffee art on top of your latte, delicious pastries, and traditional dishes. This is a great place to stay or just to visit to learn more about the history of the area and enjoy a cup of coffee in a gorgeous mansion.

$25-50

An orange stone wall covered in plaques with the names of famous Alegrians on them surrounds **Cabañas la Estancia de Daniel** (Calle Manuel Enrique Aruayo and 2 Av. Sur, Alegría, tel. 2628-1030, $30 d), a hidden garden property just a block west of the *parque central*. Five *cabañas* sit inside a small garden with flowers, hammocks, and picnic tables. Each room is decorated with colorful Salvadoran art and bedspreads and has a private bath, hot water, fan, Wi-Fi, and a TV. There is no formal restaurant, but breakfast can be requested.

$50-100

Far from the town center, **Vivero y Restaurante La Cartagena** (Final Barrio El Calavario, 3 blocks downhill from *parque central,* Alegría, tel. 2628-1131 or 7886-2362, restaurantecartagena@hotmail.com, $60 *cabaña,* maximum 4 people) is definitely the most peaceful place to stay in town. Wooden *cabañas* are hidden among the trees and flowers on this sprawling property with a *vivero* and an excellent restaurant with spectacular views. Each *cabaña* has four beds, fans, and a private bath with hot water, and is simply decorated with neutral colors and colorful bedspreads. The restaurant serves *comida típica,* and attached is a lovely shop with local crafts, including jewelry, ceramics from Guatajiagua, and locally grown gourmet coffee.

FOOD

Enjoy fresh home-cooked food at **La Fonda** (Av. Golgota, in front of the church, Alegría, tel. 2606-5309, 9am-9pm daily, $4-10), where delicious *comida típica,* including excellent *sopa de gallina,* seafood soup, grilled meat, and amazing coffee and *refrescos,* is served up in an idyllic garden. Stop by for coffee or enjoy a meal—either way, you can't go wrong.

Merendero Mi Pueblito (Calle Alberto Masterro, Alegría, tel. 2628-1038, 7am-7pm daily, $3-10) is an eclectic space, with sprawling plants, children's toys and books peppered across the floor, and frequent performances by local musicians. The inside seating area is a bit dark, but the tables on the outside deck make a sweet spot to enjoy a delicious early-morning breakfast, with fresh eggs, cheese, and coffee straight from the campo. Dinner does not disappoint either, with generous portions of beef, chicken, or pork drawing locals on a regular basis.

INFORMATION AND SERVICES

There is a **visitor information office** (1 Av. Norte and 1 Calle Poniente, Alegría, tel. 2628-1087, hours vary) in *parque central* where you can arrange guided hikes to and around the lake. Alegría does not have any ATMs, but there is a Scotiabank beside *parque central* in Berlín.

GETTING THERE

From San Miguel, catch any bus toward San Salvador and tell the driver to let you off in Triunfo ($1.50, 1 hour, runs every 15 minutes). From there, take the microbus to the city of Santiago de María ($0.30, 15 minutes, runs frequently until 5pm), where you can take one of the frequent buses to Alegría ($0.60, 45 minutes, runs every 30 minutes). Bus 348 runs daily between the central parks of Alegría, Berlín, and nearby Santiago de María ($0.35, runs every 30 minutes).

From the Terminal de Oriente in San Salvador, bus 303 (1.5 hours, $1.50) goes directly to Berlín at 2pm daily. From Berlín you can take bus 348 to Alegría ($0.35, 15 minutes, runs every 15 minutes). If you miss the direct bus or simply want to get moving earlier, you can take any bus going to San Miguel (bus 301) or La Unión (bus 304) and ask to be let off at Mercedes Umaña, where you can take bus 354 ($0.50, 30 minutes, runs every 30 minutes) to Berlín, and from Berlín take bus 348 to Alegría ($0.35, 15 minutes, runs every 15 minutes).

Driving from San Salvador in the west or San Miguel in the east, follow Carretera Panamericana and follow the sign for Santiago de María. From there, follow the signs to Alegría and Berlín. From Santiago de María, Alegría is three kilometers and Berlín is eight kilometers.

San Miguel

Sitting at the bottom of the imposing Volcán Chaparrastique (San Miguel), 136 kilometers east of the capital, there is a tropical intensity to San Miguel that sets it apart from the rest of El Salvador. The third-largest city in the country can be a bit overwhelming, with its narrow streets, glaring sun, and blaring music, but it's worth exploring for those who appreciate a little urban grit. The sidewalks are crowded with old men selling horse saddles and robust women wiping sweat from their brow as they furiously work their corn *masa* for tortillas. The sprawling central market takes up a few blocks, and a string of neon-lit strip clubs and discotheques create a provocative nightlife, making San Miguel a fitting pit stop to prepare you for passage into the wild east. Most people, however, don't see anything more than the bus terminal.

Tourism still has not taken off in the east, and although San Miguel may not be a top destination itself, it can be a comfortable base for exploring the surrounding areas.

SIGHTS

Catedral Nuestra Señora de la Paz

Catedral Nuestra Señora de la Paz (4 Av. Norte and 4 Calle Poniente, tel. 2661-1979, 7am-7pm daily, free) sits across the street from *parque central* (otherwise known as Parque Guzmán) and is considered the largest Roman Catholic church in El Salvador. According to legend, in 1682 merchants found a sealed wooden box on the shores of Golfo de Fonseca. They put the box on the back of their donkey and continued on to San Miguel. Once in the town, the donkey

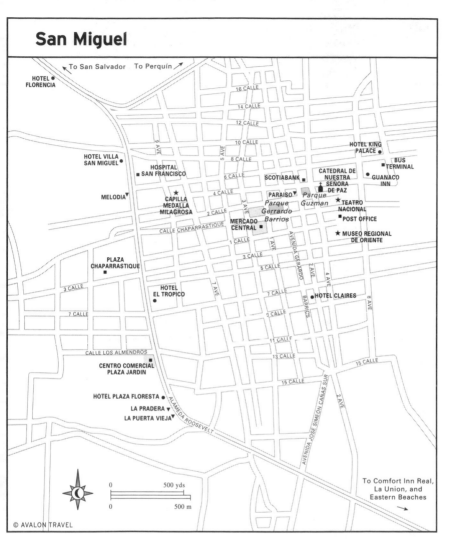

San Miguel

To San Salvador   To Perquín

HOTEL FLORENCIA

16 CALLE
14 CALLE
12 CALLE
10 CALLE
8 CALLE
6 CALLE
4 CALLE
2 CALLE

HOTEL KING PALACE
BUS TERMINAL

HOTEL VILLA SAN MIGUEL
HOSPITAL SAN FRANCISCO
SCOTIABANK
CATEDRAL DE NUESTRA SEÑORA DE PAZ
GUANACO INN

MELODIA

CAPILLA MEDALLA MILAGROSA
PARAISO
Parque Guzman
TEATRO NACIONAL

Parque Gerrardo Barrios
POST OFFICE

CALLE CHAPARRASTIQUE
MERCADO CENTRAL
MUSEO REGIONAL DE ORIENTE

1 CALLE
3 CALLE
5 CALLE

PLAZA CHAPARRASTIQUE

3 CALLE
7 CALLE

HOTEL EL TROPICO

7 CALLE
9 CALLE

HOTEL CLAIRES

11 CALLE
13 CALLE

CALLE LOS ALMENDROS

CENTRO COMERCIAL PLAZA JARDIN

15 CALLE
15 CALLE

HOTEL PLAZA FLORESTA
LA PRADERA
LA PUERTA VIEJA

ALAMEDA ROOSEVELT

AVENIDA JOSE SIMEON CAÑAS SUR

BARRIOS

AVENIDA GERARDO

0   500 yds
0   500 m

To Comfort Inn Real, La Union, and Eastern Beaches

© AVALON TRAVEL

mysteriously stopped in front of the town chapel and refused to move. They opened the box to find an image of the Virgin Mary with the baby Jesus in her hands. Nobody knew the name of the idol, but they called her Our Lady of Peace because after her arrival, the violence that had been escalating among different ethnic groups miraculously abated. The chapel was rebuilt in 1903 into a bigger church in honor of the saint. In 1787, when Volcán Chaparrastique erupted, the river of lava threatened to reach San Miguel. Locals decided to remove the image of the Virgin Mary from the altar and place it at the main entrance of the church. Legend has it that the lava changed its course, saving the town. The clean white facade and brick-red bell towers make the church the centerpiece of the bustling *parque central*. Inside, the eight-meter-tall altar, chandeliers, and stained glass windows create a grandiose and peaceful refuge.

Teatro Nacional Gavidia Francisco

Built in 1909 as part of a campaign to beautify the city, **Teatro Nacional Gavidia Francisco** (6 Av. Norte and 2 Calle Poniente, 1 block behind the cathedral, tel. 2660-7480, 8am-4pm Thurs.-Sat., free, performances $3) lacks the art and pomp of the theaters in San Salvador and Santa Ana but is worth checking out to see if there are any performances scheduled. The style of this theater, which seats up to 450 people, is neoclassic, with details modeled after Paris's opera house. The theater hosts dramas, contemporary dance, folk dance, and symphony performances.

Capilla Medalla Milagrosa

The small white neo-Gothic **Capilla Medalla Milagrosa** (7 Av. Norte and 4 Calle Poniente, no phone, 8am-noon and 2pm-4pm daily) was built in 1904 and was originally a hospital run by a group of French nuns. Today, the church is a peaceful place to visit, perfect for getting away from the bustle of this intense city. Set amid tall trees, a long walkway leads inside, where you will find high arched ceilings, stained glass windows, and an altar cloaked in the glow of bright lighting that shows off a statue of the Virgin Mary.

SPORTS AND RECREATION

Volcán Chaparrastique

Volcán Chaparrastique (San Miguel) is located 15 kilometers east of San Miguel and provides the stunning backdrop to the not-so-stunning city. Most people prefer to enjoy admiring it rather than climbing it, but for the hard-core hikers who are interested, it is possible to tackle this behemoth. The third-tallest volcano in the country at 2,130 meters, Chaparrastique provides an unforgiving 10-hour round-trip hike. The trail is a series of zigzags through coffee fields that eventually turn into thick grass, stunted trees, and scrub, and finally becomes surreal rocky terrain. It is steep and sweltering, with no shade and lots of scrambling, but you will be rewarded with spectacular views of eastern El Salvador, including the Golfo de Fonseca and Bahía de Jiquilisco. At the top there is a plunging crater more than 300 meters deep with a massive pile of boulders at the bottom.

This hike is too complicated to do on your own, and can technically be done with a police escort for free; however, you will need to organize it weeks in advance and have access to your own vehicle. You are better off paying a tour guide. Many national tour companies can arrange the hike, but they usually just hire an independent guide. You can cut out the intermediary and extra cost by contacting the intrepid independent adventure tour guide **Joaquín Aragón** (tel. 7165-2882), who guides the hike for $35 pp. You should contact him a few days in advance, as he is based in La Libertad.

Laguna Jocotál

Laguna Jocotál is popular with locals but still relatively undiscovered by travelers. This popular weekend retreat is about 15 kilometers southwest of San Miguel and is home to a wide range of birds, including pelicans, emerald toucanets, and blue-and-white mockingbirds. The lake gets busy on the weekend with throngs of locals escaping the hectic city, but if you come during the week, you will likely have the place to yourself. This glimmering lake is covered in water lilies and offers unrivaled views of Volcán Chaparrastique and its perfect reflection in the clear water. You can take a ride around the lagoon in a canoe for $8 per hour, or just hang out by the shore and chat with locals or eat some fried fish from one of the small stands that are often set up around the lake.

To get here, take bus 373 to Usulután ($1, 15 minutes, runs every 15 minutes) and tell the driver you are going to Laguna Jocotál. He can let you off about one kilometer from the shore.

SHOPPING

San Miguel's **Central Market** (west of Parque Gerardo Barrios, 6am-6pm daily) is a massive, loosely organized collection of indoor and outdoor stalls with vendors selling everything from machetes and whole chickens to pharmaceuticals and cosmetics. There are also innumerable food stalls serving *comida típica* if you are looking for some cheap local fare.

For a quieter, cooler, and significantly more costly experience, check out **Metrocentro** (Av. Roosevelt Sur 704, tel. 2640-1836 or 2640-1837, www.metrocentro.com, 7am-9pm daily), a shopping mall with lots of banks, restaurants, clothing shops, pharmacies, electronics, and more.

ACCOMMODATIONS
$10-25

By far the best budget option is town is **Hotel Claire's** (Av. José Simeón Cañas 504, tel. 2660-4503, www. hotelclairess.com, $20 d). This cheerful yellow building is attended by equally cheerful staff and conveniently located just a few blocks from the center. Claire's offers simple, very clean rooms with tile floors, private baths, air-conditioning, cable TV, and phones. All of the rooms are located along a long walkway with plants and sitting areas, facing a small courtyard and parking lot.

All of the other budget hotels in San Miguel are near the bus terminal, a smog-laced area that is crowded and chaotic during the day and potentially unsafe at night; it is not recommended that you stay in this area. However, if you must, a relatively decent budget choice is **Guanaco Inn** (8 Av. Norte 1, Pasaje Madrid, tel. 2661-8026 or 2660-6403, $10 s or d). The large rooms with tile floors, double beds, private baths, and not much else are at least clean, and there is a restaurant downstairs.

$25-50

Although a bit of a misnomer, **Hotel King Palace** (6 Calle Oriente, directly in front of the bus terminal, tel. 2660-8800, 2661-1086, or 2660-6358, www.hotelkingpalace.com, $30 s or d) is still the best bet around the bus terminal. This large security-conscious hotel offers enough amenities to be comfortable for a night or two. With a large outdoor courtyard,

a swimming pool, a business center, a *comedor,* and a parking lot, it is comfortable for a short stay. Rooms are small but clean, with two double beds, air-conditioning, tile floors, private baths, and TVs.

Hotel Floresta (Av. Roosevelt Sur 704, tel. 2640-1549, $30 s, $40 d) is a much nicer option in this price range. This simple, bright hotel has a lovely open-air space with a swimming pool surrounded by shade-providing plants and trees. The rooms are simple, with tile floors, private baths, cable TV, and air-conditioning. Breakfast is included and can be eaten in the sitting area by the pool. The friendly, attentive staff is a bonus.

$50-100

Comfort Inn Real San Miguel (Final Alameda Roosevelt, tel. 2600-0200, www. comfortinn.com, $65 d) is an excellent option, and cheaper if you stay on the weekend. Spotless white hallways open to modern rooms with king beds covered in crisp white sheets on light wooden bed frames. All of the rooms have a clean, modern style with immaculate white curtains and tile floors, air-conditioning, TVs, desks, and windows letting in plenty of natural light. There is a great little business center with Internet access, a small gym, a swimming pool, a restaurant, and even a cute little bar called Tequilas beside the swimming pool. No request is too onerous for the efficient staff, and the hotel is conveniently located next to the Metrocentro, where there are plenty of shops, restaurants, cafés, and a grocery store. If you stay on the weekend, the rates are discounted to $45 d.

Hotel Villa San Miguel (Av. Roosevelt Norte, 407, tel. 2669-6969, www.hotelvillasan-miguel.com, $45 s, $57 d) is one of the newest hotels on the strip with spotless modern rooms boasting queen beds with crisp white sheets and big fluffy pillows. This is a perfect place to relax and indulge after battling the traffic and heat of San Miguel. Check out the gym and swimming pool on the second floor before hitting your room to blast the air-conditioning and turn on the large flat-screen

TV. The staff is very friendly and helpful, and there is an excellent Salvadoran breakfast buffet included in the rates. Hotel Villa San Miguel is also located right next door to some of the best cafés and restaurants in the city.

Hotel Trópico Inn (Av. Roosevelt Sur 303, tel. 2661-1800, $45 s, $65 d) is as close to Miami's South Beach as it gets in El Salvador, complete with a rooftop bar and its glittery following. This massive, modern three-story hotel is conspicuously located on the main street and has a distinctly tropical feel, with a massive airy lobby with small souvenir shops, and a swimming pool surrounded by palms and lounge chairs where attentive staff bring you cold umbrella cocktails. The rooms are large and airy, with air-conditioning, wicker furniture, and decks that look out over the courtyard and swimming pool.

At the very entrance of San Miguel, **Hotel Plaza Florencia** (Km. 135, Carretera Panamericana, tel. 2665-5500, www.hflorencia.com, $40 s, $60 d) seems out of place beside the neon lights of the neighboring strip clubs, but don't let that deter you. This neo-colonial facade opens up to a large parking lot that is surrounded by rooms and palm trees. The rooms are a bit crowded and eclectic, with tropical-print bedspreads, antique furniture, and kitschy art on the walls, but they all have air-conditioning, Wi-Fi, and TVs. There is a swimming pool, and an excellent breakfast buffet is included, served in the formal restaurant where servers take their jobs very seriously, attending to you in dress suits and bow ties. There is also a small bar and efficient room service.

FOOD

Paraíso Comida a la Vista y Pupusería (2 Av. Norte, west side of *parque central,* tel. 2660-1852, 6am-4pm daily, $2-5) is an excellent budget option in the city center. This cheerful, brightly lit *comedor* has a great selection of salads, steamed vegetables, meat, fresh soups, and other rotating *comida típica.*

What **La Pradera** (Av. Roosevelt Sur 70, tel. 2661-4915, 11:30am-9:30pm daily, $8-17) lacks in ambience it makes up for in food. This simple steak house has been serving some of the best food in San Miguel for years and remains one of the local favorites. The specialty here is the *punta jalapeña,* a steak smothered in jalapeño salsa served with all the trimmings, including mashed potatoes and grilled vegetables.

The small, modern **La Tartaleta** (Av. Roosevelt Sur and 11 Calle Poniente, Plaza Jardín, tel. 2660-4983, 6am-10pm daily, $5-10) is an icy-cool refuge from the mean heat of San Miguel's streets. It's a perfect pit stop for a coffee, smoothie, or a bite to eat. This small café is the only place in town to find some decent vegetarian options, including soups, salads, sandwiches, and pizza, and it boasts an extensive selection of coffees and desserts.

It's a bit of a trek to get to **La Pema** (Km. 142.5, Carretera El Cuco, tel. 2661-4915, www.lapema.com, 10am-5pm Sun.-Thurs., Fri.-Sat. 10am-5pm and 7pm-midnight or later, $7-16) but worth it if you are craving seafood. On the road to El Cuco, just five kilometers south of town, this large open-air restaurant gets packed on the weekend with loyal customers. La Pema brings in only the freshest fish straight from the coast and is famous for its *mariscada,* a large creamy seafood soup with crab, shrimp, and lobster served with cheese-stuffed tortillas. There is live music every Friday night after 9pm, and there is usually dancing.

San Miguel's **Sunday Food Fair** (*parque central,* 9am-6pm Sun.) is a little-known treasure. Every Sunday morning, vendors from the surrounding pueblos set up shop in *parque central* and serve up *comida típica* from their villages. You will find traditional fare like *atol* (a warm, sweet corn-based drink), *chuco* (*atol* made with blue corn), *sopa de gallina, riguas* (small sweet corn pancakes), and tamales. It's a very laid-back and friendly vibe, and it is a great way to get to know some of the locals and their traditions.

ENTERTAINMENT
Nightlife

Papagallo Bar and Grill (Av. Roosevelt Sur, Mall 5, tel. 2661-0400, noon-8pm Sun.-Thurs., noon-2am Fri.-Sat.) serves up tasty Mexican fare, and when there is live music, some of the best nightlife in town. The dimly lit front area has a small bar and a few tables, creating an intimate space that is great for casual dinner and a beer. The back door of this space opens to a large room with a stage, where there is either live music or a DJ on the weekend. There is no cover charge.

Puerta Viejo (Av. Roosevelt, in front of Parqueo Municipal, tel. 2660-0263, 9pm-2am daily) is a popular bar that has three sections to suit your mood. In the front of the bar is a tiny dance floor that gets crowded with locals dancing to salsa or reggaeton. The center of the bar has tables where you can eat and watch the action on the dance floor. The backroom is definitely the most entertaining and a real slice of Salvadoran culture. Beer and karaoke are what this room is all about—usually involving a lot of sorrowful songs about broken hearts and unrequited love belted out with no inhibition. There is no cover charge.

Melodia (Av. Roosevelt 503, no phone, 9pm-2am Fri.-Sat.) is the local discotheque where you are "promised to be fulfilled." If flashing lights, thumping dance music, and uninhibited dancers is what you are looking for, this may prove true. The action doesn't start until at least 10pm. There is a cover charge for men that varies by the night and the entertainment; women always get in free.

El Trópico (Av. Roosevelt Sur 303, tel. 2682-1000, 6pm-2am daily) has a rooftop bar with a small indoor dance floor that gets packed with locals dancing to reggaeton and salsa. The large wraparound deck that overlooks Avenida Roosevelt, friendly staff, and a laid-back vibe make this the best spot in San Miguel for some evening cocktails. There is no cover charge.

Festivals

The biggest festival in El Salvador takes place in San Miguel the last weekend of November. **Carnaval de San Miguel** (www.carnavaldesanmiguel.net) is the country's biggest party, held in honor of Nuestra Señora De La Paz (Our Lady of Peace). The carnival began in 1959 and has been growing in size ever since. It is now considered one of the biggest festivals in Central America. Festivities include lots of live music, dancing, parades, fireworks, and general debauchery. Depending on how you feel about rowdy crowds, public drinking, and parties, you may want to plan to attend or to avoid the carnival accordingly. If you do decide to go, make sure you make reservations for hotels well in advance.

INFORMATION AND SERVICES

There are various banks located around Parque Guzmán, including a **Scotiabank** (2 Av. Norte and 4 Calle Oriente, tel. 2204-5904, 8am-4pm Mon.-Fri., 8am-noon Sat.).

For medical issues, **Hospital San Francisco** (Av. Roosevelt Norte 408, tel. 2645-2900, for emergencies tel. 2645-2955) is the first choice. As of yet, there is no tourism office in San Miguel, but for any tourism related questions, the *alcaldía,* located right in front of Parque Guzmán, may be of assistance.

GETTING THERE

From San Salvador, take bus 301 from Terminal de Oriente. There are three options: *regular* ($2.10, 3-4 hours), *especial* ($3, 2.5 hours), and *super* ($5, 2 hours). Buses leave every 15 minutes.

If driving from San Salvador, take Carretera Panamericana and head east for 138 kilometers. The drive takes about two hours.

Perquín and Vicinity

The tiny town of Perquín has gained leftist fame as the former FMLN guerrilla stronghold in the country. Today it is a modest agriculture-driven community where people get up at dawn to work the land and retire at dusk to prepare to do it again the next day. The town is marked by colorful murals promoting civil rights, a few simple *comedors* and *tiendas* where women sell heirloom beans and vegetables, and a shady central plaza where old men sit and quietly watch the hours go by.

Most people come here to see the revolution museum and the nearby El Mozote memorial and then move on, but those who take the time to balance out the somber history with some outdoor adventure are rewarded with unmapped hiking trails that most travelers have yet to discover. In and around the thick pine forests of Perquín, brilliant blue skies and lush green hills are punctuated with waterfalls and crystal-clear rivers. This is where the guerrillas hid during the war. Their intimate knowledge of the terrain was their greatest advantage in constantly avoiding military attacks during the ongoing cat-and-mouse games of the 1980s. Today, they use their unrivaled familiarity with the land to guide curious visitors off the beaten track, past bomb craters, former guerrilla camps, and cave hideouts, and offering firsthand accounts of what life was like for the guerrillas during the civil war.

Today, the town of Perquín is quiet and stable. As one elderly woman happily put it when asked what there is to do on the weekend: "Nothing. Every day is the same here." After the region's terror-filled past, the people of Perquín appreciate today's tranquility. There are no Che Guevera T-shirts or lefty bars here, just a peaceful mountain town full of ex-combatants and quiet campesinos with stories to tell, if you would like to listen.

SIGHTS
★ Museo de la Revolución Salvadoreña

The main attraction in Perquín is the **Museo de la Revolución Salvadoreña** (Calle Los Héroes, tel. 2610-6737, 8am-4:30pm daily, $1.20). Just a few blocks west of *parque central,* this museum has various displays depicting the circumstances that led to the civil war, including photos, newspaper clippings, and solidarity posters, along with artifacts such as weapons, homemade bombs, and finally a room showcasing the former underground Radio Venceremos mobile radio equipment. The radio station was famous for broadcasting caustic commentary that often ridiculed the government, and it was particularly offensive to Lieutenant Colonel Domingo Monterrosa, leader of the notorious Atlacatl Battalion and orchestrator of the El Mozote massacre. Monterrosa was constantly trying to shut the radio operation down, without any success, until 1984, when he found the FMLN radio transmitter lying on the ground. Unable to believe his luck, Monterossa grabbed the transmitter, boarded his helicopter, and took off, only to plunge to his death halfway through the flight. The transmitter turned out to be a bomb, a booby trap cleverly set by the rebels. The remnants of the helicopter are now on display in front of the museum, alongside testimonies from survivors of massacres that took place throughout Morazán during the war. This museum receives no funding from the government and is run by volunteers and ex-guerrillas who are committed to educating the public about the history of the armed conflict in El Salvador. If you don't speak Spanish, it is recommended to go with an English-speaking guide, which can be arranged through **Perkin Tours** (Final Calle Principal, tel. 2680-4086, rutadepaz.perkin@gmail.com, approx. 2 hours, $30). If you do

Memories of War

The peace talks started at a restaurant table in La Palma and ended under a mango tree in Perquín. Everywhere you go in between, somebody has a story. The way the story unfolds depends on who you are talking to, but the way it ends is always the same—the scars still run deep from El Salvador's civil war. This region was seriously affected by military massacres during the war. Many poor campesinos were already frustrated from land issues that dated back to the 19th century. Disgruntled with the government, and with the gap between rich and poor ever widening, many young people decided to join the FMLN—perhaps it was not an easy decision, but many felt there was no other viable alternative. As many people who lived through the war in this region say today, "We were tired of not being able to afford to eat."

The mountains made perfect hiding spots, and the local population's intimate knowledge of the terrain was a great advantage. Despite the army's determined efforts to gain control of the region, the red zone remained impenetrable. Well-organized guerrillas hid in the forest, huddling in *tatús* under the ground, transmitting famous underground radio broadcasts from caves and dugouts and washing in the rivers and waterfalls. The land protected them and was instrumental in keeping the movement alive. As the military's frustration with the elusive guerrillas increased, so did the gunfire, and not long after the war began, civilians began to get caught in the crossfire. In the early 1980s thousands of civilians in eastern El Salvador were killed in a military strategy coined *Quitarle el agua al pez* (Take the water away from the fish), the premise being that the rebels would not to be able to survive without the help of the people.

It was true; many villages actively supported the guerrillas, primarily by providing food. As more and more massacres took place, fear drove more villages to adopt a neutral stand, but at the height of the operation, it didn't matter whether you were truly a rebel sympathizer or not. El Salvador's war had entered the realm of senseless killing. The most tragic example of a massacre of villagers who did not support the guerrillas took place in El Mozote in 1981, when 800 people, including women and children, were brutally murdered by military troops, who unknowingly left one traumatized witness behind—Rufina Amaya Mírquez. This was the largest known massacre in Central America.

Traveling in this part of the country today, there are reminders of the war everywhere: bomb craters, bullet-pocked buildings, destroyed churches and abandoned houses with wild grass growing up and around the crumbling walls. Salvadorans are split on how to deal with the grief. Some believe it is better to let the grass keep growing until there are no more vestiges of the painful past. Others believe remembrance is essential to the healing of the nation. Many of the tours in this part of the country are not only a source of income for people who lived through 12 years of war and have few other options for employment, but also as a source of comfort, knowing that they are keeping the memory of El Salvador's past alive.

speak Spanish, there are always ex-guerrillas at the museum who will take you on a guided tour for significantly less. They can also arrange hiking tours around the area.

Beside the museum is the **Campamiento Guerrilla** (tel. 2680-4303, 7am-6pm daily, $0.50), a reenacted guerrilla camp where owner Ángel Recino has created a somehow lighthearted and fun way to learn about the war. The FMLN anthem plays from an ancient radio as you walk around and check out this coffee plantation turned park, with displays of old machine guns and bombs as well as rope

bridges and *tatús*, the multipurpose underground hideouts.

Directly across from the museum is **Cerro de Perquín,** where you can take a short 10-minute walk up to the mirador to enjoy the peaceful quiet and a view of the surrounding mountains of northern Morazán and neighboring Honduras.

★ El Mozote Memorial

El Mozote Memorial is dedicated to the hundreds of innocent civilians who were killed in one of Latin America's most brutal massacres.

It all began toward the end of 1981 when stories started circulating that military troops were making their way through northern Morazán, and that guerrilla supporters were being tortured and killed.

El Mozote was an evangelical Christian town, with no ties to the guerrillas, and word had spread that those who sought refuge there would be spared. In a matter of days the peaceful town of El Mozote received an influx of people from neighboring villages seeking safe haven.

On December 10, 1981, the battalion arrived, ostensibly to reassure everyone there that they would be protected; but instead of having their fears put to rest, villagers watched in disbelief as their worst nightmare began to unfold. The soldiers violently interrogated everyone, and then ordered them to stay inside their houses, warning that anyone who tried to leave would be shot. Every home was full of locals as well as the visitors who had recently sought refuge in El Mozote. After several grueling hours trapped inside with crying children being comforted by terrified adults, dawn broke and everybody was ordered outside, where they were lined up to be interrogated again. What happened next was one of the most notorious massacres in Latin American history, not only because of the size and brutality, but also because there was a sole survivor, left to tell the tale. **Rufina Amaya Mírquez** had escaped the line of women and hid behind a tree, where she laid for hours, motionless and terrified as she watched the whole town murdered and burned, including her husband and children. When she was sure the soldiers had left, she frantically made her way through the forest out to the main road where somebody found the traumatized 35-year-old woman, disheveled and in shock. She went to the international media with her story, and shortly after the massacre took place, American journalist Raymond Bonner showed up in El Mozote. He published an article in the *New York Times* in January 1982 describing his interview with Rufina Amaya, backed up by his personal account of seeing the skulls and bones of dozens of bodies "buried under burned-out roofs, beams, and shattered tiles." The article was refuted by both the Salvadoran and U.S. governments. The Reagan administration, which was at that time focused on obliterating communism in Latin America, continued funding the war despite the widespread accounts of human rights violations. After the peace accords were signed, the Spanish government

remnants of Monterrosa's helicopter at the Museo de la Revolución Salvadoreña

sent in an Argentine forensics team to excavate the remains of El Mozote. They unearthed the charred remains of hundreds of people, including children, corroborating Rufina Amaya's testimony. Today the church in El Mozote has been rebuilt and is covered in murals of children happily playing.

Behind the church, the **Garden of Innocents** has flowers placed above the graves of the children who were killed, as well as another mural with the names and ages of the victims. In the center of town is a memorial that lists the names of many of the adults who were killed. There is a small women's cooperative that sells crafts and books beside the memorial. You can ask them to arrange a local guide for you, provided you give a small donation. There should be at least one guide who speaks English.

Getting There

You have to leave Perquín early in the morning to catch the El Mozote bus. From Perquín, take a pickup truck ($0.25, 5 minutes) in front of *parque central* heading to the *desvío de Arambala* ("Arambala fork in the road"). Here you need to catch the Joateca-bound bus ($0.50, 20 minutes), which stops in El Mozote. The bus leaves the *desvío de Arambala* at 7:45am. This is the last bus heading to El Mozote, so make sure you don't miss it. The same bus returns from the center of El Mozote at 12:45pm.

If you are driving, El Mozote is about 10 kilometers southeast of Perquín. Head north toward Ruta de Paz, continue straight on Ruta de Paz for about six kilometers, and then take a left onto MOR 15 WB and continue for two kilometers until you see the sign for El Mozote.

RECREATION AND TOURS
Hiking and Swimming
Río Sapo

The cool, turquoise water of Río Sapo is not only pretty to look at but also a pleasure to swim in, as it is also one of the cleanest rivers

in El Salvador thanks to the continued efforts of the surrounding communities and the guidance of local environmental organization PRODETUR. Together they have rallied to make Río Sapo and its surrounding land a protected area that covers about 6,000 hectares. The river boasts a series of small waterfalls that rush over huge stones, creating dozens of deep, clear green pools that are perfect for swimming, even during the dry season. There are two trails around the river, but they are not marked. Each trail takes about 1.5 hours and you need a guide. Guides can be arranged through **Perkin Tours** (Final Calle Principal, tel. 2680-4086 or 7901-9328, rutadepaz.perkin@gmail.com), which also runs an excellent campsite beside the river. They run package tours that include transportation to the campsite, food, a tent, an hourlong hike to a nearby waterfall, and an evening fire on the rocks for $40 pp.

If you would just like to take a swim in the river, it is best combined with a trip to El Mozote. It's about a 45-minute walk from the town to the river. Ask for a local guide once you are in El Mozote.

La Cascada el Chorreron

About four kilometers east of Perquín in the small town of San Fernando is La Cascada el Chorreron, a rushing waterfall and swimming pool hidden at the end of a beautiful hike past lush green cattle fields and spotless blue skies. This completely isolated gem has a palpable fairy-tale feel, complete with butterflies and lots of shade provided by the large leafy trees. The walk takes about 1.5 hours and can easily be done on your own. It can get hot, so bring water, sunscreen, and a hat.

To get to El Chorreron, take bus 332 ($0.50, 20 minutes) from Perquín to San Fernando; buses pass by the center of Perquín at 8:40am, 10am, and noon. Once you arrive to San Fernando, look for the road that leads to the cemetery, and then walk straight for three kilometers on this road. You will see a sign for El Chorreron on the right side, pointing toward a house. Enter the gate to the house and walk straight ahead. Ask whoever is around to point you in the right direction. From there, it is a 10-minute climb down a path to the waterfall. The same bus returns from the center of San Fernando to Perquín at noon and at 3:30pm.

Llano el Muerto and Bailadero del Diablo

On the road toward the Marcala border with Honduras, the environment transforms into a dreamlike landscape displaying an immense expanse of flat granite rocks sprinkled with trees, shrubs, and creeks. This is the area called **Llano el Muerto** (Dead Man's Plains) and **Bailadero del Diablo** (Dance Floor of the Devil), marked by tall pine forest, wide-open prairies, and strange rock formations. There are walking trails that take you to the rushing Río Negro and waterfalls that create lovely swimming pools during the rainy season. There are no real difficult hiking trails here, but it's worth a visit to enjoy walking around the surreal scenery, relaxing by a waterfall, and cooling off with a swim.

La Cascada el Chorreron

It is possible to do the trip as a day trip, but there are *cabañas* in Llano el Muerto, if you feel like spending the night. About seven kilometers from where the bus leaves town, **Centro Turistico Llano El Muerto** (tel. 2660-3184, carmenmaria1223@hotmail.com, $30 d) has *cabañas* scattered on a large grassy property with a swimming pool, restaurant, and just a short walk to a waterfall and swimming hole. Each *cabaña* has three beds, a private bath, and a small porch with a hammock.

Llano el Muerto is about five kilometers northeast of Perquín and Bailadero del Diablo about two kilometers farther in the same direction. Bus 486, also known as the Marcala bus ($0.50, 20 minutes), passes by the center of Perquín at 6:50am daily and goes first to Llano el Muerto and in another 10 minutes stops at Bailadero del Diablo.

ACCOMMODATIONS
$10-25

Hotel Perkín Real (entrance to Perquín, tel.

7209-3042, $10 pp) is a good budget choice, located right at the entrance of Perquín, across from *comedors* and *tiendas,* and within walking distance of *parque central* and the museum. A long corridor is lined with simple dorm rooms, each with four single beds with very clean, brand-new shared baths. The mattresses have plastic coverings on them, which can take a little getting used to, and the rooms do not have ceilings, which means you are fair game for mosquitoes (and privy to your neighbors' conversations), but overall it's a comfortable stay for the price.

The more open-minded traveler might check out **La Casita de la Abuela** (Calle Los Héroes, on the way to Museo de la Revolución Salvadoreña, tel. 2680-4237, $10 d), where *la abuela* Alba Gladis rents out one room (her room) in the back of her eclectic shop, where you will find everything from locally collected crystals, books, and old solidarity posters to a small café with Salvadoran poetry adorning the walls. The rustic room out back has a well-worn plush double bed, cable TV, fan, and private bath. The roosters are up at the crack of dawn right outside the window, and *la abuela* is not far behind; the good news, however, is that by the time you are up, she will have a huge pot of coffee brewing.

The most popular hotel in the area is **Perkín Lenca Hotel de la Montaña** (Km. 205.5, Carretera a Perquín, tel. 2680-4046, www.perkinlenca.com, $20 d, includes breakfast), and with good reason. Not only are the rooms lovely; a portion of the proceeds goes toward running a local school for children in the area (ask owner Ron Brenneman if you are interested in volunteer opportunities). *Cabañas* are set high up on a hill and scattered among pine trees and hammocks. Each room has tile floors, two beds, fan, private bath with very hot water, and swinging saloon-style doors, which look nice but may hijack privacy. In front of each room is a porch with a hammock, and free drinking water is provided. Farther down from the rooms is a large restaurant that serves very good home-cooked food and which has Wi-Fi. The hotel is located about a 15-minute walk before the entrance of Perquín, so if you are planning on staying here, make sure you ask the bus driver to let you off at the hotel.

$25-50

Even farther away from the entrance of town than Perkín Lenca Hotel de la Montaña is **El Ocotal Hotel de Montaña** (Km. 201, Carretera a Perquín, tel. 2634-4083, www. hotelocotal.com, $25 d, includes breakfast), about a 25-minute walk from the entrance of town. This hotel offers a peaceful vibe among the tall pines that are interspersed with short walking trails, a swimming pool, and a restaurant. *Cabañas* are set high up and away from the main road, with a lovely view of green hills and forests. Each *cabaña* has a small porch with a hammock, and the inside is simply decorated with two beds, fan, and private bath with hot water. This is a nice option if you are looking to get away from it all and commune with the sounds of nature.

FOOD

Antojitos Marisol (main road, no phone, 7am-5pm daily, $2-5) serves tasty *comida típica* at very economical prices. This small, simple *comedor* has a few tables, a TV, and a set lunch and dinner menu that usually involves some kind of meat, rice, and salad. If you come at an odd time, just ask what is available and something (simple as it may be) can always be prepared.

If you are catching an early pickup to El Mozote, the only *comedor* open for breakfast before 7am is the tiny **Comedor Teresa** (in front of *parque central,* no phone, 6am-9am and 11am-1pm daily, $2-3), where you will find locals filling up on fast, cheap breakfast before starting their workdays. Portions are generous and items on offer include the usual eggs, beans, plantains, cheese, and tortillas.

Perkin Lenca Hotel de la Montaña (Km. 205, Carretera a Perquín, tel. 2680-4046, www.perkinlenca.com, 7am-8pm daily, $4-10) offers the best view in Perquín, alongside excellent, home cooked food, including freshly baked bread, cookies, cakes, and pies. The restaurant is large and built out of pinewood, giving it an authentic mountain-lodge feel. They serve up traditional meat dishes, tacos, soups, and salads, and the outdoor seating area is a great place to watch the moon rise in the evening.

El Ocotal Hotel de la Montaña and Restaurante (Km. 201, Carretera a Perquín, tel. 2634-4083, www.hotelocotal.com, 9am-9pm daily, $5-12) has a cute open-air restaurant near the swimming pool, with beautiful mountain views. The menu specializes in *comida típica* and is very popular with Salvadorans coming from San Miguel on the weekend especially for *sopa de gallina.*

La Cocina de mi Abuela (entrance to town, on the right side, tel. 2502-2630, 8am-5pm Sat.-Sun., $3-6) is open on the weekend only and serves up economical generous portions of *comida típica.* If you are lucky, you might catch *la abuela*'s grandson playing the piano while you dine.

172

INFORMATION AND SERVICES

There is no visitor information office in Perquín, but the **Centro de Amigos del Turista (CAT)** (tel. 2656-6521, cat.rutadepaz@yahoo.com, 9am-5pm daily) is an excellent resource with English-speaking staff who can help you arrange guided tours anywhere in the area. The office is located just outside of Jocoaitique, a small town two kilometers north of Perquín. There are no banks in Perquín, so make sure to bring enough cash to carry you through your time here.

GETTING THERE

From the San Miguel bus station, bus 332 ($1.35, 3 hours) leaves daily at 6am, 7:20am, 8:30am, 10:50am, noon, 12:30pm, 1:40pm, and 4:15pm. If you miss the last bus, you can take bus 328 ($0.75, 1 hour, every 15 minutes) to San Francisco de Gotera, and from there transfer to a crowded pickup truck to Perquín ($0.75, 1 hour, runs every 15 minutes).

If you are coming from San Salvador, you have to take bus 301 (*ordinario* $3, 3-4 hours, every 15 minutes; *especial* $5, 2 hours, runs every 30 minutes) from the Terminal de Oriente to San Miguel and then take bus 332 ($1.35, 3 hours, 6am, 7:20am, 8:30am, 10:50am, noon, 12:30pm, 1:40pm, and 4:15pm daily) from the San Miguel bus station to Perquín.

If you are driving from San Salvador, take the Carretera Panamericana. If you're driving from San Miguel, take highway CA7 heading north for 53 kilometers to Perquín.

Historic Sites near Perquín

The towns of Guatajiagua and Cacaopera and the archaeological site Cueva del Espíritu Santo can each be visited as a day trip from Perquín or San Miguel. Cacaopera and Cueva del Espíritu Santo are located in the same direction and can be visited in one day, but it will likely require an overnight in Corinto.

GUATAJIAGUA

The small town of Guatajiagua is known for its black pottery, which has been crafted by hand by the women of this town since the indigenous Lenca people populated this region as long as 3,000 years ago. Most of the women in the town make a meager living through makeshift workshops in their homes, and it is not uncommon to see three generations of women working away molding the clay into shape or setting it out to dry. The men then tend to the clay while it cooks in the wood-fired dome-shaped kiln. Once the clay hits the right temperature in the kiln, it's taken out and dyed black with the seeds of the *nacascol* tree.

If you are interested in learning about how the pottery is made, or participating in production, or if you would like to buy some directly from the source, a trip to Guatajiagua is easy enough to do if you have a few free hours. If you would like a tour, it can be arranged through the **Centro de Amigos del Turista (CAT)** (tel. 2656-6521, cat.rutadepaz@yahoo.com, 9am-5pm daily) just outside of Jocoaitique, two kilometers north of Perquín.

Getting There

To get to Guatajiagua from Perquín, take a pickup truck ($0.75, 1 hour, runs every 15 minutes) to San Francisco de Gotera. Ask where Banco Agricola is and wait in front of it for bus 410 ($1, 30 minutes, runs every hour) to Guatajiagua. From San Miguel, take bus 328 ($0.75, 1 hour, runs every 15 minutes) to San Francisco de Gotera, and from there bus 410 to Guatajiagua.

If you are driving, Guatajiagua is 44 kilometers southwest of Perquín and 25 kilometers north of San Miguel. Driving from Perquín, follow the Ruta de Paz south 29 kilometers to San Francisco de Gotera and then head east on the Carretera San Francisco Gotera, which will turn into to Carretera Guatajiagua until you see the signs for Guatajiagua.

CACAOPERA

Anyone interested in the indigenous history and culture in El Salvador should not miss a visit to Cacaopera, an area believed to be the sole surviving example of an otherwise vanished ethnic group referred to as Kakawira or Ulúa. It is thought that they arrived from northern Nicaragua sometime around 3000 BC. Invited by the Maya to come to what is now El Salvador and begin to cultivate cacao, the Kakawira settled beside the Río Torola and named their community Cacaopera, which roughly translates as "cultivate cacao by the river."

Cacaopera has been better able to preserve its indigenous culture than other parts of the country because of its relative isolation in the middle of the mountains of Morazán, and important archaeological sites have been discovered in the area. Some sites are former Ulúa communities that date roughly from 3000 BC; others, including caves with petroglyphs, date as far back as the Archaic period (8000-2000 BC).

If you are interested in visiting some of these lesser-known sites, you can contact Tata Miguel Ángel at **Museo Winakirika** (tel. 2651-0251, after 6pm tel. 7857-2036, 8am-4pm daily, donation), about one kilometer outside of town (take a motorcycle taxi, $1-2). Tata Miguel runs not only the museum but a community center where he leads different activities aimed at preserving and cultivating indigenous culture. The museum showcases indigenous artifacts, photos, traditional costumes and masks, grinding stones, and more. Tata Miguel is an incredible source of information and can arrange tours (in Spanish only) to surrounding communities that still live traditionally; he also offers permaculture courses and courses about plants indigenous to El Salvador. There are also simple adobe rooms if you are interested in sleeping here ($5 pp). This is intended to mimic traditional

living, and as such there is no water or electricity. For bathing, the river is about a three-minute walk, and food can be prepared by local women if requested. Tata Miguel also leads Mayan ceremonies honoring the earth, water, corn, and, of course, cacao. Visitors are welcome to participate.

Getting There

From Perquín, take a pickup to San Francisco de Gotera ($0.75, 1 hour, runs every 15 minutes), but ask to be dropped off at *desvío a Cacaopera* also known as *desvío el Amante*. From there, take bus 337A ($1, 1 hour, runs every hour) to Cacaopera. From San Miguel, take bus 328 ($0.75, 1 hour, runs every 15 minutes) to San Francisco de Gotera, and then transfer to bus 337A ($1, 1 hour, runs every hour).

Cacaopera is 23 kilometers south of Perquín, and the road is extremely bad. It is not recommended to drive.

★ CUEVA DEL ESPÍRITU SANTO

From San Miguel, a 3.5-hour ride along a paved but neglected road will eventually bring you to the town of **Corinto**, a cute, clean town with not much to do other than visit one of the most important rock-art sites in Central America, estimated to be up to 8,000 years old. **Cueva del Espíritu Santo** (8am-4pm daily, free) is El Salvador's most ancient archaeological site and has roughly 200 pictographs, including multicolored symbols, animals, human figures wearing feather headdresses, and various hand stencils. The cave is 60 meters wide, 30 meters high, and 20 meters deep, creating a natural gallery with the art grouped according to the varying styles (animals, humans, symbols). There are a couple of other caves within walking distance; one has more pictographs, and the other has a pretty waterfall. The guides in the park can show you how to get there; their services are free.

Because of the amount of time it takes to travel between Corinto and San Miguel, you might have to spend the night in Corinto. **Hotel Corinto** (Barrio la Cruz, tel. 7543-7520) offers basic, clean rooms ($10) with cable TV, a fan, and a private bath. There is a restaurant serving up simple, cheap food.

Getting There

From San Miguel, bus 327 ($1.75, 1.75 hours, runs every 30 minutes) runs directly to Corinto. The last one leaves at 3:30pm.

Traveling from Perquín, take bus 332 ($1.50, 2.5 hours, 5am, 5:45am, 6:30am, 7:50am, 8:30am, and 11am daily) to San Miguel, but ask to be dropped off at Kilómetro 18. On the opposite side of the street from where the bus drops you off, wait for bus 327 ($1.75, 1.75, runs every hour), which will take you to Corinto.

The road to Corinto from San Miguel is long and in extremely poor condition, and it is not suitable for driving.

Visiting Cacaopera and Corinto in a Single Day

Cacaopera and Corinto can both be done as a day trip if you get an early start. From Perquín, take a pickup to San Francisco de Gotera ($0.75, 1 hour, runs every 15 minutes), but ask to be dropped off at *desvío a Cacaopera,* also known as *desvío el Amante.* From there, take bus 337A ($1, 1 hour, runs every hour) to Cacaopera. After you are finished in Cacaopera, you can take bus 782 ($1, 2 hours, runs every hour) to Corinto.

From San Miguel, take bus 328 ($0.75, 1 hour, runs every 15 minutes) to San Francisco de Gotera, and then transfer to bus 337A ($1, 1 hour, runs every hour).

prehistoric rock art inside the Cueva del Espíritu Santo in Corinto

Background

The Landscape

El Salvador is geographically small—at 21,000 square kilometers, about the size of Massachusetts—but diverse. In one day you can see mountains, hike through cloud forest or climb a volcano, swim in the Pacific Ocean, and sleep in the valley of San Salvador. It is the only Central American country without a coastline on the Caribbean Sea, but it makes up for it with 300 kilometers of scenic, rugged Pacific coast. El Salvador is one of the most seismologically active regions on earth, straddling three of the large tectonic plates that make up the earth's surface. The motion of these plates causes frequent earthquakes and volcanic activity. The country is home to 23 active volcanoes and many more dormant, inactive, or extinct ones; in fact, 90 per cent of the country was formed by volcanic materials, creating the fertile soil that El Salvador has been built on.

Land issues have played a pivotal role in the history of the country, dating back to the arrival of the Spanish conquistadores and their expropriation of land for the commercial cultivation of cacao, balsam, indigo, and most significantly, coffee. Coffee is still grown in the western part of the country but is no longer the main product driving the economy. Land issues these days consist of overcrowding in the urban areas, overconsumption of the land's natural resources, and climate change threatening the coastline.

GEOGRAPHY

El Salvador can be split into three geographical zones: the **mountain regions,** which are two parallel ranges that cross the country east to west: the northern Sierra Madre (which includes the scenic Apaneca-Ilamatepec mountain range in the western region of the country) and the coastal range in the south; the **central plain,** which sits between the two ranges; and the **coastal plain,** which is long and slender, running 300 kilometers along the Pacific (the widest part is in the far east, beside the Golfo de Fonseca). The mountain chains consist mostly of temperate grasslands and oak and pine forests (or what is left of them). The central plain is home to many small bushes and subtropical grasslands as well as savanna and large swaths of deciduous forests. The coastal plain, which is also referred to as the Pacific Lowlands, extends from the coastal volcanic range to the Pacific Ocean. Vegetation here includes tropical fruit trees, including plenty of mango and coconut trees, as well as cashew fruit, tamarind, and *jocote* (similar to a plum) trees. The fact that the ocean is so close to the southern chain of volcanoes makes for some pretty spectacular scenery along the coast, especially around the area of La Libertad, where at some points the slopes of the volcanoes jut down directly into the ocean. This southern range of mountains is actually an intermittent series of more than 20 volcanoes clustered into five groups. The westernmost group, near the Guatemalan border, includes Izalco and Santa Ana, the highest volcano in the country at 2,365 meters. The land between these volcanoes is some of the best for coffee growing due to the rolling hills and rich volcanic soil. The northern range of mountains is part of the Sierra Madre and forms a continuous chain along the border with Honduras. Elevations in this region range 1,600 to 2,700 meters. This part of the country suffers from erosion as a result of deforestation. As a result, it is the country's most sparsely populated zone, with very little farming or other development.

In the middle of all this seemingly uninhabitable land, one might wonder, where do all the people live? Considering this is the most densely populated country in Central America, it's a good question. The central plateau between the two mountain ranges constitutes only 25 percent of the land area but contains the heaviest concentration of population and the country's largest cities. This plain is about 50 kilometers wide and has an average elevation of 600 meters. Terrain here is rolling, with occasional escarpments, lava fields, and geysers. The cities in El Salvador are under constant threat of earthquakes due to their location between these volcanic ranges, but the lack of other inhabitable areas for large settlement means they simply have to accept the looming possibility of unannounced natural disasters.

RIVERS AND LAKES

El Salvador is home to more than 300 rivers, the most important of which is the **Río Lempa.** It is El Salvador's only navigable river, and its tributaries drain nearly half of the country. Starting in Guatemala, the Río Lempa is 422 kilometers long and provides water for several hydroelectric dams, including the Cerrón Grande reservoir in Suchitoto, more commonly referred to as **Lago Suchitlán.** The river cuts across the northern range of mountains, continuing along much of the central plateau, and finally flows through the coastal volcanic range to empty into the Pacific. Other rivers are generally short and flow from the central plateau through gaps in the southern mountain range until they empty into the Pacific. Numerous lakes of volcanic origin are found in the interior highlands; many of these lakes are surrounded by mountains and have high, steep banks. The largest lake, **Lago de Ilopango,** lies just to the east of the capital. Other large lakes include the **Lago de Coatepeque** in the west and the **Lago de Güija** on the Guatemalan border.

GEOLOGY

El Salvador is known as the Land of Volcanoes, and it's pretty obvious why once you are here. The southern part of the country consists of a string of volcanoes that span the country from east to west. Mighty jade-green cones create the most magnificent backdrop throughout the country, but these beauties are also responsible for a history of destructive geological activity. El Salvador sits on the **Ring of Fire,** a 40,000-kilometer line that is the most volcanically active area on earth. One of the most seismologically active regions in the world, situated atop three of the large tectonic plates that constitute the earth's surface, El Salvador experiences earthquakes on a regular basis. Most of these are referred to as tremors—enough of a shake to stir everybody up, but not enough to cause any real damage. However, when the strong quakes do hit, they can be deadly. Some of the most notable were the January and February 2001 earthquakes that killed more than 1,000 people and destroyed much of the country's infrastructure. There were also significant quakes in 1951, 1965, 1982, and 1986.

With more than 20 active volcanoes in the country, volcanic eruptions are always considered a threat. The most active volcano has been **Volcán Izalco.** Izalco erupted at least 51 times from 1770 to 1966, earning it the nickname "Lighthouse of the Pacific" because the flowing lava created a bright-orange luminous cone visible to seafarers. Thankfully its frequent eruptions were never deadly. In contrast, **Volcán Ilopango** has erupted only twice in recorded history, but its first eruption, around AD 500, was so powerful, according to American paleoecologist Robert Dull, it may have been the catalyst for the Dark Ages, sending a thick dust and ash cloud over the northern hemisphere, cooling parts of the earth, and resulting in millions of deaths. Its effects at home were especially catastrophic. It blanketed much of central and western El Salvador with pumice and ash and decimated the early Mayan cities, forcing inhabitants to flee. Trade routes were rendered inaccessible, and the centers of Mayan civilization shifted from the highland areas of El Salvador to lowland areas to the north and in Guatemala. Most recently, while Hurricane Stan dumped record levels of rain on El Salvador in 2005, **Volcán Santa Ana** decided to erupt—adding to the chaos and mudslides. **Volcán San Miguel,** also known as Chaparrastique, is one of the most active volcanoes in the country and has erupted half a dozen times since 1994, most recently in 2013.

CLIMATE

El Salvador has a tropical climate with distinct wet and dry seasons. The wet season is referred to as *invierno* (winter) and typically runs from May to October. The dry season is known as *verano* (summer) and runs from November through April. The Pacific lowlands are the hottest region, with annual averages ranging from 25°C to 29°C. San Salvador and the rest of the central plateau has an annual average temperature of 23°C. The mountain areas are the coolest, with annual averages from 12°C to 23°C, and minimum temperatures sometimes approaching freezing. At the highest point in the country, El Pital, sometimes there is even snow.

Almost all of the annual rainfall and humidity happen during the wet season, with southern-facing mountain slopes the hardest hit and the central plateau receiving the least amount of rain. The average annual rainfall in El Salvador is 183 centimeters in the coastal areas and up to 203 centimeters in the central plateau. During the wet season, there is a tendency for the rain to come every afternoon around 3pm and continue throughout the evening. As a result of climate change, hurricanes are more frequent in El Salvador, usually accompanied by heavy rains that can result in floods and mudslides. The year 2009 was especially destructive in terms of extreme weather. Heavy rains caused floods and mudslides that killed hundreds and displaced approximately 15,000 people. Hurricane Ida hit that year, and mountainsides collapsed after the relentless rain, killing 124 people and cutting off mountain communities from the rest of the country.

ENVIRONMENTAL ISSUES

When traveling in El Salvador, it is not uncommon to spot large belts of land peppered with the stumps of trees that have been burned or cut down. **Deforestation** is a problem here and highlights the biggest environmental threat that faces El Salvador today: the growing number of people and the limited amount of land. This tiny country has the highest population density and the smallest amount of primary forest remaining in Latin America. The demand for firewood is outpacing the number of trees, but people need to eat, and wood and charcoal are their primary source of energy for cooking food. Charcoal is produced by heating wood in makeshift kilns and reducing it. This process is one of the most environmentally destructive, and the emissions created are detrimental to human and environmental health. Thankfully, the number of people burning wood to make charcoal has decreased in El Salvador, but it is still common in some areas.

The long-term impacts of deforestation are varied and serious. When forests are logged or burned, that carbon is released into the atmosphere, increasing the amount of carbon dioxide and other greenhouse gases and accelerating the rate of climate change. Erosion results in reduced soil fertility and sediment deposition in streams and rivers causes an increased risk of floods.

The government has halfheartedly tried to control trees being cut down, but with the growing number of people in need of energy sources, this is becoming increasingly difficult. One point of interest is that the strongest advocates of forest preservation are ex-guerrillas. Many of them say that the trees protected them during the civil war, and now it is their turn to protect the trees. Cinquera in Las Cabañas is a wonderful example of a place where the protected forest is monitored by ex-guerrillas who make sure that no more trees fall victim to human needs.

Some people cut down trees to supplement their income and some do so simply to be able to feed their families. Either way, the underlying issue is poverty, and the problem of deforestation cannot be solved without also addressing the root issues that drive people to short-term solutions with long-term consequences.

The high level of deforestation in El Salvador has contributed to its second-biggest environmental challenge: **climate change.** El Salvador is one of the most vulnerable countries in the world when it comes to climate change, not only because of its location but because of its small size and dense population. The primary effects of climate change include rising sea levels and increased frequency and severity of extreme weather events such as tropical storms, hurricanes, and floods. El Salvador's coastal areas are especially vulnerable and have already seen an increase in hurricanes and floods in recent years. Areas such as the **Lower Río Lempa** and **Bahía de Jiquilisco** are especially at risk, as the sea rises and submerges the mangroves that sustain villages in these regions. The mangrove forests provide the only source of livelihood for these impoverished communities, who make a subsistence living from fishing and crabbing. If sea levels continue to rise, soon it will not just be their livelihoods but their homes as well that will be swallowed up by the ocean.

Another potential environmental threat to the mangroves in this region is the recent proposal for the development of high-end resorts. Plans for these resorts are in the works with the help of money from the U.S. Millennium Challenge Corporation (MCC), a bilateral American foreign-aid agency established by Congress in 2004. The program strives to donate aid money to country-led projects that target problems specific to that area. In El Salvador, the proposal is to improve the economy through tourism in one of the country's most beautiful and undeveloped areas. Some

people believe that the project will bring revenue to the area, providing jobs and much needed income, but environmentalists and those in local communities fear the worst. They say the effect this kind of heavy development may have on the fragile ecosystem and the people who coexist with it will mostly likely be grim. Local communities are populated by subsistence farmers who largely want to continue this kind of work, rather than seeking employment as cleaners or cooks in hotels. They also want to protect the bay and mangrove forests and fear that development will jeopardize the biodiversity. Government officials do require that developers meet minimal environmental standards, but considering El Salvador's track record on enforcing environmental laws, whether or not this will be honored remains unknown.

Another major environmental issue in El Salvador is the problem of toxins in the soil. All of the land is aggressively farmed, even on the steepest slopes, and the volume of agrochemicals leaching into the soil is building. In recent years, a number of farmers across Central America have mysteriously fallen victim to kidney diseases. Studies have shown a strong correlation between the illness and the amount of pesticides being used by farmers. A study by the El Salvador Health Ministry shows that the rate of kidney failure in El Salvador is significantly higher than in neighboring countries, and most of it is concentrated in one part of the country, Bajo Lempa in the eastern department of Usulután. This is likely largely due to the heavy exposure to pesticides and herbicides in this area during the cotton boom period, when chemicals like DDT—an insecticide that is now illegal—were heavily used. There is still residual DDT in much of the soil, and although DDT is now banned, highly toxic agrochemicals continue to be used. Most of the pesticides are sold by foreign companies, and under a 2004 executive order, sellers, crop owners, and importers were held responsible for ensuring that the people who handle the agrochemicals receive training and use appropriate safety gear; sadly, this is not enforced. In fact, if you travel to this region, you are likely to see farmers working with little more than a bandana around their faces.

Solutions

It's not all doom and gloom when it comes to the environment in El Salvador. This country has many dedicated and qualified people working toward building a sustainable future. **EcoViva** (1904 Franklin St., Suite 902, Oakland, CA 94612, tel. 510/835-1334, www.eco-viva.org) is an organization that is spearheading a community movement to protect people and the land from environmental degradation. They work mainly in the Bajo Lempa area and focus on community empowerment and "climate-proofing" local agriculture. Methods for doing this include the increased use of agroforestry, specifically the intercropping of trees to prevent soil erosion and increase biodiversity; adaptation of native seeds to weather extremes; installation of drip-irrigation systems for the dry season; and crop diversification, so that no single crop is wiped out completely by a drought or flood. However, they also believe it is important to be realistic, and as climate change shows no signs of slowing down, and agricultural damage continues, it is becoming more critical for local communities to have other sources of income besides subsistence farming. EcoViva is helping communities build a green economy through the implementation of small livestock projects, ecotourism, and sustainable fisheries.

SalvaNatura (33 Avenida Sur, Colonia Flor Blanca, San Salvador, tel. 2202-1515, info@salvanatura.org, www.salvanatura.org) administers **Parque Nacional El Imposible** and partners with the **Rainforest Alliance,** an international NGO that works to preserve biodiversity, to protect coffee forests and curb deforestation. The project works by providing information and tools to coffee growers to improve their management practices and make them more responsible toward the environment; this focuses on, but is not limited to, the practice of cutting down trees to make room for coffee. The project works in all coffee-growing areas of the country.

Voices on the Border (4000 Albemarle St. NW, Suite 200A, Washington DC 20016, tel. 202/505-2850, voices@votb.org) is another excellent organization that strives to promote sustainable development in El Salvador. Over the course of the last few years, they have worked hard to protect a section of forest near the community of Amando López beside the Río Lempa. They have raised awareness about how valuable the forest is to the community and secured protected status from the government. Through grants and the support of El Salvador's Ministry of Environment, they now provide salaries to a team of local forest rangers and run energy forests (stands of fast-growing trees planted specifically to provide quick sources of firewood). The benefits of this project were seen in October 2011 when other communities in the same region suffered the worst flooding in the region's history. Amando López, however, escaped with only minor damage. Community members thank the forest for absorbing the majority of floodwaters from the Río Lempa.

ECOTOURISM

Ecotourism has caught on in theory but unfortunately not in practice in El Salvador. Many tour companies or hotels tag the word "eco" onto their names, but all it really means is that the tours take place outside in a natural setting, or that the hotel is built with natural materials. For example, it is not uncommon to find a hotel with wood cabins, bars, and furniture calling itself eco-friendly, but considering the problem of deforestation in the country, the use of more wood should be a red flag rather than a sign of sustainability. For information on how to organize a truly eco-friendly trip in El Salvador, you can contact **SalvaNatura** (33 Av. Sur, Colonia Flor Blanca, San Salvador, tel. 2202-1515, www.salvanatura.org, info@salvanatura.org).

For true community tourism, contact

Green Trips (tel. 7943-5230, greentripselsalvador@gmail.com), where English speaking bird aficionado Benjamin Rivera organizes tours that focus on community development. The tours include sleeping and eating with local families, fishing trips in nonmotorized boats, and visiting local NGOs and women's groups. El Gringo Tours (Calle Francisco Morazan 27, Suchitoto, tel. 2327-2351, rpbroz@gmail.com), run by the very sociable transplanted Californian Robert Broz, also offers unique tours that focus on bird-watching and local community development, specifically in the artisanal areas of San Sebastián and Ilobasco.

For volunteer tourism that is eco-oriented, contact Eastern Pacific Hawksbill Initiative (ICAPO) (www.hawksbill.org) and EcoViva (1904 Franklin St., Suite 902, Oakland, CA 94612, tel. 510/835-1334, www.eco-viva.org). Both offer programs in the Bajo Lempa area that focus on environmental projects, sustainable development, and preservation of the endangered hawksbill turtles.

Plants and Animals

El Salvador's flora and fauna can generally be split into three regions: the interior plateau (the massive Parque Nacional El Imposible provides the most biodiverse representation of this region), the coast, and the cloud forests of the highlands. However, it is also worth noting that the type of flora and fauna you will see in El Salvador has more to do with the altitude rather than the region. For example, Cerro Verde is technically located in the interior part of the country, but because of the high altitudes, it has the same flora and fauna as the cloud forest region of the country.

One constant in El Salvador are the gorgeous flowering trees, in particular the *maquilishuat* (*Tabebuia rosea*), the pink-tufted national tree; the beautiful *roble colorado* (*Tabebuia schumanniana*), with its fuchsia flowers and dark-gray branches; and the *árbol de fuego* (*Delonix regia*), a tree with brilliant orange flowers, all of which flower in the spring. Mango and coconut trees can also be found all over the country, especially along the coast.

PARQUE NACIONAL EL IMPOSIBLE (INTERIOR PLATEAU)

Located in the coastal elevations of Ahuachapán, Parque Nacional El Imposible is the largest and most biologically diverse protected area in the country. Given the size of El Salvador, though, it is still not a large enough area to guarantee the survival of its species. Pressure from surrounding communities encroaching on the land has diminished the amount of space in the park, affecting many species, most notably the puma. Pumas used to roam freely in the area, but now there is only space in Imposible for one family of pumas. Lack of genetic variation, vulnerability to natural disasters and disease, and illegal hunting have seriously threatened the possibility of the species' long-term survival. Unfortunately, pumas are not seen in the park anymore; they are likely to have migrated to neighboring Guatemala, where there is more space. Although you won't find large mammals, the biodiversity of flora and fauna is still impressive, and a hike through the mosaic of different ecosystems is one of the highlights of a visit to El Salvador.

Plants

The first thing you will notice in Imposible are the towering trees with massive trunks and roots. The giants that dominate the lowlands of Imposible are the *conacaste* (*Enterolobium cyclocarpum*) and the much revered *ceiba* (*Ceiba pentandra*), which can grow up to 70 meters tall. The ceiba was sacred to the Maya; its roots were believed to go to the underworld. The *conacaste* fruit could come in handy if you are camping in the park and have some washing to do. It is one of the best natural soaps found in the region; simply add a little water and friction to produce a sweet-smelling white foam.

Palms and tree ferns abound in Imposible, including the **pacaya** (*Chamaedorea tepejilote*), which flowers in the beginning of the rainy season in May and June. It produces edible florets that Salvadorans enjoy in savory tomato sauces.

A number of plants valued in El Salvador for their medicinal properties are found in Imposible. One of the endemic plants you will likely see is called **guaquito de tierra** (*Aristolochia salvadorensis*), which can be found along most hiking trails. It is distinguished by its beautiful burgundy-colored flowers with white spots and grows on trees near the base of their trunks. Its roots are used for healing stomach problems. Some other important medicinal plants that can be found in the forest include **ujushte** (*Brosimum alicastrum*), referred to as *ramón* in other Latin American countries; in El Salvador the plant's name has retained a connection to the Mayan root *ox,* which means corn. The towering tree can grow as tall as 37 meters, and the sprawling roots extend as far as 1.5 meters. The nutrient-rich seeds can be dried and ground into flour and are capable of being stored for long periods of time, making them an important supplement to corn in the Mayan diet. The bark of the fruit-bearing **sálamo** tree, recognizable by its broad crown and multicolored bark, is used for snake bites, and the red flowers of the **chichipince** plant are prepared to prevent infections and skin problems, inflammation, menstrual pain, and insect bites.

More than 40 species of **orchids** have been identified in Imposible, but the most aromatic and lucrative of these is **vanilla,** a succulent vine originally used by the Aztecs.

Birds

El Imposible is one of the most interesting places in the country for bird-watching. It has more bird species than any other park in the country, and of the 282 species reported, six occur nowhere else in El Salvador. These include the **white hawk, crested guan, great curassow, ruddy quail dove, tody motmot,** and **green shrike vireo.** Sadly, all of these birds likely inhabited the entire country at one point, but high levels of deforestation left them homeless and restricted to the forest of Imposible. The best time to look for the park's resident birds is April to June, when the rain begins to fall and breeding season begins.

Reptiles and Amphibians

The extra-long dry season in El Salvador is especially hard on amphibians and reptiles, and most species estivate (spend the summer in torpor, similar to hibernation) during the dry season, making it very hard to spot them during these months. Similar to all seasonally dry environments on the Pacific coast of Central America, the species diversity of amphibians and reptiles is quite low. In total, there are 53 known species in the park, and they are mostly drought-resistant.

Most of the amphibians in the park are frogs and toads. Four species of frogs and seven species of toads have been found. The most common are **aquatic frogs,** not surprisingly, as Imposible is full of streams and ponds that act as the watershed that feeds into Barra de Santiago. These frogs have long, powerful legs for jumping and intricate webbing between their toes for swimming, and they can often be seen during the day, unlike most other amphibians, which are typically nocturnal. **Leaf litter frogs** have varied patterns and colors that blend in with the leaves on the forest floor. They lack adhesive pads on fingers and toes and do not have webbing between their toes. They can usually be found hanging out in piles of leaves in the more humid parts of the forest.

You are likely to see lizards darting around the forest floor while hiking in Imposible, scurrying through the leaf litter in open spaces. The largest species of lizards are iguanas—the **black-tailed spiny iguana** and the **green iguana,** which are misnomers as both can range in color from green to dark gray. Not so conspicuous are the 21 species of snakes known to exist in the park, three of which are venomous: the **Central American coral snake, jumping pit viper,** and the **neotropical rattlesnake.**

Insects

El Salvador is teeming with beautiful **butterflies,** and Imposible is a particularly popular hub for these colorful creatures. There are at least 5,000 species in the forest, and most of them like to flutter around the lower zone of the park. This is the part of the forest where there has been the highest degree of disturbance. In the parts that have been cleared, wildflowers have taken up residence, attracting the butterflies into these wide-open spaces. Some of the most common butterflies found in the park include the **white morph, great prepona, bluish wanderer,** and the **torquatus swallowtail.**

Mammals

The largest species that historically inhabited the El Imposible forest are in danger of extinction, and sadly, visitors have little chance of seeing them. The majestic puma that once roamed the forest has likely relocated to neighboring Guatemala, where there is more space. For more than 50 years it was believed that the **Baird's tapir** was extinct in El Salvador; however, the skull of a tapir was found in 1987, and in 2002 the tracks of this large mammal were identified in the low-lying humid area of the park, suggesting that the tapir has possibly reappeared. It is unknown whether the tracks were made by one of the original inhabitants of the forest or if tapirs from Guatemala have recolonized the area; either way, it is promising news. Mammals you are more likely to see while in the forest include **armadillos, foxes,** and **pacas,** similar to guinea pigs, with small forelimbs, large hind limbs, a cone-shaped body, and pretty white spots like those of a deer that run the length of its body.

THE COAST

Where the land meets the sea, the roots of the **mangroves** rise up out of the saline water in strangely beautiful twists and turns. There are two major mangrove forests on the coast: **Barra de Santiago** in the west, and **Bahía de Jiquilisco** in the east. The flora and fauna of these two forests are similar, with more

El Salvador is teeming with butterflies.

species variety in Bahía de Jiquilisco, where the lower Río Lempa estuary covers an area of 63,000 hectares, making it the largest remaining mangrove forest in Central America.

The mangroves are one of the most biologically complex ecosystems on earth. **Fish** (common species include snook, red snapper, and corvina) and **shellfish** such as crabs and shrimp all depend on mangrove roots for their nesting grounds, and the trees also provide habitat for thousands of **marine and coastal birds** as well as a refuge for several endangered species, among them the **spider monkey,** the **hawksbill sea turtle,** and **crocodiles.** In Bahía de Jiquilisco, there are three additional species of **sea turtles: olive ridley, leatherback,** and **green.**

One of the most important functions of the mangrove forests is that they are highly effective carbon sinks. They absorb carbon dioxide, taking carbon out of circulation and reducing the amount of the greenhouse gas in the atmosphere. Coastal wetland areas like Bahía de Jiquilisco can sequester up to four times more carbon dioxide per hectare than rainforests, making them one of the earth's best carbon storage facilities, a major natural bulwark against worldwide climate change. Their location on the coast, however, also makes them one of the most vulnerable areas in terms of the effects of climate change. As climate change accelerates, more and more natural disasters are hitting coastal areas, including hurricanes, tropical storms, floods, and landslides. Longer periods of drought, coupled with storms that are more intensive during the rainy season, threaten to wipe out crops each year. Half of the world's mangroves have disappeared in recent history, and with the current global rate of greenhouse gas emissions, their protection is especially critical, not only for people but for all the other species who thrive in this habitat.

HIGHLAND CLOUD FORESTS

The highlands are cool, misty, verdant, and ideal for hiking. These areas offer a great

Flowers abound in the damp, mountainous regions of the country.

array of natural vegetation, ranging from **semideciduous tropical forest** at lower altitudes, **pine-oak forest** at middle altitudes, and the misty **cloud forest** at the very top.

The cloud forests of El Salvador are full of **epiphytes,** plants that survive from moisture in the air and depend on other plants for structural support. Epiphytes include the **mosses, lichens,** and **brackens** that cover the forest floor as well as lush green **tree ferns** that can grow as tall as eight meters. The cloud forests also have an enormous array of gorgeous **orchids,** which thrive in the moist highlands.

Chances of seeing the elusive green and red **quetzal** are highest in the cloud forest regions of the country. The best time of the year to see the bird is during the March-June mating season, and the best time of day is at sunrise.

Other colorful birds found in the highlands include the **blue-throated motmot,** a beautiful green bird with a teal throat and tail, and the **collared trogon,** with its green and teal head, striking red body, and black- and white-striped tail.

The highlands of El Salvador are also visited by migratory species such as the globally threatened **golden-cheeked warbler,** a small, dainty bird with distinctive mustard-yellow cheeks.

Some mammals that you might spot while in the highlands include red and gray **squirrels, porcupines,** and **agoutis.**

History

EARLIEST CULTURES

There is a gap in the knowledge of prehistoric activity in El Salvador, most likely due to the poor conditions of preservation at the populated sites and the fact that most of the remains from that time have been buried deep in the ground, making it hard to recover them. However, considering its location on an isthmus and the wealth of natural resources, it is almost impossible that the area wasn't inhabited, or at least occupied temporarily by people in transit, very early on. The earliest evidence of human activity in El Salvador can be found in the eastern part of the country in the form of cave art; the most popular and accessible site is **Cueva del Espíritu Santo** in Corinto, where the drawings are estimated to be 8,000 years old.

The first known inhabitants of what is now El Salvador occupied the coastal plain, an area that proved to be strategically important. It was narrow enough that they could easily walk to the mountains to hunt animals or gather plants, but also close enough to the sea to take advantage of the marine life, so they never had to spend long periods of time away from the settlement. This access to ecological diversity led to a high-protein diet rich in fish and meat, and the fertile plain provided an opportunity for agricultural development.

By 1500 BC the inhabitants had created new tools such as projectile points for hunting as well as knives for skinning animals, and they had established small villages where they lived in simple adobe huts. Soon after, the appearance of pottery helped advance the society, as they were able to store and transport food. The small villages grew until an elite emerged that took over key roles in the development of these communities, and what had been a community without social stratification became a chieftaincy with a powerful ruling class.

From 900 BC onward, the population of farmers grew rapidly. New settlements began to appear throughout the west and in the center of the country.

THE MAYA AND THE LENCAS

Around 500 BC, there was a major population explosion coupled with an expansion of settled land, especially in the lowlands of the country. Important sites of this time include **Santa Leticia** in Apaneca and **Tazumal** in Chalchuapa. Although the Mayan sites in El Salvador in general were not as grandiose as the sites in Guatemala or Mexico—El Salvador was a bit of a backwater—the area of what is now Chalchuapa was culturally important. Evidence from Tazumal suggests a strong relationship with the Olmec Empire in Mexico. The Maya who lived there produced major ceramics and controlled the obsidian trade with Guatemala. Additionally, glyphs found in the tombs of Tazumal suggest that important knowledge originated in this area with regard to the calendar and writing systems.

The settlement of Santa Leticia began around the same time and was located in the foothills of Apaneca; it covered about six hectares of very fertile land. In addition to being an agricultural settlement, it was also thought to be an important ceremonial and religious center because of the large round female sculptures that were discovered there. The two sculptures weigh 7 and 12 tons and can be seen at Hotel Leticia. More than 70 similar sculptures have been found in other significant archaeological sites in Guatemala, Mexico, Honduras, and Nicaragua. Mystery shrouds the figures found at Santa Leticia, but it is thought that they date from the early preclassic period and have Olmec influence.

Santa Leticia also provided important information for the reconstruction of daily life during this time. The variety of corn that was cultivated here was common among classic Mayan populations in Belize and Mexico. The discovery of bell-shaped holes in the ground known as *chultunes* were used to store grains or water and were also found in other Mayan settlements.

Around the same time, in eastern El Salvador, the site of **Quelepa** was being developed. Located in the valley of the Río Grande beside San Miguel, this land was used for the cultivation of maize, beans, cacao, and cotton. The Quelepa population maintained relations with the Maya in western El Salvador; this is evidenced by discovery of ceramics likely to have come from Chalchuapa as well as a jaguar head very similar to another found in Cara Sucia in the west. Despite this evidence of contact with the Mayan west, all other cultural features were similar to their Honduran neighbors, the Lenca, and as such it is generally assumed that this was a Lenca settlement.

There was also a settlement in the center of the country where the artificial Lago Suchitlán now is, but very little is known about it other than that the land was fertile and likely used predominantly for maize cultivation. The people who lived here were Lenca, but findings in these sites also indicate trade and contact with the Maya in the west.

ILOPANGO BLOWS, AND EVERYBODY FLEES
The eruption of Ilopango volcano around AD 500 completely changed the distribution of people in El Salvador. It sent large amounts of volcanic ash flying over an area of 10,000 square kilometers, forcing everyone within that range to flee and relocate. Many large and small population centers were completely abandoned, and most people moved to the mountains of Apaneca, where the land was high enough to avoid the flooding caused by large amounts of ash blocking the channels of the rivers.

The centuries after the eruption are known as the classic period (AD 250-1000). During this time, Chalchuapa was eventually repopulated, but it never returned to its former prominence. Cara Sucia reached its peak during this time, becoming wealthy from the salt trade between 650 and 950. The central region was completely abandoned after the eruption, and small communities did not return to the area until about 200 years later, when San Andrés eventually became the Mayan administrative capital of the region, with a large central settlement surrounded by many smaller villages.

But as luck would have it, just as the Maya had returned and resettled, another volcano, called Laguna Caldera, located in the department of La Libertad, erupted around 600. Thankfully this was not nearly as catastrophic as Ilopango, but still managed to decimate some villages. Fortunately for archaeologists, many of the buildings in the small Mayan village **Joya de Cerén** were perfectly preserved by the ash, and because of this, important information has been discovered about the daily life of the inhabitants. A wide variety of wildlife was also preserved, including a dog's tooth, two species of ants eating beans inside pottery bowls, a duck, and some bones, probably of a deer, that appeared to be cooking instruments similar to spatulas.

Beginning in 800, there was a process of destabilization in the Mayan areas, during which large centers were abandoned. This phenomenon, known as the collapse of classic Mayan civilization, ended around 1000, and produced a complete reorganization of society in the Americas.

ARRIVAL OF THE PIPILES

It was not until 600 years after the Ilopango eruption that the western part of the country was resettled. The new inhabitants, the Pipil people, are thought to have migrated from central and southern Mexico. Archaeological evidence suggests that the first migration of Pipiles to El Salvador was sometime between 900 and 1200.

The Pipiles established themselves in the central and western part of El Salvador and called the land Cuscatlán: the land of precious jewels. They cultivated cacao and established trade with the Lenca in the east.

THE SPANISH CONQUEST APPROACHES

During his last voyage in 1502, Christopher Columbus found a Mayan trader's canoe off the coast of Honduras. It was full of gleaming goods never before seen by the Europeans in the Caribbean—obsidian weapons, shiny copper axes, and colorful fine fabrics. His interest was piqued; it was clear that this canoe belonged to a people completely unknown to the Spanish. No one could have imagined that the few goods on this canoe were just a sample of what was about to be discovered.

In 1519 Hernán Cortés led his troops into the Yucatán in Mexico. After consolidating control of the Aztec Empire, the Aztecs told him of the area to the south, in the Guatemalan highlands, where a group of people called the Kaqchiquel lived. To lead the conquest of the land to the south, Cortés chose his lieutenant, **Pedro de Alvarado.**

Alvarado's group set out on their mission in 1522 and succeeded. Once the Kaqchiquel were under the control of the Spanish, Alvarado used them to help conquer their enemies in the east, the Quiche. After the successful conquest, he asked the Quiche who their enemies were to the south; they said it was the Pipiles. Armed with this information and his retinue of recruits, Alvarado set his sights on the newest mission: to find out who the Pipil people were, what they had, and how they could be conquered.

CONQUISTADORS ARRIVE IN EL SALVADOR

In June 1524, Alvarado led the first effort by Spanish forces to extend their dominion to the nation of Cuscatlán (now El Salvador). Alvarado left for Cuscatlán with 250 Spanish and nearly 6,000 indigenous recruits from Mexico and Guatemala. They made their way down to the Pacific coast and entered modern-day Salvadoran territory via the Río Paz on June 6, 1524.

On June 8, they reached the port of Acajutla, where they were faced with thousands of Pipil warriors who had gathered there to meet the Spanish, presumably to prevent their entrance into the Río Grande valley of Sonsonate, which led directly into Pipil territory. The defenders were dressed in thick cotton padded armor, referred to in Mexico as *ichcahuipilli*. The *ichcahuipilli* offered excellent protection against arrows but were cumbersome and prevented the Pipiles from moving quickly. As a result, many fell and became easy prey for the Spanish. They were defeated, but the Spanish did not escape casualties. Most notably, during the **Battle of Acajutla,** Alvarado was hit with an arrow that fractured his femur and left him with an infected wound for eight months. The injury would remain with Alvarado for the rest of his life, a reminder of the fearlessness of the people of Cuscatlán. After their victory, the Spanish rested in Acajutla for five days, nursing their injuries and planning the rest of the conquest.

The next battle, in Tacuzcalco, was led by Alvarado's brother due to Alvarado's leg injury. Alvarado watched the battle from the hills and was pleased to see an easy victory. After defeating the Pipil population here, they moved on to Miahuatlán, which had been abandoned by its inhabitants fleeing in fear. Alvarado was renowned for his skill as a soldier, and also for his cruel treatment of the indigenous people. Word had spread about the mass murders committed in subjugating the indigenous people in Mexico. Finally, the army reached Atehuan, where the Spanish received the good news they been waiting for—an invitation from the rulers of Cuscatlán to enter the main city.

On June 17, 1524, Alvarado's army came to the city of Cuscatlán, where they were received by the spear-wielding population, who tenuously granted them entrance to the political and cultural center of the Pipil people. However, as soon as the Spanish made themselves comfortable, most of the indigenous population abandoned the city. When Alvarado took some Pipiles as servants and put them to work panning for gold, his intentions to subjugate the local population became clear, and any indigenous people who were left fled to the nearby mountains.

Alvarado sent messengers to the mountains to convince the leaders of Cuscatlán to come back and negotiate, but the messengers returned with the news that if he wanted to talk, they would be waiting for him in the hills with their weapons. Alvarado attempted once more, sending a new group of messengers up to the hills, but they never returned. He then commanded his army to attack several hills where the indigenous people were hiding. During the attacks, many people were killed on both sides, but the Pipil warriors had cleverly put themselves in a position of power, as they were familiar with the terrain up in the hills. Defeated, Alvarado abandoned the attack and returned to Guatemala on July 21, 1524, with the news that the Pipil people were a force to be reckoned with.

In 1525 they returned with reinforcements, more weapons, horses, and dogs. The conquest of Cuscatlán was completed, and the city of San Salvador was established. Over the course of the next few years the conquest continued with a scorched-earth strategy, as homes were burned and the population was murdered en masse. In eastern El Salvador the Lenca people also fiercely resisted the Spanish, but by the late 1530s a smallpox epidemic had hit, killing much of the indigenous population. Alvarado saw this as his chance to strike. He invited the leader of the Lenca people, Lempira, for peace talks in 1537, and when he arrived, Alvarado shot him dead. With this, the ruthless conquest of El Salvador was complete.

THE COLONIAL ERA

In the eerie calm after the battles, the colony was born, and Cuscatlán—the land of precious jewels—ironically became El Salvador, "the Savior." During the two decades following the conquest, Spanish settlers began exploiting the local resources, hoping to get rich quickly, as they had in Mexico and Guatemala. Their thirst for gold was insatiable. They were disappointed, however, to find only negligible amounts of gold that was accessible only through the laborious and time-consuming method of panning. The Pipil were put to work delivering cargo and panning for gold in the riverbeds; this was the primary economic activity for the first two decades of the conquest. Panning for gold eventually took its toll on the indigenous population: It took the men away from their traditional roles as providers, and the fact that they could not cultivate corn the way they had before disrupted the family routine and exhausted the men. Feeling demoralized after the violent conquest and decimation of their culture, they were reluctant to have children and subject them to the same oppression. As a final blow, plagues of European origin began to affect the indigenous population throughout the 16th century. The labor force was dwindling, and the Spanish were forced to look at alternative sources of income that did not require so many laborers and so little return. They eventually realized what the Pipil already knew: The real economic potential was in the soil. This discovery would irrevocably change the course of El Salvador's history.

Large tracts of land were granted by the crown, much of it preexisting cacao plantations that had been there since pre-Columbian times. As the Salvadoran population decline was already considerable, Guatemalan workers were brought in, and as many as 1,000 enslaved Africans were brought to live on the haciendas and provide manual labor. They cultivated cacao, cotton, and balsam, but they discovered that the most lucrative crop was indigo. Indigo produced tremendous profits during the 18th century. Largely as a result of the importance of the indigo trade, by the turn of the 19th century the colonial capital of San Salvador had come to be the second city of the Captaincy General of Guatemala, the Spanish administrative unit that encompassed most of Central America during the colonial period. Things were looking good for the Spanish in El Salvador, but events were about to take a turn for the worse.

THE ROAD TO REVOLUTION

By the early 19th century, the political landscape in Europe was deteriorating. The Peninsular War, a military conflict between France and the allied powers of Spain, Britain, and Portugal, destabilized Europe and by extension its colonies. The war was fought for control of the Iberian Peninsula and started when French and Spanish armies occupied Portugal in 1807, escalating in 1808 when France turned on Spain, its ally until that point. The result was a major shift in power in Europe that would have widespread reverberations in the Spanish colonies. The worldwide Spanish Empire began to unravel as French occupation of Spain weakened Spain's hold over its colonies, providing an opportunity for nationalist revolutions in Latin America.

This chaos in Europe, coupled with economic hardship due to a chapulin plague that destroyed indigo crops in 1802 and 1803, created an increasingly tense atmosphere in El Salvador. The people of San Salvador had been hit hard by the economic crisis and were fed up with the fractured and weak leadership from Spain. The success of the American and French Revolutions had changed perceptions about who should control government, and movements began to form in the Spanish colonies. The seeds of revolution had been sown.

INDEPENDENCE FROM SPAIN

On November 5, 1811, Salvadoran priest **José Matías Delgado** rang the bells of the Iglesia La Merced in the center of San Salvador and called for insurrection, in what would become known as the *primer grito de la independencia,* Central America's first shout of independence. It had been brewing for a long time and was primarily the result of ever-increasing discontent in the middle classes, specifically a class of people called criollos. The criollos were people of Spanish descent born in the Americas; they had grown tired of being governed by their equals from afar.

The rebels assembled in the town square outside the church, where one of the independence movement's most passionate leaders, **Manuel José Arce** (son of Spaniard Bernardo José de Arce, the colonial intendant of San Salvador from 1800 until 1801), famously proclaimed: "There is no king, nor intendant, nor captain general. We only must obey our *alcaldes*"—meaning that since Ferdinand VII of Spain had been deposed, all other officials appointed by him no longer held any legitimate power.

The protest was dramatic but short-lived. The insurrection was suppressed, and many of the participants were jailed. Another protest took place in 1814 but again the participants were jailed. After this, however, many groups began meeting secretly and strategizing about how to successfully untether the country from Spain. Finally, on September 15, 1821, in light of unrest in Guatemala, Spanish authorities conceded and signed the Acta de Independencia (Deed of Independence) that released Guatemala, El Salvador, Honduras, Nicaragua, Costa Rica, and the Mexican state of Chiapas from Spanish rule and declared the region's independence.

The following years would entail numerous power struggles among the various actors in the fledgling nation. In the beginning, Mexico took over rule of the region and founded the First Mexican Empire, led by **Emperor Agustín de Iturbide,** despite strong resistance from El Salvador. In 1823 a revolution in Mexico ousted Iturbide, and a new Mexican congress voted to allow the Central American provinces to decide their own fate. El Salvador declared independence from Mexico together with Guatemala, Honduras, Nicaragua, and Costa Rica. The **United Provinces of Central America** was born under the leadership of **General Manuel José Arce.**

The federal republic was short-lived and marked by power struggles between liberals and conservatives. This infighting, coupled with the government's lack of resources, made the federation extremely unstable. In order to raise money to support the federation, a number of new policies were implemented, most notably the expropriation of uncultivated land. Previously, land that was not being used as haciendas was considered communal and was available for indigenous people to practice subsistence slash-and-burn agriculture. Now the haciendas expanded, usurping the communal land. Circumstances for the poor, mostly indigenous peasants became even worse than they had been during Spanish rule.

Several popular uprisings took place in the major agricultural areas of San Miguel, Chalatenango, Izalco, and Sonsonate, but they were all suppressed. The most famous of these was the peasant uprising of 1832, led by **Anastasio Aquino,** a fiery worker on an indigo plantation. He organized other peasants and began a campaign of attacking army posts, recruiting the indigenous conscripts and burning haciendas. Legend has it that the spoils were collected and given to the poor. By the end of January 1833 Aquino had managed to assemble an army of between 2,000 and 5,000 men, armed mostly with spears. They headed to San Vicente, where many of the exploitative landowners lived.

His army sacked the city, but soon Aquino was talked into peaceful negotiations by a former boss. The rebels took control of the town and proclaimed the famous **Declaration of Tepetitán** on February 16, 1833, in which,

among other things, they demanded the abolition of forced labor. After several failed attempts by the government to negotiate with Aquino, they finally approached San Vicente with an army. Although Aquino initially escaped, the government offered to spare the life of anyone who would divulge the location of the rebel peasant. After somebody revealed Aquino's location, he was found and executed by firing squad. His head was cut off and put on display in an iron cage, with the message written on a sign: "Example for Rebels."

THE COFFEE REPUBLIC

By 1840 the Central American republic had collapsed and newly independent El Salvador made a crucial discovery. The mineral-rich volcanic soil in the mountainous parts of the country was perfect for growing one of the world's most coveted crops: coffee. Coffee would soon replace indigo as El Salvador's commercial crop of choice, and as the world's thirst for the addictive elixir grew, so did the economy of tiny El Salvador. Sadly, only a small segment of society reaped the benefits. The introduction of coffee would prove to be a continuation of the colonial paradigm that set the elite in charge of large tracts of land and forced the indigenous to work it. By this point the country was being run by an oligarchy that consisted of a small group of wealthy families who were inextricably linked with the government. A series of presidents throughout the last half of the 19th century supported the seizure of communal land so that it could be used for coffee production. In addition, an antivagrancy law was passed, leaving the displaced campesinos with no other option than to work for a pittance on the new coffee plantations.

Although the coffee industry itself was not taxed by the government, ample revenue was raised indirectly through import duties on goods purchased outside the country with the money earned from coffee sales. From 1870 to 1914, more than half of government revenue came from coffee. The campesinos who worked the land did not see any of the profit, and as rural discontent grew, the fledgling Salvadoran armed forces shifted its focus from external defense to maintaining order within the country.

Between 1907 and 1911, **President Fernando Figueroa** gave special attention and increased funding to the army, and foreign military advisors were hired to educate and train Salvadoran officers. In 1912, **President Manuel Enrique Araujo** won the presidency with the support of outgoing Figueroa. Under his presidency, the **Guardia Nacional** (National Guard) was created. Trained by former officers of the Spanish civil guard, its sole purpose was to provide security on the coffee fincas. Most fincas enjoyed the services of their own Guardia Nacional units posted on their property; and regional commanders were compensated by the finca owners to ensure the continued loyalty of the guardsmen. Of course, this internal repression only served to foment tension between landowners and peasants.

On February 9, 1913, during a concert in San Salvador's Parque Bolívar (now Plaza Barrios), two farmers attacked President Araujo with machetes. He was critically wounded and died five days later. The motives of the attackers, who were executed after a military trial, were never investigated.

MILITARY DICTATORSHIPS

Araujo's death was followed by the **Meléndez-Quiñónez dynasty.** The Meléndez and Quiñónez clans were two of the most powerful families among the Salvadoran oligarchy, and their unquestioned rule lasted from 1913 to 1927. After this, **Pío Romero Bosque,** former Minister of the Government and a trusted collaborator of the dynasty, succeeded President Jorge Meléndez and in 1930 finally announced free elections.

On March 1, 1931, in what was considered the country's first freely contested election, **Arturo Araujo** came to power. His presidency did not last long; Araujo faced general popular discontent from people expecting economic reforms and redistribution of land. When it became clear that he had no intention of broaching either of these subjects, there were demonstrations in front of the Palacio Nacional from the first week of his administration. The unrest spread among military officers, and in December 1931, with the collapse of coffee prices, the military's dissatisfaction peaked. A group of young officers, led by vice president **Maximiliano Hernández Martínez,** staged a coup d'état and ousted Araujo. Araujo fled the country, and Martínez assumed power.

The presidency of Martínez would be the first of a succession of military dictators who sustained the status quo through swift and savage suppression of any kind of dissent. A vegetarian fascist, he was famously quoted as saying that ants do not reincarnate but people do, so it's better to kill a human than an ant. He certainly proved loyal to these words, ending his presidency with more than 30,000 deaths at his order. He is legendary among the extreme right, and had one of the deadliest death squads of the civil war named after him. His personal quirks are also legendary; a believer in mystic creeds, he is often remembered for once having strung colored lights throughout San Salvador in an effort to ward off a smallpox epidemic.

THE 1932 PEASANT REVOLT AND MASSACRE (LA MATANZA)

When the Great Depression hit, coffee sales started to drop dramatically. Plantation owners were no longer able to pay their workers. Desperate, many peasants begged for work in exchange for food alone. Eventually, not even that was available, and thousands of landless peasants were left unemployed and starving. All of the arable land had been taken up to grow coffee, so food shortages also came.

Rural discontent was widespread, but rural people lacked a leader who could really galvanize the masses, until **Agustín Farabundo Martí** appeared. Martí was the son of wealthy landowners. As a child he had recognized the exploitation of the country's poor and decided he wanted to do something about it. Sharp, passionate, and hardworking, he fit the profile of the people's voice, and appeared just when he was needed. Martí was strongly influenced by the socialist movements of Cuba and Nicaragua, and even though his purpose was to turn Salvadorans onto communism, most of the peasants only started to listen to him out of desperation. The movement was fueled by hunger, not ideology.

Martí studied political science at Universidad de El Salvador, but dropped out so that he could dedicate his time to working with landless peasants in rural El Salvador. After being expelled from the country and spending time in the United States and Mexico, including time spent working closely with **Augusto César Sandino** of Nicaragua, he returned to El Salvador to help organize and lead what would become known as the peasant revolt. On January 22, 1932, led by the communist leaders, thousands of rebels, mostly disenfranchised indigenous Pipil people in the western coffee-producing part of the country, attacked government forces. Within three days, they had succeeded in taking control of several towns, disrupting supply lines to many of the country's towns and villages, and attacking a military garrison. The military reacted swiftly and mercilessly. Promising open discussion and pardons for those involved in the uprising, they called all the rebels to a large public square. As thousands of people gathered in the square, waiting for negotiations, they were brutally slaughtered. Estimates are that 30,000 indigenous peasants were killed that day, and in addition, the towns of Nahuizalco, Juayúa, Apaneca, and Izalco were all attacked by the military. **Feliciano Ama,** an indigenous leader, was hanged, and an image of the execution was printed on postage stamps of the time. After this, indigenous people abandoned their clothing, last names, and any other signs that betrayed their heritage.

GUIDED REFORM UNDER MILITARY RULE

From the 1930s to the 1970s, El Salvador was led by authoritarian governments who maintained power through very limited reform and political oppression. The status quo under all of these regimes was keeping the majority of the land in the hands of the elite and quashing any kind of dissent. Among the military there was a divide between the older, more conservative military leaders and the younger generation, who pushed to loosen up the system and enact limited reforms to lessen the likelihood of another violent disruption like that of 1932.

The practice of guided reform, instituted and controlled from above, generally came to be accepted as the best course for the military to maintain the status quo and avoid radical movements. Guided reform emphasized economic development, public works, and social security (including medical and hospital care). However, no steps were taken to threaten the elite-dominated system. Agrarian reform was still out of the question. The country coasted along without any major outbreaks of violence, doing just enough under guided reform to keep popular dissent at bay.

This all changed in 1959, during the presidency of **José María Lemus.** The name **Fidel Castro** was gaining a reputation, and news of a popular revolutionary movement in Cuba began to spread throughout Latin America. Student groups in El Salvador were particularly inspired by the example of Castro and his revolutionaries. Public demonstrations in San Salvador called for Lemus's removal and the imposition of a truly democratic system. All earlier attempts at reform were quickly jettisoned in favor of increased repression. Public protests were prohibited, and political dissidents were summarily detained. The country was in chaos, and the middle class began to worry. Lemus was deposed in a bloodless coup on October 26, 1960. The junta who overthrew Lemus was soon overthrown by a group of young military officers who promised a proper election.

In March 1964 the first election took place under the new system. The main contenders were the **Partido de Conciliación Nacional (PNC),** a conservative political party closely associated with the Salvadoran military, and the **Partido Demócrata Cristiano (PDC),** which sought to find a middle ground between extreme right and extreme left. Although the PNC retained an unchallenged majority in the Asamblea Legislativa, the PDC won a significant victory in the election of **José Napoleón Duarte** as the mayor of San Salvador.

Duarte built a strong base of popular support in this post through improvements in municipal services and the organization of local self-help groups to promote small-scale civic improvements such as school renovations, establishment and maintenance of parks, and adult education programs. He was reelected in 1966 and 1968, and his successful leadership of the capital city strengthened his political profile and made him a well-known national figure.

THE SOCCER WAR

Although social progress was being made in the capital under Duarte in the late 1960s, the rest of the country was in turmoil. To make matters worse, tensions were growing between El Salvador and neighboring Honduras. As a result of the lack of arable land in El Salvador, hundreds of thousands of people had drifted over the border to the much less populated Honduras, squatting on small plots of land while providing much-needed manual labor for United Fruit Company's banana plantations. However, things turned sour when Salvadorans, being the industrious business-savvy people that they are, established many successful businesses, most notably a multitude of shoe stores. Although the economic situation in El Salvador was dismal, it was still quite enviable by Honduran standards, and many Hondurans were put off by the influx of successful Salvadoran businesses on Honduran soil. Tension between the two

countries grew as Hondurans suffered economic stagnation while Salvadorans thrived. The Honduran government decided to kick the Salvadorans out under a land reform law that gave the central government and municipalities much of the land occupied by Salvadoran immigrants and redistributed it to native-born Hondurans. Thousands of Salvadoran laborers were expelled from Honduras, including both migrant workers and longer-term settlers.

Images of displaced refugees appeared in the press, and as the stories of violent treatment of Salvadorans by the Honduran military reached home, anger escalated. Tension between the two countries continued to build until it reached a breaking point during the North American qualifying round of the 1970 FIFA Cup soccer game between the two countries in San Salvador in June 1969. During the game, rowdy fans from both nations taunted each other until full-blown riots broke out. On July 14, 1969, Salvadoran planes dropped bombs on the airport in the Honduran capital, Tegucigalpa, effectively declaring war. Four days later, most of the fighting in the "100 Hours War" was over, and as many as 2,000 people were dead. In the aftermath, an influx of returnees landed on Salvadoran soil only to find their homeland was even more hostile than it was before they left. There was no available land and little assistance from the government, and the country was increasingly plagued by overpopulation and extreme poverty.

THE 1972 ELECTIONS

The returnees only placed more pressure on the government for some kind of land reform. The PDC took this as their opportunity to turn unfair land distribution to its political advantage. They began to push the idea of full agrarian reform, calling for the expropriation and redistribution of land. Not surprisingly, this quickly gained popular support. In the lead-up to the 1972 legislative and presidential elections, the PDC stood a chance at chipping away at the long-running PNC majority, but the presidential election results were in the favor of **Colonel Arturo Armando Molina,** the PNC candidate. The election results were widely contested as blatantly fraudulent. Once again, Salvadorans were left feeling angry and disillusioned. One faction of the armed forces was outraged by the fraud and launched a coup led by **Colonel Benjamin Mejia** on March 25, 1972. The officers were in favor of installing Duarte, the popular PDC mayor of San Salvador, as president.

Some residents of the capital took to the streets in support of the young officers, but not long after that, the thunderous sounds of aerial bombardment reverberated throughout the capital as the air force demonstrated its loyalty to the government. Once again, the military maintained power through brute force. Duarte was soon tracked down by government security forces, who detained him briefly, before he was beaten, interrogated, then dispatched to Guatemala. From there, he flew into exile in Venezuela. He left behind a country teeming with widespread discontent and inequality.

BEFORE THE CIVIL WAR

The government of President Molina used the usual coercive control that had become the norm in El Salvador, but a new, dark element was introduced: **Organización Democrática Nacionalista (ORDEN),** the eyes and ears of the security forces in the rural areas. ORDEN provided counterinsurgent training to commandeered peasants throughout the country, and by the late 1970s its membership reportedly totaled 100,000. While this was happening in the countryside, left-wing terrorism was growing in the city: Kidnappings for ransom and hit-and-run attacks on government buildings and other targets became increasingly common in San Salvador.

The groups who claimed responsibility for these actions were the **Ejército Revolucionario del Pueblo (ERP)** (People's Revolutionary Army) and the **Fuerzas Populares de Liberación Farabundo Martí (FPL)** (Farabundo Martí Popular Liberation Forces). Popular support for radical leftist groups was quickly growing, and these organizations drew much of their leadership from radical Roman Catholic groups known as **Comunidades Eclesiasticas de Base (CEBs)** (Christian Base Communities) that had been established by activist clergy throughout the country.

President Molina tried to quell activism with land reform, but it proved to be too little too late. He passed a law in 1974 calling for the forced rental or potential expropriation of inefficiently used land, but the law was never enforced. Two years later, he declared that 60,000 hectares of land in San Miguel and Usulután departments would be split up among 12,000 peasant families. This did not sit well with the large landowners, who created a delegation to meet with the president. It likely did not take much arm-twisting to get Molina to agree to exempt lands serving a "social function," which essentially could apply to all the land in question, and the plan never came to fruition.

Fear of losing control became a real issue for the military and landowners, and as a result, a deadly right-wing force was taking shape: the **Escuadrón de la Muerte** (Death Squad). Funded by landowners and businesspeople in the oligarchy, the squad specialized in assassinating subversives. The government considered the CEBs to be the most dangerous threat and increasingly targeted outspoken religious leaders. The run-of-the-mill repression also continued with deadly crackdowns on public protests in the center of San Salvador, the worst of which happened after the 1977 election of Carlos Humberto Romero. Once again, electoral fraud was obvious and rampant. Thousands of angry protesters gathered in Plaza Libertad in the center of San Salvador and as many as 50 of them were killed by security forces. It seemed things couldn't get any worse, but sadly the worst was yet to come.

Under the new presidency of Romero, the government dropped its charade of reform and unapologetically increased politically motivated violence. In response, the leftist guerrillas also stepped up their game. Bombings, kidnappings, and assassinations continued to rise. At this point the church was also getting involved. Many priests, including **Óscar Arnulfo Romero,** the archbishop of El Salvador, were followers of **liberation theology,** a Roman Catholic school of thought that had its origins in Latin America during the 1950s and 1960s. It advocated taking action against oppression and addressing the immoral factors that lead to injustice and poverty.

Archbishop Romero was deeply disturbed by the brutality employed by government forces against innocent civilians as well as the clergy. As the suffering of the poor worsened, Romero became an outspoken activist, using his status to try effect social change. He frequently called on his congregation to take action against injustice and urged soldiers not to carry out their orders to kill. He argued against U.S. military aid and wrote an open letter to Jimmy Carter asking him to stop aid to the Salvadoran government as it was only fueling the war and stripping innocent people of basic dignities. This kind of social activism was too close a cousin with communism in the eyes of the military, and on March 24, 1980, Romero was shot dead while giving mass at a

small church in San Salvador. For many civilians, this was the pivotal point at which real terror set in. If the archbishop could be so ruthlessly eliminated, was anybody's life considered sacred?

SALVADORAN CIVIL WAR (1980-1992)

As government-sanctioned violence increased in both rural and urban settings, previously nonmilitant mass political groups metamorphosed into guerrilla fronts. In May 1980 the Salvadoran revolutionary leadership met in Havana, where they were advised by Fidel Castro to unify into one guerrilla group. In October they founded the **Frente Farabundo Martí para la Liberación Nacional (FMLN)** (Farabundo Martí National Liberation Front), honoring insurgent hero Farabundo Martí, who was killed by the military while leading the peasant uprising of 1932. In late 1980 the FMLN announced plans for an insurrection against the government of El Salvador, and on January 10, 1981, the FMLN launched its first major attack. The guerrillas quickly established control of most of Morazán and Chalatenango departments, and would remain in control of these areas for the rest of the war.

civil war memorial in Cinquera

Some of the worst massacres would take place in these areas of the country as the military forces sought to eliminate the guerrilla forces living in the mountainous region. In December 1981 the Alacatl battalion began its **Operación Rescate** (Operation Rescue) in Morazán, an attempt to systematically destroy all support that enabled the guerrillas to survive. This included one of the most violent massacres of a civilian population in Latin American history, the **El Mozote massacre,** in which 800 people, including noncombatant women and children, were murdered. Despite these gross violations of human rights, the Carter and Reagan administrations continued to send millions of dollars in military aid to the government. The fear of communism took precedence over concern for human rights.

The fighting continued for 12 years and cost close to 70,000 lives, forcing thousands of Salvadorans to flee to refugee camps in Honduras or to try their luck in the United States. Children were used by both the military and the guerrillas, and once boys reached the age of 12 they were conscripted into the national army. Many women joined the FMLN and fought in the war as well, and many civilians supported the guerrillas for no other reason than that they were hungry and tired of being poor and landless.

The violence was not restricted to rural areas, and although many tend to romanticize the revolutionary movement, there was plenty of innocent blood on the hands of the guerrillas as well. The people of conservative towns such as San Salvador and Suchitoto also lived in terror and were victims of frequent guerrilla attacks that involved stealing cars, breaking into homes, dropping bombs, and killing civilians.

A UN-backed peace process began in 1990. The **Chalpultepec Accords** called for a 70 percent reduction of the armed forces, the dissolution of the Guardia Nacional and the Policía Nacional, the end of military dictatorships, and the transfer of the state intelligence agencies to the presidency of the republic. All armed FMLN units were also demobilized. A nine-month cease-fire took effect on February 1, 1992, and has not been broken since.

POSTWAR TO PRESENT DAY (1992-2014)

In the years following the signing of the Chalpultepec Peace Accords, Salvadorans went to work rebuilding their country. In 1994, El Salvador held its first election that included candidates of the FMLN and other parties. The conservative **Alianza Republicana Nacionalista (ARENA)** party, originally formed by rightist military officers and landowners, won the presidency, as well as the next two presidential elections after the war. The ARENA leadership put rebuilding the country at the top of its agenda, investing in basic infrastructure, most notably constructing an excellent highway system that remains the best in Central America.

Many Salvadoran entrepreneurs returned from the United States, eager to invest in their home country now that there was peace. The *colón* was replaced by the U.S. dollar, and the economy started to flourish. However, the same underlying issues were at play, the same people were in power, and there was a huge discrepancy between the rich and the poor. Land reforms did finally happen, but many people were given small plots of land in the most untenable parts of the country, susceptible to flooding and other natural disasters. A middle class was virtually nonexistent.

In the 2009 presidential election, the people of El Salvador elected the first left-leaning president, **Mauricio Funes,** a former journalist and member of the FMLN party. His presidential campaign was driven by the slogan "safe change," and he was careful to endorse moderate political policies. Conservatives voiced concern that Funes's election would mean a turn toward Venezuelan influence, but he insisted that strengthening relations with North America was a touchstone of his foreign policy.

The FMLN party has implemented social reforms designed to combat poverty and inequality, some of which include free health

a sign of support for the FMLN outside a home in Cinquera

fight crime. The brutal past cannot be erased from the national psyche, and violence and crime continue to plague the country. Many Salvadorans live in fear due to the heavy presence of gangs throughout the country. In March 2012 a truce was reached between rival gangs **Mara Salvatrucha (MS-13)** and **Barrio 18.** The truce saw the transfer of many high-profile gang members to a luxury prison with access to conjugal visits, phones, TVs, and other amenities. Rumors that the government granted gang members these and other concessions in exchange for a drop in crime circulated around Central America, but they were flatly denied by Funes.

There was a drop in crime for the first year, but in mid-2013 homicide rates started looking more like they did before the truce. The reality is that the culture of violence is so deeply embedded in El Salvador that it could take just as long to dissipate as it took to cultivate. Most Salvadorans limit their entertainment outings to secure places such as malls, movie theaters, and pedestrian areas that are guarded by police. The government has done a good job of creating more of these spaces, notably **Paseo El Carmen** in Santa Tecla. As for the future of El Salvador and its gangs, only time will tell if the collective fear continues to grow or if this relatively new democracy can finally overcome the vicious cycle of violence.

care, the distribution of property titles to hundreds of families, monthly stipends and job training for those who live in extreme poverty, and pensions for the elderly.

These were all positive steps, but the biggest concern for all Salvadorans today is security, and some say Funes did not do enough to

Government and Economy

GOVERNMENT
Politics

After a series of coups, military repression, and a 12-year civil war between the military-led government and left-wing guerrilla groups, the 1992 Chapultepec Peace Accords marked the official end of the war. The Chapultepec Accords called for a ceasefire, a reduction of the armed forces, as well as demobilization of guerrilla units and the creation of a new civil police force. The Comisión de la Verdad para El Salvador (Commission

on the Truth for El Salvador) was created to investigate serious acts of violence during the civil war as well as to identify methods of reconciliation. This Truth Commission delivered its human rights violations findings for both sides in 1993, but an amnesty law for all acts of violence committed during the civil war was passed five days after the report's release.

El Salvador held its first democratic elections in 1992. The right-wing ARENA party won the country's first election and stayed in control until March 15, 2009, when the election of FMLN candidate and former journalist Mauricio Funes as president of El Salvador broke the 20-year hold on power.

Funes began his five-year term emphasizing his centrism, identifying himself as neither a Marxist nor a Socialist. Significant emphasis was placed on implementing wide-reaching social reforms and poverty-alleviation initiatives. A notable achievement during Funes's presidency was a temporary decline in the country's homicide rate as a result of a controversial gang truce. However, Funes left office with a mixed legacy on economic and political fronts, contributing to a disenfranchised middle class.

Politics in El Salvador remains a polemic topic and fanaticism runs deep, which was reflected in the country's 2014 elections, in which the country was almost evenly split between conservative ARENA and the leftist FMLN party. In March 2014, former Marxist guerrilla leader Salvador Sánchez Cerén of the FMLN won El Salvador's presidential election by a slim margin, demonstrating the country's continued political divisions. Sánchez Cerén is the country's first ex-rebel president.

The country's economic growth and crime rates are issues that most concern and affect Salvadorans. The FMLN has a stronghold with poor working-class citizens who still hold strong revolutionary associations with the party. However, many also believe that the administration has lost its loyalty to the poor working class.

In short, Salvadorans are becoming increasingly disenchanted with politics, which is often reflected in conversations. Much of the real, lasting development that happens in the country is a result of remittances sent from abroad, which account for about 20 percent of GDP. The Salvadoran diaspora remains strongly connected to their roots and involved in the country's politics.

Organization

El Salvador is a democratic republic governed under the constitution of 1983. The president, who is both head of state and head of government, is popularly elected by universal suffrage by absolute majority vote and serves for a five-year term. A second-round runoff is required in the event that no candidate receives more than 50 percent of the first-round vote. The members of the 84-seat unicameral Asamblea Legislativa are elected based on the number of votes that their parties obtain in each department, and members serve for three-year terms. The country has an independent judiciary and Corte Suprema de Justicia (Supreme Court). The country is divided into 14 departments, which are similar to U.S. states. Each department is headed by a governor appointed by the president. Mayors control individual municipalities and are elected.

ECONOMY

Compared to other developing countries, El Salvador has experienced relatively low rates of GDP growth, and the trade deficit is one of the highest in the region, at almost 20 percent of the GDP, in comparison to the size of its economy.

In 2004, El Salvador's original currency, the *colón,* went out of circulation and was replaced by the U.S. dollar. The price of everything went up, yet wages stayed the same. Many blame this as the nail in the coffin of an already failing economy due to years of war and natural disasters that had stripped the country of its farmland and infrastructure. Today, 38 percent of the population lives below the poverty line, and the richest 10 percent of the population receives approximately 15 times the income of the poorest 10 percent.

A Free Trade Agreement signed with the United States in 2006 resulted in job production in the manufacturing industry, which created jobs cutting and assembling clothes for export to the United States, but one of the highest crime rates in the world and corruption still deter direct foreign investment.

Most experts agree that this lack of investment is the number-one reason the economy of El Salvador has not been growing. Investment has never been high, but in recent years it has taken a turn for the worse. Gang violence and negative media coverage continue to deter foreign investment, and the basic costs of running a business are high.

In addition to the lack of foreign interest, new growth sectors for a more diversified economy have not been developed. For many years, El Salvador was considered a monoexporter, an economy that depended heavily on one type of export, initially indigo, then coffee. When the demand for both of these products petered out, tourism became the next logical next step in building the economy, but negative media images of the country and lack of infrastructure have prevented many possibilities from being properly exploited.

The return of Salvadorans who have inherited the consumerist ideals of the United States has created a strong market for fast-food chains as well as other international goods. One only needs to head to one of San Salvador's famously carnival-like malls for proof of this. The upper echelon of Salvadoran society is obsessed with shopping, name brands, and the newest technology.

Instead of choosing an investment path and creating incentives in sectors like alternative energy or technology, what is growing in the country are commercial centers, car sales, and cell phone consumption. An estimated 20 percent of El Salvador's GDP is made up of remittances from abroad, and according to the Migration Policy Institute, 1 in 5 Salvadorans live in the United States.

People and Culture

DEMOGRAPHY

El Salvador's population currently stands at 6.2 million, making it the most densely populated country in Central America. Most people are of a mixed European and indigenous background, with small pockets of indigenous people concentrated mostly in Izalco and Nahuizalco in the west, Cacaopera in the east, and Panchimalco, just outside of San Salvador.

Due to the abundance of volcanoes and mountains, habitable areas are limited, putting a tremendous amount of pressure on urban spaces. Rush-hour traffic in San Salvador is a good indication of the ever-growing urban population; traffic after dark, however, tells a different story—this is when everyone has retreated to their homes, nervous about crime and violence. Some of these homes may be luxurious, on the outskirts of the center near the volcano, where the air is clean and security is provided 24 hours daily, but the majority head to one of the many sprawling shantytowns or apartment buildings teeming with families living in tiny, claustrophobic spaces. El Salvador's population continues to grow and doesn't show any signs of slowing down anytime soon—many people joke that Salvadorans are just as fertile as their soil. One in every three babies is born to a mother under age 18. It is the norm for teenagers as young as 15 to have babies, and often the young mothers work while the grandmothers take care of the children. Only in the upper classes are women waiting longer to have children, focusing on education and career first.

RELIGION

The majority of Salvadorans are devoutly Roman Catholic. Religious idols adorn most people's homes, and it is normal to see rosaries hanging from rearview mirrors in cars and crosses worn around the neck. A belief that the events of one's life are God's will is prevalent and is demonstrated in the frequent usage of term *Ojalá*, which finds its root in the Arabic *Insha'Allah*, meaning "God willing," and is used mostly to express a want or desire for something to happen in the future.

All indigenous religious practices were pushed underground after La Matanza in 1932 and never openly reappeared, but that does not mean they do not exist. There are still people who practice indigenous religions, most notably in the primarily indigenous areas: Izalco in the west, Panchimalco in the center, and Cacaopera in the east. This is most evident during festivals or religious holidays, when there are elements from both Roman Catholicism and indigenous traditions.

In Panchimalco, for example, during the Festival de las Flores y Palmas (Festival of Flowers and Palms) in May, the town celebrates its two patron saints with a spectacular festival. The origin of this event is in pre-Columbian Mayan culture, when it was used to commemorate the start of the rainy season. Women strip the palm branches of their leaves and replace them with colorful flowers, creating huge fronds that they then carry through the town. In the afternoon, a group of boys and men perform a religious dance drama that reenacts the Spanish conquest, and afterward a large altar to the Virgin Mary is adorned with flowers and carried through the town by women dressed in traditional clothing.

LANGUAGE

Spanish is the official language of El Salvador and is spoken by virtually all inhabitants. The local Spanish vernacular is called *caliche* and is considered informal slang. Like most other Latin American countries, Salvadorans have an extensive list of words that are not used anywhere else. That is why even visitors who speak Spanish may have a hard time understanding the lively banter among Salvadorans.

The indigenous language is Nahuatl and is only spoken by about 1 percent of the population. The language was all but eradicated when most of the indigenous population was killed in 1932, striking terror into those remaining. They spoke only Spanish in order not to betray their indigenous roots and risk being murdered. However, there is a movement to revive the language, and young people are spearheading it. They call themselves *neohablantes,* which refers to someone who is not indigenous but has studied Nahuatl with indigenous teachers.

Many Salvadorans speak English, and not just in the city. This is because of the large numbers of people who emigrated to the United States during the war and later returned of their own accord or were deported. In the upper classes, pretty much everybody speaks English, as they attend private bilingual schools. For those who study in the public system, primary and secondary education involves English classes, so they usually have basic English skills. Many Salvadorans prefer not to speak English unless they absolutely have to, either as a point of national pride or personal modesty. Oftentimes someone will tell you they don't speak English, but when the pressure is on, they perform like a pro.

EDUCATION

The government provides free education up to grade 9, but only 82 percent of children in El Salvador make it this far. School is mandatory from the age of 7 to age 15, but in many rural areas, choosing between getting an education and helping your family survive is all too common a dilemma. The FMLN government has been responsible for some notable achievements when it comes to education, including government provision of uniforms, shoes, and supplies to public school children, as well as financial assistance to low-income people. These strides have definitely marked some education reform, but several problems remain. In rural areas, many students must walk for hours just to get to their school, sometimes not returning home until after dark. There are many cases when children work instead of going to school, to supplement the family income. It is very common to see young children selling food on the bus or washing windshields in the city. In addition, young boys are often recruited by gang members whose method of operation is to go to school grounds throughout the country and talk kids into joining the gang. For young people living in a cycle of poverty and domestic instability, the feeling of being part of a group and being taken care of is sadly sometimes a more attractive option than going to school.

ARTS AND ENTERTAINMENT
Music

Music was often suppressed during the civil war and maybe this is why many Salvadorans seem to be stuck in the 1990s when it comes to their musical preferences. The most popular radio stations lean toward '90s grunge and rock music.

Traditional music in El Salvador uses marimba, flutes, drums, scrapers, and gourds as well more recently imported guitars and other instruments. On the weekend it is not uncommon to see a group of men traveling on foot with a combination of these instruments and performing in restaurants. Sometimes it is upbeat and fun, but Salvadorans, especially the older ones, seem to love a sad love song, full of longing, with lyrics about lost or unrequited love. Marathon drinking sessions are often fueled by such melancholic music.

Colombian music has also influenced El Salvador, especially **salsa** and **cumbia.** The famous **La Sonora Dinamita** is a Colombian salsa group with Salvadoran vocalist, **Susana Velasques.** Many nightclubs throughout the country have salsa or *cumbia* nights, and even if they don't, by closing time it's usually salsa or *cumbia* that ends up being played for the stragglers.

Live **reggae** and **funk** bands can always be found at La Guitarra in Playa El Tunco or Trenchtown Rock in Santa Ana, and the younger generation has found its voice in the gritty social commentary of the popular hip-hop group **Pescozada.**

Finally, El Salvador's **National Symphony Orchestra** often performs in the national theaters in San Salvador and Santa Ana. The cost is usually around $2, and it is a wonderful way to take in the theaters as well as some beautiful classical music.

Literature

El Salvador's literature is full of interesting characters. Front and center is **Roque Dalton,** the revolutionary poet who was assassinated in 1975 by his own compatriots when the paranoia of the war spun so out of control that they turned on him when they thought he was a spy. Dalton is one of Latin America's most compelling literary figures. His poems were equally political and deeply romantic, and are as relevant today as they were in the 1970s.

Salvador Efraín Salazar Arrué, known simply as **Salarrué,** was a painter, writer, and diplomat who wrote *Cuentos de Barro* (Tales of Clay), a series of short stories that provide an intimate window into idealized rural life in El Salvador. Published in 1933, it became one of El Salvador's best-known literary works and made him one of the founders of the new wave of Latin American folkloric narrative called *narrativa costumbrista.*

Alfredo Espino wrote one of the most published books of poetry in El Salvador, *Jícaras Tristes* (Sad Vessels), a collection of simple poems about love and life in rural El Salvador that was published in 1977. The more sophisticated **Alberto Masferrer** claimed he was never formally educated and instead attended the "university of life." He was a well-known and well-liked essayist, fiction writer, and journalist. In 1928, Masferrer founded and directed the newspaper *Patria,* which published social criticism and called for justice for those most in need in the context of widespread poverty in the country. After La Matanza in 1932, Masferrer was exiled to Honduras and never returned.

If you happen to feel like the scenery in El Salvador conjures images of the classic allegory of love and friendship *The Little Prince,* you are onto something. The rose in the story represents **Consuelo de Saint-Exupéry,** the Salvadoran wife of **Antoine de Saint-Exupéry,** the French writer who penned the famous novella in 1943. The two met in Buenos Aires in 1931 and were married shortly after, only to have a long and tumultuous relationship marked by fighting and extramarital affairs. During the course of their marriage they frequently visited the family home of Consuelo in the small town of Armenia in Sonsonate. From that home there was a view of three prominent volcanoes in the Ilamatepec range, inspiring the backdrop for the novella. Consuelo de Saint Exupéry was also a writer and penned her own memoir of their life together called *The Tale of the Rose,* which was published posthumously in 2000 and became a national sensation in France.

Holidays, Festivals, and Events

Salvadorans are festive folk and celebrate a number of holidays during the year. Depending on how you feel about crowds, you might want to plan your travels to coincide with holidays and festivals or to avoid them. For a moderate taste of Salvadoran party culture, you should try to make it to at least one of the *fiestas patronales.* These parties last several days and celebrate each town's patron saint. They are generally religious in nature and involve special masses and processions as well as carnival rides, beauty contests, live music, and general levity.

For a more debauched holiday, the **Carnaval de San Miguel** tops the list with a weeklong party the last week of November that includes live music, heavy drinking, and dancing. Santa Ana's **Fiestas Julias** celebrate patron saint Santa Ana and take place during the last week of July. Events include carnivals, sporting events, live music, rodeos, parades, and masses. **Semana Santa** is the week leading up to Easter and is when you want to go or stay away from the beach depending on your mood. It seems as if the entire country migrates to the coast to drown themselves in ceviche and *cerveza* for the duration of the week. Finally, San Salvador celebrates its patron saint, the Divine Savior of the World (a.k.a. Jesus Christ) during the **Fiestas Agostinas** in the first week of August. Although the holiday is religious in nature, many Salvadorans take this time as their annual vacation, and many businesses shut down for the week. Again, the beaches get crowded, and there's live music accompanied by heavy drinking, while parties take place throughout the capital.

FOOD AND DRINK

Comida típica (typical Salvadoran food) involves a lot of rice, tortillas, beans, cheese, and grilled meat. *Comedors* (small, inexpensive eateries) are found everywhere throughout the country and have set menus for breakfast, lunch, and dinner, with rock-bottom prices of $1.50-3. All meals are served with tortillas or bread and a small side salad of lettuce, tomato, and cucumber. Some of the better *comedors* have more variety, including steamed vegetables, pasta, or pizza, with a slightly higher price of around $4 or $5 for a plate.

Staples

First things first: The *pupusa.* Anywhere you go in the country, no matter how remote or how elite, you will be able to find this delicious national favorite. *Pupusas* are eaten in *pupuserías,* very basic restaurants consisting of a few tables and a grill behind which two or three women expertly shape the corn dough into a bowl shape and then fill it with cheese, beans, or meat and then slap it all together into a small pancake and grill it. Staple fillings include beans, cheese, *chicharrón* (pork), and *loroco* (an edible flower). Vegetarian *pupusas* include the traditional beans and cheese that are available everywhere, but depending on where you go, it is also possible to find *pupusas* filled with *ayote* (a type of squash) or garlic. Cutting-edge *pupuserías* have fillings that run the gamut from spinach to seafood. *Pupusas* are served with *salsa roja* (a simple yet flavorful tomato sauce) and *curtido* (a pickled cabbage slaw). They are very cheap and filling and an amazing boon to backpackers sticking to a budget; a meal of two or three *pupusas* will cost about $1.

A *desayuno típico* (typical breakfast) consists of *huevos revueltos* (scrambled eggs) or *huevos picados* (scrambled eggs with finely chopped tomatoes, onions, and green peppers), *queso duro* (a hard white cheese similar to feta), or *queso crema* (essentially a dollop of cream), mashed beans, boiled or fried plantain, and tortillas. Breakfast beverages include *refrescos*, hot chocolate, and coffee.

Lunch and dinner options include some type of meat, usually chicken, beef, or fish, served with plain rice or *casamiento* (a combination of beans and rice), salad, and tortillas. In some of the more rural areas, it is common to eat some combination of beans, eggs, cheese, and tortillas for dinner as well.

Meat can be prepared with a variety of sauces. *Al ajillo* is garlic sauce and is often served with seafood. *Encebollado* is a preparation in which the meat (almost always chicken) is simmered and smothered in onions. *Alguashte* is a seasoning typical of Salvadoran cuisine made from ground pumpkin seeds and is used on both sweet and savory dishes.

Street Food

Salvadorans are full of the entrepreneurial spirit and as a result, there is no shortage of delicious snacks being touted at nearly every street corner. Among the most common is *yuca con chicharrón* (cassava with pork); a starchy root vegetable similar to a potato is served fried or mashed, sprinkled with fried pork, and topped with *salsa roja* and *curtido*. Vegetarians can simply ask for their yuca *sin carne* (without meat).

Panes rellenos or *tortas* are another favorite. These are basically hot submarine sandwiches filled with chicken or turkey. Soy meat is also available, making them another vegetarian option. Tacos are the popular late-night snack around the major cities, with thin corn tortillas topped with meat, cheese, and *chirmol,* a mild salsa made of diced tomatoes, onions, and peppers. Tamales are a traditional Mesoamerican food that are made with a corn based *masa* (dough). Filled with meat, cheese, or vegetables, they are steamed or boiled after being wrapped in a banana leaf.

Soups

Soups are quite popular in El Salvador and are eaten frequently for both lunch and dinner. If the thought of eating feet and innards puts you off, stay away from *sopa de pata*, a hearty Salvadoran soup that is made with cow's feet, tripe, *yuca, chayote* (a green squash-like vegetable), sweet corn, bananas, and green beans, and seasoned with coriander, lemon, and chilies. *Mariscada* is a seafood soup that can be ordered as a creamy chowder or as a *caldo* (broth). It comes with mussels, prawns, crab, and often lobster—all with bones and shells. Expect it to get messy.

Sopa de gallina india is probably the most popular soup in El Salvador. It is a chicken soup that comes with vegetables and herbs, made special by virtue of the fact that the hen is free-range. Unless you go to a restaurant that specializes in it, it's usually only available on the weekend, and it's a very popular hangover cure on Sunday. *Sopa de res* is a beef soup that comes with vegetables and corn, topped with cilantro and chilies. *Sopa de frijoles* is a simple black bean soup. *Sopa de tortilla* is a Mexican soup but tastes so good that it has made its way to many menus in El Salvador. It has a creamy tomato-chipotle base with chicken, tortilla chips, cheese, and avocado.

Specialties

Gallo en chicha is definitely not fast food, but it is worth the wait. The best of its kind usually take about two days to prepare, and this is why Salvadorans only have it for special occasions. It is a rooster stew similar to coq au vin, except instead of wine it's made with Salvadoran *chicha* (a fermented drink made of maize) and *panela* (unrefined whole cane sugar). Making excellent *gallo en chicha* is a point of culinary pride for Salvadorans, and many claim to have "the best in the country." The official best remains to be determined, but the unofficial best can definitely be found at La Lupita del Portal in Suchitoto.

Drinks

Refrescos are cold drinks made with local

El Salvador's Best Coffee

Considering El Salvador is a coffee producer, it's disappointing how variable the quality can be—although it's always easy to find a cup of coffee, how good it's going to be is unpredictable. For coffee aficionados, these are the places where you are guaranteed to find the best coffee in the country.

· **Viva Espresso** (La Gran Via, San Salvador, tel. 2289-5052) serves the best coffee in the big city in a tiny, contemporary space in La Gran Via shopping mall.

· On Ruta de Las Flores, the best coffee is at **El Cadejo Café** (Calle Monseñor Romero, Juayúa, tel. 7536-9334 or 7528-6848) in Juayúa and at **Jardín de Celeste** (Km. 94, Carretera Ataco-Apaneca, tel. 2433-0281) between Concepción de Ataco and Apaneca.

· In Suchitoto, **La Lupita del Portal** (*parque central*, Suchitoto, tel. 2335-1429) serves a big, strong cup of excellent brew. Farther east, the small mountain towns of Alegría and Berlín both have very good coffee, with **Casa Mía** (2 Av. Norte 10, Berlín, tel. 2643-0608 or 2663-2027) standing out in the crowd.

fruits and spices, and are often included with *comida típica*. The most ubiquitous *refresco* is *horchata*. Although every Latin American country has its own particular brand of *horchata*, the exact ingredients vary. The Salvadoran version of this drink includes peanuts, *moro* seeds, sesame seeds, cacao, cinnamon, and rice, all ground into a powder and then blended with water or milk and sugar to create a delicious beverage. Other popular *refrescos* include *rosa de Jamaica*, a striking red juice made from hibiscus flowers. It is extremely high in vitamin C and cooling for the body on a hot day. *Jugo de tamarindo* (tamarind juice) is known for its distinct sweet and tart flavor, and *cebada* is a sweet drink made from barley and sugar. Sometimes you might find a pinch of tiny gray seeds in your *refresco*; these nutritional powerhouses are chia seeds and they are full of protein, fiber, and omega-3s, making them a great energy fix.

Hot drinks are just as common as *refrescos* and can be found early in the mornings and in the evenings, especially in the cooler areas of the country. *Atol* is a very popular beverage in El Salvador with roots in Mayan cuisine. It is a thick, hot, sweet drink often eaten with a spoon. *Atol de elote* is the most common and is made with fresh corn (*elote*) and traditionally served in a bowl made of a dried calabash gourd. Even better is *chilate*, which is *atol* with cacao added to it. *Atol de marañon* is made with cashew nuts instead of corn. It's harder to come by but is especially delicious. *Atol de chuco* is made with purple corn and ground pumpkin seeds, giving it its dark color, which is why it's called *chuco*, which means "dirty" in Salvadoran slang.

Hot chocolate is available anywhere *pupusas* are sold, which is basically everywhere. The hot chocolate in El Salvador is always good; it's made from ground cacao beans, sugar, and cinnamon. Keep in mind that *pupusas* and hot chocolate are considered morning and evening fare, and lunch time is for *platos fuertes* (main plates that include meat, rice, and salad) and *refrescos*.

Chicha is a fermented beverage made from corn, and can be alcoholic or not. If you want the nonalcoholic version, ask for *chicha sin alcohol*. It is usually very sweet, and if it does have alcohol, it's strong. Proceed with caution, as it is impossible to know exactly how strong until it may be too late.

Essentials

Transportation

GETTING THERE

Air

Aeropuerto Internacional Comalapa (SAL, tel. 2339-9455, www.cepa.gob.sv/aies) is 44 kilometers southeast of San Salvador and is the only international airport in El Salvador. Like any international hub, it has all the usual airport amenities, including duty-free shops, restaurants, and hotel information. The airport is closer to the beaches of La Libertad than to the city, which works out nicely for surfers and anybody else looking to head straight to the coast.

El Salvador is not a country where you are greeted by hordes of taxi drivers or shuttle companies touting their services as soon as you exit the airport. There should be a line of a few official taxis, and you can rest assured they will provide safe, reasonably priced transportation to your hotel, no matter what time you arrive. A taxi to San Salvador should cost $25-30 during the day and $30-35 at night, and take 1 to 1.5 hours. A taxi to the beaches of La Libertad should cost $20-25 during the day and $25-30 at night, and take around 20 to 30 minutes depending on which beach you are going to.

From North America, there are several airlines that fly to and from San Salvador. They include **American** (www.aa.com), **Delta** (www.delta.com), **Avianca/TACA** (www.avianca.com), **United** (www.united.com), and **Copa** (www.copaair.com). There are no direct overseas flights from Great Britain, Australia, or New Zealand. You have to fly to North America and catch a flight, most often from Miami or Houston. Departing international passengers must pay a $32 departure tax, although this may already be included in the cost of your ticket.

Car

If you are driving into El Salvador in a vehicle, you need a driver's license from your home country or, even better, an International Driving Permit in addition to your license, as well as full registration papers for the car in the driver's name. If someone else holds the title, you have to obtain a notarized letter authorizing you to drive the vehicle.

International Bus

If you arrive in El Salvador from any of the neighboring countries, there are international buses that run frequently.

Guatemala: Pullmantur (tel. 2526-9900, www.pullmantur.com) and **Ticabus** (tel. 2222-4808 or 2243-9764, www.ticabus.com) run from Guatemala City to San Salvador daily, cost $25, and take around four hours. From Antigua, several tour companies offer direct shuttle buses to the beaches of La Libertad for $30; the trip takes about four hours.

Nicaragua: From Managua, **Ticabus, King Quality** (tel. 2271-3330, 2271-1361, or 2257-8997, www.kingqualityca.com), and **Del Sol** (tel. 2243-1345 or 2243-8897, www.buses-delsol.com) all run daily to San Salvador, cost $27, and take 11 hours.

Honduras: From Tegucigalpa, **Ticabus** and **King Quality** run daily to San Salvador, cost $15-30, and take around seven hours.

Costa Rica: King Quality and **Ticabus** run from San José to San Salvador, cost $88-116, and take 25 hours.

Boat

It is also possible to reach El Salvador by boat, coming from Potosi, Nicaragua, and arriving in La Unión. The trip can be booked through **Cruce del Golfo,** which can be

---

Previous: Parque Nacional El Imposible; view of islands in the Golfo de Fonseca from Conchagüita.

contacted through any **Vapues Tours** office in Nicaragua (info@crucedelgolfo.com). The trip takes two hours, crosses a distance of 55 kilometers, and costs $65.

GETTING AROUND
Car or Motorcycle

Driving in El Salvador is easy and straightforward. New, well-paved, and well-signed roads run across the country east to west and north to south. The Carretera Panamericana (Pan-American Highway), or CA1, runs across the country from east to west, and the Carretera Litoral runs parallel to it along the coast. From the Carretera Litoral, there are three well-paved highways that run from the south to the northern part of the country. Although most of the roads are well maintained, some areas in Morazán and Chalatenango require a 4WD vehicle.

In El Salvador, cars drive on the right, as in the rest of North America. Remember that speed limits are shown in kilometers per hour. The speed limit is 90 km/h on freeways and 40 km/h in cities. Take extra precaution around bus drivers, as they tend to drive erratically. Gas stations are widely available.

Driving in San Salvador is at best an exercise in frustration and at worst rage-inducing. You need to drive aggressively if you actually want to get anywhere. This is one of the most densely populated cities in the Americas, and Salvadorans tend to lose their altruistic nature when behind the wheel. There are frequent accidents, and your defensive driving needs to be employed, as this is also one place in the country where all the rules are broken. Signals are barely if ever used, last-minute lane changes are common, and speeding is normal.

Police tend to be lenient with minor infractions such as running a red light, but very stringent when it comes to having your documents on order. There are checkpoints across the country, marked by orange pylons and armed police officers. They will randomly pull vehicles over and ask for your license and registration. If you have these, the check takes no longer than a few minutes. If you are missing either (but especially the registration), there can be serious consequences. Your car may be impounded at the nearest police station, where it will most likely be stripped of its parts by opportunistic thieves. You will then have to return to the station with the registration and pay a hefty fine to get your car back.

In case of a traffic accident, remember never to move your car away from the scene of the accident until after the insurance agent arrives. Insurance companies require photos to process the claim, making this especially crucial if the accident was not your fault. If you do not have insurance, you will have to try to sort things out with the other driver involved, which will involve agreeing on who is to blame and the costs incurred. If that is not possible, you will have to call the police, and you could end up waiting up to four hours for them to arrive. If you hit a person while driving in El Salvador and the person is injured, you will be sent to a detention center while the person is assessed and will only be released when the person claims no further damage.

If driving along the Carretera Litoral on the weekend, be aware that many Salvadorans are coming and going from the beach where they have spent the day drinking. Drunk driving is not heavily monitored, and the legal repercussions are minimal, so stay alert and take it slow.

If you decide to ride a motorcycle through El Salvador, the same rules apply. Be aware that the air quality can be suffocating in some parts of the country, especially San Salvador. It is worth investing in some sort of face mask that can reduce the effects of air pollution.

Car Rental

Most rental car companies are based in San Salvador, and also have offices at the airport. The daily rate is $25 per day, and in general you must be 25 years of age and have a valid driver's license and a major credit card to rent a car. Make sure you check everything on the car, take photos if you can, and make a note of any preexisting damage before signing anything. It is unfortunately quite common for companies to try to claim that the car is damaged when you return it, in an attempt to finagle more money. Make sure all the paperwork is up to date, especially the Tarjeta de Circulación ("circulation card," the vehicle registration) and that insurance is included.

Bus

There are no big bus companies in El Salvador. Instead, all the buses are owned and operated privately. As a result, it is very difficult to get bus information from a unified source. Buses do run reliably to schedule; the problem is figuring out what the schedule is. Because all the buses have different owners, the times and fares are not collected in one place. One way of getting information is to go to the bus terminal and ask the bus drivers or the men standing in front of the buses screaming out destinations. This method is accurate but inconvenient. Hostels that provide excellent information about bus fares and schedules include **Joan's Hostel** (Calle del Mediterráneo 12, San Salvador, tel. 2519-0973) in San Salvador, **Casa Verde** (7 Calle Poniente, between 8 and 10 Av. Sur, Santa Ana, tel. 7840-4896) in Santa Ana, and **Casa Mazeta** (1 Calle Poniente No. 22, Juayúa, tel. 2406-3403) in Juayúa. A good online resource is **Waves Tours Fiestas** (www.wtf-elsalvador.com).

Traveling by bus in El Salvador is cheap and straightforward, and it's a completely authentic way to see the country. Buses literally run from the most isolated villages at the end of bumpy dirt roads to the heart of San Salvador and beyond. For the most part, they are old school buses from the United States that have been decked out with neon lights, colorful tassels, prayers (you may come to feel you need them), and pictures of bikini-clad women. There seems to be no limit to the number of people that are permitted on a bus, and just when you think they couldn't possibly fit one more body, the driver slows down at the next stop. All kinds of people take the bus: farmers, office workers, young families, teenagers, and the most beautiful elderly Salvadoran *abuelas* (grandmothers), who, despite the fact they look as frail as a bird, seem to have unparalleled determination and strength when it comes to getting on and off the bus. Equally admirable are the fare collectors, who somehow make their way through this eclectic mass of bodies, remembering who has paid and who still needs to pony up the fare.

Needless to say, there is often not much room for luggage, but if you want to travel on the local buses with your luggage, it is possible. It can be a bit intimidating boarding a crowded bus with all eyes on you and your baggage, but for the most part, other passengers will be helpful, and in many cases the bus driver will store your big bags up front or in the back. Otherwise, you will have to find a way to fit your luggage on your lap or at your feet.

Keep a close eye on your belongings, but in general, people are helpful not harmful, and it is not uncommon for someone sitting next to you with a bit more leg room to offer to hold something for you. If you are uncomfortable with handing anything over to a stranger, just politely decline. It is also not unheard of for other passengers to pay your fare as an act of hospitality. This usually only happens in rural areas where tourists are rarely seen. It can be nerve-racking being on a packed bus, pinned into your seat, and not knowing how far you are from your stop or how on earth you are going to get off. You can ask the fare collector to let you know when you reach your stop. Sometimes they forget, so make sure you maintain eye contact with him and remind him. The bus will stop at every stop, so you don't need to signal to the driver when you want to disembark; you just need to know where you want to get off. When it is your turn to get off, other passengers will somehow maneuver their bodies so that you can squeeze your way out.

Salvadorans are natural salespeople, and the bus is as good a place as any to see many of them in action. On any given trip, you will likely witness a series of vendors board the bus and politely ask for your attention before proceeding to launch into an impassioned introduction to whatever product they are touting. Promoters will very seriously wax poetic about the perfect texture and taste of a tiny toffee candy or the incredible pant-saving antileak function on a pen. Natural remedies as well as antiparasitic medication are also extremely popular. Whatever it is, it never costs more than $2, and you will be amazed at the number of people who do a good deal of shopping on the bus. In addition to this, there are the regular vendors touting fruit, nuts, sweets, plantain chips, french fries, *pupusas,* empanadas, coconut water, *horchata,* and more. Most of these snacks are safe to eat, but it's better to err on the side of caution when it comes to fruit, as you never know how clean the place was where it was prepared.

There have been some reports of robberies on buses, and although this is much more common in San Salvador, it could happen anywhere. Do not keep any valuables in your pockets and keep a close eye on your belongings at all times.

Visas and Officialdom

ENTERING EL SALVADOR

Entering El Salvador is usually pretty easy and straightforward. Immigration officials are friendly and like to do things by the book. You will need to pay $10 for your tourist visa, whichever way you enter the country, and you must have a passport that is valid for the next six months. In theory, you should have a return ticket or some other proof of when you will leave the country. In practice this is rarely enforced, but consider yourself warned.

TOURIST VISAS

El Salvador is part of the CA-4 agreement that also includes the neighboring countries of Nicaragua, Honduras, and Guatemala. Once you enter any one of these countries, you are granted a 90-day visa to all four countries for a $10 fee. This is important to remember when moving among countries. If you enter El Salvador after being in Guatemala for two months, for example, you will have one month left for El Salvador. If you want to reenter with a fresh visa, you have to leave the CA-4 region for 72 hours. Most people go to Mexico to do this.

If you overstay your visa without extending it, you will have to pay a fine of $114 when you leave the country, regardless of whether you overstayed two weeks or two months. If you would like to get an extension, the process is relatively painless. You need to go to the **Dirección General de Migración y Extranjería** (Av. Olímpica and Alameda Enrique Araujo, San Salvador, tel. 2213-7778, 8am-4pm Mon.-Fri.) and wait a long time for a short interview, during which you will be asked what your reason is for requesting the extension. You will need to provide a passport-size photo of you, photocopies of your bank card and passport, and $25. Most applicants are granted an extension; technically this can only be done once, but depending on your reason for needing a second extension, it is not impossible.

LEAVING EL SALVADOR

When you leave El Salvador, your visa will be checked. If you have overstayed without extending, you will be charged the $114 fine, so if you know you have overstayed, make sure you have this money ready when you are heading out of the country.

If you are flying out of El Salvador, you will have to pay a departure fee of $32, which is often included in the price of your ticket; if it is not, you will be asked to pay this at the airport when you leave the country.

CUSTOMS

Customs is not overly strict in El Salvador. Articles up to a value of $500 are permitted into and out of the country, and if you are 18 years of age or over, you are permitted to bring in and take out 200 cigarettes or 50 cigars, and up to 2 liters of alcohol.

An import permit is required if you want to bring a pet into the country, for a fee of $9, which can be obtained ahead of time or on arrival at the animal quarantine department at the airport.

EMBASSIES AND CONSULATES

Most countries have embassies or consulates in San Salvador, most of which are located in the tree-lined streets of upscale Colonia Escalón.

- **Embassy of Belize:** Calle La Mascota 456, tel. 2264-8024, embsalbel@yahoo.com, 8am-4pm Mon.-Fri.

- **Embassy of Canada:** Centro Financiero Gigante 63, Av. Sur and Alameda Roosevelt, tel. 2279-4655, ssal@international.gc.ca, 8am-12:30pm and 1:30pm-4:30pm Mon.-Thurs., 8am-1:30pm Fri., after-hours emergency contact information for Canadian citizens only call collect tel. 613/996-8885

- **Embassy of Costa Rica:** 85 Av. Sur and Calle Cuscatlán 4415, Colonia Escalón, tel. 2264-3863, www.embajadacostarica.org.sv, 8am-4pm Mon.-Fri.

- **Guatemalan Embassy:** 15 Av. Norte 135, tel. 2271-2225 or 2222-3903, embelsalvador@minex.gob.gt, 8am-4pm Mon.-Fri.

- **Embassy of Honduras:** 89 Av. Norte between 7 and 9 Calle Poniente, No. 561, Colonia Escalón, tel. 2263-2808

- **Embassy of Nicaragua:** 71 Av. Norte and 1 Calle Poniente 164, Colonia Escalón, tel. 2223-7729 or 2298-6549

- **Embassy of Panama:** Calle Los Bambúes and Av. Las Bugambilias 21, tel. 2298-0773, embpan@telesal.net, 8am-4pm Mon.-Fri.

- **Embassy of United Kingdom:** Torre Futura, 14th Fl., Colonia Escalón, San Salvador, tel. 2511-5757, britishembassy.elsalvador@fco.gov.uk, 7:30am-4:30pm Mon.-Thurs., 7:30am-11:30pm Fri.

- **Embassy of the United States:** Bulevar Santa Elena, Antiguo Cuscatlán, tel. 2501-2999, congensansal@state.gov, 8am-4:30pm Mon.-Fri.

Conduct and Customs

El Salvador is an extremely social country, and cultivating interpersonal relationships is considered the most important priority. Family and friends always come first. Despite this, or perhaps because of this, Salvadorans are also extremely successful at business endeavors. Business relationships often start out by getting to know someone and building a rapport. Salvadorans are incredibly industrious, and you will notice that if you need help with just about anything, complete strangers will come to your aid, with smart, action-oriented solutions.

Salvadorans have a strong sense of personal pride and dignity and can easily get offended by direct communication that they may consider abrasive or rude. Be aware of how you talk to people and what you say about people. If you have something negative to say, or a personal subject to discuss with someone, always do it in private. Any kind of public comment that may jeopardize somebody's reputation are considered inappropriate. If you do end up offending someone, it is likely that they will not let you know directly, but get somebody else to politely inform you of the affront. Apologies are greatly appreciated and grudges not likely to be held.

You will notice that Salvadorans are always making jokes and teasing each other. It is very common for people to have *sobrenombres* (nicknames) that their friends have come up with. It could be something based on a memory, as in *el muerto* (literally "the dead one"), poking fun at someone who once got so drunk time that it was impossible to wake him up, or *tristeza* (sadness) for someone who is sad all the time. In some areas, *sobrenombres* are so prevalent that often people don't even know the birth name of their friends. It may seem a bit cruel but it is not unusual for a nickname to be based on someone's appearance, even if it is something negative that is qualifying it. They can be as harsh as *feo* (ugly), *gordo* (fat), or *flaca* (skinny). On that note, Salvadorans do not consider it rude to make direct comments about your appearance. Don't be surprised if someone tells you have gained weight, lost weight, or look tired and worn out. Try not to let it ruin your day.

GENERAL RULES OF POLITENESS

Salvadorans are very kind and will often go out of their way to help others. If somebody does something for you, be sure to express your gratitude, and if possible, try to return the favor. It is not necessarily expected, but this kind of reciprocity is what fuels relationships here. If somebody invites you to their house for dinner, the same rules of etiquette apply as in your home country. It is considered polite to bring a bottle of wine, flowers, sweets, or some small token of appreciation. If you are invited out for a meal, it means that the person who has extended the invitation expects to pay for the meal. Listen for the phrase *te invito*, which literally means "I

invite you." Likewise, if you invite someone, you will be expected to pay.

Respect is expected to be given to older people by younger people, and to higher-status people by lower-status individuals. This includes using titles of respect such as *Señora* (Madam) or *Señor* (Sir) before people's names and using the formal form of "you," *usted*, instead of the informal *vos*.

As in all of Latin America, time tends to be a loose term in El Salvador, and tardiness is not considered rude. Expect most people to show up about an hour after your scheduled meeting time.

When entering somebody's home or any commercial establishment, it is expected that you greet everyone who is there with a simple *buenos días* (good morning), *buenas tardes* (good afternoon), or *buenas noches* (good evening or good night), depending on what time of day it is. Failure to greet a person is considered offensive. You can also use these greetings when passing people in the street, and it will always be appreciated as a sign of friendly politeness. You can also use *adiós* or *salud* as a way of greeting when you are passing by someone on the street.

When you see people eating, you should say *buen provecho*, which loosely translates as "enjoy your meal," and they will say *gracias* (thank you). And vice versa, if you are eating and somebody says *buen provecho*, say *gracias*.

Although Salvadorans are generally very open to talking about most things, there are a couple of topics that are best to avoid when first getting to know someone. Salvadorans are very religious people and don't tend to question Roman Catholicism too much. If you are getting to know someone, it is best to not broach the subject of religion. Most people are not into theological philosophizing—all of the good and bad things that happen are the will of God, and that's that. Of course, there are definitely exceptions, especially among younger and more urban Salvadorans, but it's best to feel it out before launching into a conversation about God and religion.

Secondly, most Salvadorans do not talk too much about the war. It was extremely brutal and touched everyone's lives in some way, regardless of whether they lived in the suburbs of San Salvador or in the mountains of Morazán. This is another topic that should not be broached lightly, as you never know what painful memories it might bring up. Wait until somebody else mentions it before you ask questions.

GENDER AND SEXUALITY

El Salvador is no different than the rest of Latin America when it comes to machismo culture. It is prevalent, and by and large considered the norm. At its best, the macho attitude is connected with taking on the role of provider and problem solver; at its worst, it can transmute into aggressive and controlling behavior directed toward women. Unfortunately, El Salvador has a very high rate of violence against women, most of which happens in the privacy of people's homes in the form of marital disputes. Crimes of passion are frequent, usually as a result of the dangerous combination of alcohol and infidelity. El Salvador has one of the highest rates in the world of women killed by men.

Sexism is deeply entrenched in the system. For the most part, stereotypical gender roles are accurate. Quite often, women are expected to take care of the children and duties in the home as well as to work outside it to supplement income. In families with both sons and daughters, it is common for the son to get special treatment, and the girls can even be expected to cook and clean for their male siblings. There is no resentment about it; that's just the way it is. It is also considered normal for men to make comments on a woman's appearance, even in professional settings, and many women accept the compliments in silence, perpetuating the stereotypical roles.

The good news is that attitudes are beginning to change, and a new term has arisen in recent years. *Caballerismo* is starting to replace machismo. *Caballero* translates as "gentleman" and is somebody who embodies all of the best attributes of a macho man. He shows strong leadership and is a good father and provider. Some men have even started going to workshops where they are taught how to be a more sensitive, less macho man.

At the same time, younger women are refusing to take on the same roles as their mothers and opting for more independent lifestyles. Most recently, shelters for victims of abuse have been established, and anti-domestic violence campaigns have taken off and helped to open up discussion about the once taboo topic on TV and radio shows.

Sports and Recreation

HIKING AND CAMPING

The best hiking is in the national parks, which are also the only areas with proper campsites. You can usually rent tents for around $5, but better to bring your own if you can, as the condition of the tents may not be that great. Campsites in the national parks are equipped with toilets, running water, and barbecues.

There is also decent hiking around Ruta de Las Flores, especially near Juayúa, where guided hikes cost $10-20. In other parts of El Salvador, there is not much in the way of organized hikes, but there is certainly no lack of possibilities. Basically anywhere you go in the country, there are mountains nearby that may not have distinct hiking trails but can usually be climbed with the help of some locals or the tourism police. One great thing about El Salvador is that the tourism police will accompany you to any place you want to go. Just go to the local police office and ask. Sometimes they have someone ready to accompany you right away; other times you may have to wait a few hours. But the option is always there, and it is free. The same rules apply for camping. Although there are not many official campsites, there are plenty of areas in the country where you are able to pitch a tent and spend a few nights without bothering anyone (or anyone bothering you). Ask around when you arrive somewhere where might be a good place to camp. The locals as well as the local police can advise you on secure areas.

SURFING

El Salvador is a year-round surf destination with equally warm water and weather. The entire coastline is marked with right points and beach breaks, and even during the rainy season, waves still break cleaner than most beach or reef breaks around the world. The dry season runs November to April and typically sees offshore winds, sunny skies, and consistent surf. Large waves still roll through at this time of year, albeit less frequently than during the wet-season months of May to October, when waves can reach up to three meters high. Surfboard rentals are available at almost all of the hotels along the coast.

There are many options for surfing spots, and nobody knows them better than the local guides who can help you get the most out of your surf trip. Some highly recommended English-speaking guides in El Salvador include: **Joaquín Aragón** (based in La Libertad, tel. 7165-2882), **Luis Rivas** of **Zonte Spanish S'cool and Tours** (Playa El Zonte, tel. 7297-6003), and **Juan Carlos Rodezno** of **Paradise Adventures** (Playa El Sunzal, tel. 7670-5266, www.paradiseadventures.biz).

SCUBA DIVING

Although not an obvious scuba-diving destination, El Salvador offers some unique lake diving in Lago Coatepeque and Lago Ilopango, as well as around Los Cóbanos.

Lago Ilopango is El Salvador's largest and deepest lake and can make for some interesting dives, where you can see boilers, dry lava rocks, and the unique formation and topography of a volcanic crater lake. **Lago Coatepeque** is less frequented by divers, but still may be of interest to those curious about more crater lake diving. Around **Los Cóbanos,** you can explore the massive coral reef and see humpback whales, whale sharks, dolphins, and manta rays as well as the country's only underwater archaeological site, which includes shipwrecks from the 19th century.

El Salvador Divers (3 Calle Poniente and 99 Av. Norte, 5020, Colonia Escalón, San Salvador, www.elsalvadordivers.com) is the original and best diving company in the country. They have bilingual staff and can help you arrange diving trips as well as PADI certification. Remember that visibility is best November through January.

FISHING

El Salvador is gaining popularity as a fishing destination and offers a variety of fishing methods, such as jigging, casting, trolling, and deep-sea fishing. For those who want to keep it simple, many guides can offer artisanal fishing trips that may involve standing in the surf and casting nets or going out in a simple *panga* to fish for some of the local favorites such as *boca colorada* (red snapper) or *corvina* (white sea bass).

Los Cóbanos is a great fishing destination due to the coral reef and the marine ecosystem that it supports, attracting a variety of fish to the area. Here you can find artisanal fishing trips or deep-sea fishing trips. If you don't feel like heading out onto the deep sea, a fun option at Los Cóbanos is **reef fishing,** which is great for catching mackerel, barracuda, and snapper. **Rock fishing** can be done close to coral beaches in Los Cóbanos, where cliffs make great casting spots for the strong roosterfish and jacks.

For **deep-sea fishing,** many people head to **Costa del Sol,** where El Salvador is becoming one of the top sportfishing destinations for species that include blue marlin and tuna.

BIRDING

El Salvador is fast becoming a birder's paradise. A two-week birding trip here can cost less than half the price of a similar trip in Nicaragua or Costa Rica, and the variety of birds is just as impressive. The geographic diversity coupled with the small size of the country means birders can hit all the best spots in a short amount of time.

Because of its location, El Salvador is a major throughway for migrating birds, making it a prime location for both endemic species and others that are just passing through on their annual journeys. The country has a rich ornithological history and more than 540 species of resident and migratory birds, and half of those species can be seen throughout the year in the different national parks, protected natural areas, and wetlands and along the Pacific coast. The largest number of the endemic species can be found in the cloud forests.

El Salvador's prime birding locations include **Cerro Verde** and **Montecristo** cloud forests. Cerro Verde is very accessible and close to accommodations, making it a popular stop for birders. The shade-grown coffee plantations and forest patches at mid- and lower elevations create a buffer zone that makes this one of the most important sites for birds in the country. Older second-growth cloud forest surrounds this site where it is common to find species such as the rufous-browed wren, the blue and white mockingbird, and the slate-throated redstart. If you are lucky, you may even spot a singing quail.

Located in southwestern El Salvador in the Department of Ahuachapán, **Barra de Santiago** contains approximately 2,000 hectares of protected coastal mangroves, beaches, and mudflats and has been designated as **Important Bird Area (IBA)** by BirdLife International. Important Bird Areas are recognized as being globally important habitat for the conservation of bird populations. Some beautiful birds you can expect to see while quietly cruising through the mangroves include the American pygmy kingfisher, orange-chinned parakeet, lineated woodpecker, and shorebirds such as the mangrove swallow, Wilson's plover, and lesser yellowlegs.

Parque Nacional El Imposible is another great bird-watching zone. The park contains some of the largest tracts of virgin Pacific slope forest in Central America, and nearly 300 species of birds have been recorded here. Some birds you might spot while hiking through the forest include the ivory-billed woodpecker, lesser ground cuckoo, long-tailed manakin, banded wren, mottled owl, and gray hawk, among others.

Suchitoto has excellent bird-watching in and around **Lago Suchitlán,** especially known for the great egret, great blue heron, American coot, blue-winged teal, ringed kingfisher, and green kingfisher. Finally, **Bahía de Jiquilisco** is one of the top spots for bird-watching in the country, but a lack of tourism infrastructure means bird-watching excursions can be a little more difficult to organize.

Benjamin Rivera of **Green Trips** (tel. 7943-5230, greentripselsalvador@gmail.com), based in San Salvador, is El Salvador's top bird-watching tour guide and can arrange unique tours around the country. **Robert Broz** of **El Gringo Tours** (Calle Francisco Morazán 27, Suchitoto, tel. 2327-2351, www.elgringosuchitoto.com) offers excellent bird-watching adventures around Suchitoto.

Travel Tips

OPPORTUNITIES FOR STUDY AND EMPLOYMENT
Volunteering in El Salvador

There are plenty of opportunities for volunteer work in El Salvador if you are willing to work with small organizations. Many of the opportunities are in remote areas and do incredible grassroots work with local communities. Listed below are some reliable options.

The **Centro de Intercambio y Solidaridad (CIS)** (Av. Bolivar 103, Colonia Libertad, San Salvador, tel. 2235-1330, www.cis-elsalvador.org) is an excellent resource if you are interested in volunteering or studying Spanish. The organization focuses on education and social-justice issues and has a Spanish school inside its office in San Salvador.

There are also volunteer opportunities in Suchitoto at the **Centro Arte Para la Paz** (2 Calle Poniente 5, Suchitoto, tel. 2335-1080, www.capsuchitoto.org), where you can speak with the director and tailor your own program according to your skillset. Also in Suchitoto, the **Permaculture Institute of El Salvador (IPES)** (2 Calle Oriente 13-A, Suchitoto, www.permacultura.com.sv) offers volunteer opportunities to learn and practice permaculture.

On the eastern coast, the **Eastern Pacific Hawksbill Initiative (ICAPO)** (www.hawksbill.org) organizes volunteer programs that focus on preserving the endangered hawksbill turtle. **EcoViva** (1904 Franklin St., Suite 902, Oakland, CA 94612, tel. 510/835-1334, www.eco-viva.org) offers volunteer programs that focus on sustainable development of rural communities around the Bajo Lempa region.

On the western coast, **Sueños Pacíficos** (Playa el Cocal, 5 minutes' drive west of La Libertad, tel. 7112-0662) offers excellent volunteer opportunities in an enthusiastic eco-community just a few kilometers from one of the best surf breaks in the country, Punta Roca. The project aims to involve visitors directly with the local community and to provide training and scholarships to local people so that they are able to make a sustainable living through tourism. Sueños Pacíficos is always looking for volunteers to share their skills and knowledge with the local community as well as other travelers, or just lend a hand with tasks that need to be done in the eco-community. This is an excellent opportunity to learn about organic farming and permaculture, natural building, and environmentally appropriate technologies.

Work Opportunities

There are not many work opportunities for foreigners in El Salvador, apart from teaching in one of the international schools. Almost every formal job requires a preexisting visa or an already-hired expatriate. Leading headhunters in the region might be able to help expatriates look for jobs. Popular websites for this are **www.latintopjobs.com** and **www.tecoloco.com**.

ACCOMMODATIONS

In the more touristed areas you will find hostels that are geared toward international backpackers, but in less frequented towns, if you ask for a hostel, they will likely not understand what you need. It's best to ask for a hotel or a *hospedaje* (lodging).

When many places say they have hot water, they are referring to electric showers. Although this is more common in less expensive places, it can also be found in some of the pricier hotels. If you are someone who loves a *hot* shower, the electric shower just may never fully satisfy your need for heat. To optimize the heat in an electric shower, you need to sacrifice water pressure, bringing your shower down to a lighter sprinkle, but at least it will be hot. Remember never to touch the electric showerhead when your hand or any other part of your body is wet. It is electric, after all. If piping hot water is a deal breaker for you, always ask to see the shower before you decide on a room. If there is a bulbous, beige plastic showerhead with a sliding button, this is an electric showerhead. If it is a regular showerhead, they likely have gas-heated water.

As in most of the rest of Central America, the plumbing in El Salvador cannot handle toilet paper, so remember to place it in the trash instead of flushing it down the toilet.

Central America is known for its scores of Auto Hotels, and El Salvador is no exception. Auto hotels are ubiquitous and uniform, and if you are driving through El Salvador, you are likely to become very familiar with them. For the most part, they look like and function as any other generic roadside motel, except they are specifically designed for illicit sexual encounters. The hotels provide absolute anonymity, including an enclosed space exclusively for your vehicle that has one door leading to a small, usually cement-walled room with no windows. All communication and financial transactions are done through a darkened sliding window or a revolving drawer in the room. If you are driving and desperately in need of a cheap, safe place to sleep, an auto hotel will serve the purpose.

Always check rooms to see if they are facing the street. Salvadoran buses and traffic can be noisy, and it usually starts around 4:30am. Always try to secure a room as far away from the street as possible.

Salvadorans are security conscious and like to know who is staying with them. You will be asked to provide your passport details upon checking into any hostel or hotel.

TRAVELERS WITH DISABILITIES

Travelers with disabilities can expect to be seriously limited in El Salvador. With the exception of the highest-end hotels and restaurants, wheelchair ramps and disabled toilets are virtually nonexistent.

WOMEN TRAVELING ALONE

Hermosa. Princesa. Niña. If you are traveling as a single woman in El Salvador you have likely heard all of these terms of endearment. Depending on what kind of mood you are in, and how many times you have already heard it that day, you may smile and laugh it off or grimace and rage inside. Traveling as a single woman in El Salvador can be equal parts charming and infuriating. The macho culture means that men are always expected to be the hero, and in El Salvador men seem to take this to the next level. Don't be surprised to find men running after you to help you carry a large item, holding doors for you, or offering to drive you to wherever you are going. Basically, if there is a problem, they will help you solve it. This makes traveling a lot easier, and sometimes a lot of fun. But be careful—normal social interactions between men and women in your home country may not be the same in El Salvador. For example, if you are out in a social context with a group of people and a man asks if you would like a ride home, this can easily be misinterpreted as you wanting to go home with him. Always make sure you are clear about what you want—and what your expectations are regarding a relationship with a man. Pay attention to how you dress. It is a sad reality that unless you want to be ogled and catcalled, it is wise not to wear revealing clothing such as short shorts or low-cut tops. Even at the beach, you will notice that with the exception of the touristy surf spots, most Salvadoran women bathe in shorts and a T-shirt.

If you do find that someone is making you uncomfortable with their comments, say something to them in no uncertain terms. Salvadorans are very sensitive about their reputation, and if you make it public that you do not appreciate the attention, it is likely to stop. Take the normal precautions as a single woman traveler: do not take rides with unknown men, always take a taxi at night, and keep an eye on your drink when you are at a bar. You might want to invest in some pepper spray once you arrive. Thankfully, sexual assault of foreigners is almost unheard of, but with the rise in tourism, you never know how things could develop.

TRAVELING WITH CHILDREN

For Salvadorans, children are life's deepest source of fulfillment and joy. Concessions are constantly made in honor of keeping kids happy and comfortable; when it's clear that you're foreign, the desire to coo, coddle, and cuddle your child will be magnified even more. Although at times it might drive you crazy, it is all done with only the best intentions, so try to be gracious and smile. Hotels and restaurants will generally go out of their way to accommodate kids, and you will be amazed at the number of places with small playgrounds, swimming pools, and toys available.

Safety issues are not exactly a priority in El Salvador. Car seats are not required by law, and you should keep a watchful eye at playgrounds and amusement parks because the equipment and rides could be unsafe.

LESBIAN, GAY, BISEXUAL, AND TRANSGENDERED TRAVELERS

Given its religious conservatism and macho culture, El Salvador is not a comfortable environment to be openly gay, and discrimination and violence directed to anyone who is not heterosexual is common. A national law does exist to prohibit discrimination on the basis of sexual orientation, but discrimination remains widespread. Same-sex marriage is not recognized, and the national constitution defines marriage as only between a man and a woman. However, activism and visibility are on the rise. Gay pride parades and national conferences on LGBT rights have started to take form, and a dedicated minority is working toward a more just society. If you do decide to weather the discriminatory storm as an out LGBT traveler in El Salvador, there is a wonderful community of people that you can connect with. Start with **Las Dignas** (Av. Bernal 16S, San Salvador, tel. 2284-9550, www.lasdignas.org), a women's rights organization that is deeply involved with LGBT issues and events. There is also a collection of gay bars near the Metrocentro in San Salvador.

Health and Safety

BEFORE YOU GO

Travelers to El Salvador should take certain health concerns into consideration. There are various risks of diseases that are nonexistent in your home country, however with the proper preparation and precautions your chances of falling ill are minimal. Before you leave, make sure you find a **travelers clinic** that can help get you prepared. Don't leave it to the last minute, though, as some medications and vaccinations require some time for completion.

Vaccinations

You do not have to have proof of vaccinations to enter El Salvador, but you should always travel with your International Certificate of Vaccination (Yellow Card). You never know when you may be asked to show proof of your immunizations. Some of these shots take several months to complete, so make sure you allow yourself enough time.

There is no **yellow fever** in El Salvador, but the government of El Salvador requires proof that you have been vaccinated against it if you are arriving from an area where there is yellow fever. **Hepatitis A** can be contracted through contaminated food or water in El Salvador, regardless of where you are eating or staying. It's a good idea to get vaccinated before you go. The vaccination is given as two shots, six months apart. **Hepatitis B** is contracted through sexual contact, contaminated needles, and blood products, so it's a good idea to get this vaccine if you plan on having sex with a new partner, getting a tattoo or piercing, or having any medical procedures. The vaccination is given as three to four shots over a six-month period.

Typhoid fever is also contracted through contaminated food or water in El Salvador. This vaccine is recommended for most travelers, especially if you are staying with friends or relatives (you are more likely to be infected if in close quarters with people who live in the country), visiting smaller cities or rural areas, or if you are an adventurous eater. Typhoid is one shot and will last 5 years. **Rabies** can be found in dogs, bats, and other mammals in El Salvador. You might want to consider getting this vaccine if your travel will involve a lot of outdoor activities such as camping, hiking, and biking, or you plan to be around a lot of animals. A rabies shot is also a good idea for children, as they are more likely to play with and potentially get bitten by an animal. The vaccination includes a series of three shots over one month.

WHEN YOU ARE THERE
Air Quality

The air quality in some parts of the country is extremely poor, the worst area being the capital. The fact that San Salvador is located in a valley and is so heavily populated is bad enough; factor in the old buses expelling heavy, toxic exhaust and the result is a heavily polluted city. Asthmatics should take note of this and make sure to travel with appropriate medication.

Diseases from Food and Water

El Salvador is no different than any other tropical country and is teeming with potentially hazardous germs, especially near the coast. Always drink bottled water and never from the faucet, and ask for drinks *sin hielo* (without ice). You will likely be unable to resist

a cold *licuado* (fruit shake) on a hot day, and you shouldn't, because they are delicious. You can ask for your *licuado* with milk or water. If you choose water, ask if they are using *agua pura* (purified water) just to be sure. Your best bet is to avoid cheap, unhygienic-looking places and keep a close eye on the preparation of your drink. To be absolutely certain you won't get sick from drinks, stick to bottled beverages. When drinking alcohol, remember that the sun adds to dehydration, and without proper hydration the tropical hangover can hit you like a ton of bricks. Try to alternate alcoholic drinks with water.

Be careful when it comes to salads and fruit. It is impossible to know whether fruits and vegetables have been washed with purified water or not. All side salads come with a wedge of lime: use it and ask for more to squeeze on your salad, as the lime helps kill bacteria. Try to stick to fruit that you can peel, such as mangoes and bananas. Pre-prepared fruit can be very enticing, but you do not know how clean the person's hands were who prepared it, or how long it has been exposed to potential risks such as disease-carrying insects or airborne bacteria. It is a good idea to carry around a bottle of **grapefruit seed extract (GSE)** when traveling. This natural antibiotic can be found in any health food store in your home country and, when added to your water a few times a day, can do wonders to protect you from bacterial infections. Make sure you wash your vegetables thoroughly, as many of them are sprayed with toxic agrochemicals. You can contact **Soya Nutribar** (Av. Las Palmas, Pasaje 6, No. 114, tel. 2566-6835) or **Café El Botón** (Av. de la Capilla 210, tel. 2264-9738) to purchase local organic produce.

Cholera is spread by drinking contaminated water and by eating raw or undercooked food. It is an intestinal infection that causes diarrhea and vomiting, and the most important recourse if you contract it is rehydration through lots of water and rehydration salts. Rehydration salts are not easy to find outside San Salvador, so make sure you bring some with you. Chances of contracting it in El Salvador are low, and if you do, it is unlikely it will be severe enough to warrant seeking medical attention. **Traveler's diarrhea** is an inescapable reality when traveling in tropical countries. Most cases are mild and do not last more than a couple of days. The best thing you can do for diarrhea is drink plenty of fluids and rest.

Insect-Borne Diseases

Transmitted by mosquitoes, **Malaria** is found in rural areas around Ahuachapán, La Unión, and Santa Ana; however, even in those areas, the risk is extremely low. It is not necessary to take antimalarial drugs while traveling in El Salvador unless you are in a high-risk category, such as the elderly and pregnant women. **Dengue fever** is also transmitted by mosquitoes and is most common in rural areas along the coast. There has been a spike in the number of cases of dengue fever in El Salvador in the last few years, and unfortunately there is no vaccine. Dengue fever mimics the flu with symptoms such as headaches, high fever, and joint pain, and the treatment is the same as for the flu: plenty of rest, fluids, and painkillers.

Chagas' disease is found in very rural areas of El Salvador and is spread by a bloodsucking triatomine insect known as *chinche* or the kissing bug. An infected insect, which hides in dwellings made from mud, adobe, straw, or palm thatch, falls from the ceiling onto a sleeper's face and bites, hence the name kissing bug. Symptoms can include swelling around the bite area along with fever, fatigue, body aches, headaches, rash, diarrhea, and vomiting. But sometimes there are no symptoms at all until decades later, when the disease can cause deadly heart problems. If you think you may have been kissed by the deadly bug, it's best to take a course of antiparasitic medication, which can easily be picked up in any pharmacy in the country.

Leishmaniasis is carried by tiny sandflies and is one of the world's most common parasitic infections. Small, itchy red bites develop into skin sores, allowing the parasite to enter through mucous membranes into the blood, where it then spreads to the internal organs, causing deadly damage to the spleen and liver. Try to use an extra-fine mosquito net to avoid getting bitten and look out for any bites that turn into lesions. This is a red flag for Leishmaniasis. If you do contract it, it can be treated with antiparasitic medication available in pharmacies.

Onchocerciasis, commonly known as river blindness, is caused by a parasitic worm, *Onchocerca volvulus*. This worm is transmitted by fly bites, specifically from the notorious blackfly that breeds in rivers, which is where the disease's common name originates from. After initial infection, it may take more than a year for symptoms to develop. They include an autoimmune response that causes skin lesions, swelling, severe itching and burning, and gradual blindness in less than 10 percent of cases. There is no vaccine for river blindness but it can be diagnosed through a simple blood test and can be treated with antibiotics easily found in pharmacies throughout the country.

MEDICAL SERVICES

Hospitals and English-speaking doctors are available in the major cities. You can try your luck finding English-speaking doctors at the public hospitals, or go to a private one, where there will likely be someone who speaks English fluently. In rural areas, you will be hard-pressed to find a doctor who speaks English, and often there won't be a hospital nearby. People in remote areas usually depend on pharmacies and small clinics for health care. Because of this, pharmacists are often knowledgeable about illnesses and appropriate treatments. Pharmacies are very well stocked with medications that would often require a prescription in your home country, especially antibiotics. The one exception is medication for psychological conditions; medications such as benzodiazepines are strictly regulated in El Salvador.

CRIME

Crime is an unfortunate fact of life in El Salvador, and determining a potentially dangerous situation can be tricky, so it is better to be alert at all times. The fact is, for all the negative media about crime in El Salvador, it is a surprisingly safe country for travelers. This is not to say that the stories of violence are not true; considered the epicenter of the gang crisis, along with Guatemala and Honduras, El Salvador has one of the highest rates of crime in Latin America. Although the murder rate dropped after a gang truce in March 2012, sadly it seems to be on the rise once again. Strangely, it is rare for a visitor to see this underside of the friendly face that El Salvador presents to the world, but rest assured that it is there.

Common Crimes and Dangerous Areas

Armed robbery seems to be on the rise in El Salvador. This could be either at knifepoint or at gunpoint and usually does not go any farther than threats; however, there have been a few rare incidents where robberies have turned violent. As in any country where there is rampant poverty, petty theft can also be a problem. Buses are the most common place where you may be robbed by a pickpocket, and any place where there are crowds of people can be risky. The most dangerous parts of the country are in San Salvador, and more specifically in the eastern area of Soyapango, where there is a well-known gang presence. The historic center can also be unsafe simply because of the sheer number of people. The well-heeled neighborhoods of Zona Rosa and Escalón are generally safe, but robberies also take place here, mostly at night and on dimly lit side streets. Along the coast, there has been a rise in armed robberies near El Tunco, specifically along the stretch of beach between El Tunco and El Sunzal, at nighttime. Do not walk between any beaches at night.

Safety Tips

Always be aware of your surroundings and trust your gut. If something seems suspicious, remove yourself from the situation. Be especially watchful on crowded buses, especially in the city. Do not keep any money or valuables in your pockets, and keep your bag closed and close to your body at all times. Make a copy of your passport and carry that around with you; keep the original in a secure place at your hotel. Do not wear flashy jewelry or carry expensive gadgets or cameras in plain view, especially on buses or in crowded areas in San Salvador. Always take a taxi at night, even if you are moving a short distance in a nice neighborhood—robberies happen on side streets no matter where you are. If you are driving at night, keep your doors locked, and remember that if you feel threatened, it is legal to run a red light. Dormitories are generally safe in El Salvador, but it is best to use security lockboxes if they are available.

If you do happen to get approached by a thief, do not try to resist or argue; hand over your money, and most likely the only damage you will receive is financial.

If Something Happens

If something does happen, go directly to the nearest police station and fill out a *denuncia* (police report). It is not likely that you will retrieve what you lost, but at least they will be able to look for the criminal. There are tourist police in El Salvador, but when it comes to reporting a crime, it doesn't make much difference whether you go to them or the regular police, because most of them do not speak much English anyway. It is good to note that the police in El Salvador are generally not corrupt and usually do things by the book. Contact your embassy right away in the case of a stolen passport. Embassies can also sometimes help with wiring emergency funds.

Information and Services

MONEY
Currency

In 2001, El Salvador adopted the U.S. dollar as its official unit of currency. The switch to the dollar resulted in an economic boom and an increase in prices. Compared to its neighbors Guatemala and Nicaragua, El Salvador is a bit pricey, but it is still cheaper than Costa Rica and Panama. For American travelers, the use of the dollar means that there is no need to worry about currency exchange.

Outside the major cities, cash is easiest, as not all places accept credit cards. Finding small change is always a problem, and often people will tell you they do not have change for bills. It is considered your responsibility to have the correct change for a purchase. It's a good idea to keep a change purse and try and collect as much as you can for small purchases and bus travel.

Traveler's Checks

Traveler's checks are gradually becoming obsolete, but you may want to carry a few hundred dollars' worth in case of an emergency. Most major banks, including Banco Cuscatlán, Scotiabank, and Citibank, will cash traveler's checks. Don't forget to bring your passport.

Money Transfers

If you need to get money wired to you, there is no shortage of Western Union offices in even the smallest of towns. The country's economy runs on remittances from the United States.

Credit Cards and ATMs

Most establishments will charge a 6-12 percent surcharge for credit card purchases. Visa and MasterCard are widely accepted.

ATMs are widely available in the major cities and also in the main tourism destinations, including Juayúa and Concepción de Ataco along Ruta de Las Flores as well as Suchitoto and La Libertad and El Tunco on the western coast. ATMs are harder to come by in the eastern part of the country, so it is best to make sure you have enough cash for the eastern leg of your trip when you stop in San Miguel. ATMs usually have a limit on how much you can withdraw per day. Typically the maximum amount you can get is $250, but occasionally you can find machines that will dispense up to $500. There is really no way of knowing except through word of mouth.

Tipping

A *propina* is not required when dining out in El Salvador; however, unless you are eating at a *comedor,* it is usually expected. Some restaurants add a 10 percent tip onto your bill. If it is not included, consider leaving it anyway. It may be a small amount of money to you but could make a big difference for somebody making minimum or less than minimum wage. Plus, with the excellent customer service in El Salvador, it is usually well merited.

It is a good idea to tip guides a few dollars, as they only make a small percentage of what you pay; most of it goes to the tour company or the hotel you hired them from. Hotel staff do not expect tips, but will be very grateful for them. Use your own judgment as to whether someone has gone above and beyond their regular duties (which is often the case in El Salvador). You are not expected to tip taxi drivers, but again, if someone is very efficient or speaks English, it is a good idea to leave a little extra in exchange for the added value.

Taxes

Hotels in El Salvador charge an 18 percent tax, which is usually included in the price and sometimes waived if you pay in cash. There is a 13 percent sales tax on all goods.

Prices and Bargaining

You are much less likely to get ripped off

in El Salvador than you are in other Latin American countries with well-trodden gringo trails. That being said, of course, in the more touristy areas such as El Tunco, you will not get the same price as a Salvadoran. For the most part, though, the price given to travelers will never be too much higher than the real price, and bargaining is not really common in El Salvador. In rural areas, people are very honest and will give the correct price. Don't aggressively haggle with people; they work very hard and make very little money. Let them renew your faith in humanity instead of you tarnishing theirs.

Budgeting

El Salvador can be as cheap or expensive as you want it to be. If you sleep in dormitories and eat *comida típica* (typical Salvadoran food), you can get by on less than $15 a day. If you want to sleep in a private room and have a little more variety in your food, you are looking at about $30 a day. For $50 or more, you can stay in quality hotels, hire guides, and eat at international restaurants.

COMMUNICATIONS AND MEDIA
Mail

Post offices can be found in nearly every small town in the country as many Salvadorans still rely on snail mail for both sending and receiving goods to and from other parts of the country as well as the United States. Prices for sending mail are quite reasonable, but the regular mail system is very unreliable. Packages are often opened and searched by customs, and it is not uncommon for things to go missing from El Salvador's postal system, especially in incoming mail. If you need to send or receive anything of any value, it is strongly recommended that you use a courier service such as DHL or FedEx.

Telecommunications

The country code for El Salvador is 503, which you only need to use if you're calling from outside the country. International access codes for calling El Salvador are 011 in the U.S. and Canada, 0011 in Australia, 0170 in New Zealand, and 00 in Great Britain.

To place a call within El Salvador, dial the eight-digit number, which begin with a 2 for landlines and a 9 for cellphones. To place a direct international call from El Salvador, dial 00 for international access, plus the country code for the country you are calling, followed by the area code and local phone number.

Internet

Salvadorans in the city are very connected, and most places you go in San Salvador will have Wi-Fi. However, in rural areas and at the beaches, it is harder to find wireless connections. All four leading mobile phone companies here (Movistar, Digicel, Tigo, and Claro) offer USB devices that you can plug into your computer and access the Internet even in the remotest areas. If you are going to be traveling a lot in El Salvador, these are worth the investment. The initial purchase will set you back about $15 and then you can simply buy prepaid cards from any *tienda* to recharge them.

Newspapers and Magazines

The major daily newspapers in El Salvador are *La Prensa Gráfica* and *El Diario de Hoy,* and they are available everywhere. Some Spanish-language versions of magazines are available in the cities, such as *National Geographic* and *Cosmopolitan.* In general El Salvador is not a reading culture, so your options are usually limited.

Television and Radio

Salvadoran TV is heavily influenced by Mexico, and as such has a lot of *telenovelas,* Mexican soap operas that involve heavy drama centered around the elite class of Mexican society, and histrionic talk shows that focus on celebrity gossip. Luckily for travelers, if there is TV in your hotel, it will have cable, and this includes a few English-language movie channels as well as American comedies and dramas. In more rural areas, radio is a very popular form of entertainment among older Salvadorans.

MAPS AND VISITOR INFORMATION

The **Ministerio de Turismo (MiTur)** (Ministry of Tourism, www.elsalvador.travel) has offices throughout the country and they provide brochures, maps, and other information about visitor activities. They are well-staffed, and some offices have fluent English speakers. The main MiTur office is located in **San Salvador** (Alameda Dr. Manuel Enrique Arauajo, Pasaje and Edificio Carbonell 2, San Salvador, tel. 2243-7835), where you will find the most complete selection of maps and brochures. **La Libertad** (Km. 34, Carretera del Litoral, La Libertad, tel. 2346-1898) has a MiTur office located at the entrance to town that offers information about the western beaches. **Suchitoto** (Calle San Martín, beside *parque central,* Suchitoto, tel. 2335-1739) has a very helpful MiTur office with loads of information about what to do in and around Suchitoto. Added bonus: It is one of the few places in town with icy cool air-conditioning. **La Palma** (Calle José Matias Delgado, La Palma, tel. 2335-9076, cat.lapalma.corsatur@gmail.com) has an excellent office beside the *parque central* with information about La Palma, El Pital, and Miramundo. The very enthusiastic staff can arrange guided hikes and has a good selection of maps and brochures.

WEIGHTS AND MEASUREMENTS
Electricity

Electricity in El Salvador is 115 volts and 60 hertz alternating current, the same as in the rest of North America. The flat pronged outlets do not have the third grounding socket. Power outages do happen, especially during the rainy season, so remember to back things up on your computer.

Measurement

El Salvador uses the metric system, but there are still some residual Spanish terms such as *manzana,* a word used to describe the size of land, equivalent to about 7,000 square meters.

Time

El Salvador is six hours earlier than UTC or Greenwich Mean Time, and daylight saving time is not used. That means in winter, El Salvador's clocks are the same time as North America's central standard time, and in summer it is the same as mountain daylight time.

Resources

Glossary

aguacatero: street dog
aguas termales: hot springs
alcaldía: mayor's office
almuerzo: lunch
artesanías: handicrafts
bicho/a: a slightly disrespectful term for a young person
birria: beer
bolado: to be drunk
bolo: a drunk
buxo: to be ready
cabal: exactly, perfect, right on
cabaña: cabin
caliche: Salvadoran slang
campesino/campesina: rural resident
campo: countryside
Carretera Litoral: coastal highway
casamiento: rice and beans
cerveza: beer
chapín: slang for someone from Guatemala
chela: beer
chele/a: someone with light skin
chicha: fermented maize drink
chivo: cool
chocolate: hot chocolate
la chota: the cops
chupar: to suck; slang for to drink alcohol
cipote: a child
combo: container
comedor: small restaurant serving typical Salvadoran food
comida a la vista: pre-prepared typical Salvadoran food
comida chatarra: fast food
comida típica: fast food

finca: farm
gringo/a: foreigner; usually used to refer to Americans, but can refer to any foreigner with light skin
guanaco/a: slang for someone from El Salvador
guaro: alcohol
huésped: guest in hotel
lancha: small motorized boat
lavandería: Laundromat
licuado: smoothie
mara: gang
la mara: slang for a group of friends, "the gang"
mestizo: someone of mixed ethnicity
moreno/a: someone with dark skin and hair
paleta: ice pop
panamericana: Pan-American Highway
paseo: pedestrian area
pisto: money
propina: tip
puchica: way of expressing amazement, anger, frustration
pupusería: restaurant that sells only *pupusas*
quesadilla: dense cake made with cheese, milk and sugar
refresco: juice or soda
salchicha: hotdog
salu: good-bye
sorbete: ice cream
tienda: small store with basic goods
torta: submarine sandwich
zancudos: mosquitoes

Spanish Phrasebook

Spanish is the language of El Salvador, and if you speak even just a little, it will greatly enhance your experience and understanding of the culture. Fortunately for beginners, Salvadorans are very patient—even if your Spanish is abominable, most people will simply appreciate the fact that you are trying. The more you speak, the more your self confidence will surge, as Salvadorans have a lovely way of making you feel like your Spanish is fabulous and fluent, even when they can barely understand you. Since so many people who live here have spent time in the States, they understand what it is like to try and learn a new language, and as a result are very sympathetic to those who make an effort. You will notice that, with just a few phrases under your belt, you will hear more and more often, *pero habla bien español!* (but you speak Spanish well!). With this kind of friendly encouragement, El Salvador is an ideal place to study and practice. Remember the key to success is to have no shame. You will make many awkward mistakes along the way, but it's all part of the process. One day you just might be amazed to find yourself spontaneously having a fluid conversation with someone, and the feeling of triumph will make all the hard work and embarrassing moments worth it.

Spanish commonly uses 30 letters—the familiar English 26, plus four straightforward additions: ch, ll, ñ, and rr, which are explained in "Consonants," below.

PRONUNCIATION

Once you learn them, Spanish pronunciation rules—in contrast to English—don't change. Spanish vowels generally sound softer than in English. (*Note:* The capitalized syllables below receive stronger accents.)

Vowels

a like ah, as in "hah": *agua* AH-gooah (water), *pan* PAHN (bread), and *casa* CAH-sah (house)

e like ay, as in "may:" *mesa* MAY-sah (table), *tela* TAY-lah (cloth), and *de* DAY (of, from)

i like ee, as in "need": *diez* dee-AYZ (ten), *comida* ko-MEE-dah (meal), and *fin* FEEN (end)

o like oh, as in "go": *peso* PAY-soh (weight), *ocho* OH-choh (eight), and *poco* POH-koh (a bit)

u like oo, as in "cool": *uno* OO-noh (one), *cuarto* KOOAHR-toh (room), and *usted* oos-TAYD (you); when it follows a "q" the **u** is silent; when it follows an "h" or has an umlaut, it's pronounced like "w"

Consonants

b, d, f, k, l, m, n, p, q, s, t, v, w, x, y, z, and ch pronounced almost as in English; **h** occurs, but is silent—not pronounced at all

c like k as in "keep": *cuarto* KOOAR-toh (room), Tepic tay-PEEK (capital of Nayarit state); when it precedes "e" or "i," pronounce **c** like s, as in "sit": *cerveza* sayr-VAY-sah (beer), *encima* ayn-SEE-mah (atop)

g like g as in "gift" when it precedes "a," "o," "u," or a consonant: *gato* GAH-toh (cat), *hago* AH-goh (I do, make); otherwise, pronounce **g** like h as in "hat": *giro* HEE-roh (money order), *gente* HAYN-tay (people)

j like h, as in "has": *Jueves* HOOAY-vays (Thursday), *mejor* may-HOR (better)

ll like y, as in "yes": *toalla* toh-AH-yah (towel), *ellos* AY-yohs (they, them)

ñ like ny, as in "canyon": *año* AH-nyo (year), *señor* SAY-nyor (Mr., sir)

r is lightly trilled, with tongue at the roof of your mouth like a very light English d, as in "ready": *pero* PAY-doh (but), *tres* TDAYS (three), *cuatro* KOOAH-tdoh (four)

rr like a Spanish r, but with much more emphasis and trill. Let your tongue flap. Practice with *burro* (donkey), *carretera* (highway), and Carrillo (proper name), then really let go with *ferrocarril* (railroad)

Note: The single small but common exception to all of the above is the pronunciation of Spanish **y** when it's being used as the Spanish word for "and," as in *Ron y Kathy*. In such case, pronounce it like the English ee, as in "keep": Ron "ee" Kathy (Ron and Kathy).

Accent

The rule for accent, the relative stress given to syllables within a given word, is straightforward. If a word ends in a vowel, an n, or an s, accent the next-to-last syllable; if not, accent the last syllable.

Pronounce *gracias* GRAH-seeahs (thank you), *orden* OHR-dayn (order), and *carretera* kah-ray-TAY-rah (highway) with stress on the next-to-last syllable.

Otherwise, accent the last syllable: *venir* vay-NEER (to come), *ferrocarril* fay-roh-cah-REEL (railroad), and *edad* ay-DAHD (age).

Exceptions to the accent rule are always marked with an accent sign: (á, é, í, ó, or ú), such as *teléfono* tay-LAY-foh-noh (telephone), *jabón* hah-BON (soap), and *rápido* RAH-pee-doh (rapid).

BASIC AND COURTEOUS EXPRESSIONS

Most Spanish-speaking people consider formalities important. Whenever approaching anyone for information or some other reason, do not forget the appropriate salutation—good morning, good evening, etc. Standing alone, the greeting *hola* (hello) can sound brusque.
Hello. *Hola.*
Good morning. *Buenos días.*

Good afternoon. *Buenas tardes.*
Good evening. *Buenas noches.*
How are you? *¿Cómo está usted?*
Very well, thank you. *Muy bien, gracias.*
Okay; good. *Bien.*
Not okay; bad. *Mal or feo.*
So-so. *Más o menos.*
And you? *¿Y usted?*
What's up? *¿Que onda?*
Thank you. *Gracias.*
Thank you very much. *Muchas gracias.*
You're very kind. *Muy amable.*
You're welcome. *De nada.*
Goodbye. *Adios.*
See you later. *Hasta luego.*
please *por favor*
yes *sí*
no *no*
I don't know. *No sé.*
Just a moment, please. *Momentito, por favor.*
Excuse me, please (when you're trying to get attention). *Disculpe or Con permiso.*
Excuse me (when you've made a boo-boo). *Lo siento.*
Pleased to meet you. *Mucho gusto.*
Do you speak English? *¿Habla usted inglés?*
Is English spoken here? (Does anyone here speak English?) *¿Se habla inglés?*
I don't speak Spanish well. *No hablo bien el español.*
I don't understand. *No entiendo.*
How do you say . . . in Spanish? *¿Cómo se dice… en español?*
What is your name? *¿Cómo se llama usted?*
My name is . . . *Me llamo…*
Would you like . . . *¿Quisiera usted…*
Let's go to . . . *Vamos a…*

TERMS OF ADDRESS

When in doubt, use the formal *usted* (you) as a form of address.
I *yo*
you (formal) *usted*
you (familiar) *tu*

he/him *él*
she/her *ella*
we/us *nosotros*
you (plural) *ustedes*
they/them *ellos* (all males or mixed gender); *ellas* (all females)
Mr., sir *señor*
Mrs., madam *señora*
miss, young lady *señorita*
husband *esposo*
wife *esposa*
friend *amigo* (male); *amiga* (female)
sweetheart *novio* (male); *novia* (female)
son; daughter *hijo; hija*
brother; sister *hermano; hermana*
father; mother *padre; madre*
grandfather; grandmother *abuelo; abuela*

TRANSPORTATION

Where is . . . ? *¿Dónde está . . . ?*
How far is it to . . . ? *¿A cuánto está . . . ?*
from . . . to . . . *de . . . a . . .*
Can you give me a ride? *¿Me puede dar un ride?*
How many blocks? *¿Cuántas cuadras?*
Where (Which) is the way to . . . ? *¿Dónde está el camino a . . . ?*
the bus station *la terminal de autobuses*
the bus stop *la parada de autobuses*
Where is this bus going? *¿Adónde va este autobús?*
the taxi stand *la parada de taxis*
the train station *la estación de ferrocarril*
the boat *el barco*
the launch *lancha; tiburonera*
the dock *el muelle*
the airport *el aeropuerto*
I'd like a ticket to . . . *Quisiera un boleto a . . .*
first (second) class *primera (segunda) clase*
roundtrip *ida y vuelta*
reservation *reservación*
baggage *equipaje*
Stop here, please. *Pare aquí, por favor.*
the entrance *la entrada*
the exit *la salida*

the ticket office *la oficina de boletos*
(very) near; far *(muy) cerca; lejos*
to; toward *a*
by; through *por*
from *de*
the right *la derecha*
the left *la izquierda*
straight ahead *derecho; directo*
in front *en frente*
beside *al lado*
behind *atrás*
the corner *la esquina*
the stoplight *la semáforo*
a turn *una vuelta*
right here *aquí*
somewhere around here *por acá*
right there *allí*
somewhere around there *por allá*
road *el camino*
street; boulevard *calle; bulevar*
block *la cuadra*
highway *carretera*
kilometer *kilómetro*
bridge; toll *puente; cuota*
address *dirección*
north; south *norte; sur*
east; west *oriente (este); poniente (oeste)*

ACCOMMODATIONS

hotel *hotel*
Is there a room? *¿Hay cuarto?*
May I (may we) see it? *¿Puedo (podemos) verlo?*
What is the rate? *¿Cuál es el precio?*
Is that your best rate? *¿Es su mejor precio?*
Is there something cheaper? *¿Hay algo más económico?*
a single room *un cuarto sencillo*
a double room *un cuarto doble*
double bed *cama matrimonial*
twin beds *camas gemelas*
with private bath *con baño*
hot water *agua caliente*
shower *ducha*
towels *toallas*
soap *jabón*
toilet paper *papel higiénico*

blanket *frazada; manta*
sheets *sábanas*
air-conditioned *aire acondicionado*
fan *abanico; ventilador*
key *llave*
manager *gerente*

FOOD

I'm hungry *Tengo hambre.*
I'm thirsty. *Tengo sed.*
menu *carta; menú*
order *orden*
glass *vaso*
fork *tenedor*
knife *cuchillo*
spoon *cuchara*
napkin *servilleta*
soft drink *refresco*
coffee *café*
tea *té*
drinking water *agua pura; agua potable*
bottled carbonated water *agua mineral*
bottled uncarbonated water *agua sin gas*
beer *cerveza*
wine *vino*
milk *leche*
juice *jugo*
cream *crema*
sugar *azúcar*
cheese *queso*
snack *antojo; botana*
breakfast *desayuno*
lunch *almuerzo*
daily lunch special *comida corrida* (or *el menú del día* depending on region)
dinner *comida* (often eaten in late afternoon); *cena* (a late-night snack)
the check *la cuenta*
eggs *huevos*
bread *pan*
salad *ensalada*
fruit *fruta*
mango *mango*
watermelon *sandía*
papaya *papaya*
banana *plátano*
apple *manzana*

orange *naranja*
lime *limón*
fish *pescado*
shellfish *mariscos*
shrimp *camarones*
meat (without) *(sin) carne*
chicken *pollo*
pork *puerco*
beef; steak *res; bistec*
bacon; ham *tocino; jamón*
fried *frito*
roasted *asada*
barbecue; barbecued *barbacoa; al carbón*

SHOPPING

money *dinero*
money-exchange bureau *casa de cambio*
I would like to exchange traveler's checks. *Quisiera cambiar cheques de viajero.*
What is the exchange rate? *¿Cuál es el tipo de cambio?*
How much is the commission? *¿Cuánto cuesta la comisión?*
Do you accept credit cards? *¿Aceptan tarjetas de crédito?*
money order *giro*
How much does it cost? *¿Cuánto cuesta?*
What is your final price? *¿Cuál es su último precio?*
expensive *caro*
cheap *barato; económico*
more *más*
less *menos*
a little *un poco*
too much *demasiado*

HEALTH

Help me please. *Ayúdeme por favor.*
I am ill. *Estoy enfermo.*
Call a doctor. *Llame un doctor.*
Take me to ... *Lléveme a...*
hospital *hospital; sanatorio*
drugstore *farmacia*
pain *dolor*

fever *fiebre*
headache *dolor de cabeza*
stomach ache *dolor de estómago*
burn *quemadura*
cramp *calambre*
nausea *náusea*
vomiting *vomitar*
medicine *medicina*
antibiotic *antibiótico*
pill; tablet *pastilla*
aspirin *aspirina*
ointment; cream *pomada; crema*
bandage *venda*
cotton *algodón*
sanitary napkins use brand name, e.g.,
    Kotex
birth control pills *pastillas*
    anticonceptivas
contraceptive foam *espuma*
    anticonceptiva
condoms *preservativos; condones*
toothbrush *cepilla dental*
dental floss *hilo dental*
toothpaste *crema dental*
dentist *dentista*
toothache *dolor de muelas*

POST OFFICE AND COMMUNICATIONS

long-distance telephone *teléfono larga*
    distancia
I would like to call ... *Quisiera llamar*
    a...
collect *por cobrar*
station to station *a quien contesta*
person to person *persona a persona*
credit card *tarjeta de crédito*
post office *correo*
general delivery *lista de correo*
letter *carta*
stamp *estampilla, timbre*
postcard *tarjeta*
aerogram *aerograma*
air mail *correo aereo*
registered *registrado*
money order *giro*
package; box *paquete; caja*
string; tape *cuerda; cinta*

AT THE BORDER

border *frontera*
customs *aduana*
immigration *migración*
tourist card *tarjeta de turista*
inspection *inspección; revisión*
passport *pasaporte*
profession *profesión*
marital status *estado civil*
single *soltero*
married; divorced *casado; divorciado*
widowed *viudado*
insurance *seguros*
title *título*
driver's license *licencia de manejar*

AT THE GAS STATION

gas station *gasolinera*
gasoline *gasolina*
unleaded *sin plomo*
full, please *lleno, por favor*
tire *llanta*
tire repair shop *vulcanizadora*
air *aire*
water *agua*
oil (change) *aceite (cambio)*
grease *grasa*
My ... doesn't work. *Mi... no sirve.*
battery *batería*
radiator *radiador*
alternator *alternador*
generator *generador*
tow truck *grúa*
repair shop *taller mecánico*
tune-up *afinación*
auto parts store *refaccionería*

VERBS

Verbs are the key to getting along in Spanish. They employ mostly predictable forms and come in three classes, which end in *ar*, *er*, and *ir*, respectively:

to buy *comprar*
I buy, you (he, she, it) buys *compro,*
    compra
we buy, you (they) buy *compramos,*
    compran

to eat *comer*
I eat, you (he, she, it) eats *como, come*
we eat, you (they) eat *comemos, comen*

to climb *subir*
I climb, you (he, she, it) climbs *subo, sube*
we climb, you (they) climb *subimos, suben*

Here are more (with irregularities indicated):

to do or make *hacer* (regular except for *hago*, I do or make)
to go *ir* (very irregular: *voy, va, vamos, van*)
to go (walk) *andar*
to love *amar*
to work *trabajar*
to want *desear, querer*
to need *necesitar*
to read *leer*
to write *escribir*
to repair *reparar*
to stop *parar*
to get off (the bus) *bajar*
to arrive *llegar*
to stay (remain) *quedar*
to stay (lodge) *hospedar*
to leave *salir* (regular except for *salgo*, I leave)
to look at *mirar*
to look for *buscar*
to give *dar* (regular except for *doy*, I give)
to carry *llevar*
to have *tener* (irregular but important: *tengo, tiene, tenemos, tienen*)
to come *venir* (similarly irregular: *vengo, viene, venimos, vienen*)

Spanish has two forms of "to be":

to be *estar* (regular except for *estoy*, I am)
to be *ser* (very irregular: *soy, es, somos, son*)

Use *estar* when speaking of location or a temporary state of being: "I am at home." *"Estoy en casa."* "I'm sick." *"Estoy enfermo."* Use *ser* for a permanent state of being: "I am a doctor." *"Soy doctora."*

NUMBERS

zero *cero*
one *uno*
two *dos*
three *tres*
four *cuatro*
five *cinco*
six *seis*
seven *siete*
eight *ocho*
nine *nueve*
10 *diez*
11 *once*
12 *doce*
13 *trece*
14 *catorce*
15 *quince*
16 *dieciseis*
17 *diecisiete*
18 *dieciocho*
19 *diecinueve*
20 *veinte*
21 *veinte y uno* or *veintiuno*
30 *treinta*
40 *cuarenta*
50 *cincuenta*
60 *sesenta*
70 *setenta*
80 *ochenta*
90 *noventa*
100 *ciento*
101 *ciento y uno* or *cientiuno*
200 *doscientos*
500 *quinientos*
1,000 *mil*
10,000 *diez mil*
100,000 *cien mil*
1,000,000 *millón*
one half *medio*
one third *un tercio*
one fourth *un cuarto*

TIME

What time is it? ¿Qué hora es?
It's one o'clock. Es la una.
It's three in the afternoon. Son las tres de la tarde.
It's 4am. Son las cuatro de la mañana.
six-thirty seis y media
a quarter till eleven un cuarto para las once
a quarter past five las cinco y cuarto
an hour una hora

DAYS AND MONTHS

Monday lunes
Tuesday martes
Wednesday miércoles
Thursday jueves
Friday viernes
Saturday sábado
Sunday domingo

today hoy
tomorrow mañana
yesterday ayer
January enero
February febrero
March marzo
April abril
May mayo
June junio
July julio
August agosto
September septiembre
October octubre
November noviembre
December diciembre
a week una semana
a month un mes
after después
before antes

Suggested Reading and Viewing

BOOKS

Argueta, Manilo. *One Day of Life*. New York: Vintage, 1992. This novel follows the daily life of several women in a rural village in Chalatenango during the 1970s. The book was released in 1980 and was immediately banned by the government for its descriptions of human rights violations by the Organización Democrática Nacionalista (ORDEN), the government's paramilitary intelligence organization.

Brockman, James. *Romero: A Life*. Maryknoll, NY: Orbis Books, 2005. A thorough and personal biography of Óscar Arnulfo Romero, the archbishop of El Salvador, until his assassination in 1980.

Consalvi, Carlos Henríquez. *Broadcasting the Civil War: A Memoir of Guerrilla Radio*. Austin: University of Texas Press, 2010. In this first-person account, Carlos Henríquez Consalvi, a.k.a. Santiago, the legendary voice behind guerrilla radio station Radio Venceremos, tells the story of the rebellion of poor peasants against the Salvadoran government. This memoir also examines the war in a broader context, looking at the Cold War and the heavy U.S. involvement in El Salvador under President Reagan.

Dalton, Roque. *Poemas Clandestinos/ Clandestine Poems*. Milwaukee: New American Press, 1984. *Small Hours of the Night: Selected Poems of Roque Dalton*. Willimantic, CT: Curbstone Books, 1996. For anyone interested in the work of revolutionary poet Roque Dalton, these are two of the only books that are widely available with his work translated into English.

Danner, Mark. *The Massacre at El Mozote*. New York: Vintage, 1994. This excellent work of investigative journalism follows the events of the infamous 1981 El Mozote massacre in Morazán. It first appeared as an article in the *New Yorker* in 1993 and exposed the searing details of one of the most brutal massacres in Latin American history. The story caused shockwaves in the United States, as it also brought to light the fact that the U.S. government was sending aid to the military in El Salvador despite gross human rights violations. The article is now expanded into a book with new material and sources.

Didion, Joan. *Salvador*. New York: Vintage, 1994. Joan Didion traveled through El Salvador in 1982, at the height of the civil war. In this long essay she examines the state of war-torn El Salvador through interactions with all sectors of society—from poor rural peasants to the president of the country. Didion pulls no punches as she creates a descriptive, chilling, and acerbic commentary on the role that the U.S. government played in perpetuating the bloody conflict.

Martín-Baró, Ignacio. *Writings for a Liberation Psychology*. Cambridge, MA: Harvard University Press, 1996. Written by the Spanish-born Jesuit priest and psychologist Ignacio Martín-Baró, this book examines the psychological aspect of political repression, the impact of violence and trauma on child development and mental health, and the use of psychology for political ends. Martín-Baró was devoted to his adopted country of El Salvador and to making psychology accessible to the rural communities. In November 1989 a Salvadoran death squad assassinated him.

McClintock, Cynthia. *Revolutionary Movements in Latin America: El Salvador's FMLN and Peru's Shining Path*. Washington DC: U.S. Institute of Peace Press, 1998. Examines how and why the FMLN were able to overcome massive revolutionary challenges during the civil war.

Romero, Óscar A. *The Violence of Love*. Maryknoll, NY: Orbis Books, 2004. A collection of Archbishop Óscar Romero's homilies and other works.

Romero, Óscar A. *Voice of the Voiceless: The Four Pastoral Letters and Other Statements*. Maryknoll, NY: Orbis Books, 1985. This book contains Romero's last sermon as well as letters and official and public statements that include university addresses and the famous letter to the U.S. president, Jimmy Carter, that demanded an end to all U.S. aid and military involvement in El Salvador.

Sheets, Payson. *The Ceren Site: An Ancient Village Buried by Volcanic Ash in Central America (Case Studies in Archaeology)*. Boston: Cengage Learning, 2005. This book is about the ruin of Joya de Cerén, often called the Pompeii of the Americas, and was written by the archaeologist who discovered the site in 1976, Payson Sheets. It provides a detailed portrait of the life, houses, artifacts, and activities of the Mayan people who lived here. Full of art and images from Sheets's own collection, the book also talks about the personal trials and triumphs he experienced while working in the field in El Salvador.

Towell, Larry. *El Salvador*. New York: W. W. Norton, 1997. This book of photography is full of stark black-and-white images taken toward the end of the civil war. Towell's shots get close and personal with the reality of living in both San Salvador and the rural areas of the country. Photos include scenes of the daily activities of guerrillas, government forces, and civilians, and all include a short summary of the background of the photo; it is a tragically arresting and hauntingly beautiful look at the truth of the civil war.

FILMS

El Lugar Más Pequeño (*The Tiniest Place*, 2011) is set in the mountain town of Cinquera, Las Cabañas. During the war the town was completely decimated and abandoned. In the film the director interviews survivors who returned and rebuilt this tiny town in the forest. Evocative interviews and images are spliced together seamlessly to create a visually and emotionally powerful film.

In the Name of the People (1985) is a documentary that follows four filmmakers who secretly entered El Salvador and followed guerrillas across the country as they fought against government forces. This is some of the only video footage of the guerrillas' daily life during the war.

La Vida Loca (2008) is a documentary filmed by journalist Christian Poveda, who captured rare and disturbing footage of the rival gangs Mara 18 and Mara Salvatrucha. Poveda was assassinated on September 2, 2009, on his way to an interview in a gang-ridden slum close to San Salvador.

Romero (1989) is an American biopic depicting the life of Archbishop Óscar Romero.

Salvador (1986) is a sensational drama written and directed by Oliver Stone. The story follows an American journalist who drives to El Salvador to chronicle the events of the 1980 military dictatorship. During this time he forges relationships with both guerrillas, who want him to get photos out to the U.S. press, and the right-wing military, who want him to bring them photographs of the rebels.

Sobreviviendo Guazapa (*Surviving Guazapa*, 2008) is a movie about two men on opposite sides of the civil war who are forced together by circumstances.

Voces Inocentes (*Innocent Voices*, 2004) is a riveting and heartbreaking look at how the civil war affected children in rural El Salvador. Written by Salvadoran Oscar Orlando Torres, the movie chronicles the story of his childhood living in Cuscatazingo, a small town in a strategic location between government and rebel forces. Told through the eyes of innocent children, the film serves as a visceral commentary on the use of children in conflict and the effect of war on innocent civilians. Highly recommended.

Internet Resources

GENERAL EL SALVADOR WEBSITES

Waves Tours Fiestas (WTF)
www.wtf-elsalvador.com
El Salvador's best source of online information, written for travelers by experienced travelers who know the country well. The bilingual magazine should be your first stop for all the information you need to organize unique tours, accommodations, transportation, and more.

El Salvador Impresionante
www.elsalvador.travel
This is the bilingual website of the Ministerio de Turismo.

Fundación Clic
www.clic.org.sv
Online magazine that focuses on art, history, and culture.

Voices on the Border
www.votb.org
Excellent online magazine that covers social justice issues in El Salvador.

The Other El Salvador
www.theotherelsalvador.com
An eclectic site with photos and suggested tours.

NEWS AND MEDIA

La Prensa Gráfica
www.laprensagrafica.com
The biggest newspaper in El Salvador provides online content.

El Faro
www.elfaro.net
An online digital newspaper, founded in 1998 by the sons of political exiles. It claims to be the first exclusively digital newspaper in Latin America.

El Diario Latino
www.diariolatino.biz
A slightly sensationalistic news site that focuses on breaking news.

Index

List of Maps

Photo Credits

MAP SYMBOLS

Expressway	★	Highlight	✕	Airfield	⚲	Golf Course
Primary Road	○	City/Town	✈	Airport	🅿	Parking Area
Secondary Road	◉	State Capital	▲	Mountain		Archaeological Site
Unpaved Road	⊛	National Capital	✛	Unique Natural Feature		Church
Trail	★	Point of Interest				Gas Station
Ferry	•	Accommodation	🐾	Waterfall	〰	Glacier
Railroad	▾	Restaurant/Bar	⚑	Park		Mangrove
Pedestrian Walkway	■	Other Location	🚩	Trailhead		Reef
Stairs	⋀	Campground	⛷	Skiing Area		Swamp

CONVERSION TABLES

°C = (°F - 32) / 1.8
°F = (°C x 1.8) + 32
1 inch = 2.54 centimeters (cm)
1 foot = 0.304 meters (m)
1 yard = 0.914 meters
1 mile = 1.6093 kilometers (km)
1 km = 0.6214 miles
1 fathom = 1.8288 m
1 chain = 20.1168 m
1 furlong = 201.168 m
1 acre = 0.4047 hectares
1 sq km = 100 hectares
1 sq mile = 2.59 square km
1 ounce = 28.35 grams
1 pound = 0.4536 kilograms
1 short ton = 0.90718 metric ton
1 short ton = 2,000 pounds
1 long ton = 1.016 metric tons
1 long ton = 2,240 pounds
1 metric ton = 1,000 kilograms
1 quart = 0.94635 liters
1 US gallon = 3.7854 liters
1 Imperial gallon = 4.5459 liters
1 nautical mile = 1.852 km

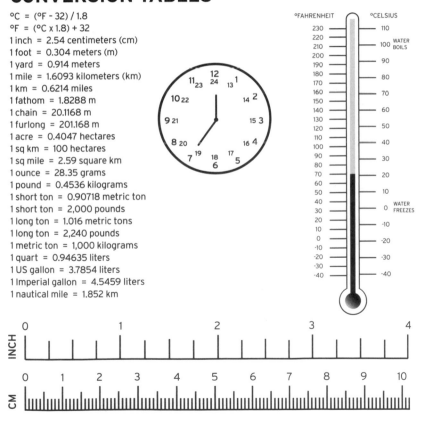

MOON EL SALVADOR
Avalon Travel
a member of the Perseus Books Group
1700 Fourth Street
Berkeley, CA 94710, USA
www.moon.com

Editor and Series Manager: Kathryn Ettinger
Copy Editor: Christopher Church
Graphics Coordinator: Lucie Ericksen
Production Coordinator: Lucie Ericksen
Cover Design: Faceout Studios, Charles Brock
Moon Logo: Tim McGrath
Map Editor: Mike Morgenfeld
Cartographer: Stephanie Poulain
Indexer: Greg Jewett

ISBN-13: 978-1-61238-561-7
ISSN: 2374-698X

Printing History
1st Edition — December 2014
5 4 3 2 1

Front cover photo: Tamanique Waterfalls, near
Playa El Tunco © Lucas Paolo Krainz
Back cover photo: crater of Volcán Santa Ana
in Parque Nacional Los Volcanes © Hugo
Brizard/123RF

Printed in Canada by Friesens

All recommendations, including those for sights,
activities, hotels, restaurants, and shops, are
based on each author's individual judgment.
We do not accept payment for inclusion in our
travel guides, and our authors don't accept
free goods or services in exchange for positive
coverage.

Although every effort was made to ensure
that the information was correct at the time of
going to press, the author and publisher do not
assume and hereby disclaim any liability to any
party for any loss or damage caused by errors,
omissions, or any potential travel disruption
due to labor or financial difficulty, whether
such errors or omissions result from negligence,
accident, or any other cause.